Master *of the* Mission Inn

A Life

Maurice Hodgen

Copyright © 2013 Maurice Hodgen
All rights reserved.

ISBN: 0976278510
ISBN 13: 9780976278511

Library of Congress Control Number: 2013908353
CreateSpace Independent Publishing Platform
North Charleston, South Carolina
Ashburton Publishing

To My Family

*For Rhona, Victoria, Mary,
Philip, Allie, Jack, and Annie.*

"It is easy to describe second-rate talents, because they fall into a class, and enlist under a standard; but first-rate powers defy calculation or comparison, and can only be defined by themselves. They are *sui generis*, and make a class to which they belong."

William Hazlitt, *Character of Cobbett*, 1836.

Table of Contents

Preface	ix
Part One: The First Boy	1
1. Going West	3
2. Seventeen Years in a Frontier Village	11
3. Almost Like Starting Over	23
4. Going I Don't Know Where	33
5. So Here Goes for Business	43
6. Like a Duck to Water	53
7. For Sale at a Bargain	65
8. Telegraph in Cipher	75
9. Influence Without Office	85
10. Wide-Ranging Enterprises	97
11. Practically a Gift to Riverside	107
Part Two: Master of the Mission Inn	117
12. In Clear Over My Head	119
13. Frank Is Proud of His Hotel	129
14. A Trying and Busy Time	139
15. A Tumble of Ideas	165
16. Much Sweetness of Character	175

Part Three: The Return of Laughter — 187

17.	Propinquity Does It	189
18.	Big, Jovial, and Genial	201
19.	A Play, a Hotel, and a Gallery	211
20.	Peace, Race, and Ceremony	221
21.	A Gorgeous Creation	233
22.	Hospitals and Egotism	243
23.	Go on a Long Sea Voyage	253
24.	The Things We Believe In	263
25.	Peace Plans and Straws in the Wind	273

Part Four: No Currents of Despair — 283

26.	Medals, Minarets, and Flying Buttresses	285
27.	Advancing Years	295
28.	Master No More	305

Epilogue	315
Acknowledgments	321
Abbreviations	327
Chapter Notes	329
Bibliography	429
Index	445

Preface

Who was this Master of the Mission Inn? Did he think up all the architectural variety in his hotel, putting stained-glass windows in unexpected places and adding tiny balconies, parapets, spiral columns, and Asian courtyards? And all those paintings—were they his choices? And the variety of the decorations? It's enough to encounter them at almost every turn as one visits the inn, but why such variety, and who paid the bill? And why build a hotel so different from all others?

The Mission Inn in Riverside, California, the handiwork of the Master, is indeed unique in so many ways that people seeing it naturally wonder about the man and the mind that put it all together. They have very good reasons for their curiosity. Even in the grounds of the hotel, they almost immediately see a miscellany of decoration—a Saint Francis shrine, the builder's statue, and macaws of lively and sometimes noisy brilliance. Visitors pass a pair of eighteenth-century ship cannons, a bust of Booker T. Washington, and a huge Chinese bell paneled in mysterious calligraphy. Inside the hotel, the motley continues with colorfully decorated Chinese ceramics and portraits of US presidents, from William Henry Harrison to George H. W. Bush, all of whom came as guests. Then visitors move into the heavily beamed and chandeliered Music Room, church-like with a pipe organ and stained glass honoring the builder's wife as Saint Cecelia. Farther along, twisting stairs, balconies overlooking an enclosed patio, and a medieval chapel of gilded splendor give stimulus enough for more questions, even before the visitors walk, unsuspecting, from a Spanish baroque setting into an Oriental court with its huge Buddha and water-spouting dragon.

Curiosity prompts a score of questions, especially about the man who imagined all this, built it over thirty years, died there, and now, if known at all, is merely a name.

He was Frank Augustus Miller, and even for me, after forty years in Riverside, several of them spent guiding tours and hearing questions, the man that built the hotel is still fascinating. I, too, wondered what led him to choose an architectural style so different among California's hotels. And why, having chosen the mission-revival style, did he add on another style and then another and another, joining them all to fill a city block? And why did he choose the variety of decoration? That embellishment began to make sense as I learned of bric-a-brac gathered up during his two European visits, especially the several weeks in Spain, and his 1920 trip to Mexico. But why the increasing ecclesiastical emphasis, with sculptured saints, bells, crosses large and small, and his last addition, a chapel of gilded Baroque splendor? And why did he add the Asian architecture and decoration, so different from the rest?

Then I discovered that his influence and activity in town, quite apart from the hotel, excited more attention, raised more quarrels, and influenced more buildings, ceremonies, and attitudes than any of his contemporaries. And given all that, why did he slip silently out of public memory? Here was a life to be looked into and a story to be told.

Others before me, just as fascinated, have offered some answers. Frank Augustus Miller's authorized biography appeared in 1938, three years after his death, his memory fresh enough then. The book, in spite of poor reviews, supported two printings. More recent and readily available writing for general readers gives catalogs of events, artifacts, and building sequences but tells little of the man, sharing almost nothing of the inner man or of the surprising breadth of his activities in the town and the state. Besides, all of these are out of print.[1]

My intention is to look at the life of Frank Augustus Miller the man, to understand his lifework, and, in his work, to find expressions of the man in his time and place. In other words, I'm trying to answer the question about the kind of man who built the Mission Inn and did so much else to define the town of Riverside, California. In doing so, I have the advantage of new material, perhaps not easily accessible to earlier writers and certainly not exploited, even if they had the perspectives I have chosen. My quest revealed over and over the truth of what Miller, as an introspective twenty-year-old diary keeper, said of himself: "I am made Independent [sic] in disposition and am willing to fight my own battles…Life is a battle in which I am going to win or die."[2]

Let us take him at his word and follow his claim in what became a self-fulfilling prophecy.

PART ONE:
The First Boy

1

Going West

When Christopher Miller left the village for California in the bitter February weather of 1874, neighbors suspected that sooner or later all the family would follow him. So many people were moving in and through the state; so few ever came back.[1] Besides, Miller's work at railroad surveying in Wisconsin had disappeared as depression spread across the nation in the wake of the 1873 Wall Street collapse. Then there was his wife's health; "up and down" was how the family explained it.[2] Perhaps he'd find work and the California climate would help Mary Ann, even if she already harbored the dreaded tuberculosis.

By summer, every one of about eight hundred people in Tomah, Wisconsin, knew the family's plans. The remaining Millers would leave early in October, planning to meet Christopher in Los Angeles. With them gone, there would be a noticeable gap in the community: Christopher and Mary Ann Miller were an influential couple, college graduates and residents since Tomah, a frontier village, began eighteen years earlier. Their four children had grown up there. Emma, the oldest, moved there as a three-year-old, but all the others had been born in the village—Frank born within a few months of the family's arrival. Alice was now fourteen, and Edward age ten.

The small drama of a family moving from one place to another had been played out countless times and in countless places across the frontiers. It would continue to be enacted in Wisconsin and elsewhere for many years: the packing; the Saturday auction at the house, itself up for sale; and then the quiet of Sunday. And before the leaving, there was always a host of last-minute things to be taken care of—visits to be made, neglected words that needed to be spoken. For the Millers, the swirl of these details during their last days in the village disappeared in the daily brevity of seventeen-year-old Frank's diary entries: "Busy," "Busy," "Busy."

On the October evening of their departure, ten or fifteen close friends joined the family at the dimly lit railroad depot; all were bundled up against the frost that settled in early. The farewells ended; friends called last good-byes into the chill darkness as the family settled into a night of train travel. Frank checked the time: 7:38 p.m. The sudden absence of company added to the wrench of parting. Later he wrote, "Done a deal of crying but couldn't help it." The pain of severing bonds formed in childhood and youth came in waves and was repeated in his diary over several years. For now, however, as the train pulled steadily though the night, the comfort of his family around him eased his tearful grief. He recorded nothing of their experience in leaving; they left us no records of their own.

By morning they arrived in an early rising Chicago. Frank's mother, Mary Ann, and his oldest sister, Emma, had been there several times before and were able to guide the others though the maze of hurrying travelers, baggage handlers, express agents, and hotel boosters toward ticket offices and baggage-transfer platforms. Frank, however, now the manager of travel arrangements, bought tickets, checked the baggage, and squired the family to their railroad car.

From Chicago the family traveled west to Omaha, Nebraska. From there the Union Pacific would carry them to Cheyenne,

Wyoming, into the Rocky Mountains, to Ogden, Utah, and then north around the Great Salt Lake and almost due southwest through northern and central Nevada. It would then take them over the last great pass and into the descent through California's Sierra Nevada to Sacramento. Eighty miles more would bring them to Oakland to a ferry across the bay to San Francisco. From there, they'd steam by ship south to San Pedro, ride the railroad to Los Angeles, rejoin husband and father, Christopher Miller, and travel on to their new home.

The Millers were a railroad family; they knew the rails before they traveled them. Christopher had surveyed new railroad routes since his college graduation in 1852, some twenty-two years before. Young Frank had worked alongside him in Wisconsin. They knew about derailments and the effects of severe weather, collisions, fires, personal injuries, and accidental deaths. They had traveled in Wisconsin, with Frank and his father riding in the cars, the cabs, and the cabooses as need arose on freights and passenger trains. The family shared closely in the national triumph of the completed transcontinental link in 1869, an event now setting their own lives in a different direction.

A new sense of authority placed Frank in charge. Early in the journey he headed a diary page, "Expencs [sic] to San Francisco from Tomah, Wis Oct 5 1874." This was to be a detailed extension of the record keeping he'd begun with his first diary in 1871. In early entries he noted four and a half fares from Tomah to Chicago at $34.20, bus fares at $2.00, three cups of tea at $0.30, four and a half tickets to San Francisco at $55.50, and a total of $249.75. But by the family's arrival in San Francisco, details had thinned out. His later record was of little more than notes for small amounts for food—grapes, apples, peaches, and bread, petering out in "etc." as memory and diligence waned. But however sketchy his record of the journey, he and his habitually sociable family savored all the democracy of railroad travel in the cheapest of accommodations, emigrant class.[3]

Little outside the railroad-car window caught Frank's eye for notice or drew him into reflection. In coming years he'd cross and recross the continent many times by train, sail to Europe twice, and cross all or some of the north Pacific half a dozen times. But he left only the thinnest record of places he had visited or of the people he encountered, despite his reputation as a genial companion. Even in maturity, he revealed little of the inner experience of his travels.

The changes of routine and surroundings challenged Frank's health. As he traveled west, he experienced a "very bad sick headache" on Wednesday, which eased somewhat over Thursday and Friday and was gone by Saturday as the train moved slowly through northern Nebraska and across the North Platte River at night. The hollow, pulsating clatter and roar of iron wheels crossing the long, wooden trestle bridge seemed almost endless in the dimly lit car.

Nine days out, Frank suffered another distressing headache, his recovery slowed by the movement, grit, smell, and smoke of the train. A week later in Nevada, there was another headache and then another two days after that, between Sacramento and San Francisco. This latest headache grew in punishing intensity to be "the worst sick headache I ever had in my life." In San Francisco, he found comfort and recovery overnight when the family stayed briefly in a rooming house.[4] Remarkably, Frank rarely slowed his pace because of these repeated illnesses, which appear now to be classic, recurrent migraines.

"California for Health," a widely popular booster slogan for many years, may have entered the family's thinking about Frank's recurrent sick headaches, but it certainly influenced the family's thoughts about Mary Ann's health. She had "been up and down, up and down," stirring family fears of tuberculosis, a familiar scourge throughout the nineteenth and early twentieth centuries. And whatever complex of motivations drew the family west, hopes for Mary Ann's improved health was remembered later as a main reason for the migration.[5] Not surprisingly, her reserves wore thin over the first ten days of train travel, and only then did Frank note, "Ma a little tired." Her patient nature may well have concealed a greater fatigue than he saw, oppressed as he had been with his own discomforts. Perhaps both fell victim to skimpy diary keeping.

Ignoring his own distress as much as he could, Frank wrote letters as the train went into Nevada. He began writing in Chicago and continued as the family traveled west through Illinois and Iowa, giving each letter two or three sessions as he worked it to completion. His letters were in a neat hand and generous in being rarely fewer than three pages. During the trip west he wrote seven letters, three to adult friend Mr. Graham, two for his sweetheart, Mattie Weed, one to age-mate Eddie Erwin, and one ahead to "Pa." He mailed all en route at railroad-depot letter drops. The letter-writing habit would persist, his lifetime output numbering thousands.

Only brief comments in Frank's diary hint at what must have been on the family's more varied and active travel calendar. Other travelers recalled card playing—Frank would resist on moral grounds but would seek instead games of checkers or chess at which he had recognized skill. Other rail passengers on long journeys took along books, among them travel guides crammed in small type with railroad schedules and lists of the depots named in mileage sequence. There were places to see along the way, even predictions of future glories to be brought into existence by the mere presence of the railroad. The passenger cars were moving islands of humanity, and any social reserve on a short journey among strangers would surely melt into easier sociability among a group sharing long days and nights together toward distant destinations.

After twelve nights and eleven days on wheels, an overnight stay at what Frank called the Brobling House[6] gave the family its first release from the rumble and closeness of the train. Little could steal from the reassuring comfort of walking on solid floors, using customary furniture, opportunities for personal care in comfortable space and privacy, and, especially, the restoring luxury of rest in regular beds.

Early on a foggy Saturday morning in October 1874, Frank saw to loading the family luggage onto the steamer *Salvador*, which would take them south. The *San Francisco Daily Evening Bulletin*[7] recorded, "Sailed, Steamer *Salvador*, [Captain] Howes, Panama, PMSS Co." She sailed on schedule toward Panama and way ports, one of them San Pedro/Wilmington, the family's next destination. Travel south by boat made sense. The other choice, four hundred and fifty miles by stagecoach along the Butterfield route, took about five days, was rarely accident-free, and was always harsh in its dusty, endless swaying and jolting; it was ruinous of rest and sparsely served, with long stretches lacking even the most rudimentary conveniences.

Boats habitually crowded on more passengers than there were bunks or even any kind of ordinary sleeping arrangements. So the cabin provided for Mary Ann Miller and the two girls, given at the captain's discretion, tells of the Millers' careful arrangements and influential friends. The added comfort, however, provided no antidote for their seasickness. Frank slept on a platform of luggage the first night and on a table after that. His younger brother, Ed, escaped Frank's comments on this and every other part of the journey. The robust food provided matched the sailors' appetites, offering no temptation to queasy stomachs—beef, bread, beans, rice, pork, yams, the cook's own soups, and meats and poultry slaughtered on board.[8]

In this floating world, the Millers lived from Saturday noon until Monday morning. Frank, at least, remembered the Sabbath day, recording two of his characteristic Sunday activities—studying the *International Uniform Sunday-School Lesson* and enjoying the quiet company of new adult acquaintances, a Mr. and Mrs. Conkling, names that appear and disappear with this voyage. And except for them and the ladies' distress, little else merited diary mention.

These strangers to the West had a network of friends along the way. San Francisco merchant E. M. Root, of Root and

Sandborn, handled banking matters for them. Someone had influence enough to secure the comfortable cabin space for Mary Ann and her daughters. In Los Angeles, Frank and his father visited a "Mrs. Mappa and family," and next day spent time with "Mr. Wilson about a mile out of town." A little over a month later, Christopher Miller traveled north to San Jose to visit Charles Herman Allen, a friend from Wisconsin who was president of the San Jose State Normal School in California's central valley. Nine months earlier a friend must have guided the senior Miller from San Francisco to Southern California and to employment at an isolated tin mine in the hills of remote, empty, and vast San Bernardino County, a journey suggestive of much more than mere happenstance.

In Los Angeles the gathered family looked briefly at the town and shopped, and Frank had his picture taken for the then-popular two-and-a-half-by-four-inch *carte-de-visite*, the initial currency of friendship handed out among sociable youths. The cost was five dollars for the dozen.[9]

The next afternoon they all boarded the train in shambling Los Angeles for the two-hour ride twenty-four miles due east to the end of the line at Spadra, two miles west of present-day Pomona. Travelers wanting to go from there to anywhere in the expansive valley walked, rode horseback, bounced about in a stagecoach, or sat as best they could on loaded freight wagons pulled by six horses. This end of the line provided the entrepôt for a broad valley stretching east for fifty miles to the mountains and the small San Bernardino settlement. The few tiny, widely separated ranch houses, timber crews in the nearer mountains, and mining camps in the high desert all connected through Spadra, where by day people, animals, and goods came and went; by night only the empty, quiet of the desert remained.

This was the West. The Millers stayed overnight at Rubottom's, the home/hotel/post office, a large, single-storied wood building. Verandahs that were eight or more feet deep extended on three sides of this clean-lined building in a desolate setting among low, treeless hills. A few well-weathered wood buildings served as shelter for animals and storage. The place denied everything the Millers knew of Wisconsin's architecture, green meadows, forested hills, and their compact frontier village of Tomah. This new home, empty among barren hills, remote mountains, and desert seasons, would reshape their lives. With their neighbors in the desert valley, they would share the novel circumstances of this frontier.[10]

On a brisk, clear October morning, the Millers left Rubottom's, climbed aboard the hired buggy with their luggage, and headed east then southeast toward the Santa Ana River, some twenty-five miles away. The sun would be ahead of them almost all the way, the horizons far and high, treeless and sharp-edged against a blue-gray morning sky and the purple, western glow of evening. A neighbor later remembered that isolation as putting him "out of the world by weeks."[11]

Near the end of the tedious day, the Millers headed toward a river crossing. In the dimness of a rising moon, the horses hauled the wagon up from the river, onto a mesa, and to the settlement called Riverside. Christopher Miller drove them toward one of the few scattered houses in the village, the home of their host, Riverside's resident clergyman. When Frank later brought his diary up to date, he noted, "Reached River Side at six p.m." Quite by coincidence, that evening arrival in Riverside almost matched to the hour their evening departure from Tomah, seventeen tedious days before.

Much lay ahead and unsuspected on the family's October 1874 arrival. And yet, because their future lay cradled in their past, we must look back before we look ahead to understand their lives in this place, in those times, especially the life of Frank A. Miller.

2

Seventeen Years in a Frontier Village

Frank Augustus Miller lived his first seventeen years in Tomah, Wisconsin, growing up with the village. He was the first boy born there, in June 1857. Just when he learned that as a fact we don't know, but a sense of *firstness*, of independent self-awareness, appears early in his youthful diaries and is explicit in early manhood self-appraisals, written as he sought direction for his life. Years later he launched into his reminiscences for the Pulitzer Prize–winning playwright and novelist Zona Gale by saying, "I was the first boy born in Tomah, Wisconsin."[1]

Memories of child life in a frontier-village family, however, were fragmented, the return of his father from army service in 1865 one of the few memories recorded. Frank was nine at the time. Seventy years later, he said of that homecoming, "The first thing that I can remember of my father is that he had come home from the War and came into our room all dressed in his uniform." A photograph of that uniformed soldier further preserved the image for Frank and all the family: the long, sober face, a high brow above sunken eyes that were fixed calmly on a distant prospect, cheeks hollow above a well-trimmed mustache and beard that obscured the mouth, so much a mirror of mood.

Christopher Miller, a civilian again after eight months of military service, returned to doing field surveys in Wisconsin as railroad building boomed for a decade after the war. His experience and professional training gave him a superior status among surveyors. In the village, it had assured his election as county surveyor. He stood professionally with attorneys, physicians, and seminary-trained clergy. His position as an elder in the Methodist Episcopal Church, as a Mason, and as a veteran officer of the Union Army assured widespread recognition. Mary Ann Miller's college training at Oberlin, long acquaintance with the founders of the village, and role as mother and wife all placed her also in a respected position. For the children, days were defined by schooling, whether at home or in the one-room school, and home tasks, what young Frank phonetically called his "chowers." These took on even more importance with their father often absent from home on survey again, especially as their mother's health began to seesaw.[2]

Home routines were sometimes flexible, falling within a general routine in village households: Monday was washday; on Tuesday, if the clothes had dried, they were mended, flat ironed, folded, and put away. Wednesday or Thursday was baking day—making large quantities for growing appetites and weekend guests. On Saturdays, housecleaning had extra care, a necessity and a ritual preparation for the Sabbath with its slower pace, church attendance, and frequent visits. Days overflowed with mending, cooking and baking, daily cleaning, and all the demands of a family of six in a home without indoor plumbing, electricity, gas, refrigeration, vacuum cleaners, or telephones.

Young Frank's diary, though frequently sparse and telegraphic, does give occasional windows on his days. He recorded it at twelve, but certainly much earlier he had become the family grocery boy and managed a flourishing kitchen garden for home and selling.[3] His chores provided a setting for his emergent initiative and autonomy, described in miniature in unusual detail in his diary for one day:

> *March 10, 1874*
>
> *Got up at 6:30. Built a fire. Planted tomato [seeds] in a box in the house. The tomato was Hubbard's Curled Leaf. Then gave the cow and heifer calf [undecipherable] and old mangy [dog?] and Miss Underwood [a horse]. Also gave the cow and my horses feed and the horses some water; milked the cow and had just finished when she kicked the milk over and bedaubed me with manure. Then eat my breakfast Miss UN hitch up, went to the back house and to school. P.m. Gave horses feed and water. Eddie gave the cows water. Eat my dinner [i.e., lunch], went to school. P.m. 4 fixed the wood box fixed a new place for the calf in the lower barn and nailed him up in his place, milked, watered and cleaned the upper barn; eat my supper after fixing the calf up. Just as I got through with my chores calf got out and I fixed him in his place again. Helped Eddie cut a little wood. Eddie helped me in the morning. Went shopping for Ma down in the town from 7 to 9. Studied from 9 to 11.*

Beyond home and school, he contracted hay sales from land they owned, hired day labor for fencing, arranged marsh grass burn-off and plowing, and sold his garden produce street side on public holidays and pedaled them house to house in the village.

The Miller family's social class allowed Frank to defer direct entry to regular work and receive more schooling at home and in the local upper grades. For many on the frontier, schooling was fit in when convenient among the demands of family, farming, and earning. The Miller parents, both college educated, had little incentive to trust their children solely to the crowded, grossly inadequate local school, a place described locally on one occasion as "an evil," something demanding remedy. State reports make similar judgments about dozens of rural schools like those of Tomah.[4] Mary Ann likely supervised as the children learned to read to her and to each other. She read the classic *Uncle Tom's Cabin* to them, forming a memory for Frank that lasted a lifetime.[5] Christopher guided Frank in arithmetic and record keeping, using simple, orderly columns, which were often included in the end pages of Frank's diaries. Christopher also read aloud to Frank—history and enough of Edward Eggleston's *Hoosier Schoolmaster* to get Frank started on his own.

At age fourteen, Frank began a record of books he read, doing so for almost ten years. His choices included history, fiction, biography, travel, and self-improvement, some chosen from a small library of 348 books left over from a short-lived venture into community education called the Tomah Institute.[6] Sunday reading included a lifelong program in the *International Uniform Sunday-School Lesson* and the magazine *Family Circle*. The family took the weekly *Inter-Ocean* from Chicago, a publication described as Republican, patriotic, morally upright, and predictable. Seward's *Travels Around the World*, published in 1873, with pages describing the transcontinental railroad journey, caught the family's notice, given their interest in California. Reading, and especially having someone read to him, remained a source of pleasure throughout Frank's life. These were years when elocution flourished to make oral reading a performance and before the movies cast the presentation of public readings among the antiquities of popular entertainment.[7]

Frank and his sister Alice both developed journeyman skills in public speaking and debate at the Lyceum—a community organization, not a place. At these meetings, prepared topics of current interest included the uneasy relations among Indians, African Americans, and whites and the political status of women.[8] Frank's first book purchase, a four-hundred-page, leather-bound copy of *The American Orator* by Increase Cooke, offered self-improvement "to the youth of America with a view to their general excellence in knowledge, taste and virtue..."[9] As an adult, he liked to excuse himself as inept at public speaking. This was not the case. There are reports of his forceful, occasionally belligerent advocacy for projects and legislation that drew on all his energies. His persuasive powers were formidable. In youth his skills strengthened as he took to heart the critiques given by Lyceum judges. Their decisions as to winners and losers gave him opportunities for reflection and self-evaluation, aids alike to skill and to emergent self-identity. Diary comments of "We beat" or "My side lost" are small mirrors, reflecting self-worth from brief encounters in which he clearly aimed to prevail, to be first. He also measured himself for *firstness* in other youthful enterprises: throwing snowballs for distance, racing on the ice, turning a tidy profit selling vegetables, being captain of pickup baseball teams—all self-measurements of his public presentation, performance, and achievement.

Entertainment and culture came to Frank's frontier village, the rails bringing a sizeable itinerant army of public speakers, all notable then though long since forgotten, each adding richness to frontier culture and welcomed by energetic and inquiring youth. He heard notable visiting speakers;[10] he traveled to hear a Civil War general in Saint Paul, Minnesota, a hundred and fifty miles away.[11] In Tomah, the tiny Walter's Troupe played a cut, three-act version of *Othello*.[12] From a makeshift stage with travel-worn props, the actors carried him into their world, briefly transforming the shabby, rustic hall into a forum for alarming human passions. This first encounter with Shakespeare touched Frank deeply enough to draw him seventy-five miles north to Eau Claire a year later to see and hear the same company in the same play. His judgment again: "The best I ever saw."[13] That dark, Shakespearean play offered much to engage a youthful listener, with its varied themes of love, jealousy, and betrayal. His later theater and opera house associations, not as an audience member or performer but in management, could well have had roots in those chilly halls.

At home, he and Alice joined the Good Templars Lodge, a moral-uplift organization that required total abstinence from alcohol and placed no membership restrictions of gender or race;[14] its openness was unique among lodges of the time. Frank's membership lapsed in California, but he lived by his early Templar pledge and promise to his mother, repeating on many occasions, "I never took a drink over a bar or treated a man to a drink in my life."[15]

As Frank turned fifteen, his life took on the usual added complexities of adolescence: the need to move toward a life-work, to face the demands of formal schooling, and to cope with vaguely recorded but undeniable inner struggles with erotic impulses and interests. Together this trio consumed his energy and most waking hours; separately and unevenly each called for introspective note in his youthful diaries.

Just when Frank first joined his father on the survey team is uncertain. But in the second week of 1872 and for several months thereafter, at age fifteen, he was in the field. This marked a new maturity, something more extensive in time and farther away from home. Starting then, father and son together took the train or rode horseback to survey camps ranging as far north from Tomah as Saint Paul, Minnesota, for days or a week at a time, coming home again most weekends and for periods of Frank's schooling. At this time he gave his coerced promise to his mother not to "smoke or drink and so forth" and endured the sting of being called a sissy, tied to his mother's apron strings. The smoking or drinking ceased to be the issue. What became supremely important to him was knowing that he could give his word and keep it; in memory, the episode became an often visited monument on his moral landscape. "By the time I came of age," he recalled in retelling this teenage episode, "I was proud of the fact that my kind of boys were pretty scarce. I feel that kind of pride was not on a very high plane, but I am very sure that it came pretty near being the making of me." This episode, he thought, instilled confidence and fortitude against unnamed temptations later in life.[16]

In the months away, he had begun, however gradually, to sever home ties and reshape his roles in work, worship, school, village, and family. He had become a regular wage earner, living away from home and doing a man's work in a team, in a man's world. Church attendance depended on the availability of a convenient congregation; a new diligence enveloped sessions of schooling. He was with his father and away from his mother more than he'd ever been. For her part, she would sense the absence of both her men, feeling, as mothers do, that she was losing him. Perhaps in wresting the promise from him not to smoke or drink, she had deeper motivations than either of them sensed fully, something more intimate than mere abhorrence of the filthy weed and the devil's brew.

On December 25, after running survey lines several miles through a snowstorm across an already frozen landscape, father and son and two helpers retreated indoors. Frank had given no thought to lunch or holiday, merely making a note to himself that evening of "the day Jesus Christ was born" and writing his benediction: "May God bless all the family next year and forgive our sins."[17]

However glib that diary line invoking blessing and forgiveness, sin and righteousness kept prominent places in young Frank's life. With the onset of physical maturity, he became sensitive to hormones writhing within, pleasurable, almost irresistible, but feared. These feelings were thought to be impure, hence wrong. In his conflict with desire, he tried all available lines of defense: moral support from his seven-year-old brother and appeals for divine aid written again and again over the years.[18]

He confessed his failures in writing, using some variant of "Was a bad boy," in a litany pulsating through the end of 1873 with only a brief summer surcease. "Done a bad thing" became a ritual confession of this old, or even newly invasive, unspecified and irresistible attraction.[19] New knowledge from a weeklong lecture series on anatomy offered another bastion; he even attended a private lecture. But within a week after the lecture, the drama of veiled confessions disappeared from his record. Had his paper prayers been answered? Perhaps knowledge lulled his conscience, or perhaps large doses of willpower drowned evil inclinations. Even four years later, at twenty, he still wrote notes to God seeking purity as temptations persisted, but his habits of resistance stood firm: even fifty years later, friends would name purity of word and deed among his virtues.[20]

Interestingly, Frank recorded no link between the turmoil of sinning and confessing and an equally steady chronicle of warming intimacies with a succession of village girls described in entries such as "Went home with Hettie [Melloy], kiss her," and "Went home [after church] with Kate Bush," and "Sat by V. Richards at church," and "Took...Mattie Weed to prayer meeting."[21] Three years of the Tomah diary provide a succession of these burgeoning romances set in weekly congregational attendance, prayer meetings, singing schools, and berry picking and described hands held and kisses bestowed. In March 1873 came a declaration to himself: "I love Mattie Weed."[22] This early mutual attraction continued, advancing in gifts exchanged and his written prayer for her long life. Mattie Weed remained the love of his adolescent years for life. There would be other youthful liaisons, briefly as passionate perhaps, but none as enduring. Mattie kept a place in his heart and was often spoken of privately until they met again almost sixty years later, the warmth of first love still glowing.[23]

Nowhere in Frank's experience or in comments about him by others is there mention of either a religious conversion experience or a response to the emotional "calls" of evangelists, although these both were part of his regular religious scene in Tomah and in California. Much nineteenth-century religious experience centered on these often dramatic and emotional episodes ushering in the fullness of salvation, the born-again experience, and the periodic revivals of dedication and reconsecration that rekindled believers' "first love." Friends did comment on Frank's fervent pursuit of righteousness as an adult, but that was civic righteousness, right doing in civic matters and keeping his behavior consistent with conscience and what he interpreted as guidance from the exemplary life of Jesus.[24]

During 1872 and 1873, school claims on his time increased. He learned by day and prepared by night in algebra, higher arithmetic, reading, spelling, orthography, grammar, constitution, and writing.[25] At session end he usually reported perfect attendance. He crowded brief summer months with attention to the flourishing vegetable garden, football, and a few music lessons on the family's new piano. A "sick headache" marred one July 4, an early harbinger of recurrent, though not frequent, lifelong distress. Then, in August 1873, he was back to school for several months before another stint in the survey field.[26]

A month after school resumed in January 1874, Father Miller left Tomah for California. Frank settled down to the winter demands of school with five subjects, including Latin; evening study periods ran late.[27] The Latin, a college-entry subject, suggests preparation for further education. Another step toward the future came two weeks after school closed for the summer with his enrollment in a local two-week summer session called the Teachers Institute. The teaching-skills lectures given by university instructors aimed at improving the performance of employed, untrained teachers and at preparing aspirants for the qualifying examinations in October.

Frank attended the ten days of afternoon instruction, filling his mornings with the usual catalog of activities at home, harvesting and selling vegetables and joining a team of grass-fire fighters.[28]

Even by that summer, the family knew that California lay ahead. The senior Miller urged his family to travel west before more winter cold invaded Wisconsin or added extra hazards to the usual unpleasantness and danger of long-distance rail travel. There was no lack of assets. Habits of frugality had provided savings. Both parents owned Tomah land,[29] and although real-estate sales moved slowly, rentals and leases were readily arranged. There were other assets of course: the house, furniture, tools, and animals—the stuff of so many pioneer moving-on auctions, and theirs was set for an October date.

Life in a railroad surveyor's family, his own months spent in the field with Christopher, and frequent travel north and east as far as Eau Claire on the river gave Frank an intimate knowledge of railroads. Few travelers boarded the trains with as much feeling for the railroad. It is not surprising then that he'd later champion the arrival of railroads for his new hometown in California and cement personal friendships with their directors and the chief executives of the major lines when overt hostility surged relentlessly over railroad dominance in California's politics and business. He'd be middle-aged when the automobile began to redefine the national culture. One of his last journeys of any kind was by rail. By then, in 1934, he walked with a knobby cane to take his seat in the first shiny, two-car Union Pacific streamliner train at the invitation of railroad tycoons. He rolled in unaccustomed quiet and smoothness from the desert town of Victorville to Riverside and onto the frontiers of the streamlined era of railroad travel.[30]

Whatever the presence of the automobile by the thirties, his was the railroad era.

His seventeen-year frontier apprenticeship ended in the greatest rail journey then known, the family's transcontinental migration by rail from Chicago to San Francisco in the autumn of 1874. His father met them all in Los Angeles, easing their way on the last part of their long journey to their new home.

3

Almost Like Starting Over

Christopher Miller arrived in Riverside a few months before his family, surveying at a tin mine even more remote than the colony. The founders evidently welcomed his decision to bring his family there to join him, even though the mine work had ended. The colony needed Miller's expertise as settlers purchased land and needed boundaries proved.

The Millers and the colony were well met: all the family, except Emma, would live out their lives there and be interred in the Evergreen Cemetery. Seventeen-year-old Frank would become the town's first citizen, an influential political figure in California's Republican politics, and the confidante and beneficiary of some of the nation's major capitalists. His achievements for the town would bring repeated praise. His personality would spark frequent antagonisms; he would be scorned and labeled unpatriotic and a socialist. His married life would bring him deep love, profound grief, enduring happiness, and divisive family censure. He'd be honored by foreign nations and, by his own count, entertain "six presidents and six members of royal families."[1]

Much of the progress that Frank thrust himself into would have happened without him, but other achievements came to the town only because he initiated, cajoled, prompted, and pushed. And over a period of thirty years, he built a hotel that defined the town even more than its profitable citrus industry. His Mission Inn would endure long after the huge acreages of oranges and lemons had given way to suburbia. All of this and more lay far ahead and unsuspected on the family's evening arrival in October 1874.

The next morning after their arrival, his curiosity, abundant energy, and opportunity started Frank on making his own inventory of the place they'd come to. He cataloged the few buildings, a drugstore, a meat market, a blacksmith, and the largest, a brick dry-goods store. He made brief notes, promising himself to continue later, but he discovered quickly that there wasn't much more than he'd seen in his first foray.

He'd seen a community building lacking the battens between the wallboards, a gusty, dusty shell for early court sessions, church meetings, village sociables, and the euphemistically named four-grade school.[1] Other buildings, some homes smaller than two hundred square feet, were spread widely apart. Some were fringed by stunted shrubbery and spindly trees; some fronted vineyards of raisin grapes or young citrus or walnut trees, none of more than four years' growth in a dry climate.

Residents built cabins or homes for their families as soon as lumber arrived from San Bernardino. None of the homes were large: E. G. Brown's 1870 cabin floor measured sixteen feet by twelve with a nine-foot ceiling; James Boyd built his home even smaller—a ten-foot square cabin for himself and his wife.[2] As Frank walked about, he saw these few scattered cottages. One cottage was larger than the others, founder John W. North's home, with an attached colony office, and the Athertons' home, where the Millers stayed at first, stood a couple of blocks away. One settler, George Garcelon, made quite a stir in 1872 when he lined his house with lath and plaster, the only one of its kind in the village for many years to come.[3]

The dried-up landscape showed signs of the six or more rainless months. Frank walked the dusty village path from the Athertons' home to the nearby hotel for meals. He climbed what would later be named Mount Rubidoux, a prominent, rocky, treeless hill on the northwest edge of the colony boundary, and looked down on the older Jurupa Rancho, just north across the Santa Ana. He explored the river bottom. On several mornings he hunted fowl along the river, something for the pot in a crowded house. What he saw of the semidesert and scattered homes in the four-year-old colony allowed easy and unfavorable comparison with the nearly twenty-year-old Tomah set in Wisconsin's greenness.[4] He'd learn soon enough that had the family arrived four years earlier when the colony had begun, the scene would have been even more desolate—a treeless, shrubless, and denuded sandy plain, an open range stripped bare of any springtime grazing.

Frank would notice the simpler fare served at home and in the hotel; recognize the comfort of lighter clothing, even in October and November; and observe the active lives among the small population, perhaps two hundred families. Homegrown and local defined much of the diet and social life. San Bernardino lay northeast twelve miles away, offering the diversions of an older, more rough-and-tumble town. Getting there required a close to two hours' ride, river crossings, and an incentive to go at all for shopping, business, pleasure, or just fresh contact with a larger community. Getting to Los Angeles took a very long day, requiring a stage ride and about the same amount of time when the railway track reached Colton. San Francisco lay a week away.

A week after the Millers' arrival, Frank visited the home of the colony's founder, John W. North. If he had not already read the two *Ho! For California* broadsides that the founders had published, he would hear about their aspirations from Judge

North. He'd also see the future on paper as it was surveyed for the founders. The Mile Square, geometrically platted in the commonest contemporary grid pattern, resembled ten thousand other villages and towns across the nation. On paper, in Riverside a nod went toward the region's distant Spanish heritage (or the Los Angeles home of the surveyors)—with a more-or-less central plaza the size of a city block. Two streets, Main and Market, tracks in reality, connected casually with the two routes to Colton and San Bernardino. Christopher Miller must have remembered seeing a similar plat of Tomah in the same state of optimistic creation seventeen years before. He and the family were starting over.

North and his colleague James P. Greves had given serious thought to their colony. The cost of arrival and membership and the descriptions of settlement patterns and social institutions made for selectivity. They envisioned prohibitionist Christians living in a clustered village, engaging in intensive agriculture.[6] The people in their colony would be "good people"; they would be intelligent, industrious, and enterprising people who were expected to join in building an institutional infrastructure of civilized living—schools, churches, and reading rooms, as well as a lyceum and library. Their efforts for their own prosperity would benefit the community, a mutually strengthening relationship. Whether Frank caught this notion later or as he talked with North, Frank adopted this motif as his own. He'd grasp opportunities that promised benefit to himself and to the village, saying and doing so repeatedly.

The founders' idealism attracted some; capitalist goals drew others, probably most. All who came needed some financial reserves to carry them through for a year or more until a home was built and paying crops could be sold. All, however, wanted success for the infant enterprise located on 8,600 acres. Frank could see without being told that, contrary to North's hopes for a clustered village, most settlers buying land built their cabins or homes farmer fashion, centrally on their five- or ten-acre purchases. The houses were well spaced, close to plantings of vines, citrus, or grain crops, all requiring protection from wandering livestock, wild animals, and human predators. The Millers, village dwellers by habit, would also place their home centrally but in what was to be the town center.

Settlers tended to want acreage, one of the allurements offered in North's *Ho! For California* broadsides. They favored regenerative wealth[7] in the hoped-for rewards of fertile soil and the consequent increase in land values. In these respects, Riverside held out the promise of hopes likely to be fulfilled but not fitting the pattern that North had in mind.

Whatever young Frank heard from North or others, few would discuss openly the intense and divisive loyalties left over from the Civil War. Sharp lines separated Republicans and Democrats; the North and South lived on in the West to provoke community discord and conflict remembered almost fifty years later.[8] Then there were incipient confrontations between squatters and colonists over water, a matter that would soon force North out of management and lead to his leaving Riverside.

The Millers encountered other new social gradations in the presence of two small Mexican communities nearby, Indians in the Spring Rancheria community beside the river, and Catholic and Protestant religious loyalties drawn mainly along ethnic lines. A Chinese helper arrived to do the lifting and carrying when their furniture came.[9] The fault lines of these social divisions, however well garbed in good manners, were more complex than what Frank had lived with in his other frontier home.

Disadvantages revealed themselves slowly to the Millers: the remoteness, plagues of grasshoppers, and relentless desert winds, blasting in summer, chilling in winter, always with clouds of penetrating dust. At the nearby riverbank, Spanish residents of La Placita and Agua Mesa allowed their stock to wander; squatters on the borders of the Mile Square that comprised Riverside agitated for equal treatment with colonists, especially over water.

In this blending of newness and the familiar, Christopher Miller stayed with his profession over the next eighteen years, with only a short diversion into hotel keeping. Work seemed assured for him and his already competent helper, Frank. The Riverside Land and Water Company wanted the original survey lines checked and corrected; property buyers wanted accurate boundaries pegged; developers wanted large subdivision tracts platted outside the Mile Square that defined the colony. There were additions and corrections to be made to irrigation canals, those lifelines of agriculture that would distinguish Riverside then catapult many residents into affluence within a short span of years. Design and construction required an expert eye and practiced skills. Streets on paper must become realities. The senior Miller began work again within a few days of arrival, with Frank on the team. Only one rainy day kept them out of the field between then and Christmas.[10]

The colony fitted the Millers' habits of Protestant Christian morality and civic virtue and work skills. At age fifty, Miller brought years of experience as an engineer, surveyor, and community leader, and all of this enlarged his capacity for success in this new location. But in many ways he was beginning over again—guarding his wife's health, guiding four maturing children in their Protestant convictions, building a home, and supporting a family financially. As in Tomah, his professional skills were lacking in the colony. Like a few others, he was a Mason;[11] like many, he was a Civil War veteran; and like almost all, he was white, Republican, and Protestant. His arrival with Mary Ann, his college-educated wife, and four energetic, attractive children could only have pleased everyone in the colony.

Wife and mother Mary Ann knew that she too was beginning again in Riverside, hoping, no doubt, that it would be easier in seasons generally kinder to her health than Tomah, Wisconsin.[12] California's climate had lured her and thousands of others West in hopes of just such a reprieve. And although Riverside's burnt-up, boulder-covered hills offered nothing of the rural beauty of Wisconsin, the long, cold winters were a thing of the past: Riverside weather continued to be almost balmy while letters from Tomah told that frosts had given way to snow and months of freezing cold. And there might have been reason to hope that in Riverside Christopher would be working closer and be home more often with the family.

A few days after the Millers' arrival in Riverside, Mary Ann went to visit with a family some miles east, heading toward the present-day Redlands.[5] There, without her family around her, she relaxed for a few days, a travel-weary guest shedding the fatigue of transcontinental noise and grit, days of seasickness, and the jolting, eight-hour-long buggy ride from Spadra to her new home. For now Mary Ann was a guest, free of family cares and refreshed through pleasant autumn days and brisk nights in the drier airs of the semidesert climate. With Mary Ann away, even for a short time, daughter Emma took charge in Riverside as capably and smoothly as she had so many times before when Mary Ann's health ebbed. The difference now was living in a crowded house that was not her own and called for even smoother efficiency.

At forty-five, Mary Ann had a happy and successful marriage and a family of healthy, helpful children. Even the youngest, now ten, could share all the home duties under her direction. Emma, the oldest, would marry soon; the two younger children must be in school as required by a new California law.[13] She had guided their schooling in Wisconsin out of necessity in the early years; now she did it almost from habit. Shortly after school began, she visited the classroom several times, inscribing her name in the visitor column of the register.[14] Frank, beyond school age at seventeen, did need polish, she knew, especially with his spelling. At times she thought him just a big, overgrown boy, though he was always responsive to her wishes.[15]

Because of the housing shortage when they arrived, the Millers had moved in with the Athertons. If they gave thought to it, moving in with the Athertons after twenty-one years of comfortably housed homelife, property ownership, and village status may have seemed like another way in which they were starting all over again. The mere numbers in the Atherton house would change almost everything about domestic routines, no matter how considerate the newcomers or tolerant the hosts. The Millers' immediate choice to eat at least some of their meals at the nearby hotel and Mary Ann's visit elsewhere for a week or more were as much out of necessity as acts of forbearance and tact.

The Millers needed a home of their own, large enough for six and with room to spare for the guests they habitually welcomed[16] and would continue welcoming in so isolated a community. The prospect of income from boarders influenced their thinking, and when the Athertons left town and they began renting the home, they took in a boarder. When they did begin to build, less than a year after their arrival, these thoughts took material form in a large home well able to receive friends, guests, and boarders.

One of the first to join them was Gustavus Olivio Newman, who was coming, he said, "to claim his bride."[17] He had wooed and won Emma's heart in Tomah where he had met the family while he was the director of survey for the Wisconsin Valley Railroad. Their love drew him west in early 1875. His arrival, marriage, and later partnership with Christopher Miller in survey and boardinghouse operations in Riverside made for a comfortable association for a few years. Frank liked Newman; he wished Newman were more "a temperance man and loved the Bible," but these small failings were more than covered by his observed kindness and love for Emma.[18]

Frank's liking for the new had not diminished his love for the old; letter writing linked this chain across the continent, not only for him but also for all the family. His father and mother wrote, in one instance frankly taking up John North's idea of personal and community benefit when the local pulpit fell vacant. They campaigned directly with their former clergyman and his wife, the Reverend and Mrs. W. H. Cross, urging the opportunity for the pastor and the benign climate for his afflicted wife. In the long run, the Millers' campaign succeeded; Rev. W. H. Cross came to occupy the congregational pulpit for six years,[19] doubly rewarded as his wife's health responded to easier weather.

Young Frank had joined the Cross campaign, part of vigorous letter-writing activity that must have filled many an evening and Sunday. He gave most letters several writing sessions before considering them finished. Most went to adult friends, slightly fewer to age-mates, all in Wisconsin. As would any newcomer, he'd fill pages with descriptions of the place they had come to, about work, recreations, the family, and, when writing to the girls of his infatuations, he'd send circumspect but unequivocal words of his love. He had much to tell in those epistles of six and eight pages in his tidy handwriting.[20] In these and in his diary, Mattie Weed above all others became the focus of a pleasurable obsession. It pulsated steadily from almost the first week in Riverside, passionate when he sent a rose in mid-November and shortly thereafter as he inscribed her name in his diary within a wavy frame followed by a line of advice to himself: "Have faith and trust in God and all will be well."[21] Did he sense the cooling passion of love strung taut over so many miles or a competitive presence in Tomah, someone with more attractive educational or vocational prospects? He thought of her every day and reminded himself of it; fourteen separate diary entries detailed the waiting, receiving, and responding, the sheer luxury of her letters and his fantasies.[22] In his love life, Riverside was a desert, for him a place of separation, his youthful love requited only by slowly arriving mail, lean sustenance indeed for a passionate youth.

The last day of the year 1874 he worked all day on the transit. In the evening he took up an unfinished letter to an adult friend in Tomah, a Mr. Beebe. Writing it had already absorbed parts of two evenings, and when he finished it, he turned to his daily diary entry, still thinking of the envelope just addressed and its destination: "One year ago tonight I was at my old home in Wisconsin." Since beginning his first diary, Frank had closed each year by writing a short prayer or pious hopes for family blessings or eternal salvation. This year his final thoughts were different—work and its weariness, gifts exchanged within the family. He paused in his writing, skipped a line on the page, and then continued: "Mattie, Mattie, Mattie, Home Sweet Home." The same words were repeated as on previous days. Now as he wrote them, a small, inky smudge appeared on the page.[23]

4

Going I Don't Know Where

For Frank, as for the family, their new home brought continuity, change, and newness. His ties with Tomah, the home sweet home of his diary, were indeed loosening. The flow of letters had thinned. A little regretfully, he noted, "I feel that I am fast making friends but that I am forgetting my old friends at home."[1] In fact he had mailed away twice as many letters to old friends as he received, so the forgetting wasn't all one-sided or greater on his part. Even his postal devotion to Mattie Weed waned; she became "my dear good sister," a more manageable emotional tie.[2] His diary received short, increasing reflections on his frustrations with work, friends, recreation, and his own ethical standards. These were not new thoughts perhaps but evidence of his growing maturity. These changed family and social circumstances and his reflective nature sent him searching for at least fresh resolutions if not new dimensions.

Work took a high and clear priority—finding it, keeping it, and earning enough to meet obligations to himself and the family. Something bigger loomed: settling on a lifework that fitted his convictions. From home, school, and the pulpit, he knew the gospel of work and the stewardship of time with their imperatives of personal virtue, assured prosperity, and moral safety, even divine approval. The immediate need, however, was cash in his pockets and his contribution to boost the family income. His seemingly boundless physical energy and gregariousness provided powerful potential, but steady employment and a sense of vocation waited.

He took the clear path. His experience made him a valued member of any survey team, so he worked on survey with his father six days each week, sometimes in the village and at other times several miles away, lugging instruments, checking alignment down in the irrigation ditches, and correcting depths and gradients for water flow over the canal's many miles.[3] For days on end in his diary he recorded his fatigue. Then, beginning in late January 1875, he complained of a succession of illnesses: carious teeth ached in spite of "smoke oil" treatment; recurrent sick headaches sent him home from the field; an ear ached internally; a "sty" erupted on one ear; he had "piles quite bad"; neck muscles tightened to painful stiffness; and gastric upset "from eating oysters" at a party brought him even more discomfort. Most mornings he'd awaken sore and lame, but work put no crimp in his social life, which on at least one occasion kept him up till one in the morning.[4]

From his wages at a dollar a day—his father earned five—some went regularly on deposit at interest with the local general store.[5] Already careful with money, he relentlessly pursued by mail a $1.10 bequest from Tomah.[6] Savings accumulated slowly, but as soon as he could, he made the initial $110 deposit on a twenty-acre corner lot at the present Magnolia Avenue and Jefferson Street. Frank's father signed the papers for him, a purchase that tied him to quarterly payments of twenty-five dollars, though he sometimes added more—a lifetime habit—to more quickly reduce the balance on the $550 purchase. Around the edges of what became at times a spotty work schedule and through the hottest part of the year, he cleared the scrubby bushes, broke up the caked, virgin soil, and then planted and irrigated his fruit trees.

In so small a village, everyone knew about his hard work, his consistent habit of saving, and the land purchase and development. These were sterling values to be admired. With characteristic energy, he was setting a business pattern that served him well for the rest of his life: personal frugality, security assumed by a third party, and scrupulous repayment and reinvestment—all done with those who had proved trustworthy. Though he still lacked a vocational fix, his entrepreneurial streak signaled an independent disposition.

His imagination for self-improvement and vocational exploration also responded to a gift copy of the nationally popular *Hills Manual of Social and Business Forms*.[7] No sooner had he received the book than he began the exercises provided in it, which were intended to improve his handwriting. At the same time he sought double benefit, selling copies door to door, COD, in Riverside. He sold a few and collected then deposited the profit as savings. But his interest in it paled. He liked the money well enough, but the life of a book peddler was not for him, he wrote, adding a little obscurely, "Man makes the profession, not the profession the man."[8]

Family obligation rather than emerging enterprise drew him into helping build the family home in mid-1875. The Millers' block of land, bounded by Sixth, Seventh, Orange, and Main Streets, cost Christopher Miller and his prospective son-in-law and partner G. O. Newman[9] $250, the going rate for property sold by the colony.[10] A few weeks after his eighteenth birthday, Frank hauled rock for the foundation of the home he would share in one form or another for the next sixty years.[11]

The Millers built large. They had in mind an essential service to newcomers found in any village or town: temporary living with others while getting established. In memory Frank described the new house as "the largest and finest in the Valley" and also remembered bumping his head on the sloping ceilings in the upper bedrooms.[13]

Frank worked at backbreaking labor, carrying adobe blocks as his father and Newman built. He recorded shingling, laying floors, and the tedium of lifting and carrying adobe blocks. Inwardly he rebelled at such menial tasks, his feelings gently soothed, he thought in later maturity, by his father's understanding comments.[14] Fond memory, however, stretched the adobe experience into brick, making it far beyond his diary record. The story slipped, enlarged, into family mythology, even injected carefully into his reminiscences for the 1922 *History of San Bernardino and Riverside Counties*[15] and rehearsed as opportunity arose.

Settled in their new home, the family cast about for a suitable name. Emma recalled "Esperanza" as the choice.[16] Frank recorded a different family decision: "We have name[d] our home Glenwood Cottage," he wrote, giving no precedent,[17] but an earlier event suggests at least an association, if not an origin. He had earlier asked the local, blue-eyed charmer Annie Eastman to choose a name for his own twenty acres, a request she declined. The Eastman family had chosen "Englewood" as the name for their property. Without too much ingenuity, the name "Englewood" becomes "Glenwood," and my guess is that's just what happened: in the surges of his swelling infatuation for the Eastman daughter, Frank settled on "Glenwood," for him at least a linguistic pairing.

Shortly after his first night in Glenwood Cottage, Frank hired on as a mule driver at the tin mine in nearby Temescal. He could reasonably expect continued work, regular hours, pay, and a degree of independence by being away from home. As is so often the case, there were unexpected developments. After a tearful leave-taking and a brave diary entry of "San Jacinto

Tin Mine San Bernardino Co," he and a friend moved into the mine bunkhouse, took charge of their mules, and began hauling loads of ore during the late shifts.

At work, at meals, and in the bunkhouse, he recoiled inwardly from the miners' uncouth ways, fisticuffs, and vulgarity.[18] The mine boss kept his eye on the newcomers, cutting short their reading as they drove, giving them full care of the mules, and filling their off time with a seemingly endless list of odd jobs. Mining, he made clear, went on every day year round. Frank, in his innocence, followed his own conscience in doing no work on Sunday. Rather, even though the mine superintendent had warned him against Sunday rest,[19] he entertained his visiting sister Emma and G. O. Newman with a tour and picnic lunch on his first Sunday. The next week the boss called him away from his day of rest to sign a wage receipt. Frank refused; he'd do no work and no business on the Sabbath. He relented when the boss pointed out that the check was dated for Monday, not Sunday. But he worried, pricked in conscience. Later that week, fired from his mule driving and back home, he asked his diary, "Did I do wrong?"

The story of his plight circulated beyond the family, enough that an adult friend in Riverside commiserated, calling him "a Sunday martyr." Frank liked the phrase well enough to record it in his diary.[20]

He had been away less than two weeks, going the twenty miles to the mine with some sense of adventure. And although he gave only a little space to reflecting on his time there, his work habits later suggest lessons learned and not forgotten. And as far as we know, he left only two recorded descriptions of the mine experience, both recitals intended for his biography. In one he remarked his learning a solid defense of principle; in the other he compared early rigidity in Sunday observance with later flexibility, especially as the owner of a flourishing hotel. Either way, the episode generated lasting ethical reflection.[21] Moreover, he never again accepted day labor from which he could be fired or any work in a regimented, supervised position. Nor did he ever again work with an equal partner as he had done with the other youthful mule driver. He'd work alone, or he'd be in charge. He did take on manual labor, but of his own choosing and fitted to his own pattern.

Back in Riverside in late 1875, he cast around for work: he helped build the family adobe, worked on surveys, and talked occasionally of going away again to find work in San Francisco or Arizona.[22] He took a brief stint or two in local stores; one ended quickly in a "little organization debate" with the owner about how to stack goods for storage. He looked about for work, any work, he said, "even if I have to go into the ditch and shovel."[23] He took on a plowing contract, filled an order for a thousand grape cuttings, hauled sand, cut firewood, built a chicken house, and planted citrus and decorative trees on three home frontages. He acquired skill in budding and briefly prospered in lucrative contracts with newcomers, who knew only that their citrus trees needed his skill.[24] But whenever his father and G. O. Newman found lucrative engineering contracts away from home, they left the Glenwood to him and the rest of the family, without pay.

Frustrated and still without other prospects, he made the break, turning "all the papers and books over to Pa," determined to have nothing to do with running the house. He regretted cutting loose to leave his mother, Ed, and Alice, now seventeen, to manage as they could. He would "work hard to raise the note [on my property] this year. Life is hard sometimes but my [fight] is nothing compared with the life of some young men." He would not be satisfied until clear of debt.[25] He faced a tissue-thin credit balance, lacking funds to fully develop his lot[26] and even borrowing to make his quarterly payment.

Perhaps deeper concerns than earning money and paying off the note prompted his recognition that "Things are going I don't know where."[27] Nothing seemed to point toward his calling or lifework. No occupation beckoned to fit his temperament and personality or affirm his identity and support the autonomy needed by his unflagging energy and optimism.

His experience and family social status ruled out life as a day laborer or hired help; he'd shown no inclination for skilled craftsmanship or the trades. He lived a Victorian Protestant imperative: to follow some divinely appointed task. "Oh God," he wrote, "give me more will to do what thou hast put me in the world to do." Eighteen months after arrival in Riverside, he lacked conviction that he had taken the path in life that God had for him.[28]

Even so, resolute determination flourished; the first boy born in Tomah would not slacken in his awareness of *firstness*. "I am getting desperate," he wrote, "and I am not going to give up." He would get a good education and become "Good and Great," perhaps a statesman, he wrote on a hot August Sunday afternoon in 1876. Months later, still adrift, he repeated his determination: "I am resolved to work hard, and become something in this life. I pray God that this may be no empty thought. Live to work, do good and be happy, but I can do no better."[29]

If the bastions of Protestant morality challenged him in work and finding a lifework, so, surprisingly, did it invade his leisure, particularly baseball. He had joined the local Blues team, almost immediately becoming team captain as he had been in Tomah. Soon after the first competitive game, his already scrupulous conscience raised questions about his stewardship of time. He sensed selfish indulgence: "Oh there's a great deal of pleasure in [baseball]." He berated himself, writing, "I must not play ball so much," and, "I must not spend so much time playing base ball as I have." Repeated self-condemnation led to resolve; he told his teammates he'd resign and did just that.[30]

Though the circumstances in Riverside were different from those in Tomah, the same very sensitive conscience fueled Frank's vacillation between indulgent pleasure and self-accusation. Baseball gave greater pleasure than anything else. But he knew that play was only just that, something always to be taken in moderation after all other obligations were met. So resign he did, amid whatever the crosscurrents of motivation. In doing so he also ceded his leadership to others, something he repeated when moral anxiety stirred at the risks of joining in what he regarded as bad company.[31]

Such an active adolescent conscience led to socially isolating judgments. "So many fast young men," he noted. Frank feared "fast." He yearned in his diary, for example, over a rejected companion from work and hunting trips. "Oh how fearful is the future for [him], *poor boy*. Would God that fires or some awful means would come to blot out from Riverside the saloons which are the open gates to Hell."[32] Riverside's saloons were indeed blotted out a few years later but by nothing more awful and fiery than a popular vote in which the prevailing small majority did indeed see God's hand.

Throughout life Frank tested people by their moral worth, approving of them in the language of the times as being "clean" and "straight" in character. He strove ardently for exactly these virtues himself. He looked for them in others that asked for favors or sought introductions, in employees, in political aspirants, and in potential business partners. For many, age brings a mellowing and even compromise. Miller never gained a clear victory over this conscience, although geniality, even graciousness, smoothed the testy insecurity of early manhood. In maturity he sustained moral sensitivity, testing his behavior in a practical ethical pattern widely recognized in its public expression as "civic righteousness," the habitual effort to apply Christian principles to civic life, something by no means free from its own dilemmas.

※

The demons of erotic fantasy invaded Frank's young manhood, urgent and disturbingly ambiguous threats to a conscience that yearned and prayed for purity of thought while drawn by the sirens of worth and beauty in young women. His journey toward mature friendship, love, and intimacy led through the all-too-familiar youthful turmoil. Though giving and receiving the sweets of infatuation he walked the straight and narrow path, blameless, his record without mention of an improper act, sexual or otherwise.

En route he passed through a succession of passionate attachments, which, however intense, usually ran their course within about twelve months. He'd left Mattie Weed in Tomah in October 1874. The remorseless logic of distance transformed Mattie into his "sweet sister" by the next year-end; then in December 1876, he learned of her marriage to Adolph Schulz in Tomah.[33] A sweetly banal diary comment wishing her "happiness complete" lay lonely on his page."[34] Whatever his thoughts and memories then, the passage of years revealed engraved affection for this first adolescent love, perhaps made even more enduring because of the parting.

But already in 1875, two warmly admired young women had appeared in his life and diary, partners for walking, riding out, learning to dance, and exploring each other's worlds. Late in the year, the warmth of infatuation cooled, yielded to friendship, dwindled to acquaintance, and by year-end disappeared from his diary.

Into the ascendant came another, a Miss Wooster, and then Annie Eastman, she of Englewood, blue-eyed, blonde haired, and alluringly unresponsive to the smitten and aroused Frank. "Oh God," he prayed in thoughts about her, "Keep me Pure and Noble."[35] Almost on schedule after an agonizing twelve months, by January 1877, Annie became for him his "sister of golden hair." But passion would not die, resurrected occasionally in the colors of upwelling desire.

Then another appeared, and her coming would be more freighted with consequences. Isabella Hardenberg, one of the local schoolteachers, earned public praise: "Miss Hardenberg deserves great credit for the manner in which the school has been conducted for the past term."[36] She gained a growing place in Frank's attention. In the local dancing school, Frank and Isabella practiced graceful deportment and correct foot placement, their harmony allowing him to ask her the favor of the last dance at the close of the school, after which she would leave for summer at home in Wisconsin.

Whatever these swirling currents, Frank continued his habits of self-improvement. At the Lyceum he polished his speaking and debating skills, stretching his mind on topics of current importance. Both he and his sister Alice launched themselves as effective public speakers in this forum, its formal framework a restraint on his occasional outbursts. Later in life he'd excuse himself as an inept speaker. The record shows otherwise. Reported private conversations; his steady stream of political, social, and business correspondence; and three notable public speeches fully reported in the local papers all confirm a superior command of language and persuasive skills.

The friendship that grew between Frank and Isabella benefitted Frank's intellectual development, but his initiative also sought self-improvement to fill the place of privilege. He read and loved to be read to[37] from novels and self-help books crowded with information, strategies, and encouragement. Not unrelated, he chose as close friends only individuals better educated than himself, a habit that had telling consequences for him and for the growing village that he called home.

5

So Here Goes for Business

Even in 1876 as Mattie Weed married, Frank and Miss Isabella Demarest Hardenberg danced together, their sedate steps the first toward a loving partnership that ended only in death. About the same time, his search for a lifework began to take on direction that would lead with few detours to a successful business then to hotel keeping. Love and vocation converged, flowing smoothly together.

Isabella—intimates called her Bell[1]—had come to teach in Riverside from Wisconsin. Frank saw her at church and met her socially at home in December 1876.[2] He glowed, "a fine lady and a noble girl." He willingly gathered the financial pledges due the next June that assured her return to her one hundred dollar a month position after summer at home in Wisconsin.[3]

As she left, her gift to him of a rosebud transported him beyond himself: "She I know is an Angel woman to lift up degraded man. Woman alone is pure Good often times when man is but a Brute."[4] Returning in September, she gave him her photograph, a modest token of friendship. She moved into the Glenwood Cottage as a boarder, promptly setting him to work on a program of reading and grammar, with recitations to her on alternate nights.[5] Guiding hands must have paved the way;

his father served on the school committee, and his mother, already personally close to Isabella, was ever watchful of her older boy.

Mutual attraction between Frank and Isabella blossomed into a friendship altogether different from his earlier amours. He recorded no swelling passions. Rather he admired her social ease and her self-direction in employment. Her place in his intellectual life offered far more than merely conversations on rides or walks or at Sunday school. She scheduled him into her life. And perhaps best of all for Frank, she lived right there, under the same roof at the Glenwood.

Early in the autumn of her return, they had already grown comfortable enough with each other to move from the formal "Miss Hardenberg" and "Mr. Miller" to calling each other Frank and Isabella, or Bell occasionally. She rode with him to San Bernardino on buying trips. Once, as they bumped through the dusty sand, Isabella improved the shining moments by reading to him from Dickens's *Bleak House*. He listened then talked, not so much about Dickens, but to his own surprise, he poured out more and more of the thoughts he'd kept to himself and his diary. His feelings tumbled into confusion: a swelling love for Isabella, waves of sadness and loneliness coming unbidden, tearfulness at the remembered beauty of her singing, and admiration of her goodness. All this came under an umbrella of surging closeness to all his friends and especially his family.[6] Here indeed was a young man smitten. She, however, remained composed, inscribing in his diary for 1877, "That these pages may be the record of a noble life is the wish of your friend Isabella."[7]

Frank's other trips away from Riverside took supplies to his father whenever he worked on contracts at a distance. On one such trip to a Santa Ana River camp in September 1877, his father and Newman took Frank to Anaheim, where they met Collis P. Huntington of Central Pacific Railroad fame. His diary marked the event: "I was entertained by Mr. Huntington."[8] None could anticipate the significance, especially for Frank, of that brief meeting with Huntington. It would lead to other meetings and introductions to two other Huntingtons, Henry Edwards Huntington and Archer Milton Huntington, both of whom became arbiters of Frank's financial and aesthetic evolution.

Under the December moon of 1877, Frank and Isabella rode together to his father's survey camp and thence to Tustin in Orange County. As the pair drove down the chilly canyon, Isabella taught him the words and melody of that Christian worship standard, the "Doxology," "Praise God from whom all blessings flow." Together these two competent singers intoned the solemn cadences, much to the amusement, he thought later, of anyone who might be near enough to hear—a slight chance in that empty canyon.

By nine thirty that morning they were in Tustin. With business completed, their return trip took them back to the survey camp then up the canyon, where they paused to rest the horse and eat a "very romantic" picnic breakfast. They arrived back in Riverside very early Sunday morning, having welcomed the Sabbath by singing the "Doxology" many times over.[9]

Whether he knew it or not, this newest friendship spelled an end to his adolescent infatuations strung out over the previous half-dozen years. These trips to San Bernardino and Tustin were rich with pleasure and the stuff of memories, happiness beyond anything Frank remembered. Intuition convinced him that Isabella felt the same. Just as important to both in this time of social conservatism, they had gone and returned unchaperoned with public approval—their friendship affirmed, trusted, and even blessed. That in itself was reason enough for singing thanks.

Boarders moved into the Glenwood Cottage when the Millers did. Others sought them out, more than they could accommodate in the dozen or so rooms. The success suggested expansion, a move that required capital. The partners, father Miller and son-in-law Gustavus Newman, raised the money by taking on survey contracts and then built,[10] thereby becoming more able to meet the sharp competition from the two other hotels in town.

The new construction was attached to the original large home and had the look of a hotel. Now many more guests could enjoy the Glenwood's garden setting and the large, friendly home with its suggestion of privilege in the semiprivacy of the curving, treelined driveway. Family members welcomed guests, radiating a rare friendliness and concern for their comfort.[11] No bar stood ready, but beer, wine, and hard liquors were served at an already distinguished table, telling distinctions with travelers. The dancing parties, a dancing school of about six weeks' duration, and Saturday night sociables were perhaps not the only ones in the village, but they certainly had their own touch of quiet elegance.[12] When Frank adopted a Spanish house motto, "*Entre, es su casa Amigo*" ("Enter, friend, it's your home"), years later he belatedly put into words the attitude the hospitable family shared from the first and as accommodations grew.

Several times during that year, Frank reminded himself, "Things look rather bleak ahead but I said that on this new year I was going to step on to it with a firm step and go through it like a boy of some spirit."[13] His determination held. Diligent saving allowed him to pay off the balance owed on his land and provoked a year-end exaltation: "I got my deed to my land on December 29, 1877."[14] More than this, the glowing joy of Isabella's friendship had come almost unsought in a year that began with such dismal prospects.

While the partners pursued their contracts in the field,[15] Frank had the very unpaid assignments at the Glenwood that he wanted to avoid: hotel management and maintenance.[16] Very soon, however, Miller and Newman, surveyors with more work than they could handle, hired Frank away to supervise a survey crew, something his experience fitted him for very well.

Another larger contract followed; his pay was fifty dollars a month and board.[17] He was in business but in something that never once took his interest as a lifework.

The course of true love never does run smooth. Unexpectedly for Frank, Isabella decided to end the physical affection they were enjoying together in private moments. No details appear in the diary, just the prohibition. Then followed an added privation. "Bell decided…that she could kiss me no more. Oh, Bell," he wrote, "It shall not be so. Do not have it so Dear Bell."[18] Protests failed, and that was not yet the end. That same month, in March 1877, Isabella told of her plan to leave Riverside for a year in Santa Barbara. Perhaps earlier she had shared this with the Miller parents and his sister Emma, but to Frank the announcement came unexpectedly and was incomprehensible. If Isabella explained, nothing of her logic or his understanding ever went into his diary.

Why move away? Her reputation assured employment in the fall. Living at the Glenwood was secure. Mutual affection bound her and Frank's mother, Mary Ann Miller,[19] who would be protective of her courting son. Perhaps maternal wisdom advised a hiatus, sure of enduring commitment. Isabella's restraints on their private intimacy, whatever their shock to Frank's feelings, did not appear to undermine their committed friendship. Did she foresee a drift toward marriage while still uncertain about its attractions or about Miller's potential and what he meant to do in the world? Would a year's absence allow her, or both of them, the time and space to know the metes and bounds of their closeness, to measure their feelings and focus on plans for the future?

Frank wept.

In April, at the end of the school year, they went to church together; he was very happy and proud. "She looked handsome in her new black silk, almost proud, yet, no—so far above those we meet...but I may be blind yet no one seems so noble and sweet to me...each day I am made to love her more when I do not know why." That written, his next sentences lamented within inky frames of funereal black: "Bell is going away in two weeks and forever. Only she says for a year but I feel different."[20] With that his diary keeping ended.

In Santa Barbara Isabella easily shed the constraints of a village schoolmarm, writing to her sisters of dressing in a calico dress, finishing her hair in a knot, and doing as she pleased. She had arrived without the promise of a position but knew also that she had influential relatives with friends among the school trustees. She told her sisters that she would never go back to Riverside; earlier she assured them and herself that she had lifelong friends there.[21]

Three months later, Frank followed her north for a week's visit,[22] about which the record is silent. And whatever her early resolution never to return to Riverside, she spent her Christmas holiday there.[23] By the time of her return to Santa Barbara, Isabella had asked for and signed a teaching contract in Riverside for the next year, 1879–1880. As a member of the school committee, father Christopher Miller weighed in with his public endorsement.[24] So much for going away forever.

༺

Frank Miller's diary keeping ended with Isabella's first departure on April 28, an abrupt end to nearly eight years of almost daily writing, itself part of his personality, or so it had seemed.[25] For whatever reasons, he stopped. The new directions he found after Isabella's departure provided more than enough challenge to his time, crowding out even a small daily summary of his yearnings.[26] A later beginning in diary keeping petered out in the early months of the year it began.

༺

When the hotel expansion was completed, it added a two-story adobe and wood structure set directly behind the original house, toward Sixth Street.[27] I believe their choice of materials was dictated by not only cost but also taste. Observers began talking about a regional architectural identity. If Miller and Newman kept on, said the local editor, their use of adobe as a material of choice in building would produce "a structure equal in size and superior in beauty to the old Catholic missions' cathedrals."[28] This exaggeration of size and style veiled an interesting inference: Western hotel builders usually chose wood for cheaper hotels and fired brick for most others. In the colony very few home builders used adobe, as did some farmhouses in nearby Corona, but most in the nearby Mexican villages of La Placita and Agua Caliente by the river used adobe. And, of course, the crumbling Franciscan missions were adobe. Wood, brick, and stone spoke of modernity, progress, Protestantism, and the majority; adobe looked both back toward an almost consciously obliterated Spanish era and looked down on the social and economic scale. As for the emphatically regional California mission-revival style of architecture, quite unknown in 1878, almost a quarter of a century would pass before that would become popular, the signature of a new Glenwood and, indeed, of Frank himself, though by no means his only choice.

In what for most was a surprise move, Frank A. Miller became a merchant while Isabella taught school in Santa Barbara. He set up a lively "Cash Grocery Store!" announcing in the local *Weekly Press* on November 23, 1879: "I would respectfully inform the citizens of Riverside and vicinity that I have leased the store formerly occupied by Dr. Carroll and filled it with a stock of Groceries, Candies, Fruits and Nuts and everything usually found in a first-class Family grocery Store." Village gossip savored the news, another energetic venture by this popular village youth.²⁹ He reminded himself of this as he broadened his earlier hearty declaration: "So here goes for business."³⁰

When he described the beginning five years later, he wrote that his capital investment of $750 had developed "one of the finest retail grocery stores in the State," a consequence of "strict attention to business and honorable dealing." There was no lack of *firstness* here. His investment, in fact, amounted to much more than $750, but his remarkable success did begin on a thin-enough basis, and his assiduous habits of attractively honest value came easily.³¹ He allowed no credit buying. In the small print, he lured customers another way: "The highest prices will be paid for country produce in exchange for goods."³² In a year when gardens flourished in plentiful rains,³³ his offer pleased thrifty growers and gave him double benefit: produce for the store and for the hotel kitchen.

Prosperity and friends allowed him soon enough to build his own new brick store on Main Street. He shared a common wall with a newly arrived local jeweler and watchmaker.³⁴ The village drugstore was next door and in a year or so would also house the village's library.³⁵ This cluster, with the newspaper office across the street, offered shoppers convenience that merchants all hoped would attract customers, and it did. On a hot June day, Miller walked across the street to watch the first pressrun of a local newspaper. He talked for a while with the owner and walked away as the newspaper's subscription agent.³⁶

Miller painted his new storefront an arresting blue, becoming the Blue Front Store,³⁷ a color and name that provoked lighthearted comment,³⁸ just the attention he wanted. He advertised specific items, not merely groceries. He made space in his store for two sisters to sell their fresh bakery goods. The Blue Front became home for the telegraph office, the oracle of local and distant information. He bought in bulk on site in San Francisco, shipping frugally through Newport Beach³⁹ rather than Los Angeles. Public comment thought all this comprised "rather novel arrangements" ahead of the times, as indeed they were. Frank's newly expressed facility for profitable innovation continued as a successful business style and a mark of his personality, though it sometimes ruffled more tranquil minds.

"Strict attention to business" brought prosperity to the novice groceryman, however much he mused otherwise later in life about success through chance, accident, and simply "forces beyond control."[40] His success testified to his reach for opportunity and his timely vigor in grasping to advantage the forces of a social revolution in which he lived—a communications revolution. The striking blue color of his grocery store, his pithy newspaper messages, the telegraph office in the store, the post office next door, his newspaper subscription agency, his use of etched printing plates in display advertising—all of these reached deep into the core of a changing culture where people talked more often and in new ways and in the process shared greater detail than ever before. Success attended his ready grasp of resources at hand, even emerging in the village. This, rather than following distant visions, brought him the success that gossips relished and his competitors envied.

Frank Miller had changed directions. No longer the itinerant surveyor, he'd joined the staid world of grocers; he offered goods and services and not day labor. He no longer participated in the simple exchange of work for cash, but he showed a lifelong knack for seeking profit and community benefit. He had moved his place of business to the center of village life and gossip. With it all his status changed in his village of some 1,300 residents, most of them as conscious as people always are of their own social and economic differences. From this time on, his name appeared more often in the local paper. Now almost never printed as Frank, his name almost always appeared as Frank A. Miller.

In its own way, the village changed with the Millers. Flourishing pepper, cottonwood, and eucalyptus trees now shaded the widely scattered homes; citrus trees had rapidly replaced raisin-grape vineyards. More roads, formerly only on paper, had become sandy paths. Increasing real-estate deals indexed growth, and convoys of freight wagons brought building materials through masses of spring flowers, the horses bedeviled by swarms of villainous horseflies.[41] A rail connection in 1876 linked Spadra and Colton near San Bernardino.[42] Boosters lauded the virtues of Riverside in outlandish praise.[43] The same writers rarely mentioned the cruel desert winds, hot in summer and cold in winter; the clouds of dust; the long, blistering summer heat; or the necessity of capital reserves for newcomers building and waiting for their first crops.

Neighbors would see the Millers as settled and prospering, a family with a reputation for hospitality and solid community membership. But the senior partners at the Glenwood, Miller and Newman, were quietly restless, their outdoor surveying and engineering far more attractive to them than the desk register and management of the boardinghouse, however prosperous.

6

Like a Duck to Water

The senior men at the Glenwood were restless. Christopher Miller, at age fifty-three, lived a divided life between the hotel and field survey,[1] not settled on either. G. O. Newman, his son-in-law and partner in the boardinghouse, wanted full-time survey employment elsewhere, preferably with the US government. Their families must have felt the tension, but fortunately resolution for both men came smoothly. Newman sold his interest to the senior Miller for $3,200 and moved away to Arizona in 1880.[2] Frank, in his turn, bought out his parents' interests for $5,000 in promissory notes, becoming, at twenty-three, the youngest hotelier in Riverside, possibly in California.[3] Christopher Miller and Mary Ann eased into more agreeable lives with their daughter Alice and youngest son, Ed, at the hotel. Their older daughter, Emma, was married to Newman and continued living on the Newman ranch just over a mile away.

Frank's growing assets assured his financial survival and easy repayment of his debt. He sold his already productive twenty acres for $7,300, a tidy profit sweetened by the prior sale of five hundred pounds of figs from his trees.[4] Paying guests came and returned to the Glenwood, and the Blue Front prospered.

Tables do turn. Young Miller had left behind those years he had seen as "going I don't know where," those times of vocational, even social wandering. As hotel owner, he had not become *pater familias*, replacing his father's strong presence, but he now owned the roof over the family and was proprietor and at least titular host at the hotel. His beloved Isabella, back in Riverside as a teacher for the 1879–1880 school year, lived under his roof, and like his parents, she would do so for the rest of her life. His sister Alice would live there and work for him; his brother, Ed, would also, though intermittently. It is no surprise, then, that he would later grasp a title tossed off by a friend, claiming for himself and his letterhead the designation "Master of the Inn."

Nor were any surprised at the wedding announcement for the popular schoolteacher back from Santa Barbara and the energetic, young groceryman, who was now a hotel owner. The ceremony would be the highlight of the summer. Family members loved to tell how business threatened his composure as Miller dressed for the ceremony on June 8, 1880. A wagonload of groceries arrived at his Blue Front; the driver, weary from his daylong haul in ninety-degree heat, wanted Miller and was eager to unload. In despair, the groom begged for at least enough time to get married.[5] No doubt someone else unloaded the wagon.

"A Brilliant Wedding," said the local paper, which ran eight column inches telling of friends decorating the church, witnessing the ceremony, and spreading joy in the community. The reporter waxed wise about the large floral bell hung in an arch over the couple during the service. "Whether the bell should remind the congregation of the marriage bell which always chimes so merrily, or whether it suggest the bride's name, or whether it referred to the many Riverside belles there present who endeavored to peep down into the future and get a glimpse of the time when they were to figure conspicuously on such an occasions—our reporter failed to find out." After the ceremony Mr. and Mrs. Frank A. Miller received their friends informally at the Glenwood.[6]

Beyond those details we know nothing. Perhaps the reporter in so small a community assumed that everyone knew from having been there. What the bride or the groom wore, who attended, and the form of the ceremony—nothing of these details remains. Nothing in the Miller family record allows us to revisit this evening wedding that attracted as many, possibly more, than could crowd into the little wooden chapel. We can be sure that the Miller parents and brother and sisters attended, with Emma there alone because her husband had already gone to his new employment. Isabella's sister Rose, a recent arrival in town, would certainly have been a bridesmaid.

Marriage changes everything. Isabella came a thousand miles from her Wisconsin home to Riverside. Self-reliant, she traveled alone and farther than many women might do, whatever the inducements drawing her to so remote a place. Now twenty-seven, as a respected teacher and public servant, she managed a school, responsive to the trustees and parents and expected to validate herself in her pupils, especially in their year-end performances. She supported herself financially, even though at the mercy of public fund raising in a poorly budgeted town. And although her superior professional competence had twice won her public recall to Riverside, she shared the modest social status of all elementary-school teachers.

Marriage changed much else for Marion. It denied her a private income, ended her independent management of her life, put limits on her movement, and could have made her as invisible in the community as almost all other women became at the time. In the close Miller family, she'd be the live-in daughter-in-law, the sister-in-law of Alice, the hotel manager, and the wife of Frank, the proprietor, all of whom had well-formed family and hotel fiefdoms and carefully cultivated relational boundaries.

Communities also have their tiers of prestige. In the late nineteenth century, hotel keeping ranked low on these scales.[7] In Riverside this seems to have been true for the Millers for many years. Their names rarely appeared among Riverside's "best people," those named in the social columns. A prominently announced eightieth birthday, for example, just days before the Miller wedding, specifically named thirty-six guests—including the Evans brothers, Albert S. White, Mr. and Mrs. James Bettner, several Norths, and the Rudisills, who'd been joined at the party by "many others." The Millers may have attended among the "many others," but they were not named. Many of those named had entertained their visiting relatives and friends at the Glenwood's tables; all had, at some time or another, hired either father or son as paid labor. Further, when local pretensions called for ladies to publish their "days at home," to guide social visiting, none of the Miller or Newman names ever appeared. In that sense also, the Millers were not seen as society.[8] Ten years after its founding, Riverside already lived in clearly stratified social patterns and would continue to do so. The Millers had a niche almost entirely their own, even set off from the layered community and from the commercial hotels by the distinctiveness of their lives and the definitions that the hotel took on, carefully scripted by the Master of the Inn and his wife.

The newly married Millers delayed their wedding trip until April of the next year then traveled east. Never far from thoughts of business, Miller mailed a card from Deming, New Mexico, reminding the Riverside newspaper, "The Blue Front is the place to buy groceries. All well. Frank A. Miller."[9] Good-naturedly, the editor published the card, just the advertising Miller intended. Other squibs followed.

The couple visited Chicago and then Isabella's mother and three sisters in their hometown of Lone Rock in southern

Wisconsin. There Isabella could show off her husband to the home folks who had seen only pictures.[10] Then they went on to Tomah, Wisconsin, where Miller could show off Isabella, visit old friends, and sell land for cash.[11] They met a Grandma Shultz; she now was the mother-in-law of his adolescent sweetheart Mattie Weed, who was the wife of her son Adolph. Mattie and Adolph lived in Tomah, and I cannot imagine that the two couples did not meet, however briefly, chatting and silently appraising each other as couples will do in such circumstances.

Riverside had fared better than Tomah in the intervening years, its economy cushioned by careful management of the water supply, profitable citrus and raisin crops, and, as the locals liked to hear it said, "men of energy, enterprise, intelligence and wealth" who had settled in the village. (Those who lacked the wealth on arrival had fared much less well.) Disinterested observers agreed. Even a decade later, the *San Bernardino Gazette* saw Riverside as "particularly fortunate," in that while "Nature [had] done little for her, skill and well directed energy [had] done much."[12] Other Southern California towns had also prospered—Anaheim and Pasadena had a similar economic resilience, though for different reasons, and they also rode out the depressed times with little distress.

By moving to the West, both Isabella and Frank had seen the elephant, as said at the time—the excitement of the West with its rewards and sometimes hard lessons—and whatever their fondness for the scenes of childhood, they returned to Riverside telling of their satisfaction with their place in the world after two months of travel together.[13]

While the couple traveled, Alice Miller managed the hotel. Congressman William McKinley from Ohio, later to become president of the United States, came with his wife and sister. Alice introduced them to another guest, Collis P. Huntington of

Central Pacific and Southern Pacific Railroad fame. Later the nationally known travel writer Charles Nordhoff came seeking material for his popular books promoting California.[14] The Glenwood's notability attracted them and others in a steady parade of nationally notable guests whose names remain important in the twenty-first century. With them came scores of now unknown but then influential women and men—politicians, capitalists, businessmen, entertainers, and social reformers—all welcomed through the doors of the Glenwood and its successor, the Mission Inn; all spreading its fame; and a very few becoming Miller's friends and advisers.[15]

Back from his wedding trip, Miller's hustle and bustle generated the comment that he had "taken to business again like a duck to water."[16] He advertised. The grocery business benefited from short, punchy newspaper pieces, one- and two-liners: "Fresh crackers at the Blue Front" or "I have the largest and best stock of cigars and tobacco in town at the Blue Front. F. A. Miller." His hotel advertising also differed from his competition, using a steel engraving of the hotel in a short two-column-wide layout. He played to his strengths: central location, the one-block setting among citrus and shade trees, easy access to public rooms, daily sunshine in every guest room, and verandahs on all sides. The advertising language defined patrons selectively as active, healthy, affluent, goal oriented, and upper middle class, describing patrons as "business men, tourists, travelers, and pleasure seekers" seeking the "best accommodations to be found in Riverside." Alice early became the hotel's manager, named in advertising and letterhead alike.[17] The hotel's solid reputation, its warm family hospitality, and its fine table in those years were recalled even fifty years later.[18]

Miller added to the grocery store with display windows, sliding glass shelf covers, a large basement and storeroom, and a papered and carpeted office. Here was *firstness* or more. Local opinion had it that he moved "a little in advance of the demands of the times, but he [had] built up a very lucrative business by always exhibiting a judicious amount of energy and push." He was the companion of opportunity in any setting, a comer and possessing, as was said, American "goaheadativeness" [*sic*].[19]

Many didn't expect his innovative independence, finding it an uneasy fit into the convenient box of conformity but an easy target for editorial witticisms. A month after the wedding, for example, he left his horse hitched to his delivery wagon all night. The editor could not resist an oblique comment linking his apparent forgetfulness to the happiness marriage brings.[20] His frequent visits out of town led to a comment about his being back in town "for half an hour."[21] The blue of his storefront and its later galvanized tin roof, both novel in Riverside, drew lighthearted notice in local newssheets.

Free from the hotel after his son's take-over, the senior Miller soon took a surveying contract on the Colorado River near Blythe. There he endured summer on the river again for three or four months the next year. The harsh desert climate tanned his face, bleached his beard, and aged his clothes. On an unannounced return visit back to Riverside, and I suspect well aware of his bedraggled appearance, he went directly from the coach to his friend James Roe's store looking for a jackknife. Roe failed to recognize him but watched him guardedly. By then I believe Miller sensed the irony of his situation and went next door to the Blue Front and asked his son Frank for provisions on credit for a prospecting trip. The younger Miller flatly refused, giving no sign of recognition. Now abundantly sure of his unplanned disguise, father Miller continued around the village, to a physician for a prescription, to the railroad office seeking work, and to the land office wanting to be shown land for purchase, always unrecognized and each time promptly turned away. He went home to the Glenwood and to a room, discovered there by one of his daughters, who called to her sister to announce a tramp in the house. As they prepared to show him out together, his wife, Mary Ann, came to his rescue with belated recognition. The *Daily Press* loved the story, ending its tale by drawing its own curtain of privacy over the details of "a family scene."[22]

In his usual appearance, almost everyone in the village knew Christopher Miller, received him as an amiable gentleman, remembered his quiet dignity, and respected him as a veteran and Mason. His few surviving letters reveal a subtle and kindly wit. He likely enjoyed some of the small drama of his brief anonymity as much as anyone reading about it, yet like them, he must have wondered.[23]

༄

A year after purchasing the Glenwood from his father Frank Miller decided that competition from other hotels and his own increasing patronage were reasons enough for more expansion.[24] Within a month he let a $10,000 contract, fixing completion dates for the first of June. As April began, the foundations went in. By July 4 Miller hoisted his large, new "Glenwood Hotel" pennant to announce completion.[25]

The addition, with its plain roof lines and verandahs, looked like dozens of other timber construction-settlement hotels in the West. Miller landscaped the block, building a delightfully secluded patio on the southeast side and seating areas sheltered by grape arbors and glass enclosures, summer and winter havens for quiet conversations. Where else could guests have baskets of fruit in their rooms, much of it picked from orange trees outside their windows?

Frank and Isabella had also put their stamp on the Glenwood in the decorations throughout.[26] The "back of the house," where vendors and employees came and went, took on a newly organized appearance. The Glenwood had settled into itself and the community, notable for sociability and select festivity.[27] Much later a close observer and lifelong resident in the town assured his listeners that even before a new hotel had been built in 1903, in those earliest years the Glenwood held pride of place among Riversides hostelries.[28] Indeed, no other hotel in Riverside, and few in California, received such sustained praise in travel and leisure magazines whose messages reached far beyond the town.

Miller decided to sell the Blue Front, apply the capital to the hotel, and focus his efforts more sharply. That done—Miller retained the Blue Front real estate—he thanked the community for their patronage, urged support of the new owners, and turned his attention to the Glenwood. The pontifical newspaper editor thereupon reviewed the history of the store and of the Glenwood and then gave his blessing on the whole arrangement.[29] The *Los Angeles Times* endorsed evidences of success.[30] From then on news from the Glenwood appeared often in the metropolitan papers.

Even more happiness for Frank and Isabella came with the birth of their daughter, Allis, at home in the old adobe on April 19, 1882. Unable to resist a verbal flourish that exceeded his other reports of births, the now good-natured local editor described her arrival as "in a very destitute condition but carefully provided for and Frank A. is passing cigars to all his friends." Just a month earlier Miller had insisted that the local phone line, up until then only at the Blue Front and half a dozen other Riverside businesses, be connected through to the Glenwood,[31] more than a coincidence.

At twenty-six, Miller had become active in community affairs. He had represented his church congregation at a regional meeting; he'd helped plan the annual Citrus Fair in Riverside. He joined in protesting a postmaster appointment. His long-standing Republican Party affiliation[32] involved him enough for his name to appear with the local party leaders petitioning their central committee.[33] But his full immersion in politics lay ahead: he would have to earn his place among the influential. That came within two more years, when he became one of five elected county delegates to the state's Republican convention, then a member of a permanent Blaine and Lincoln Club.[34] These growing involvements took him away from the hotel, but his sister Alice's management made him less needed. His eye, however, seldom wandered far from the business details, and his pen was ready in a stream of correspondence, as surviving records and letter books reveal.

Success is its own herald. Word of Miller's acumen in the hotel business brought offers of management from owners of newly opening or struggling hotels. The first, in April 1884, came from the local Park Hotel, which he promptly leased for two years.[35] The venture thrived but not enough to lure Miller to renew the lease. Rumors in Los Angeles had it that Miller would take over the new Southern Pacific Railroad hotel beside the ocean in Santa Monica. Nothing came of it. He did, however, take on furnishing and opening the oceanfront Long Beach Hotel.[36] Isabella and two-year-old Allis joined him for the summer; it was cooler for them all, and for Isabella, it was a release from demands on her at the Glenwood with a tiny daughter in tow.

The twenty-first century opinion of Miller as merely Riverside's extraordinary hotelkeeper would surprise his contemporaries. They knew him early for far broader interests and achievements around the town and county, even on a national stage, all played out against the hotel as a backdrop. From his own point of view, his interests were all organized around an amalgam of personal gain and community betterment. "I do not mean to take to myself an undue amount of credit for the success of any public enterprise," he said to the town trustees much later. Any benefit to him, he added, had been "solely that which [came] by reason of the progress, the building up and successful development of Riverside," all of which he had pushed.[37] This focus, proclaimed in the town, separated him, he thought, from others involved in change or seeking their own advantage.[38]

7

For Sale at a Bargain

In June 1885, on a financial upswing,[1] Frank Miller offered the Glenwood for sale by simply adding a line in his long-running newspaper advertisement: "This property for sale at a bargain." To those whose surprise prompted inquiry, he said that he wanted to retire from the business of hotel keeping.[2] But up to that time, he had done nothing to signal thoughts of retirement. Rather, he had honed his competitive edge by adding indoor bowling, roller-skating, and target shooting in a new building,[3] attractions his fellow hotelkeepers did not offer. And over the thirty months while the for-sale notice was out, he would bring in other attractions and improvements to his hotel. Were these inducements to buyers? I believe they were hints of ambivalence about leaving the hotel-keeping profession.[4]

Miller wanted a resort clientele. He convinced Walter Raymond of the distinguished Raymond and Whitcomb Tour Company of the Glenwood's allure, getting commitments that brought tour groups in large numbers, their arrival made even easier when Riverside's railroad connections doubled. The arrangement paid off all around: the railroads wanted more passengers, and tour-company profits increased. Miller had tapped into a new seasonal clientele,[5] and the overflow of guests benefitted other hotels in the community.

By coincidence or intention, the Glenwood fit tourist expectations of the West. Guests arriving by stage in that railroad-and-trolley age delighted in the adobe and its board-and-batten construction and sat in vine-covered lattices among citrus surroundings and exotic vegetation.[6] Doing the town, as local, guided touring was called, took little time because there was so little town to see, but the long, horse-drawn ride along the treelined Magnolia Avenue offered the seemingly endless green of citrus orchards, fruit laden in winter, and the ride was a pleasant two hours with pauses for refreshment along the way. Here, indeed, was the West as Eden.

Word of Miller's willingness to sell the Glenwood circulated rapidly among the hotel fraternity and traveled all across the country in the widely distributed Riverside newspapers. Miller waited. Thirty months passed. No buyers came.

Why, after five prosperous years, would he want to sell or retire? His hotel expertise spoke for him; his hometown business and political stature had grown. Walter Raymond's tourist groups sometimes overflowed his hotel's capacity.[7] And why no buyer? In the fluid world of hotel ownership and management, the prosperous Glenwood, with its sixty-five rooms, location, and select clientele, suggested a quick sale, especially in good times and with its recently added attractions.

What else might Miller have had in mind? Citrus ranching? Becoming a canny capitalist, investing and lending in a growing economy? Going more deeply into real estate or becoming active in trolley lines?[8] He predicted collapse for the two local street railways in 1886,[9] but full of his own *firstness*, he incorporated the Riverside and Arlington Railroad Company a year later. Did that promise the attraction he needed?

And if he retired, what would happen to the family? True, Miller's responsibilities at the hotel had shrunk as Alice and Frank Richardson, both proven managers, moved in courtship toward marriage. His younger brother, Ed, had finished school and gone exploring the world of survey with his father on the banks of the Colorado River.[10] His mother's health no longer caused him worry. Though incomplete now, the records suggest that all of Frank Miller's large debts had been paid. But even so, talk of the sale and the turmoil of uncertainty if it should happen must have been unsettling for the rest of his family[11] and for him.

Meanwhile the Miller and White real estate and insurance office in Riverside did very well indeed, taking commissions that hovered at about 8 percent and on occasions more than 10 percent.[12] Albert S. White took up residence in the Glenwood as it opened in 1876; his business experience in New York and his friendship with the younger Frank served well as the basis for this joint venture. The partners took exclusive listings, did all the promotion, and drove buyers to and from property in their buggy and pair. What it all amounted to in dollars and cents is now impossible to know, but Miller's brief returns to diary keeping for the years 1886–1887 recorded what appears to be an 18 percent profit after all expenses. He noted an additional $4,400 from the Park Hotel.[13] A miscellany of other scribbled calculations strongly suggests even more impressive returns.

But why retirement? Had he concluded from observation or from advice from his railroad contacts that the existing Glenwood Hotel had exhausted its potential or nearly so? Miller and others all liked to call their hostelries first class, but they knew better: they all had seen the service, luxury, and opulence of the genuinely first-class resorts[14] and knew very well how far short Riverside fell. If he were to keep ahead in the business, he must invest in a first-class hotel and do so first in Riverside.

Whatever else stirred Miller's ambitions during the years while the sale announcement ran, he took on a succession of activities away from home, the first in Pomona some twenty miles away. There he furnished and opened the dozen-room Palomares Hotel, taking Isabella and Allis to live in it while he worked. When his sister Alice and Frank Richardson married in Riverside, Miller sent them off immediately after the wedding as managers in Pomona.

At the same time he went into a real-estate venture in what became Claremont, near Pomona. Few prospects even came to look at Claremont's river rocks and scrubby bushes. Sales were scanty, leaving Miller and other sponsors with that remnant of many a failed land-development scheme—an empty hotel. He, with others, donated his interests in the hotel to the fledgling Pomona College,[15] keeping the connection for the rest of his life.

Despite Claremont, he was popular in Pomona. The *Pomona Progress* commented, "Frank Miller is in Pomona and we hope he is here to stay. He is a live man and will make a first class citizen," to which the Riverside editor replied, "What yer givin' us? Take Frank away from here? Not much! We can no more spare him than we can spare our glorious climate."[16] Miller's gracious geniality allowed the editors comfort enough as they indulged in their exchanges. They, and indeed all the business community, recognized Miller's untiring activity and the value of his ever-widening acquaintance with significant developers, administrators, railroad magnates, and capitalists. Few would encourage his selling of the Glenwood or moving away. There were not many like him, none in Riverside.

Local businessmen didn't need to be told that tourism boosted their local economy,[17] and calls for a first-class hotel sounded in escalating editorials, with comments such as, "Wake Up Riverside," and "Shall we Progress or Retrograde?" A syndicate formed, announcing a hotel more splendid than anything anticipated, grander than anything seen within fifty miles.[18]

Then came a proclamation: "Hurrah for Hotel Rubidoux," a $250,000 resort hotel for the lower slopes of Mount Rubidoux. Here was luxury far beyond the tens and even the twenties of thousands being spent serially on the Glenwood, the Rowell, and others. I believe Miller anticipated this, that it influenced his for-sale sign, and that he watched developments, reading the implications for himself and the planners. Headline assurances promised a January 1, 1888, opening.[19]

Mount Rubidoux rises about four hundred feet above Riverside, northwest along the Santa Ana River. It is rocky, treeless, and has a generally symmetrical form. Construction of the splendid hotel began in August, just five months before the proposed opening date. Like everyone else in town, Miller felt the shocks of the blasting for the hotel's foundation.[20] Moreover, he knew that he had no part in the hotel or the corporation. That same month Miller took down the for-sale sign that had been displayed for two and a half years.

What would that grandly designed new hotel mean for him and for his family? What would it mean for the promising arrangements he had hammered out with Walter Raymond and his tour company? We can only speculate. One hint of his possible anxiety remains in sketches he made of subdivisions of the hotel property behind the Glenwood.[21] And although nothing came of it, the sketches suggest at least his passing thoughts about other uses for his land, more than hint of some perplexity about the future.

Adding to that, another hotelkeeper proposed an upscale commercial Arlington Hotel for Eighth and Lime Streets, to be completed and serving its first guests on Sunday, December 17. Completed in the Victorian mode, made of contemporary materials, and better than anything so far in Riverside, the Arlington welcomed its first guests and served its first meals in mid-December 1888.[22] If fear of raw competition prompted the offer of sale three years earlier, the reality of the Arlington and the proposed Mount Rubidoux hotel confirmed what Miller saw as a worst-case scenario.

Illness added to the mists of anxiety: neither Isabella nor Frank was well. The deterioration of Isabella's health is unexplained; Miller himself suffered a painful surgery for hemorrhoids that had bothered him since adolescence. A slow and painful recovery kept him housebound for two months. Then, taking the family with him to San Diego, he sought hot seawater therapy for himself and rest and quiet for Isabella.[23] Both benefitted, though recovery was slow.

Construction on the Mount Rubidoux Hotel lagged in a disturbed economy; getting behind schedule in 1888, the construction slowed then stopped. Investors begged off their promises, and even attractive house lots at the base of the mountain didn't sell to help finance the project. The hotel's wood framing stood naked and exposed, its unseasoned lumber warping in the sun, buffeted further out of true form by the dreaded, dust-laden "Northers" gusting strongly from the desert. Timbers collapsed. What would have been a hotel just slightly smaller than the renowned Hotel del Coronado in San Diego died before even taking on the look of its promise, a victim of slowly vanishing investment and perverse weather, its chief promoter financially ruined.[24]

Miller must have sighed in relief as he looked and learned. In the future, whatever his own promises and projections in building, he'd turn no sod and drive no nail until he had cash in hand or credit from proven sources, often not local. Even so, in future projects he too would see financial support slip away from him. Perhaps when he talked late in life about events shaped by "forces beyond our control," he had in mind not only providence and destructive weather but also investors' fickle promises. Now, with the Mount Rubidoux Hotel in ruin, he faced only the Arlington and his own capabilities.

Miller conditionally donated a Main Street site on his block to the YMCA, requiring a three-story building valued at least at

$18,000, with the two top floors his to rent out and retention of the title to the land. Some on the YMCA board balked at the strings he attached, but with the almost immediate appearance of $7,000 in donations and a little time to think about their options, all signed.[25]

Miller's rentals on the upper floors later took an unexpected turn. The rapidly growing Church of Christ, Scientist congregation rented from him for worship space.[26] Mary Ann Miller had befriended the local church founder, experienced healing, and, with several family members, joined the new congregation.[27] Community hostility became bitter indeed, but the thriving congregation was at first harmoniously received at the YMCA, in part because they had contributed generously to the building program. But the relationship soured. Protestant orthodoxy on the ground floor saw heterodoxy, even heresy, upstairs. Protests led to the expulsion of the Christian Scientists, something at least approved by landlord Frank A. Miller.[28] This complicity in the eviction could only have strained family relationships. Interestingly, when he began to record his family history in the 1930s, he never mentioned the family's memberships in the Church of Christ, Scientist or his mother's fervent Christian Science loyalties; he persisted in his unsupported claims that his mother was a Quaker, something for which there is no evidence.

Miller served alcohol at the Glenwood, something far more public, contentious, and long-drawn-out than the eviction of the Christian Scientist group. The town voted dry in April 1888, by only a small margin. A forced compromise arising from hard business sense allowed hotels of twenty or more rooms to serve alcohol at meals. Miller himself supported prohibition (with one notable exception) and liked to repeat well-practiced lines about never having taken a drink at a bar or of standing a man to a drink.[29] But in Riverside, Miller, hotelkeepers, and voters generally knew that guests insisted on beer, wine, and hard liquor—temperance hotels fared poorly. This issue was revived with every election, not always requiring an up and down vote but linked to candidates campaigns and ordinances regulating alcohol sales in drugstores, prescription or otherwise.[30] The "drys" wanted a drought, not a damp. In Miller and others, they saw either hypocrites or souls in need of conversion experiences.[31] With the federal constitutional amendment of 1920, Miller remained contrarian enough to cast his only antiprohibition vote: "I always voted the prohibition ticket except when the state and national issue came up in 1920 and the prohibition friends were not willing to pay the liquor interests for the damages they were inflicting."[32]

Just days after the city went dry, if business kept him in town, Miller would have watched the Pavilion, the community hall, burn to charred ruins[33] across from his hotel on Main Street. Many watching the blaze knew the community hall from the inside, having attended Citrus Fairs, heard visiting speakers, watched plays, and chuckled at vaudevillian humor high and low. Some had skated their fancy turns and glides on its dusty board floor. Those watching who scorned theater and had voted for prohibition may have seen the consuming fire as a second blessing in the same week. How it burned!

But Riverside would have its pleasures. Within days an iron-sided livery stable on Eighth Street opened, called the Riverside Opera House, then, sensing irony, renamed the Lawrence Pavilion. At least one visiting troupe looked inside then left town, refusing to play in the shabby venue.[34] But the short line trains to San Bernardino readily carried patrons there to see and hear the "the most glamorous woman of her time and the most awful actress," Lilly Langtry.[35] In Riverside the ever-opportunistic Frank Miller again seized the moment, with a well-enough-developed plan in mind and on paper and his financially robust partners in the wings.

Just eight days before the blaze, Charles M. Loring, Miller's winter visitor from Minneapolis, had written to the paper suggesting a replacement building. Surprisingly in a town of divisions and delays, his offer met positive responses all around.[36] With the fire as added incentive, Miller, his real-estate partner Albert White, and Loring together gambled on a chance worth taking. In unusual thoroughness, nimbleness, and secrecy, they had sketched a construction budget and proposal for what became the Loring Building and Opera House. They offered the town not only a state-of-the-art opera house but also offered to provide for a city hall, the fire department, a courtroom, a library, rentable offices, and a jail in the basement.

They had every reason to be nervous about their plan's sweeping scope and blunt competition from a proposal by H. B. Everest, owner of the local Arlington Hotel. The trustees pondered then accepted what was known as the Loring proposal. Miller and White were not mentioned publicly, but their alacrity showed in assured financial backing, having sets of complete drawings in hand, and naming a small group of influentials ready to buy into the centrally located project. They had outpaced Everest. Miller also plucked another plum: he would be secretary to the board and manage the opera house and building located so conveniently across the street from his hotel.[37]

Local residents believed, correctly, that the completed opera house, seating almost nine hundred, outshone almost all in Southern California, a devastating contrast with the Pavilion.[38] The lavishly decorated theater interior with a high-rounded proscenium arch and deep stage catered to all local tastes and cared for all but the most extravagant traveling shows. Because it housed the theater, business offices, the inevitable corner drugstore, and, at first, Miller's office, the building became a nexus of community activity.[39] The chance taken paid off in steady annual dividends for Miller, Loring,

White, and their fellow shareholders. For the community, it marked the end of an era.

Miller, now thirty-one, had winning strategies for the opening and programming of the building. He reserved a room for a subscription library and from his office booked opera-house performances, becoming, in effect, a cultural guide in the town. Did a thread of motivation lead back to his fascination with long-ago performances of Shakespeare's *Othello*, seen in wintry Wisconsin? If so, it energized him, not merely his viewing of stage performances but rather his managing and controlling. His tactic for the opening performance assured the greatest possible community approval. He booked a local production of *Iolanthe* by Gilbert and Sullivan, a show already widely popular that had captured local loyalties. The mix of local talent, middlebrow intellectual content, and foot-tapping melodies delighted a capacity audience and may have soothed even some who feared theatrical depravity.[40]

The 1890 January opening night glowed with a warm radiance from the heating stoves, another contrast with the drafty Pavilion. The brilliance of the walls and ceiling decoration competed for admiration with the spanning proscenium and seemingly vast stage. Carefully scripted opening ceremonies allowed social leaders to rehearse local history, sprinkle praise on the financiers, and catalog the town's cultural advancement. Whenever the performance allowed, the energetic Miller himself took every chance to perform "like a winged angel from box to stage, from stage to lobby," greeting and congratulating without restraint. His new venture would continue for fifteen years, and in the process Miller would meet, entertain, and be known by some of the greats of the theater world.[41] Success reigned.[42]

8
Telegraph in Cipher

Soon enough some theater greats and not so greats came to the sparkling, new Loring Opera House. Some came as performers, often as Miller's guests at the Glenwood. But in church every week he sat with people who believed that theatrical performances, anywhere, were wrong, morally wrong. Their belief was no mere cavil but something deep-rooted and widely shared in Protestantism.[1] Theater as a degrading presence spoke danger to their sober minds.

Miller felt the tensions of his position. "It is true," he said in 1934, "I started out a Quaker boy but I built a theater and ran it for twenty years."[2] He was never a "Quaker boy"; he was pointing at the gulf he sensed between presumed Quaker boy morality and the theater.[3] He was no stranger to ethical dilemmas and compromise: a decade earlier he had uneasily signed the tin-mine payroll on a Sunday morning. He had earlier abandoned baseball as a moral choice. He served alcohol and voted prohibition; an egalitarian in marriage, he opposed women's suffrage.[4] He had chosen the theater knowing the polarities; it was a dilemma fraught with principle and material, even personal, gain. A San Francisco friend framed Miller's opera-house quandary: "Are you going to set up a high and lofty standard, or do you propose to play everything that comes along? It would be rather incongruous to see you running a certain class of shows."[5] Miller avoided that "certain class of shows." He was savvy enough in the ways of success, the theatrical world, and Riverside, to find shows that would fill the house as often as possible and avoid controversy.

His programming included events that frequently gathered full-house audiences—visits by aspiring or sitting governors or senators and the heavy oratory of Independence and Memorial Days. He booked some events selective of smaller audiences. One such event brought Dr. Mary Wood Allen in a series of five lectures exclusively for women. The lectures discussed higher education, public health, the necessary study of physiology, dress reform, hostility to the corset, and practical instruction on hygiene.[6] All this drew audiences and local praise.[7] But praise and income from guileless events would not alone provide for the costs of operations or fund loan repayments and dividends.

He scheduled a score of Shakespeare's plays, and he booked widely praised and frequently performed productions known coast to coast—including *The Secretary*, *The Honeymoon*, and *Three Guardsmen*, adapted from Dumas's novel, *The Three Musketeers*. He invited nationally known performers such as pianist composers Amy Beach and Rudolf Friml, the theatrical charmer Madame Modjeska, and dramatic actors Frederick Warde and Otis Skinner. For the hoi polloi, he provided a roster of vaudevillian performing dogs, balancing acts, jugglers, comics, clowns, ventriloquists, and blackface minstrels. Naysayers did not disappear, but they left no public record of their complaints.

Miller drew on his entrepreneurial skills to advertise and court Californian theatrical agencies. He sent national and West Coast theater chat the local press—with titles like "Stage Notes" and "In Dramatic Lines"—that heralded coming attractions, announced their presence, and warned of their closings.[8] He met star performers, offering them guaranteed fees and a barrage of advertising and luring their audiences with door prizes and reduced ticket costs, avoiding a public "black eye" from poor attendance.⁹

Miller, at thirty-three, guided himself by a canny blend of a maturing and more secular conscience, a sense of the public taste, and what he thought best for the city. This amalgam came to be called "civic righteousness" and blended Christian morality and utility independent of sectarian conformity. For sixteen years Miller drew satisfied audiences to the opera house and generated returns for the investors. Anyone with a mind to criticize, however, could find an easy target in his application of colony founder John W. North's credo about advancing the colony's interests along with his own.¹⁰

Less than a month after he'd opened the opera house, Miller hurried through a chilly February night, called to his father's bedside. He and Frank Richardson found there was little they could do to ease the senior Miller's pain and labored breathing. Christopher died before dawn, his unexpected passing sending shock and surprise through the family, staff, hotel guests, and town. Friends recounted conversations with Christopher at church the day before, trying to make sense of what seemed so hard to believe. Many others knew him with warm regard; many more recognized his still soldierly bearing. He was a warmly respected pioneer, widely acquainted.

After Unitarian Universalist services at the Glenwood, elaborate Masonic rituals provided graveside burial, with words gently intoned reminding all "We spend our days as a tale that is told…" Fraternal brothers moved quietly, placing apron and evergreen on the casket, keenly aware of the brevity of life as they said farewell to their friend and brother, Sir Knight Miller. His small grave marker in the family plot with but the single word "Father" denied him his elegant names, his officer rank,¹¹ and even years of birth and death, a marker unique at the time in Evergreen Cemetery.

The first death had come to the Miller family, who closeted their grief, leaving no record in letters written or condolences received. His father's death came suddenly and was close, personal, even confusing for Frank, a human hurt unrelieved by anything he had known before. I believe that Miller mourned inwardly, as a son never fully reconciled with his father. Much later he told of his shame on hearing his father admit poor business acumen. He believed that his father had vacated the paternal role by being away so much and that he, the son, must take on the burden. He thought his father too optimistic, even gullible. Whatever his belated respect for his father's professionalism, strength of character, and loyalty to comrades,[12] when Miller wrote to his youthful grandson, he strangely described the senior Miller as his "mother's husband," as defenseless among deceivers, and as one "who would buy any gold brick ever made if a fellow had a chance at him."[13] This all seems, at this distance, to be an unnecessarily harsh burden of memory, lacking the softening mention of redeeming traits.

As the colony grew, residents sought increasing independence within San Bernardino County. City incorporation in 1883 was one step toward separation. Miller supported that and stood emphatically for an autonomous Riverside County.[14] But only by late 1890 had local interests jelled enough for action during the three-month 1891 California legislative session.

Miller packed off to Sacramento in January with all his usual enthusiasm, one of the local delegation primed to lobby assembly and state senate.[15] Every legislator received a colorful five-by-seven-inch triple-fold brochure displaying an orange outside and containing ten brief facts validating Riverside's case.[16] In countering moves, San Bernardino opponents of division orchestrated delays. Then cries of "boodle" sounded when a suspicious list of names and dollar amounts appeared, rescued from a wastebasket. All debate halted while the state senate met to hear the evidence. In testimony Miller passionately affirmed honesty among his associates, then his blood boiled as he heard contrary opinion from a San Bernardino attorney, Perkins by name. Both men left the senate hearing room at the same time but by adjacent doors. Turning, they confronted each other in full view. "They met, and without a parley of words they went at each other. Miller had decidedly the best of the fight when they separated. Perkins received a cut nose." Shocked amusement buzzed in political Sacramento, only thinly veiled in anonymity elsewhere in the state.[17]

Because of the delays, Riverside's well-publicized bill died without formal consideration. But Miller's highly informal political fracas suited the public taste. A brass band greeted his arrival home, and there was praise for him and all who had "sacrificed business, personal comfort, and stood the dastardly insults of the three greatest rogues in the [San Bernardino] County. All hail to Frank Miller."[18] It was declared that "The disagreeable duty Mr. Miller performed on [Riverside's] behalf would not soon be forgotten."[19]

Miller himself seems to have hugely enjoyed most of his "disagreeable duty" and was more than ready to face the 1893 session in Sacramento. "To have a thing go with vim and enthusiasm get Frank Miller behind it," said the newspaper. His voice joined many, but his visibility exceeded most.[20] His political star shone brightly.

While waiting between 1891 and 1893, Miller received in writing what every politician longs for: the promise of a favor from a powerful friend. Miller had successfully squelched a San Bernardino supervisors' inquiry into Southern Pacific Railroad activities. He'd done so at the covert request of a senior Southern Pacific Railroad executive, successfully cloaking everything in secrecy. The request itself was surprising, given Miller's bad press in San Bernardino and the long-standing animosity between the two towns. Equally surprising, Miller succeeded in shutting off the inquiry quickly and quietly. The appreciative railroad executive immediately offered Miller future benefits "in a more appropriate manner," adding in his letter, "Please request some favor at my hands."[21] Here were precious words indeed to Miller, who had county formation on his mind and knew the immense power of railroad influence among Sacramento assemblymen and senators of whatever stripe.

During the waiting period, Miller actively promoted county formation and with his unbounded energy tended his political interests.[22] He kept his hand on the Glenwood's affairs and a medley of other interests. "It is pretty hard to tell," wrote a friend, "whether you are a real estate man, a hotel proprietor, an orange grower, a church manager, a politician or a theatrical manager. You have only to become the Lord High Executioner and then you are fixed. Look out that some of the irons don't burn."

One of his "irons" had in fact burned, all his own doing. With the Perkins fisticuffs in mind, his political colleagues encouraged him to lobby and buttonhole any and all in Sacramento but seem to have kept him from speaking on the floor of the assembly and state senate. Embarrassment must be avoided. But Miller, always the "first boy," could not be content merely as one among other delegates. So in Sacramento, weeks ahead of all the others, he plunged into the thick of the movers and shakers, endlessly pursuing any and all who had or should have an interest or influence in support of the Riverside bill. According to one report, he hadn't "taken his clothes off since arrival...never sleeps...doing a power of good."[23]

The Riverside delegates moved planfully. Miller received encouragement and cautions. A Southern Pacific executive counseled care.[24] From home, a politically influential and sober friend urged Miller to be diligent, move systematically, and to scrupulously use the detailed plans they had prepared. "Don't knock us out or put us in jeopardy. Look this up [i.e., See to this] carefully" [emphasis in original].²⁵ A telegram to Miller in Sacramento had the postscript: "Telegraph in cipher." Thereafter, encoded notes and telegrams passed north and south. A typical example of one read, "Muffling monsoon luster modality," and another, "curator connubiate plus addicting few civilize replunged imprint frolicsome pilatism win moody. Dyer and McIntyre." There surely were others, not preserved.²⁶ Even Miller's pastor weighed in, cautioning mostly about the corrupting power of politics.²⁷ All this suggests nervousness lest Miller veer off track or burst forth in unsettling enthusiasm or turn his attention to other issues while the success of the bill still hung in the mists of influence and the airy oratory of legislators. Even after the bill had passed both houses, Miller's colleagues cautioned him against impatience, slackening, or dividing attention while waiting in Sacramento for the gubernatorial signature.²⁸

Newspapers thrived on the drama, especially in Sacramento, remembering the 1891 tussle and Riverside's first effort at separation. The *Los Angeles Tribune* published its bold assessment of each Riverside delegate. When the ink of the governor's signature had dried, Los Angeles judged the Riverside delegation "active, alert, and above all discreet in their advocacy." The *Tribune* commented, "Then there is Frank Miller," and described his energy, diligence, and enthusiasm all as "a power of good."²⁹ Some Miller watchers recalled earlier assessments: "Frank has not always shown the wily politician's tact, and sometimes blurts out the truth in a way that may seem injudicious."³⁰ Anxiety about Miller in Sacramento in 1893 seems well placed, however much he radiated hometown loyalty, knowledge, or persuasive arguments.³¹ His colleagues willingly used him but needed to harness his volatile streak, channeling its energy and safeguarding their shared goals.

Somewhere in the political mix, the Southern Pacific executive who earlier had promised Miller a favor made good on his offer. Railroad influence assured passage of the Riverside bill. Miller clearly thought and said so: "I was quietly, but very much a factor through the good will of Mr. Henry Huntington and the Southern Pacific, in making Riverside County." On another occasion he spoke more directly: "County division would have been absolutely impossible except for the goodwill of Mr. [Henry E.] Huntington."[32]

With the approving vote, orange-colored "Riverside County" badges erupted on coat lapels all over the capitol, no alert politician wishing to be caught unbuttoned. Just over two weeks later, Governor H. H. Markham signed the bill. He named the five members of a board of county commissioners, Miller among them, to manage the legal steps toward activating the new county. Miller's telegram to Isabella, reading, "Thank God," mixes appreciation, a sigh of relief, and perhaps a suggestion for Isabella.[33] She herself was applauded as she entered the hotel dining room with her own "Riverside County" button and orange-colored streamers.[34]

Even before Miller arrived home, festivities in Riverside surged unrestrained with bunting-draped buildings, bonfires that flamed and smoked in streets and on Mount Rubidoux, and shotguns fired randomly under a waning moon. Newspapers responded,[35] including Miller's name among the leaders and heaping praise on the small group that carried the arguments to the assembly and state senate. Miller, they said, "has done herculean work for our county bill,—watchful, sleepless and vigilant, and deserves thanks and commendations of our citizens for the grand success he aided so materially in securing." Miller accepted only the "aided" role, turning some of the praise aside and rightly identifying the diligence of colleagues active on the legislative floors.[36] Even forty years later, he added the word "quietly" when assessing his part. Though not in later recollections, some details must have been etched in memory: that combative encounter with Perkins, his exclusion from the legislative floors, the blunt newspaper comments about him and his fellow delegates, and their repeated instructions to him about staying on task.[37]

His perhaps self-created appointment as a commissioner linked him with four others in arranging all the preliminaries for the first county convention on April 6, 1893.[38] They handled details large and small, down to folding election ballots as they came from the printer and even delivering them to the polling places, closely watched for deviations by newspapers and neighbors.[39] His commissioner position ended when the newly elected county supervisors took their oaths of office a few months later. There were obvious benefits to Miller: personal recognition from Governor Henry Harrison Markham[40] and his feeling that justice could be done at his hands. Further, the brief appointment came without continuing obligation. But he never forgot the unseemly clamor for office by so many of his fellows, who he believed were unqualified by merit or effort.[41]

One political favor always requires another. Early the next year, Miller received a letter from railroad vice-president and general manager B. A. Worthington reminding him of favors exchanged and debts incurred in support of "your most cherished measure," referencing the railroad's support for county formation. Now the time had come to "reciprocate in this matter of much importance to us." The Southern Pacific wanted rail access to Riverside. Miller agreed; his public endorsement appeared, and Riverside responded favorably in spite of some grumbling. Within the year Southern Pacific crews were on site,[42] their presence forecasting increased railroad tourism in Riverside as well as competitive rates and extended market access for the citrus growers.

Miller's prominence in the county's formation gripped local notice enough to elicit military idioms: "he stood in the first rank...when the first gun was fired...and remained until victory was won"; that achieved "the campaigners" could return home, he among the last. The return provoked a burst of kudos. "To the untiring energy and splendid courage of Frank A. Miller much of the development and great improvement of the business portion of Riverside is in large measure due, and many enterprises owe much of their success to the same creative and progressive forces."[43] Miller's admirers then and later tended to say the same things, repeating a familiar catalog of energy, boldness, devotion to the town's prosperity, and creative capacity. "The gray matter of Frank's brain," said one, "is prolific of ideas."[44]

As is the case with many, repetitive praise often overlooked his contrariness and missed or obscured Miller's complexity in motivation. He was much spoken about. However, few sought or recorded his own perceptions or noted the varied intensity of his life and the evidences of growth—the very pulses by which he lived.[45]

In an opportunistic impulse, Miller and Samuel Carey Evans Jr., a local water baron and real-estate developer, patched together a proposal for housing the new county offices. They offered space in three of their own contiguous buildings downtown. The supervisors at first accepted but reversed their decision, remembering promises of frugality and choosing instead space in the Arlington Hotel.[46] Had the supervisors' first decision stood, Miller and Evans would have plucked plums: prestige as county government landlords, the tidy annual rentals, and the business generated by owning the businesses closest to county offices.

Not content, Evans and Miller cast common sense aside, challenging the reversal in a public petition. They urged the supervisors to use their "supreme power and authority" to disregard the electorate. The petition carried an attached check for $2,000 "as evidence and proof of our intention to substantiate what we allege in the petition above, [namely] a guarantee that you can save the County at least this amount..."[47] Here for all to see was blatant and shameless boodle. The supervisors, to their credit, took Miller especially to the woodshed in a stiff and public rebuke.

9

Influence Without Office

Miller came home after three months in Sacramento to a strange economic duality in Riverside, something he heard about from Isabella[1] and knew from reading the Riverside papers, something that touched his life. The Glenwood overflowed with would-be guests, more than the hotel could accommodate.[2] In contrast, economic collapse crept into Riverside from across the nation. Disquiet grew, bringing remembered industrial calamities, with trade prostrated, credit shaken, agriculture depressed, and labor elsewhere in open rebellion.[3] Riverside's resilient economy slowed the onset and cushioned the more severe shocks, but its day-labor and wage-dependent populations were especially exposed.

A strike at the World's Fair in Chicago, a meals-for-work program in Fresno, a wages strike in nearby Elsinore, and the discharge of many Southern Pacific and Western Union workers[4] were all much more than straws in the wind. The Riverside Banking Company failed in June.[5] The town stood still economically and would scarcely move again until 1899.[6] Delinquent tax lists lengthened, and foreclosures increased,[7] with all that this implied for unemployed friends and neighbors. The daily papers reported on the spreading malaise.

City trustees and county supervisors could not ignore their own economy for long.

༄

Not all was gloom as Miller returned to Riverside. For the family in 1893, a cross-country railway journey to visit the World's Columbia Exposition in Chicago promised the best birthday treat eleven-year-old daughter Allis might imagine. They visited family and friends in Wisconsin then stayed long enough in Chicago to enjoy all the fun of the fair. The exposition fertilized Miller's always alert imagination with an abundance of impressions from architecture, decoration, and the arts—the huge landscapes painted by such artists as William Keith and the crumbling California missions painted by Henry Chapman Ford, works he'd later purchase. His marketing eye noted middle-class preferences in culture and art. These were his guests, the field from which he harvested his favorite crop—tourists.[8] He absorbed the planned cityscape of the exposition, a contrast with home, offering an aesthetic and practical arrangement of streets and buildings that stayed with him. The lessons were not lost; his interest in the city-beautiful movement, city planning, and a civic center may well have taken on their new clarity at the fair.

The family returned home loaded with the trinkets of the fair, among them a fine carriage from Wisconsin and a photograph of all three: Allis with a bulky fur collar, Frank looking jaunty in a fisherman's cap, and Isabella, fashionably dressed in hat, gloves, and wrist bag, looking weary. Cool October weather in Chicago called for overcoats and a large umbrella.[9] They would return home with not only memories but also, for Frank at least, new reference points to guide his always-active imagination that shaped so much action.

༄

In his thinking, Miller often pursued a line of mutual benefit, boosting what might benefit both himself and the community. The quid pro quo of concessions to the Southern Pacific Railroad for county formation was an example, one of several publicly applauded agreements. The *Daily Press* told what most knew: "Frank is a hustler and generally wins when he sets out on a thing."[10] But a generosity of motives also came easily to Miller, whatever his pursuit of mutual benefit. He gained nothing, for example, in 1892 by supporting a Keeley Institute in Riverside, one of hundreds across the country where alcoholics were treated, many claiming cures.[11] The Riverside program had initial success[12] but disappeared from public notice, perhaps a casualty of toughening prohibition in the town. Another earlier mixing of business and philanthropy involved the federal Indian school in nearby Perris. He had donated acreage out of a land-development partnership for the school in 1890,[13] an obligation, he said later, to do his part to redress the shameful treatment of Native Americans.[14] Some then and later saw pursuit of narrow personal advantage in this and the later history of the school, a simplistic reading of this complex and generous man, in my opinion.

Miller's political pulse beat as strongly as ever, even memorably after the county-formation convention in 1893. Locally the trustees[15]—as the city council was known—heard and approved his proposals for ordinances protecting squirrels and forbidding hats from being worn in theaters. There were others—prohibiting spitting on sidewalks, outlawing fireworks in the interests of safety, restricting unseemly bill postings, but not, as local myth had it, forbidding lunch pails from being carried in the streets.[16] He weighed in early on discussions about the location of a post-office building, eager to keep it close to the hotel or have it in his own rental space.[17] His political lobbying for the Hotel Association's legislative committee[18] took him, with Isabella, to Sacramento and San Francisco, successfully pressing the association's case limiting hotel liability. Some had the impression that he and his generative imagination never rested.

A high point of Miller's party politics came when, as a member of the California Republican executive committee, he and Isabella traveled to Saint Louis in June 1896. After the Republican National Convention there,[19] they went with the delegation to Marion, Ohio, to tell McKinley formally of his nomination.[20] That done, and full of confidence that McKinley would carry California, the couple continued on a crowded itinerary of social, hotel, and financial visits in twenty or more eastern and midwestern centers,[21] a typical energetic blending of Miller's many interests. He came home with convention highlights, confident predictions of McKinley's boosting effects for tourism, and tales of fellow railroad passengers' political views, which he had gleaned in the democracy of train travel.[22]

His mind was a meeting place for opportunities and hopes that sponsored action that was carried out with almost limitless energy. The conscious, independent disposition that allowed him to conjure ideas, the ability to share to rally support, and his retreats into privacy were alike genuine expressions of his persona, impressive over the years.

Miller's response to the declining economy of the 1890s was typical. Independently, he had several long, narrow glass display panels inscribed in black and gold, saying, "Visit Riverside. The World's Greatest Citrus Growing District." These, placed in railroad depots, chambers of commerce, and elite hotels, would attract affluent visitors,[23] a source of local economic relief, he thought. He convened an elegant banquet of the leading businessmen and primed speakers to sell his other imperatives: bring more visitors to town; attract wealthy immigrants; generate visibility at the annual Winter Fair in San Francisco; get membership in the Los Angeles Chamber of Commerce; establish an effective chamber in Riverside; welcome the Southern Pacific; and support his own current whim in 1894, a promotional envelope and stationery project.[24] County supervisors caught the spirit, budgeting a thousand dollars as an immigrant attraction fund.[25] But none of this attacked relieving growing local unemployment head on.

Scores of "tramps" came west and to Riverside seeking better days. Local residents feared what this floating contingent of unemployed might mean for peace, prosperity, and property,[26] especially as the numbers increased.[27] But no plan emerged. The sticking point lay in who should act: was private or public initiative to pick up the burden? Miller came to straddle both views: local government should offer tramps quarry work and subsistence wages, relief with no inducement to stay; individual and congregational hands could reach out to local residents in distress, just as people had done in rural and frontier America as long as anyone could remember.[28]

Ethics can pull in several directions at once. In these discussions about the "shoulds" of unemployment relief, one focus offered a patriotic defense of private property and private philanthropy, whereas another led toward community obligation, local government direction, and distribution from the public purse. Some branded the latter as socialistic, a course that should be avoided because it could even lead to social revolution, whether peaceful or otherwise. Miller's friend Elmer Holmes said so publicly, fearing that Populist or socialist thinking would, in the end, bring "crazy schemes of the mentally unbalanced and lawless." But for all of Holmes's prophecies, the stark facts were that private generosity for locally unemployed (and jail time for the vagrants) just didn't work. Private charity couldn't keep pace, and jail time produced no economic remedy.

Miller and others worried. Was unemployment evidence of indolence or shiftlessness, as many said? Did private giving degrade the receiver? Did relief from the public purse open a door to socialism? Were some individuals, even groups, more equal than others in their claims on assistance of whatever kind? Miller at first rejected any shred of socialism that might threaten individualism and neighborly care, but he accepted private initiative and relief from the public purse and would live with the consequences, however complex.[29]

He knew well that most of his own hundred or so employees at the hotel were members of the most endangered groups: women, Native Americans, Mexicans, African Americans, Chinese, Japanese, and Koreans. Many in town thought he should change his employment practices.[30] But both he and especially Isabella sustained a parental care for the "family,"[31] well aware of public opinion but clear in their own beliefs that reflected a benign respect for what were then accepted social divisions in work and residence.

Paternalistic on not, Miller soon had labor troubles all his own. Not from unemployment, but disgruntled waitresses, who, when refused a raise, refused to work and wanted to quit the hotel. Negotiations failed. Miller refused to give them their trunks, because they owed him for travel fares advanced to get them to the Glenwood from the East. Scuffles followed, with accusations of angry words and tussles called "assault and battery" when legal terms were applied. Miller and Frank Richardson were summoned into court, unlikely transgressors watched on a Saturday morning from an overflowing visitors' gallery. Some kind of resolution allowed dismissal of the case, and apparent tranquility returned between Miller and his waitresses, because the usual efficient service prevailed in the dining room for Saturday lunch.[32] Miller's habitual concern and advisability likely led to increased wages for his waitresses or prospect of it—such also was his nature.

When the county offices moved into the Arlington Hotel, guest accommodations shrank. The ill-fated Mount Rubidoux

Hotel still reared its gaunt ruins. Perhaps stimulated by these facts, in 1894 Miller announced his plan to build the town's "first-class hotel."[33] He began a salvo of newspaper publicity: "A Magnificent New Hotel to be Built in Riverside. The Glenwood Hotel Grounds the Site of the New Building."[34] The only thing decided, however, was that something of the finest would be built. Miller, with Walter Raymond, the Pasadena tourist-hotel proprietor, went looking for ideas in Colorado,[35] scrutinizing hotels. Miller saw much to admire in the luxurious, new Colorado Hotel in Glenwood Springs, captivated by its architectural effects, elegance of furniture, completeness of finish, and service arrangements. He returned home with paper plans in hand.[36] Optimism surged: "if anyone on earth can do it Frank Miller can."[37] The word went out that the $250,000 needed would be forthcoming from Miller's efforts as soon as local investors raised the initial $50,000. Endorsements from local bankers and major property owners looked solid.[38] Railroad advisers concurred, and Walter Raymond of Pasadena invested $5,000 in the corporation. It was said that Collis P. Huntington had indicated "a large financial interest."[39] Miller spoke a brave economic theory of hotel operation: "The tourist crop is perennial. Frost cannot kill it; drought does not check its growth; injurious insects do not affect it. It produces a sure paying crop. There is no danger of overproduction. And the market is always good. Let us cultivate the tourist."[40]

But the crop did respond to economic drought. Moreover, in 1893 Frank Duryea had chugged and sputtered along the streets of Springfield, Massachusetts, in his gasoline-powered automobile,[41] something that would redefine the tourist crop, indeed, and much beyond.

The harvest for Miller's first-class hotel was not to be, not yet. Railroad enthusiasm waned, and purse strings tightened in the face of declining railroad solvency. Local bank support ebbed away with continuing investor caution and widespread unemployment. Lacking finance, Miller's ambitious plans faded from public discussion almost as suddenly as they had appeared but not from Miller's mind.

⁂

During the morning of August 16, 1895, Frank's mother, Mary Ann Miller, died at the Glenwood after almost twenty-one years in the mild California climate.[42] A brief notice appeared as "Local News," in the *Riverside Daily Press*. "Of interest to older citizens," it read, referring especially to those who knew her as "a woman of amiable qualities and deeply devoted to her family, warmly interested in the growth of the City with whose early development her husband was so prominently involved." The names of all her children appeared, but nothing of the date, time, place of the funeral, or obsequies was printed, a brevity surprising for so well known a pioneer. Yet the paucity of detail suited family privacy: "Not to be a public affair," said the report.[43] Years later, the doughty pioneer John Boyd offered his measured opinion. "She was a woman of refinement," he wrote, adding a sly compliment, "and transmitted some of these qualities to her son Frank, now Master of the Mission Inn."[44] Her grave beside her husband, Christopher, in the Miller plot carried but a single word, "Mother."

Mary Ann Miller achieved importance among Riverside's large congregation at the First Church of Christ, Scientist, something that neither the newspaper nor the family recorded, then or later. The family mourned privately, and none of the usual ephemeras of bereavement survive. But recorded or not, the loss of a mother wounds all in the family. Granddaughters dote on their grandmothers. Could Allis, at thirteen, have found comfort at all in her grandmother's Christian Science confidence of passing to a higher plane? Or did this sudden loss only raise fresh, painful, and unanswered questions about mortality? Isabella, her mother, lost an intimate friend of twenty years. Frank's sisters, Emma and Alice, both members of the Church of Christ, Scientist might find relief from grief in shared beliefs and mutual comfort. We know little of youngest brother Ed, who was now thirty-one, but we know enough of youngest sons to know their deep affections and special places in their mothers' love. For Frank, now thirty-eight, his mother's "crossing over" scarred a dependence that endured throughout life. Even in his last reminiscences, he pictured himself as "a mother's boy," seeing her as the wellspring of his moral fortitude and ethical attitudes.[45] For reasons never shared, he called her a Quaker for the rest of his life,[46] a strange denial of her prominence in the Christian Science community to which she and several family members belonged.

With McKinley elected in November 1896, the local *Press* headline shouted: "God Reigns." Miller, less metaphysical, revealed his own persistent certainty that Riverside's new, first-class hotel would be "one of the early fruits of the McKinley administration."[47] Then, in early 1897, the county supervisors stirred investment capital to the surface when they formally asked for bids on a county courthouse. A flood of proposals swept into their offices, Miller's among them. He had retained the distinguished office of Theodore A. Eisen and Sumner P. Hunt to prepare plans novel in concept and design. The supervisors unsealed the bids in open session and took only enough time to briefly summarize them, promptly voting to postpone action for one week. Miller sprang to his feet, asking to be heard. What he had to say—all reported word for word—had nothing of the inept, combative, blunt, or intrusive language of some of his earlier efforts. He opened with praise for the supervisors, most of them Democrats, rejecting out of hand all the "insinuations and allusions" unsympathetic to him and his interests. Surprise continued in his proposal. The supervisors and he together would build a structure combining a courthouse and hotel—such was the essence of his offer. The benefits he unrolled were impressive: increased tourist spending in the town, investment capital attracted in a time of slow growth, manufacturing industries seeking local sites—benefits already on the supervisors' own wish lists. Miller linked these blessings to his courthouse-and-hotel proposal, not mentioning much about the courthouse but rehearsing the benefits from tourist hotels, already known to be tools of prosperity in Pasadena, San Diego, and Redlands. The supervisors listened, unmoved. In anticipation they had calculated. They announced their own surprise: they would not build; they would rent.

The editor of the *Press* weighed in with one editorial after another supporting Miller's offer as meritorious because it offered the courthouse almost as a bonus. Miller also persisted; he spoke again to the supervisors, and this time he was shouted down by one of them who heaped sarcasm on his hopes and promises. Miller held his peace, perhaps remembering his earlier defeat and the public reprimand. But more astonishment was in store in a reversal. When the vote was called, the supervisors supported Miller's proposal, with five in favor, one opposed.[48]

How might we explain support for Miller's plan after five weeks of vacillating, nervous, and even abusive consideration? Did the other proposals laid before the supervisors all lack merit? No doubt the newspaper editorials had helped Miller: the supervisors did save money if he built. From another perspective, the pirouette from building to renting and around again to building signaled an uncertainty shared by most in Riverside. There was no agreement in Riverside about the future balance of agriculture, residential development, industries, and tourism. Or could the approving vote for the hotel-cum-courthouse have been a cynical recognition of the improbability of Miller's promised finance?

Whatever the medley of thinking about the future—Miller's priorities always favored tourism—the passage of very little time revealed that Miller had again, as he had three years earlier in 1894, put the cart of offer before the horse of finance. His prospective East Coast investors now had only words of encouragement, not even the promise of finance. Riverside investors remained silent. For Miller, putting bricks and mortar in place on his or any other property for courthouse, hotel, or, indeed, anything, also waited. This latest chimera, his stubborn hope to be the one to build Riverside's first-class hotel, faded but did not vanish.

10

Wide-Ranging Enterprises

Suddenly, or so it seemed to the business community in late 1897, Miller went off to Santa Monica to manage the beachfront Arcadia Hotel.[1] The announcement caught almost everyone unprepared and raised eyebrows, coming as it did so soon after his unsuccessful eastern trip to raise money for his hotel-cum-courthouse. All year he had been very visible on that and on efforts to secure a federal Indian school for Riverside. Added to that, his agitation for extensions of his Riverside and Arlington Railway Company tracks had kept many watching him closely. Surely these projects would keep him close to home, especially with the tourist season beginning.

Though others may have been mystified, Miller's family certainly knew his plans. He would have told them about some earlier "what-if" talk with the Southern Pacific, owners of the Arcadia Hotel, as he discussed with them funding the hotel-courthouse. The family knew that Frank Richardson, his Glenwood manager and brother-in-law, had already agreed to go with him to the beach. Alice Richardson would manage the Glenwood. Miller knew the now-shabby and disreputable Arcadia Hotel and its board members,[2] and he at least knew about the Pacific Improvement Company, now his boss, and its ambitions for a Santa Monica port. Many years had passed since 1875 when he had last worked as a hired hand under the direction of another. Memories do fade in the face of attractive opportunities. Might hopes of future finance from the Southern Pacific have led Miller into doing something for what looked like prospective backers? He may not have known, however, that the Improvement Company had deep financial troubles, with Hollis P. Huntington of the opinion that it may have already outlived its usefulness to his railway interests.[3]

Nothing daunted, the new managers moved in and braced the stumbling Arcadia program, using their own core staff to assure Arcadia guests of the Glenwood's hospitality. They added a slate of lecturers and presentations, hosted a Republican county convention, and announced a round of resort hotel diversions at the hotel and on the beach. A month later, Richardson and Miller, dressed in a cool linen suits, could show a reporter a guest list of respectable middle-class families from Arizona and Southern California, all enjoying the seaside. The earlier hotel gamblers and prostitutes were long gone. The Riversiders could show elegance within and flourishing geometrical landscaping without,[4] all Miller's management style: hospitality offered in refreshing settings.

After eighteen months at the Arcadia, Miller and Richardson could show reduced expenses and increased income, each by 20 percent, and a better clientele and a leaner, more efficient staff. The hotel could only prosper, he thought, on a winter-season basis. His employers, however, had other ideas. All the while, Miller divided his time unequally among the hotel in Santa Monica, visits to the hotel owners in San Francisco, and trips to Riverside supervising his street railway while diligently pursuing the possible location of a federal Indian school in Riverside. He reported at least twenty trips of one kind or another during the year.

Perhaps unknown to the two Franks in 1898, the die was already cast in San Francisco for the hotel to be closed permanently. The orders came. At year-end in 1899, Miller respectfully informed the company secretary that he had closed the hotel "in accordance with instructions," adding few terse details.[5] He also wrote impulsively to Henry E. Huntington, offering to stay on with Isabella to run the hotel successfully. But his second thoughts kept the letter unsent, retained as a personal record.

During their tenure at the Arcadia, Miller and Richardson had salvaged the hotel's reputation, reversed its downward financial and aesthetic trend, and also helped clear out community seaminess,[6] all impressive achievements. Miller's flexible and pragmatic formula of expecting success when his right methods were applied in normal circumstances had worked effectively in Riverside, in Long Beach, and at the Palomares in Pomona, and in the near future would be effective at Lake Tahoe—all places where normal meant, among other things, social and economic stability and middle-class resort-style guests. The definitions of normal at Santa Monica and the Arcadia were quite otherwise.

Within a year or so, Miller politely declined management of another coastal hostelry, the Oceanside Hotel, alluding to "this big one I now have on my hands"—meaning, of course, his hoped-for first-class hotel in Riverside.[7]

The possibility of relocating the Perris Indian School to Riverside caught Miller's attention and ardent support. Within his first six months in Santa Monica, the Riverside papers endorsed the school's relocation to Riverside.[8] Moreover, a visiting federal superintendent of Indian schools, Estelle Reed, wrote negatively about Perris, specifically talking relocation "to another locality," and mentioning Los Angeles. Several cities reached for the prize.[9]

Miller knew well the issues that swirled around the school and Indians, remembering clearly that when the school began in 1892 no one within miles of Riverside had wanted to sell property for it.[10] At that time a local developer group calling itself the Riverside Tract stepped in to give the eighty-acre location in Perris to the federal government. Miller bought into the Riverside Tract and also invested in the Perris water company,[11] both located in an empty, treeless stretch of mostly flat land, the lonely railroad depot visible for miles around. Between the school's opening and 1898, some local opinions about the school changed, softened in face of its general success.[12] But unreliable domestic and agricultural water surfaced as an important reason for relocating the school. With talk of relocation in the air and with the school's more socially acceptable image, many hands reached to capture so fine an asset that came with federal funding and as a validation of a growing middle-class humanitarian concern for Native Americans.

Miller and his fellow school advocates prudently avoided topics of bitter debate such as religious versus secular schools, assimilation and Americanization of Native Americans, school location on or off reservations, and contention about what the curriculum should or should not include. Instead they enlarged on what Riverside could offer: available acreage on Magnolia Avenue in Arlington, abundant agricultural and domestic water, the "thrifty community" of Riverside with "the busy life of commerce, manufactures [and] agriculture,"[13] and an educative environment accessible to students. Miller freely acknowledged his interest in the tourist attraction of the school.

In his advocacy Miller appears to have walked both sides of the political street, supporting two contending senatorial candidates, hoping one or the other would carry Riverside's bid to success.[14] In the process he thought he put on "a monkey and parrot" show trying to get supporters lined up, but he confessed failure, although he'd never before worked to influence people with more energy, letters, and telegrams and "had spent money like water."[15] His raw disappointment showed as Miller wrote to a firm supporter about the two in Sacramento he had expected to bring him success: "One is a —- and has been bought body and soul, the other is a coward and does not represent his constituency." The same was also true, he lamented, of locals previously sent to Sacramento.

All this time he still shared the Arcadia management with Frank Richardson. And even though this initial political effort failed to carry the day—success came later—the skirmish made their formidable intentions clear to all and made it clear that Frank Miller would bring on energetic, tactical, and even contrarian action backed by Riverside advocates and others in high places of government and business.

Local street railways also filled his agenda in these years. In 1886 Miller had incorporated the Riverside and Arlington Railroad, the R&A, knowing that mules pulling rickety, little trolleys down dusty streets didn't fit his impression of the way it should be in Riverside.[16] He also believed that electric trolleys could prosper.[17] Over the years the demands of the street railways for street construction and then electrical power put pressure on an often overwhelmed board of city trustees. The tensions generated between the trolley company and the trustees were real, public, and at times explosive.

Adding to these raw materials of conflict, Miller's closeness to the major steam railroads led to suspicions of collusion with them. Railroad dominance in California bred strong hostility. Miller framed the issues in larger, locally familiar terms: the home economy depended on tourists and citrus; tourists and citrus depended on the railroads, so collaboration with railroads of all kinds just made sense.[18] Electrification, beginning while Miller journeyed back and forth from Santa Monica in 1898, took three years. All the while the trustees were nervously aware of increased popular demands for expansion, and Miller was often the irritant. Even his eloquence did not blunt the hostility. He hammered away, gaining little by little and generating enduring ill will from the trustees, one of whom eventually said he'd not vote for anything Miller brought up.[19]

But the trustees knew the value of streetcars in other towns, and they read the supportive local press and could not ignore the abundant community support.[20]

In the early light of an April morning in 1899, before many were awake, Miller and the directors of R&A made the first electrified run, going from downtown eight miles west to Van Buren Street in Arlington and returning, comfortably successful, before most of the town sat down to breakfast. Later that day a carload of city fathers and company directors made the same return trip ceremonially, reassured by the success of the dawn run. The grand public opening of the electrified service had brought experienced crews from Los Angeles, Pasadena, and even San Francisco, where the California Electric Company of San Francisco representative wanted to enjoy and assure the success of its financial investment.[21] For the rest there was a gala of bunting, refreshment booths at both ends of the line, and a brass band to play marches and popular melodies. Festively dressed young women smiled and spoke their welcomes to hundreds from Los Angeles, Pasadena, Colton, and towns in the county, who came to ride the cars until late in the moonless evening, all in popular celebration of the practical and symbolic importance of the electric trolley in Riverside. Miller and his board could not help but be happy.

In early 1901, argument over another Miller application to the trustees dragged on for weeks as the trustees added here, removed there, and imposed restrictions widely seen as efforts to kill the franchise. In sheer frustration, Miller prepared a letter of more than 2,500 words to be read aloud by the clerk at the trustees' meeting.[22] He wrote bravely, well aware of being under suspicion. Anyone who thought about it knew that outside money had largely made the town and that Miller, more than anyone, had used his connections to significant capitalists to benefit Riverside, as was now the case.[23] The whitening bones of the Mount Rubidoux Hotel gave daily testimony to local inadequacy.[24] Most also realized that the town's seven thousand residents' appetites for infrastructure and the sweets of culture fell below their readiness to pay.

The letter presented the company's perspective and held Miller's own intensely personal statement. He laid out the company's view of its public-service role in one massive sentence of over 170 words. He accused the trustees of flimsy opposition for "personal and mercenary reasons," a resignation of their elected obligations. He hammered on this obligation, reminding the trustees that they took office to carry out the wishes of the people and reminding them that 1,200 of the 1,632 registered voters had petitioned passage of the franchise so far denied.

"What advantage to the city is offered by those who oppose the franchise?" he wrote. The listening chamber heard the challenge repeated: "What shoulders will be applied to the wheels of progress on Walnut Street and Seventh Street and the East Side when our opponents have prevented the railroad company from doing anything for them?" The question hung without answer, needing none.

Miller, as trolley company secretary, inserted Miller the person into the lengthy diatribe, knowing that personal animus toward him fed opposition to the company's request. "I am not disposed to call attention to the part that I have taken personally in public enterprises in Riverside; nor do I wish to call attention to those who have persistently opposed every measure which I have inaugurated." And continuing, his letter said, "I do not mean to take to myself an undue amount of credit for the success of any public enterprise but I think I shall be borne out in saying that I have advocated and aided to bring about many, and in every one of these the benefit which occurred to me personally has been solely that which comes by reason of the progress, the building up and the successful development of Riverside."[25] He named his contributions—the opera house, the Rubidoux Building, the relocation of the Indian school, and the street railway itself, and then he returned pleadingly to the stalled application for franchise. "What has the company done that it should merit such hostility?"

"Who are the people," his letter asked, "that will use this proposed street car line, if built? Not those opposing it to any great extent, as they will seldom have occasion to use it; but the great portion of those using it will be the laboring people in going to different parts of the city to their places of labor, and the school children going to school; the ladies going to trade, and all the people going to church and evening entertainments, also visiting tourists?" In asking this question and in answering, Miller touched on social cleavages not often brought out in the open. Some of his hearers drove to church in cabriolets, and others walked; some rode or were driven to the office, and others went on foot or the occasional bicycle. The streetcar routes at issue would certainly tap into less affluent residential areas of Riverside, the East Side particularly, with its mix of day-laboring African Americans, Mexicans, Asians, and Anglos, where the human foot or a bicycle carried children to school, laborers to work, and ladies to the nearest shops, all returning to modest cottages at the end of their day.

Miller's long company letter shone enough facts and figures, history, logic, and shaming into the trustees' chambers to penetrate the gamut of interests. Then and throughout life, he attempted to understand opposition; it was a genuine quandary for him that any should oppose what seemed so common sense to him.[26] Even so, he could and did face those who opposed him, steadied by a ballast of self-confidence, his own sense of independent disposition, and a readiness to fight his battles. I find the clearest statement of the man in this episode, especially the letter and its presentation.

This was called the "Franchise Squabble" by the *Daily Press* headline reporting the letter reading and later debate. Trustees admitted that their small-town restrictions would deter investors; some feared the controlling tentacles of the Southern Pacific; others still suspected Miller of secret deals with the Santa Fe Railroad[27]—reason enough, they said, for them to "hedge [his petition] about with all possible restrictions." They peppered their session with restrictive amendments that died among them, one after another, for want of agreement. Miller, in petulant frustration, interrupted the meeting to withdraw the application. In a parting shot, he addressed one trustee personally, labeling him ungentlemanly and insulting.[28] Little daunted, a month later he was back again at the trustees' meeting, fresh with petitions for street improvements and city beautification.[29]

Even though Henry Huntington's company effectively took control of the street-railway company in 1903, Miller kept himself involved, proud of his two special cars, the *Alfarata* and the *Juniata*, with their plush seats and silk window curtains, made to carry Glenwood guests the full length of Magnolia Avenue.[30] For years his name appeared on the railway letterhead as "Manager." In practice, his management style veered from masterful to micro. He mailed, phoned, and carried to Los Angeles a flock of his concerns about the unreliable local electrical supply, saying, "they have been swearing at me [about that] for two years." On occasions he assumed a blue-collar role downtown, personally dispatching trolleys and directing passengers. He negotiated half fares for schoolteachers and questioned bills and clerical errors. He asked the Los Angeles office about treatment for electric shock, personnel issues, and freight rates and suggested that all fares around Riverside be reduced by 50 percent. To this, his Los Angeles supervisor responded with surprising restraint. "It's all right," the supervisor wrote, "to advertise the city and county, or to aid in doing so, but it is not right to sacrifice the railroad and make it lose more money than it is losing to do so." Miller had cheating fare collectors investigated. The Los Angeles office again and again asked him to solve his problems locally, return documents promptly, and get his financial books in order.[31] But to an energetic mind like his, full of new ideas and often looking to others for solutions, that likely sounded too mundane.

Miller's response to the feeble municipal electrical power supply for the streetcars took two directions; first, he successfully sued the city to assure his supply,[32] and later he purchased and installed his own power plant at the hotel.[33] In 1911 the Pacific Electric Railway Company took over the streetcars,[34] ending Miller's almost quarter of a century of adventures in street railroading.

In securing franchises for himself, in confrontation with the trustees, and as an informal agent for the Huntington interests, Miller invoked whatever tactics he thought might make his case, among them his verbal agility, repeatedly urging, like a mantra, his theme of mutual personal and city benefit. In the process, if prudence suggested deviousness, he used it, committing his associates to secrecy and keeping some collaborators ignorant of others' roles in efforts to safeguard their credibility and his own.[35] His lifelong frankness and the matured capacity for compromise with a tender, youthful conscience still sensitized him toward ethical action. He knew that others, like himself, had long memories, and in his old age, he urged his biographer, Zona Gale, to defend his honesty in writing, telling her that no one had ever accused him of dishonesty or of "being a boodler" by taking or offering bribes.[36] The record appears to support his claim; there had been warnings but no accusations. He didn't mention occasional deviousness or complexity, stock in trade of the wily politician.

11

Practically a Gift to Riverside

In the years between 1897 and 1903, Miller kept more than one string to his bow. His street-railway venture began before that time and mostly came to an end with electrification in 1899. His role was incidental from then until it was fully taken over by Huntington's Pacific Electric Railway Company in 1911. Another string, the Arcadia Hotel, 1897–1899, seemed like a two-year diversion. In another direction, at least since the 1889 collapse of the Mount Rubidoux Hotel, he also saw himself as the one to build Riverside's new first-class hotel. He quietly solicited plans, keenly aware of two failed efforts and that that another contender might steal the prize. His interest in the Indian school, formed by mid-1897, was energetic, visible, and audible at home and in high places of government and business.

What drew Miller into the contest for the Indian school? Trivially, he recalled boyhood games of marbles with Indian boys and that as a youth he had worked side by side in manual labor with an Indian.[1] More to the point, in maturity he constantly worked toward social institutions that for him defined his idealized view of Riverside: the hotel, the electrified trolleys, the YMCA, the opera house, creditable business and civic buildings, better roads, and, later, an elite college for women.[2] Certainly the Indian school fit that portfolio. In memory, Miller also saw his actions as his effort to "discharge a little of the unpayable American debt to the Indians," something learned, he said, from his mother's presumed Quaker principles. These humanitarian sentiments were perhaps an afterthought, but perhaps they were not: in the early twentieth century strong humanitarian sentiment existed on the subject, hence the fervent arguments. In Riverside, throughout the campaign to capture the school, the given reasons of tourism and federal investment were much more marketable than doctrinaire sentiments or moralizing about the "Indian problem." The Southern Pacific magazine, *Sunset*, did affirm this loftier motivation and more, writing, "Sometimes the government does a thing because it is right, and, with no other compelling cause for its action deals still more generously."[3] That's true for individuals also.

"Ninety-nine hundredths of the people of Riverside want to see an Indian School established here," the local *Press* editor reported, and they "are frank enough to state why they want a school here, to wit, to give one more attraction to our beautiful valley."[4] Miller was also with this majority.[5] A few months later the editor repeated this, saying, "We take into account the future importance of the School to Riverside as...a source of thousands of dollars of business every year to the city,"[6] considerations not unique to Riverside. Indeed, all competitors pressed for local advantage; they realized equally that to get embroiled in ideological arguments would swamp any proposal deep in the turbulence of divergent views. And all knew that the institution was a school, dedicated to the assimilation of Native Americans into the majority culture.

After the earlier failed efforts in Sacramento, Miller had asked Collis P. Huntington of the Southern Pacific to use his influence in Washington on behalf of Riverside. Huntington begged off[7] but, as would appear, crucially supported Riverside. He also tutored Miller in threading the mazes of special-interest politics in Washington, with the result that a sympathetic congressman, James C. Needham, readily approached the relevant federal departments.[8] He persisted, keeping his Riverside supporters up-to-date, and in the 1900 legislative session, he worked to nail down the promised $75,000 appropriation "for a second school in California, the new one likely to be located in Riverside though half a dozen are trying for it."[9]

Riverside rejoiced. Trustee W. L. Peters proclaimed in a toast "To The City of Riverside...we wanted the Indian School and we are going to have it."[10] Needham delivered. On May 31, 1900, Washington approved the school; at the end of July, it also approved the Riverside site on Magnolia Avenue. By August mission-revival-style architectural plans for the school were on Washington drafting tables. Within two months property deeds recorded the transfer to the federal government, the site at the corner of Jackson and Magnolia.[11] The Sherman Institute, as the new school became, opened in 1902.

Miller had filled the role of the school's man in Riverside: energetic, visible, and audible in a shared effort. They had opposition, especially from General Otis of the *Los Angeles Times*, but they had even more support from powerful men of national reputation—Albert K. Smiley of Redlands and Collis P. Huntington of the Southern Pacific among them.[12] All shared in the glory of the eventual success. But most agreed that in Riverside, Miller did more than anyone. His view was that he was soldiering "out in the open field." Others saw "apathy and sometimes treachery at home" that would have deterred another.[13] Much later Miller reminisced about the arrival of the school: "The Indian School, Sherman Institute, was practically a gift to Riverside through the influence of Collis P. Huntington."[14] A different Huntington would make another significant addition to Riverside in the near future—the first-class hotel—though that would not be a gift.

The forty-acre school campus lay beside property owned by the R&A street railway, where its park provided picnic spots, polo grounds, tennis courts, and even the beginnings of a zoo.[15] The convenience of the side-by-side location of the school and park allowed easy access to recreation or relaxation in the park before making an enlightening visit to the school.

On their visits to the Sherman Institute, Miller's hotel guests saw a denial of popular stereotypes about Indians. Instead, at the institute they met the comfortably conventional.[16] Children sat in familiar classrooms, doing the things that schoolchildren usually did, frequently dressed in military-style uniforms as they worked at school subjects and vocational skills. They fielded a winning football team and a brass band that played Sousa marches and patriotic airs that got feet tapping. The children ignored the visitors, working away at schoolwork that "was a revelation to many present in regard to the ability and capacity of the American Indian."[17] Such visits offered a window on assimilation in progress, an affirmation of the dominant federal policy of the late nineteenth and early twentieth centuries. For almost all in Riverside, the institute added another strength to the community and to the tourist program.

Miller had begun his 1898 business year by incorporating the Glenwood Investment Company. This $25,000 stock company planned to buy and sell real property and build and operate hotels,[18] but activity achieved only the restructuring of a $25,000 loan.[19] This took place while Miller managed the Arcadia and pressed ahead on street railways and the Indian school campaign. Nothing moved on the primary intention of the company—building the New Glenwood, Miller's third attempt at the first-class hotel.[20] When at the end of 1898 the Millers, Newmans, Hardenbergs, and Segers all gathered for Christmas at the Glenwood, they could talk endlessly about the streetcars, the years at Santa Monica, and the Indian school.[21] But Uncle Frank, always full of enthusiasm, had moved only slightly closer to building his new hotel.

Miller's visibility in person from his frequent public involvement and the ready press that provided tended to obscure the others in the family, close as they were as a family. His sister Alice lived at the hotel with her husband, Frank Richardson, both of them self-directing in their widely recognized managerial skills, by no means working under Miller's shadow.[22] Each family took its own vacations at separate times and, until the 1920s when Laguna became a focus for their leisure, in separate places. His sister Emma lived a mile away, married to the often absent G. O. Newman, finding satisfaction in her own growing family. His younger brother, Ed, plotted his independent course, leaving Miller's employ at the hotel livery to trade in horses, join in city holiday events, volunteer in the fire brigade, and play in the municipal band, all the while entering comfortably into the life of the community.[23]

For his daughter, Allis, Miller sought the advantages of the prestigious Marlborough School in Los Angeles after her two years in the Riverside high school. She and a local friend entered together, a companionship that no doubt eased any tension of newness as they learned the expectations of that self-conscious school. Something of that Marlborough tone lives on in a small brochure, *Marlborough Don'ts*, thirty-five paragraphs intended to reshape the "verdancy" of young women who might otherwise, said the brochure, be "vulgar" or "greedy" or "ungracious" or "slovenly" or even persist as "the gum-chewing girl." An underground publication of *Mulberry Don'ts*, which hints at Allis's involvement, revised the guidance in such lively advice as, "Don't ever use slang, if you must, swear," and, "Don't yell in loud tones; if you must, yell in a whisper," and, "Don't crumble your food, swallow it whole." The family attended her graduation, an event that assured Allis's entry into Riverside society, whatever the admission given her parents. Miller, devoted to his daughter, swelled with pride at her graduation success and printed the arid graduation oratory of the school headmistress for distribution.[24]

Three of Isabella Hardenberg Miller's sisters came to the town, swelling the family circle. One musically talented sister lived on in Riverside and played piano and organ at the inn for several years. Rose, a teacher and Isabella's bridesmaid, moved to Los Angeles and became a middle-school principal; the third sister married a man of changing business choices—real estate, bicycles, shoes—and fixed alcoholic preferences. Miller abhorred his drinking and the ugly behavior that went with it, seeking a deckhand assignment for the derelict. "The further the boat goes the better it suits me," he wrote to a ship-owning friend. Regarding protecting the addict's wife and six children, he wrote, "It seems I must get him out of the country or kill him."[25]

Miller remained unforgiving of moral deviation. In another instance of drinking, he wrote kindly enough in praising the drinker's admirable traits but recommended that the drinker cut off one finger joint for every drunken bender, sure that with the loss of a few joints the drinker would be cured.[26] He threatened equally harsh treatment to an acquaintance thought to have abandoned his wife and children. Miller could understand marital discord but not abandonment.[27]

In other circumstances Miller's ethics offered redemption from lapses. An applicant wanting a recommendation to a West Point appointment offered Miller fifty dollars if the application succeeded. "From the tone of your letter," Miller wrote, "I am afraid you do not appreciate my motives any more than I do yours. I am not in politics for money." With that off his chest, Miller forgave all. "But let bygones be bygones," he wrote, "as long as you are a friend of John North's, for he is one of my dearest." Miller sent his recommendations to several highly placed politicians, his letters eloquent enough to make the candidate glow in the dark.[28]

Miller took the measure of his newspaper world. He complied his own dossier on twenty-nine Riverside and San Bernardino County newspaper editors, cataloging their editorial politics as favorable or unfavorable to his own and adding crisp thumbnails of the editors' characters: "A clean, manly fellow," was his comment about one. "Always looking for something for himself," he said about another. "He is N. G. [no good] from the ground up," and "A shifty uncertain lot," were his assessments of others. Another observation was, "Direct use of money will not influence him."[29]

All though 1899 Miller pored over hotel plans from the distinguished Los Angeles architects Theodore Eisen and Sumner P. Hunt, but he temporized, not even paying their bill[30] and not convinced about what he wanted. He turned to another architect, Arthur B. Benton, and another architectural idiom, the new style, mission revival.[31] Benton's and Miller's paths had crossed when Benton passed through Riverside in 1892. During 1902 Miller had watched Benton supervise construction of his mission-revival design for the First Church of Christ, Scientist, just a block from the Glenwood. Benton, described as "effective, efficient, competent, and garrulous,"[32] couldn't help but share his enthusiasm for the distinctive and increasingly attractive mission-revival architecture, a deliberate creation of a regional style, with Miller. Their relationship, once cemented, lasted until Benton's death in 1927. For Benton, his work in Riverside came to be seen as his best example of mission style; for Miller, the collaboration not only gave him and Riverside their long-awaited first-class hotel but achieved national distinction for both, something that I believe would not have come to Miller without Benton or to Riverside without Miller's advisability.

By 1902 the serious competitors for the first-class hotel were Frank Miller and local merchant George Reynolds, an insider on Miller's board of the Glenwood Investment Company of 1898.[33] Reynolds went covertly to Los Angeles with C. S. Evans of the water and land company to visit Henry Huntington, who promptly wrote to Miller, "Ebens [sic] and

Reynolds talked to me, I listened. Come to Los Angeles and I'll tell you [about the conversation.]"³⁴ Those exchanges are wrapped in silence, but the outcome is clear enough.

Scarcely a month after the conversations, a *Riverside Daily Press* front page fairly shouted, "Tourist Hotels Are Coming in Pairs." George Reynolds announced it first; Frank Miller came close behind only hours later. Reynolds, who had begun to raise capital, would transform the local Casa Palma Hotel on Eighth Street "to handle the large tourist business that should rightly come to Riverside." He'd remodel in mission style, adding a large plate-glass street front, an interior grass court, and an elevator from the basement to the second floor. He'd offer forty-nine suites with baths and a total of one hundred and ten rooms. His total outlay would be $50,000 in construction and $18,000 in furnishings.³⁵ Sixty-eight thousand dollars could not build a first-class hotel, even in Riverside. Skeptical readers might suspect a stalking horse, intended to test Miller's resolve: could he move beyond talk?

Miller's announcement, in the same issue of the paper, addressed "The Citizens of Riverside." He wrote, "In the event that a bonus of $25,000 is raised, I will erect on the site of the present Glenwood Tavern a hotel and furnishings to cost no less than $150,000 and guarantee to have the same open for the tourist season of 1903." Subscriptions were payable on completion of the hotel. Careful readers would note the conditions of the proposal, all promises and hopes, even for the trustees named, "if they will serve." The Reynolds challenge had been taken up promptly, set in a larger lot and larger dollars and on an immediate schedule. But again Miller's finances rested only on "a very positive assurance that he can secure the money in the East."

Both proposals required the local subscription amounts; Miller's terms were more forgiving of investors (but not Miller), because no cold cash for the New Glenwood would come due for nine months, and this was in an improving economy. But other proposals competing for local investment appeared—for a hospital by a group of physicians, a new jail for the city marshal, and a bond proposal for a county courthouse.[36] Miller could be outflanked by other local loyalties. Miller may have been caught unawares, misreading Reynolds's and Evans's readiness to act. He may have delayed too long, busy here and there, or lost his lead in detailed planning with architect Arthur Benton or even have been protectively overcautious because of his own earlier failures to deliver.

The city now had not one tourist hotel in prospect but two. Then, amazingly, a third hopeful offered to put himself "in the front rank of home-like hotels." The local editor rejoiced and anticipated a tourist boom, saying, "Riverside want[ed] all the tourist hotels that [were] coming to her." The editor added later, "This is a crisis in Riverside's history and success of these projects means a new era of prosperity for the City…Are we so lacking in public spirit and good business foresight that we will let this opportunity pass?"[37]

Then the drama changed. Reynolds withdrew, only $3,000 short of his bonus amount.[38] If Reynolds intended a spur to Miller, he succeeded, perhaps beyond his expectations. Miller reincorporated as the Glenwood Hotel Company, with a changed board. He announced the last meal in the Glenwood dining room for May 16, 1902, just two weeks later. He opened the contractor bids the first day of June and filed his papers with the county recorder's office twelve days later, a bulging file of fifty-two typewritten pages and eleven sheets of Arthur B. Benton's architectural drawings. Miller set up a scale of bonuses and penalties to spur the contractors toward demolition and construction. Reynolds may have forced his hand but clearly had not slowed his pace.

Earlier Miller had followed Evans and Reynolds to Huntington in Los Angeles. They discussed Benton's plans, Miller's cost estimates, and Huntington's readiness to finance the New Glenwood. He begged off, Miller said later. "He did not see how he could do it. I [Miller] told him he must not say no, and he answered that he was going to San Francisco and would see what could be done or words to that effect."[39] Miller, it seems, followed Huntington to San Francisco. When he boarded the southbound train, homeward bound after their conversation, he carried with him a Palace Hotel envelope bearing the penciled words:

"Mr. Frank Miller
You can go ahead on your Hotel project as outlined by you.
H. E. Huntington."[40]

Miller ordered three or four million building bricks. In June timbers were shoved under the Main Street wing of the hotel in preparation for moving it bodily to Sixth Street at Orange, there to become a service building and staff housing for nearly ten years. The Miller family had moved into a cottage on Orange Street; hotel furniture and furnishings had been stored or sold. At the end of June 1902, two weeks after laborers began digging the foundations of the New Glenwood, Frank Miller turned forty-five.

PART TWO:

Master of the Mission Inn

12

In Clear Over My Head

Those simple words on the front of an envelope assured Miller of his financing. He made his schedule, ran his cost estimates, announced the hotel's last meal, and called his contractors to the site on June 17. But those original cost estimates were wide of the mark. Four months into building, facing cost overruns from gross inaccuracies and laggard construction, Miller knew clearly enough what was happening. He had spent close to the total $150,000 of his initial announcement before the Reynolds withdrawal.[1] He confessed, "Frankly I am into this clear over my head. Instead of $150,000 the completed plant will cost nearly $400,000."[2]

He was wrong again, merely guessing. But having cast himself on Huntington, he held on, drawing funds until the middle of 1903, four months after the new hotel officially opened. By then he had committed everything to Huntington: the corporation, the hotel, all his Riverside real-estate holdings, and his Loring Opera House stock. He'd placed a chattel mortgage on all the furniture and assigned all his Glenwood Hotel stock to Huntington, a total, he said, of $236,809.64. He kept back only his life-insurance policies. "By the enclosed instruments you have absolute power and ownership," he wrote to Huntington in early 1903, adding in his perennial optimism prospects of hard cash from property sales and income from hotel shops and opera-house rentals and from the returning tourists already booked on a hotel waiting list.³

Even with a short first season, the New Glenwood showed a profit. The Huntington resources and a rising tide of prosperity in Riverside indeed lifted all local boats, without which Miller would have been, again, irretrievably high and dry. Strangely, even thirty years later, Miller still wondered about Huntington's supportive motivations,⁴ suggesting obligation on Huntington's part. I believe Miller's memory cast rosy glows of hubris on his long and notable entrepreneurial years, including his relationship with Henry Huntington. For his part, Huntington had given repeated and explicit signals of his financial interest in Riverside's continued prosperity since 1901. Through a company officer he'd said, "the question of growth [in Riverside was] already settled."⁵ Huntington matched confidence in Riverside with confidence in the Millers' expertise to manage a resort hotel there.⁶

Buildings such as Miller had been striving toward and for which Arthur B. Benton prepared plans are not the work of a single mind, whether architect or client, but an evolution with arguments joined and passions engaged as additions and erasures shape ideas into plans.⁷ The New Glenwood that emerged and, indeed, all the subsequent additions to what became the Mission Inn reveal this evolution. Miller's earliest published preferences conformed closely to the conventional and undistinguished, but the New Glenwood's mission-revival style that was chosen didn't conform. Miller's acceptance of the mission style was, I believe, a conversion at Benton's skilled hands, the work of a communicative, persuasive, and superbly competent architect for a responsive client. And although

Miller may not have given the style close attention before his collaboration with Benton, he had seen examples at the 1893 Chicago World's Columbian Exposition,[8] the 1894 addition to the Indian school in Perris, California,[9] and the blended classical and mission style of the First Church of Christ, Scientist by architect Benton, just a block from the Glenwood.[10] He read about mission motifs on the Santa Fe depot at Mission San Juan Capistrano[11] and had seen Benton's article "Architecture for the Southwest" in *Land of Sunshine*, to which he wrote an approving comment.[12] Glenwood guests arrived at the mission-influenced Southern Pacific depot on Market Street just a block from Miller's hotel. From his own observation and Benton's persuasive tutelage, Miller's knowledge informed his decisions.

Benton summarized Miller's conviction as a "desire not only to perpetuate the spirit of the old architecture but also to embody in his building details of construction and ornamentation as found in the missions, for their own beauty and historic interest regardless of their specific fitness for modern uses."[13] Those phrases, "details of construction and ornamentation" and "for their beauty and historic interest," were carefully chosen. Miller intended an environment of beauty and quiet, a place of hospitality, a backward reach to create the imagined spirit of California's Franciscan missions. He did not seek or become involved actively in the missions-restoration movement as Benton did.

The work declared the workman. Over the next thirty years, Miller sought ideal forms from traditions of European architecture, pursuing the spirit of hospitality—rest for the body, tranquility for the mind, and uplift for the spirit. He selected from among Spanish Gothic, Moorish, Italianate, and lastly Asian motifs. Only in this last, the Asian, can we see didactic intent, support for his advocacy of American amity with Asia, especially Japan. The hotel can be seen as his series of new infatuations with space and form creating atmosphere and, in each addition, redefining the hotel.

The evolution also reveals an evolving aesthetic awareness. The boy whose deep emotions stirred to *Othello* in wintry Wisconsin remained a selective consumer, even a molder of culture—attending events at the opera house he managed, continuously reading and being read to, and including and appreciating music at the hotel. He owned an increasingly selective display of paintings and patronized some of California's outstanding painters. Nothing he wrote or from what others remembered in 1902 or later suggested that Miller had an overarching vision or aficionado's keenness in culture and the fine arts. All the while, until a final illness made him merely an observer, his imagination and energy fueled new aesthetic excursions that changed the Mission Inn and, beyond that, the town he lived in.

With construction of the hotel basement and foundations well begun, Frank and Isabella went off on a buying trip to the East, carrying lists of the thousand and one things needed for the new and larger hotel, leaving only after Isabella had successfully saved the old adobe from destruction. By that time the rest of the hotel had been demolished or moved to Sixth Street.[14] In Grand Rapids, Michigan, the Millers bought furniture in a variety of styles including Asian, Indian, colonial, Dutch, and, of course, heavy orders of mission. Further east, they visited the Smileys at their Mohonk Mountain House in New Paltz, New York, eager to look at the famous hotel and take in all they could of the operations that made it so successful as a temperance hotel catering to elite guests and exclusive conferences. Miller admired the Smiley brothers for their success, their annual Conference of the Friends of the Indian, and their exemplary lives. He and Isabella stayed only a short time but caught lasting uplift and inspiration. "I may not be able to get onto the high ground on which you live," Miller wrote, "but I am surely going to try."[15] Miller shared the Smileys' high moral consciousness, their inclusion of religious observances in the hotel program, and their opening of the doors for those concerned about such social issues as the plight of Native Americans and, for Miller, the unconscionable wrongness of war.

༄

When Frank and Isabella arrived back in Riverside in August, they could see the brickwork, framing, floors, functional stairs, skeletons of halls, rooms, kitchens, dining room, parlor, and lobby—all the spaces that they had ordered furniture for.[16] Miller wrote as much to Henry Huntington, setting the opening date for January 8, 1903.

Miller scarcely rested. He inspected every detail daily and demanded that shoddy work be torn out, keeping Benton alert to his satisfactions and complaints. His letters going east to vendors and shippers fairly bristled with details, questions, orders, and requests. He talked bed lengths, mattress springs, wall mirrors, and cheap chairs. He asked for details on dishes in the Tiger Lily pattern in French gray, a Wedgwood pattern introduced in 1900. He ordered 1,185 feet of burlap for window-cushion covers, half golden brown and half olive green, all Isabella's choices. Six pages of details went to Marshall Field's in Chicago about window and skylight shades and curtains.

With Benton he inquired and informed about heating with steam-generating plants and cold storage for the perishables. He talked rental rates on shop space with an art dealer, a tailor, a shoe store, and a squirrel catcher.[17] He hassled vendors on price, responsive to their expertise in product knowledge and decorative acumen.[18] The political Miller went into recess. "In regard to the political part of your letter," he wrote to a friend, "I am absolutely out of politics. I am trying to build a hotel which will cost about $250,000 and this is taking every bit of the strength I have."[19]

He wore himself out, bringing on several days of "severe headache." Even though bedfast for most of a week, he still sent off an uninterrupted flow of letters. Out of bed he walked through the building, finding a multitude of omissions in construction, changes without authorization, and sloppy work by slovenly workmen, some of whom relieved themselves in a corner of the unfinished dining room. "It will take months," he wailed to Benton, "to get the stink out of the brick [walls]."[20]

Community distractions drew him aside briefly. Competitive trolley interests from San Bernardino and Colton threatened his territory.[21] There were trolley accidents,[22] and costs at the menageries in Arlington Park, located beside the Indian school, seemed excessive.[23] When the county supervisors opened bids for a courthouse, Miller urged mission-revival architecture. Wealthy tourists, he said, "who know what is artistic because of their extensive travel and the advantages of comparison" applaud the style. He hoped that the choices of "the brains and money of our land," would not be ignored by the supervisors.[24] That hope was as vain as his condescension was clear. They chose a beaux-arts design that brought enduring distinction to the city.

With the hotel opening date set, Miller began calling back the desirable and longer-term employees working elsewhere and recruiting the greater number needed for the larger hotel. To his bookkeeper, Miller wrote, "we are going to want you very much and you can depend on year round. You don't have to take a vacation [unpaid] unless you want to, and we can't live without you." Her assignments were to be formidable: bookkeeping, supervision of incoming shipments, and direction of the house inventory.[25] To ease the return of others, perhaps nervous about the larger hotel and expanded expectations, he brought sympathetic supervising individuals from the East.[26] He offered waitresses accommodations in a staff annex—rooms with either two double beds or a double and a single, a parlor, and shared bathrooms and toilets. His recruitment incentive included reduced fares or partial reimbursement from Chicago after a specified period of employment at the inn, usually a year. For young women wanting work in the West, the arrangement proved attractive. Complications arose when a waitress wanted to leave before fulfilling her contract, something that had already provided at least one dramatic confrontation at the Glenwood and public courtroom entertainment. A few others just rode off to Los Angeles and opportunity.

To early arriving guests, indeed to almost anyone who would listen, Miller liked to tell the factual details of his new hotel—three stories high, two hundred rooms, and one hundred fireplaces, with steam heat and electricity throughout the building. The footprint of the new open-court hotel, set midway on the city block and immediately behind the adobe, stretched from Main to Orange Streets, sidewalk to sidewalk, with wings extending toward Seventh Street.[27] A tidied up "back of the house" consolidated the miscellaneous service buildings on Sixth Street—the laundry and its drying rooms and woodsheds and storage. Here horse-drawn drays, wagons, and delivery carts delivered their jumble of filled barrels, boxes, and miscellaneous containers essential to the life of the hotel, carrying off the wastes sold to them.

Miller kept citrus plantings on his block, local icons and sources of heady perfume in their spring flowering. The Seventh Street driveway, curving into what became the Court of the Birds, suggested privilege to arriving guests. Those relaxing in the court on swings and rustic benches beside the adobe heard evensong chimes echoing among hotel walls of plain plaster. Large multipaned windows opened behind small wrought-iron balconies. Equally impressive decorations indoors included dark stained wood and colors chosen by Isabella—green trim and a yellow-tinted plaster predominated,[28] all part of the imagined mission theme in a homelike style the Millers strove for.[29]

Guests entered into the cool, dark, low-ceilinged lobby with its hefty square pillars, large open fireplace, and reception desk. Comfortable mission furniture and carpeted floors invoked immediate quiet and invited relaxation, so different from the bustle and clatter of many hotel lobbies. The hotel became a haven of peace and rest, a retreat from what many saw elsewhere as the hustling, threatening commercial and industrial world. Overall the appeal was "most alluring to the lover of luxury and taste," said a reporter after his guided tour. His words correctly read the selective patronage gathered at the New Glenwood. Reports traveled widely, reaching the *Detroit Free Press*, which described the inn as "a dream of art, a work of love and most of all a home."[30]

Even before completion, the building itself became a visitor attraction and copy for the local press.[31] Miller took delight in explaining some of the less obvious details to all who would listen: the Orange Street wing's multistory facade of rectangular windows relieved of monotony by wrought-iron and faux balconies above, the top floor set slightly back behind a tiled eyebrow roof, and the several street-level suites each sporting a different door design and each entered either from the street or from the courtyard. Miller would point out the curving mission-order arches high above, fronting each wing on Seventh Street and the high promenade on the fourth floor facing the interior court, as something "planned from the very beginning,"[32] an innovation of which he was justly proud. Could he resist reminiscing about the original adobe, now reduced to a flat-roofed single story with a stubby front overhang of old clay tiles salvaged from the Assistencia in Pala, near San Diego? Probably not. Here was homely charm, the old comfortably invoking the even older in a new regional architecture. He would point out the hotel's best suite, shortly to house the president of the United States, and perhaps he'd point out the owner's rooms close to the corner of Seventh and Orange, both places of importance, close to but separated from the main lines of hotel activity.

Additions to the new hotel would continue until 1930, each different in appearance and in function from the others. But there is a discernible pattern common to the New Glenwood (now known as the Mission Wing), the Cloister Wing of 1910, the Spanish Wing and Gallery of 1917, and the Rotunda Wing of 1930. Miller would build only as he had the finance or solid prospect of it. The hotel's steady prosperity, his growing assets, and his habit of prompt payment of debts helped, of course. He had learned from two unsuccessful efforts. Further, he habitually mulled over plans and made changes once construction was under way. Only late in life could illness keep him on the sidelines, merely watching. Adaptability and its boon companion suggestibility fit his personality. He did persist toward goals but habitually consulted expert opinion and superior achievers, open to advice and new things. This was especially so with his financiers, Huntington, of course, and his architects, Arthur B. Benton and later Myron Hunt and G. Stanley Wilson. And I see, throughout his almost thirty years of building, an aesthetic growth suggestive of what Oliver Wendell Holmes described as consciously building "more stately mansions."[33]

Final movements are often necessarily rapid; December 1902 brought just such a quickening in construction on the new hotel. Plasterers attacked the elevator tower; brick layers tackled completion of the bell-rich campanario that straddled the driveway; crews installed stoves, tables, fuel bins, laundry equipment, and the steam-room and cold-room fittings and insulation; cabinetmakers and decorators brought ground-floor and first-floor rooms toward completion. All of this was done in anticipation of the announced opening.³⁴ Upper floors would continue to receive fixtures and finish over the next many months. But the schedule had been met closely enough to justify Miller's promise to the city: his hotel was ready for the 1903 winter season, somewhat shortened. Financially Miller was clear over his head in debt, but his dividends of satisfaction covered it all.

13

Frank Is Proud of His Hotel

Theodore Roosevelt's promised visit to Riverside in May 1903 set people around town talking.[1] Of course, there was also talk about the Indian school, to be named the Sherman Institute, being built on Magnolia Avenue, and gossip about construction kickbacks at the courthouse. All the while, crews building the new hotel labored ten hours a day, six days a week, taking little account of the holiday season, though distracted at times by lookers roaming the building. Other interruptions and frustrations had almost everyone complaining. Miller himself was anxious, whatever his pride in the progress made. Even two years later, he wrote, "My ship is so heavily laden that for the coming few years I must watch everything closely."[2]

He and Isabella had planned the opening events. For the first, late in January 1903, they gathered the family, the Glenwood Hotel Corporation board, and all the laborers and tradesmen employed on the building.[3] For these laborers and their wives, the event must have been especially memorable. The banquet put them briefly into a world they were not part of; they could, indeed, enjoy the fruits of their seven months of labor. For them, dining as Miller's guests was special, probably a once in a lifetime event. For the board members, dining with manual laborers and craftsmen was unknown.

Other opening events followed. The general public crowded into the hotel court on Washington's Birthday. These outdoor ceremonies signaled social separation: some might gather in the court, met there by Miller, his board, and the architect, all to watch as the flag was raised.[4] Others would arrive in luxurious, private railroad cars or carriages, write their names in the new register, and then be wined and dined within. Miller's opening events embraced most but also affirmed a selectiveness defining the New Glenwood as elite—fully accessible only to those with the credentials of privilege.

A banquet on March 20 honored Henry E. Huntington. He sat among national and state influentials, legislators, and the leaders in Riverside. All formally resplendent, they dined on baked Spanish mackerel and hot tamales and roast turkey and cranberry sauce,[5] the menu in part Miller's gesture toward the Spanish allusions of the new hotel's ethos and architecture. Eloquent praise unfolded for Huntington, Miller, the hotel, other honorees, and Riverside. All, however, acknowledged Huntington's role, as well they should. He had, among other things, financed the hotel and two electric trolley lines and sat on a local bank board. Riverside, said one speaker, stood ready to "treat him as one of us and give him a glad hand in every way we possibly can."[6]

In October 1903, several hundred commercial travelers came at Miller's invitation to "show their new home to their wives," staying over if they chose.[7] These lively guests feasted among saintly statuettes, battle-axes, heraldic devices, monastic scenes in beaten brass, and busts of musicians in raised metal, all thought to be "striking and harmonious."[8] When a clergyman asked Miller what he thought of the moral qualities of his commercial traveler guests a few days later, Miller, not lacking in wit or an opinion of the clergy, replied, "I think they compare favorably with preachers."[9]

Theater companies and short-term tour patrons began arriving. Convention groups came, talked through their one- or two-day agendas, dined in their closing banquets, and left duly impressed. The seasonal regulars came, fewer than usual but welcomed as family. These stayed a month or more, joining in the new inn's program of rides, theater, and in-house entertainment and often participating in local congregations and fraternal organizations. A group of forty-two railway tourists arrived at the depot, met there by the Sherman brass band then ferried in groups to the hotel aboard the sparkling, new horse-drawn surrey.[10] When asked, they readily shared opinions about the warm, friendly atmosphere, the unexpectedly harmonious colors inside and out, and the unique furniture.[11] Nine such tour groups, with the seasonal regulars of Miller's core constituency, arrived before April,[12] there because Miller diligently cultivated tour operators and company employees who traveled with the groups. The tourist crop and its field workers needed to be cultivated.

Miller's carefully selected Main Street storefront renters moved in: a dentist, a laundry and tailor, an elegant barbershop, and a combination Turkish and electric baths and massage parlor. The monthly rental total? Over $650,[13] all added income at what would be a prospering hotel until the Great Depression of the thirties changed the economy, the town, and the hotel.

Even as celebratory banquets began in January, Miller welcomed other notable guests. Louis S. James, the actor, signed in on the first line in the new register, arriving with a dramatic troupe to play Shakespeare's *The Tempest* at the Loring. Andrew Carnegie's business associate Major L. F. Brown arrived for a few days on an undisclosed personal assignment for Carnegie and was interested in the Carnegie Library being built across Orange Street.[15] Among others were Wisconsin writer Zona Gale, who became Miller's biographer,[16] and Carrie Nation, the temperance activist. Nation stayed at the New Glenwood for a few days, mostly reclusive to avoid being merely a spectacle rather than listened to.[17] General Thomas J. Stewart, national commander of the Grand Army of the Republic, stayed a night, as did Admiral Winfield Scott Schley, given a hero's welcome for his role in the Spanish American War. Locals chanted the jingle: "We're glad to see your fiz/That has stood where bullets whiz/And put Spain right out of biz/Mr. Schley."[18]

Distinguished visitors continued to arrive in the opening years—Mrs. J. Pierpont Morgan; Mrs. George Pullman of sleeping-car fame; Mrs. John D. Rockefeller; the J. C. Stubbs of the Southern Pacific; the E. P. Ripleys of the Atchison, Topeka, and Santa Fe; Mr. and Mrs. Fred Pabst, he the brewer from Milwaukee; and two theater luminaries, Florence Roberts and Frederick Warde—all of them "delightful," said Miller, "unless in Riverside during the unusually plentiful rain."[19] Henry Huntington, Arthur Benton, and Miller had indeed put Riverside on the national map. This ready surge of notables so soon after opening endorsed an earlier loyalty and a widening span of notability that many Riversiders may not have fully appreciated.

Miller's partiality to guests of distinction irritated some, who linked them to the "robber barons" of industry. Miller roundly rejected this view. The New Glenwood was to be a first-class hotel, wooing elite touring patrons, upper-middle classes, and the almost aristocracy. Miller enjoyed their company, and they in turn, were good for Riverside. He chided his critics: "It is useless for me to spend my money running special [railroad] cars, ringing chimes and showing people the hotel if we can't work together on such things."[20]

※

President Theodore Roosevelt's anticipated visit in May 1903 loomed large to offer an enviable social pinnacle for Miller. As part of that, he wanted Roosevelt to plant one of Riverside's original navel-orange trees at the hotel, trees owned by the new Pioneer Historical Society.[21] Miller pleaded; the Society yielded.[22] Miller crowed in a telegram to Charles Loring in Minnesota: "We bear the orange branch of victory as regards the original orange tree."[23]

Everyone wanted more than the mere whistle-stop from President Roosevelt and were delighted to learn he'd stay overnight and at the New Glenwood. Miller himself chaired the town's Entertainments Committee,[24] and the Miller family was "so proud they [could] hardly contain themselves."[25] As chairman, Miller gave the president a tight schedule, with a home visit, a brief stop to dedicate a Washington palm honoring Queen Victoria, and an evening banquet at the Glenwood followed by an overnight stay in what forever after was called the Presidential Suite. In the morning, he'd plant the orange tree then leave, carrying a handsome portfolio of photographs of "Picturesque Riverside."[26]

Best-laid plans often go awry. But apart from a little lateness en route, Roosevelt's arrival and progress to the Glenwood through crowded streets and to the banquet flowed smoothly. Thoughtfully, Miller asked Roosevelt's willingness to have the kitchen staff see their president during the meal, a request readily granted.[27] Local retellings even now describe a cold-water banquet, and such it may have been, but not, as many like to claim, because Roosevelt eschewed alcohol.[28] Then, sometime about bedtime, the electricity failed in the president's rooms—Miller's worst fears realized. Just when it happened or how everyone responded was not recorded. Retellings placed the president protectively on the floor, surrounded by armed secret service men as the lights came on.[29]

Miller bristled to Benton next day. "Dear Sir," he began in a crisp and uniquely formal salutation given their otherwise friendly and frequent letters. Miller had begged Benton for steady lighting, especially in the president's apartments. Failure was "simply inexcusable." The scorching letter ended with the admirable restraint their friendship deserved: "It does seem to me I might have been saved the annoyance and disgrace of the trouble last night."[30]

Before leaving the hotel, President Roosevelt turned a couple of shovels of earth to replant an original navel-orange tree in the courtyard. Fruit from the tree became Miller's favorite gift to especially important guests. Roosevelt himself received a basketful of fruit in 1911 when the then-former president made a whistle-stop in Riverside.[31] There's little doubt that the visit by Theodore Roosevelt added lasting fame to the Glenwood as little else could have.[32] As the presidential train cleared the station yard en route to Los Angeles, a six-car tourist group arrived for the New Glenwood, ready to stay three days,[33] a harbinger of rail tourist patronage that would assure profitability through more than two decades.

Hearty and widely published praise for the new hotel came from David Starr Jordan, Miller's walrus-mustached friend, the president of Stanford University. "It has been left to you, Frank Miller, a genuine Californian," Jordan wrote in 1905, "to dream of the hotel that ought to be, to turn your ideal into plaster and stone, and to give us in mountain-belted Riverside the one hotel which a Californian can recognize as his own. I congratulate you on your success, not as a hotel proprietor, but as a poet and artist, as one who has done well for California and deserving of California's gratitude, for no one can leave the hospitable [New] Glenwood without a resolve to come back again to the region where such things are possible—to the region where in time all noble things shall be possible."[34]

What did Miller himself think about the hotel? What did it mean to him? He summed it up for Rev. T. C. Hunt, a spiritual adviser: "You will say that Frank is proud of his hotel."[35] He reviewed the challenges: costs had soared; financial burdens pressed; labor agitators coerced so that he "had to bend and concede everything" to get finished. The nervous and physical stress he'd endured far exceeded anything he'd ever known, bearable only because of Hunt's encouragement, he wrote. In bright prospects anxiety faded, with the feeling that the coming tourist season "ought to make us all the money we should have."[36] In another letter, Miller rejoiced to share the certainty of success and reported almost universal approval of the "simplicity and genuine appearance of the architecture,"[37] an architectural chasteness perhaps overshadowed by the visual enthusiasm of later additions.

The praise, the promising financial horizons, Hunt's support, and the private glow of satisfaction, all of these were not enough to ward off physical exhaustion. Within a few days of writing to Hunt, Miller was bedfast in his new hotel for the better part of a week.

Later judgments about the hotel, the part we know now as the Mission Wing, even exceeded Miller's own, one authority describing it as "one of the most complete expressions of the mission and Spanish revival styles."[38] The architecture and decoration generated happiness. It was "so cheerful, sunny and pleasant," according to the local press, that "it does not have the ordinary hotel air."[39] Miller would adopt a house slogan, "*Entre, amigo, es su casa*"—Enter, friend, this is your home—a sentiment that matched not only the warmth of welcome given to arriving guests but also the aesthetic appeal of the hotel, which was "not ostentatious but home like." The *Pueblo (Colorado) Chieftain* held forth on Californiua's regional architecture in general, the writer describing the New Glenwood specifically as "the most truly elegant public house I have ever been in—observe, I say, the most elegant, not the most luxurious. Vulgar minds may not recognize the distinction."[40]

The particularities of New Glenwood pleased Miller, with distinctiveness far beyond public expectations of the first-class hotel talked about over so many years. Just as his adult personality sustained the youthful conviction that "my kind of boys were pretty scarce," so the physical expression of that personality—his kind of hotel—was pretty scarce.[41] This personal achievement, a solid and public statement of dogged persistence, may have redressed any humiliation felt from earlier false starts, but it did not shrink his ambitions or generate hubris. Miller freely, even pleasurably, acknowledged his shared role; he called himself a "factor." He of all people knew that the architectural design and details were Benton's, the money Huntington's. Isabella had decorated and furnished; Frank and Alice Richardson attracted guests by their generous natures and attention to service. His shoulders alone bore the huge indebtedness, whatever the corporate status. But for the moment, as he sat that morning in his new room writing to Reverend Hunt, a trusted friend, the hotel was his, and he was proud.

Proud though he was, he remained demanding, writing edgy letters about uncorrected details: leaky roofs, improper drainage, paint washing off walls in the first rain, decks warped out of alignment, unfinished carpentry, electrical shorts, and water pressure enough to blow out "fastenings" when toilets were flushed.[42] Formal acceptance waited on corrections until January 1904.[43] In his feistiness, Miller seemed to overlook his own absences, frequent changes in plans, and the stream of substitutions and returns he insisted on, all of them slowing progress and adding complications among a miscellany of contractors and tradesmen, not all incompetent or devious.

From almost the opening, Miller's reserves of energy eroded, allowing recurrent illness to slow him down. He suffered from fatigue, eye problems, severe headaches, and bouts of fever and neuralgia, and he was bedfast in spite of seeking rest in San Diego and San Francisco. On his forty-sixth birthday, June 30, he was too weary even to enjoy the family party, going to bed after a bite of cake to wait there for Isabella, who would come to read to him—one of his lifelong pleasures.[44] For several days in October 1903, he was bedfast again.[45] As might be expected, his business vim fell victim to his illnesses,[46] the emotional and physical stress from this trying and busy time adding anxiety and nervousness as the second season for the new hotel approached.

The family talked about a name for the hotel. Miller favored adopting "Mission Inn" but vacillated for several years, asking others' opinions of "New Glenwood," "California's Mission Inn," and "Glenwood Mission Inn." Over family disagreements and his own indecision, Miller did adopt "Mission Inn," although for years afterward the old and new names were widely used in combination, often interchangeably.[47]

The hotel also needed a distinctive logo or symbol, or so Miller thought. He wanted something suggesting California's religious roots, particularly a cross of some kind, but he floundered for three or four years thinking about the kind of cross he wanted. At first he used a tiny Latin cross embossed on the skirt of a mission bell,[48] but later he remembered being told that application was "irreligious."[49] He went on searching, admitting that he was unsure even how to explain what he was looking for.[50] Finally, with help from Arthur Benton and others, he adopted a design not unlike the Roycrofter's double-barred cross or a bishop's ceremonial cross. His design put a double-barred cross surmounting a trapezoidal frame, within which was suspended a plain bell, a design that is still the hotel logo and is used in variant forms by the city.[51]

Adopting a patron saint for the hotel reflected the family's easy linking of a mission name, the architectural style, and a saint. Isabella and twenty-one-year-old Allis convinced Miller that a saint was needed, guiding him to a choice of Saint Francis of Assisi, a saint most easily recognized by Protestants and, of course, Catholics.[52] Saint Francis prevailed, becoming in effect a decorative motif much more than a symbol of devotion. The adoption remained robust: a catalog compiled after Miller's death in 1935 listed 474 objects with Franciscan content, more than a dozen in one room.[53] Small wonder that some visitors believed the inn itself had been a religious mission or that some Catholics had taken a special interest in the inn.

An ecclesiastical aura was absent in the old adobe of the 1870s. It appeared in the New Glenwood with the choice of a name and logo, in the cumulative religious decoration, and in the hymns and presentations in some hotel programs. Guests and the community approved. There was much for all to be proud of, but there was no evidence in 1903 or earlier of an unfolding or received vision, ecclesiastical or otherwise. Rather the driving forces were those that would motivate for the next thirty years—Miller's active imagination, his own need for achievement, his perception on Riverside's potential, and his advisability. In this instance, he responded to Benton's guidance toward a new regional architecture with appropriate, varied decoration. Other styles would beckon, and other, wider interests would summon his energies, but that lay untapped in 1903.

With the hotel demanding less time, Miller's town interests increased. He shared in preparations for a formal opening at the Sherman Institute on February 10 and resumed activity in the street railway, now run by an experienced crew and supervised from Los Angeles. In other town matters, Miller championed the good-roads movement but disturbingly grafted into that his own agenda of making a park of the privately owned Mount Rubidoux. This collation of interests stirred years of argument, irritation in the town, and frustration for Miller in his urgency about getting things done.

14

A Trying and Busy Time

An expansive mood gripped Riverside in the wake of the opening events of the Sherman Institute in 1902 and the New Glenwood and the Roosevelt visit in 1903.[1] Miller was part of it all, adding his own agendas to the city's. He had pushed again and again for better roads, impatiently going ahead with sidewalks and street improvement around his hotel block. He readily endorsed better fire protection—hotels were notoriously at risk. For him, the city interest in parks meant the Mount Rubidoux Park and road; he already had the trolley park and zoo in Arlington near Van Buren Street. Miller contrived his opportunity, linking talk of a city park with his Rubidoux road interest, even though at the time the mountain belonged to someone else. All this, and the completion of details in construction at the hotel, led him to label the period "a trying and busy time."[2] It was much his own choosing, but had his prophetic insight been clearer, he'd have seen even more such times ahead for himself, Isabella, and the whole family.

His attachment to Mount Rubidoux, the rocky hill on the northwest side of the town, sprang from at least the competitive impulse to match or surpass Redlands's Smiley Heights, a scenic area developed by the influential Smiley brothers.[3]

Others shared his interest. And as a realtor, Miller saw building lots in prospect on the lower slopes of the mountain. There was more. Miller was ready to convert the rocky baldness into another diversion for locals and visitors. As he talked in 1903, his strategies revised other people's budgets,[4] giving rise to squabbling that threatened to bury all discussion.[5] The rancor and his revisions turned public attention to less febrile topics.[6] Miller chafed at delays.[7] For a year the topic disappeared from the newspaper and from his correspondence, but it thrived in Miller's quiet planning.

His daughter, Allis, now twenty-one, had graduated from the Los Angeles Marlborough School for Girls in June 1901, after earlier schooling in Riverside. When she applied to an eastern college in 1904, she was placed on a waiting list, so she chose instead a year in Europe with a small study group of young women. They'd travel for two months then live in Rome to study the art, architecture, literature, and history of Europe.[8] As she left, Miller armed her with letters of introduction from the secretary of the Navy and from a US senator, commenting endearingly in his requests, "She is the only boy I have." Allis commented later, "What it is to have a famous father."[9]

Miller's agile mind turned his daughter's experience into the notion of having an elite women's college right in Riverside.[10] Pasadena and Santa Barbara had similar ambitions.[11] Because he lacked funding, he considered importing an existing private school from Los Angeles[12] then veered back to creating a select women's college modeled on Wellesley or Smith.[13] His eleven-page proposal reviewed the absence of women's colleges in the West, other than Mills in San Francisco; noted the waiting lists in the East; and commented on the dominance of coeducational institutions. He leaned on the merits of Southern California, especially Riverside, by reason of climate, available acreage, and an "educational atmosphere" in a city that spent impressively on its elementary and secondary schools. Riverside offered beauty, sobriety, and quiet and peaceful streets, he wrote, where "police are hardly needed." Outdoor recreations tempted year round. Miller praised the benefits of mission-revival architecture, saying, "Hardly any style of architecture lends itself more ready to educational and religious uses." He sent the proposal to Henry Huntington with a view to approval, and probably finance.[14]

Miller was not making an argument for women's higher education but describing a civic institution. His proposal took no leverage from rising middle-class educational expectations; the changing roles for women, especially in the professions; or from women's suffrage, all topics of discussion in this era of Progressive ideas and reforms. The Riverside young women who studied beyond high school went, well content, to Mills in San Francisco or to the coeducational Redlands College, Pomona College, Stanford, or the University of California in Berkeley. Allis, close in the bosom of European culture, stayed interested in her father's college ideas, inquiring from Rome about the site of "Miller College: is it on Rubidoux?"[15] It's a wise child who knows her parent.

The empty shell of Miller's advocacy became "nothing more than a remote hope and an alluring possibility," an amorphous educational institution without a site, finance, local enthusiasm,[16] or an anchor in the current priorities for women or education. Not until 1946 would Riverside have an accredited four-year college, and then it was as a private, coeducational, and religious venture located ten miles outside the city.

Miller kept his political lamps lit, even though busy with the hotel and briefly sidelined by a flamboyant Republican banker.[17] Back in the political lead, Miller traveled to the 1904 state convention in Santa Cruz, joined in the hoopla, and then, in San Francisco, spent political capital among the power brokers.[19] As Riverside's first boy of Republican politics, he wrote dozens of letters keeping party members on track, "programming" as they said then.[20] He advised devious tactics for some and flattered others with gifts of photographs and fruit.[21] He visited some, sent his sister Alice to lobby the governor, and made courteous, clear arguments in support of party candidates. For those willing to follow his program, Miller offered travel passes solicited from the railroads—some free, some at employee rates, and some discounted,[22] distributing gifts received from another's hands. "The rule in politics," Miller believed, "is to stand by your friends so long as they are honest and their purpose is right."[23]

Political purpose that year included much about the location of a state citrus experiment station. Miller's political labors help to bring the station to Riverside.[24] He stood to gain nothing from having the station placed locally or the political scuffling that went on. His link to the citrus growers was simply social; his hotel guests and tourists would rarely ever see the citrus station, at first remotely placed beside a cemetery on the edge of town. Yet Miller left no political stone unturned and few palms unpressed as he worked, successfully, with others to get the coveted research facility. Presumably he knew that his collaborators were honest and their purpose right.

Within months of formally accepting the New Glenwood from his contractors in 1904, Miller doubled the dining-room capacity. Less than two years later, his laborers began digging a large basement for a $30,000 services building and employee residence on Sixth Street.[25] Almost from the start, serious accidents bedeviled the builders on that project. A partly demolished wall fell on two laborers, breaking their legs; one side of a hole caved in, roughing up a bricklayer; and an oil tank exploded under the sidewalk, tossing a worker twenty feet in the air before he dropped bodily into the ruptured tank of fuel oil. Miller met all the expenses for immediate care, the long hospital stays, and rehabilitation.[26] Trying times indeed and not for him alone.

༶

Frank and Isabella went to Chicago to meet Allis as she returned from Rome in 1905. The reunion started out badly, with Allis and her mother bedfast for almost a week. Miller's own agenda stumbled. Financiers did not warm to his college idea. The twenty-one automakers Miller visited excelled in agonizing vagueness, "unwilling to put in black and white what they say,"[27] and likely amazed at Miller's proposal of a livery of twenty to twenty-five autos, each costing about $4,000 and each built to carry a dozen people. All this came from an effusive stranger from an unknown western town. Great caution would seem appropriate.

When the family traveled slowly to Yellowstone, however, success smiled on them all. Their stay there rested and refreshed them all. "The trip of our lives," said Miller.[28] In addition, he contracted in Yellowstone with Captain Hiram Chittenden of the US Army Corps of Engineers for a road survey on Mount Rubidoux.[29] Their journey home through Portland, with its Lewis and Clarke Centennial and American Pacific Exposition and Oriental Fair and a visit to the Tahoe Tavern on the lake,[30] sustained all the benefits of the Yellowstone stay.

Back home, with Chittenden engaged and Sixth Street construction progressing, Miller plunged ahead, linking hopes for the mountain road with plans for his auto livery of touring and rental cars. The jogging horses and clouds of dust from his carriages must give way, he proclaimed, to the motor world as a permanent fixture. He encouraged others to enter this future with him by financing his garage, the autos not yet ordered. His architect Arthur Benton's luxurious first sketches for the garage gave way to the much more modest and utilitarian Glenwood Garage opposite the hotel.[31] Small wonder if some looked in amazement at Miller's imagination and energy and the variety of his projects.

Miller still wanted a Mount Rubidoux Park to accommodate his anticipated road. A rival local syndicate had the same idea, proposing about what Miller offered: purchase, improvement, and use of the mountain for public benefit, then resale to the city after five years for $50,000.[32] Miller solicited his high-level railroad friends in support of what looks now like his whole agenda: the park, the road, the women's college, and real-estate development around the base of the mountain. Several chided him about vagueness on all aspects of his enthusiasms. Even so, the road alone caught interest, falsely linked to the flimsiest tissue of rumor that Edward H. Harriman of the Southern Pacific would finance it. He had not been wooed, but Henry Huntington had been.

Pressured to coherent action by friends, Miller wrote an unusually organized, detailed, and persuasive letter that grew into a formal proposal sent to Huntington and others. In essence, a Huntington Park Association would purchase and improve the mountain and later resell it to the city. Miller implored Huntington: "Can you not trust my judgment that this is the thing to do and feel assured from your acquaintance with me that the undertaking will be worked out and not only fortunately but so that it will be a credit and an honor to you... By use of your name you have made Riverside County possible. You are not ashamed of its courthouse, its library and its well-made roads? Your name and help worked the same part with the Indian School, the electric road and the Mission Hotel."[33] This was persuasion of a high order indeed.

Friends knew all too well that Miller multiplied his tasks, usually moved fitfully toward definitions, and that he was distracted easily. Drawn to sharper focus by their pointed comments, Miller wrote again to Henry Huntington: "I feel that if you don't take hold of the Rubidoux proposition in a way that will make it go it is because I have failed to make you understand clearly how greatly it will further your interests in Riverside." Sensing perhaps that he'd now claimed too much or urged too strongly, Miller closed his letter assuring Huntington that he'd follow advice, defer to Huntington's judgment, and even "quit and try to be satisfied."[34] Fortunately for Miller and his colleagues, Huntington stayed with them.[35]

By December 1905, Miller's interim representative, local businessman C. W. Barton, had incorporated Huntington Park Association and had local money in hand for the purchase and the legal documents ready for the Miller signature.[36] Bold newspaper headlines made the announcement,[37] and Miller signed and then glowed in the praise that greeted him. His faithful steward was little noticed. Barton had initiated and managed all the details and fund raising while Miller was off in the East for the second time that year.[38]

Isabella and Frank had gone east, this time on another order of business—his private ambition for a hotel in Yosemite Park. Frank, indifferent to landscape as a youth, had in maturity developed a commercial and mystical attachment—not only to Rubidoux, but also to this spectacular park. John Muir and John Burroughs both informed and influenced Miller's awareness. Later he'd tell friends that he had Yosemite on mind for many years. Just how many years is uncertain, but he had been stirring on it quietly for at least two years, visiting there to look at the hotels and gathering details from his fellow hotelkeepers. Miller told Charles Loring about his wish for a chain of Mission hotels from Yosemite south to at least Riverside, even San Diego.[39] Loring opposed the whole idea bluntly. "Don't be bothering yourself," he wrote, "about building any new hotels in Yellowstone [sic] or anywhere else. You have enough prospects and property enough to give you all the income you will require or that will be good for you for the remainder of your life. Take a little comfort and don't work, work, work." Another equally fervent letter followed, then another: "I see you still have the Yosemite bee in your bonnet but I hope you will not suffer his sting."[40] Beesting or not, Miller went on looking for financing.[41] He watched park protection legislation in Sacramento,[42] knowing that serious progress required federal intervention. Where better to get that than from the top, with the man who had been his guest in the newly opened hotel in 1903 and then camped in the valley with John Muir: President Theodore Roosevelt.

Jacob Riis, a close friend of the president, arranged the Millers' personal visit with the president in 1905.[43] Roosevelt received the Millers and their letters of introduction from David Star Jordan of Stanford University; Albert Shaw, editor of the *American Monthly Review*; and Lyman Abbott, editor of the strongly Progressive *Outlook*, a preeminent Protestant clergyman and a personal friend of Roosevelt.[44] With a typical flourish, Roosevelt scratched a note that swept the Millers on to the secretary of the interior: "I want to introduce to you my good friend Mr. Miller. He will show you the letters from President Jordan, Mr. Lyman Abbott and Dr. Shaw. Will you report to me on his request? <u>If proper</u>," Roosevelt underscored the words, "I shall be glad to have it granted. [Signed] T. Roosevelt."

Isabella came home with the note, a treasured souvenir. But the secretary of the interior stalled, largely, Miller thought, from his wish to "get technical" in asking for details,[45] something that with Miller tended to follow rather than accompany his ambitions. That delay on the very first visit boded for a trying future. For over a decade Miller's Yosemite ambitions wove in and out of government departments and representatives' offices before a resolution emerged, the slow pace equally Miller's doing because he too "got technical."

༄

While the Millers traveled to and from Washington, two solid offers to buy the Loring Building and Opera House arrived on his desk. The directors and Charles Loring were ready for

Miller to negotiate the sale. For the next two months he'd be "pressured," in fact kept close while brokering the sale, and by that kept away from the accident-prone Sixth Street building and from planning a power plant, the Glenwood Garage, and Mount Rubidoux.

He knew the business community was watching him closely; he knew also that he strongly favored one buyer and disdained the other. He moved adroitly and played one buyer against the other, himself jousting and anxious. After about six weeks, in 1906 he could write to Charles Loring: "The deed is done. It has just about used us all up and I am sorry I made the sale."

Common sense told him the wisdom of selling: the roof had to be replaced, the building front needed restoration, and moths had ruined much of the upholstery. The stage equipment and scenery showed their years, tawdry even at a distance. But what surprised Miller most were his feelings of attachment to the whole building, opera house, and office block and all that he'd experienced there. He wished that only a death—his or Loring's—had made the parting necessary, such a bond he had, especially for the opera house. "In conclusion," he wrote to his friend, "I hate this whole business [of selling]. I had no idea that I would have this feeling about it, and I wish that we had waited"[46] until mortality forced the sale.

His last booking for the opera house brought Madame Modjeska; she was ending her theatrical career. Her performance ended with one standing ovation after another, then encore followed encore, curtain calls seemingly without end. Fans filled her arms with flowers, passed more onto the stage, and piled them at her feet. Unannounced, Miller came on to drape her shoulders with a huge Polish flag, brilliant in red-and-white silk. Their tears flowed freely as Miller knelt to arrange even more bouquets at her feet in a touching tribute widely reported and long in the folklore of Riverside.[47] Whatever his pride in the still-new Mission Inn, letting go across the street brought an emotional wrench, something he agonized to describe to Charles Loring, something poured out with tears at Modjeska's feet to a full house. Few, indeed, in the house knew the double drama of what they were seeing.

Just four days later, Miller signed the bills of sale, ending in depression nearly fifteen years of living with performers and performances.[48] He had learned the business side of agents, booking, and scheduling; moved easily among actors in rehearsal and performance; and entertained the leading figures of a score of traveling companies. On occasion he swept floors and tidied up. He had safely threaded thickets of moral objection. Most of all, he had feasted on theatrical make-believe.

Miller's theatrical life continued. We can view the hotel itself as his theater, the building intricately equipped with props and scenery, its interior spaces and its program a series of stages and presentations where his carefully selected guests, the actors, moved through the acts and scenes of the seasonal drama. They entered and exited, directed in their parts on tours, at meals, and in Sunday evening hymn singing. Notable visitors spoke their soliloquies, the movements of all cued by bells and skilled prompters from the front desk and back of the house. Miller himself, Isabella, Alice and Frank Richardson, and Alexis Bjornsen, the hotel's majordomo of twenty years, knew the script to perfection as they directed. Perhaps with the opening of the New Glenwood Miller had theater enough, no longer needing the complement of the aging and public opera house.

Frank A. Miller, Master of the Mission Inn, in 1925 when he was declared Riverside's first citizen, honored also by a stone bridge and tower on local Mt. Rubidoux. The artist, W. A. Sharp, had depicted the family and the Mission Inn for many years. MIFM

From the family home in Tomah, Wisconsin Christopher Miller, father of Emma, Frank, Alice and Edward, enlisted in the 49th Wisconsin Infantry in January 1865. His rapid promotion to officer rank recognized his engineering degree and more than ten years directing railroad survey. He served in Missouri until October 1865, returning to survey work in Wisconsin until leaving for California in 1874. MIFM

Mary Ann Clark, an Oberlin College trained school teacher met Christopher Miller while both attended Oberlin. They married in 1852 and in late 1856 moved as pioneer settlers to frontier Tomah, Wisconsin with three –year-old daughter Emma. Frank Augustus was born the next year, Alice in 1860 and Edward in 1864. She was known as a woman of refinement, amiable, deeply devoted to her family and committed to the growth of the community. MIFM

Emma Miller Newman (1853 – 1932). RMM

Frank A. Miller, (1857 – 1935). RMM

Alice Miller Richardson (1860 – 1937). RMM

Edward Miller (1864 – 1922). RMM

The four children of Christopher and Mary Ann Clark Miller, from a group photograph taken in 1895. The family arrived in Riverside, California in late 1874. Emma, married, lived in Riverside at the time of the photograph, later in Los Angeles. The senior Millers and their other three children lived out their lives in Riverside.

Isabella Hardenberg (1853-1908), came to Riverside as a school teacher in 1876. She and Frank Miller married in 1880. RMM

Marion Louise Clark as a high school senior, 1902. She became Frank Miller's secretary in 1906. They married in 1910. The widespread approval given his first marriage was often withheld from Miller's marriage to Marion Clark because of the more than twenty-year difference in their ages. Both marriages, however, were eminently successful and happy. MIFM

Isabella Hardenberg Miller, 1903, photographed as she witnessed Theodore Roosevelt plant an original navel orange at the Mission Inn. RMM

Marion Clark Miller, ca. 1936. MIFM

Isabella and Frank Miller shared a love of riding. They are pictured here under the bell-rich Campanario in the front court at the Mission Inn, ca. 1905. RMM

Marion and Frank Miller on horseback at the Mission Inn, ca. 1914. Marion, an accomplished recreational rider, early adopted the astride position. MIFM

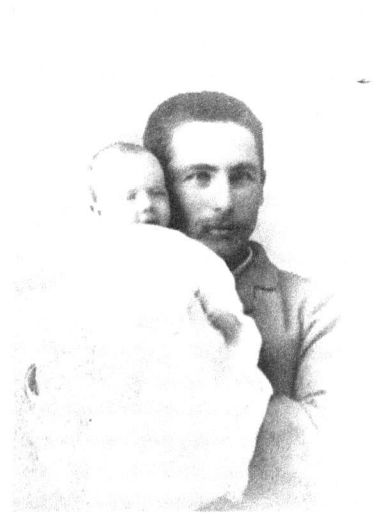

Frank Miller with daughter Allis Hardenberg Miller, 1882. MIFM

Frank Miller, wife Isabella and daughter Allis in 1893, all dressed for the fun of the fair at the Worlds Columbia Exposition, Chicago. RMM

Marion Miller and Frank Miller with his grandson Frank Miller Hutchings and his grand daughter Isabella Hutchings, ca. 1915. The portly Master of the Mission Inn enjoyed the occasional drama of appearing in costume, whether as a Franciscan friar as here or with Native American headdress or in Japanese kimono. MIFM

Frank Miller (extreme left) and Marion Miller (center) with their hosts during their visit in Japan, 1925. MIFM

Miller's locally unpopular advocacy of amity between the US and Japan, especially after his 1925 visit in Japan, influenced the award of the Japanese Order of the Rising Sun in 1929. The investiture, pictured here, was made at the Mission Inn. MIFM

Miller posed for this formal portrait after receiving an honorary Master of Arts degree from the University of Southern California in 1930 in recognition of his contributions to arts, culture and international relations. MIFM

The entrance and façade of what is now known as the Mission Wing facing Mission Inn Avenue. With its opening in 1903 Miller achieved his goal of building Riverside's "first class" hotel, himself the Master of the Mission Inn, financed by Henry E. Huntington. Steve Lech Postcard Collection

Now known as the Cloister Wing, this 1910 addition on Orange Street housed guest rooms above and the below-grade Music Room that added greatly to the hotel's cultural programming and ecclesiastical motifs. Steve Lech Postcard Collection

The Spanish Addition, backing onto Sixth Street, enclosed an inner patio, added guest rooms on upper floors and most significantly provided this imposing gallery for Miller's growing collection of artworks while providing for visiting exhibitions. RMM

The show-piece in the final addition to the hotel, known as the Rotunda Internacional, the St. Francis Chapel includes a gilded eighteenth century altar piece and seven large windows by Louis Comfort Tiffany. Still the site of hundreds of weddings annually, in 1935 Miller lay in repose in the Chapel where the obsequies he personally prepared were performed. RMM

Miller's influence and finance backed several important buildings in the city. The 1890 Loring Building, across the street from the Glenwood, (ancestor of the Mission Inn) provided a cultural impetus in the opera house and a commercial stimulus from rentable offices. As manager Miller had a formative role in local culture. Steve Lech Postcard Collection

The Sherman Institute, 1902, a federal school for Native Americans, came to Magnolia Avenue in Riverside under Miller's leadership and was located on land he brokered. Steve Lech Postcard Collection

Miller's 1911 donation to building the Congregational Church on Mission Inn Avenue at Lemon and his influence on its location furthered a widely shared vision for a civic center on the contiguous city blocks. He had joined the congregation in 1875, serving as treasurer and trustee for many years. RMM

The federal post office, opened 1912, added to the civic center on Mission Inn Avenue. Miller played the activist role as an advocate in Washington D.C., anxious that a Mission style architecture prevail. The building is home to the Riverside Metropolitan Museum. RMM

Miller traveled widely investigating modern hospital management and nurse training and donated heavily to this local response to competition from regional hospitals. Middle-class awareness of advances in medicine and hospital care stimulated local demands for a community managed hospital. RMM

The city hall opened at the corner of Orange and Mission Inn Avenue beside the post office in late 1924. An artful mayor drew Miller willingly into a promise that resulted in the gift of land for the building and an obligation to further donations toward the civic center. RMM

This 1929 building, another addition to the civic center, the Municipal Auditorium was built on Miller's and others' donations of land and incorporated his landscaping although his hopes for including an upper-floor educational center were not realized. Steve Lech Postcard Collection

Under Miller's leading influence Mt. Rubidoux, rising about 450 feet above Riverside, developed into a public park on private property and the site of community observances of Easter sunrise and patriotic memorials. RMM

The happy Master of the Mission Inn on a summer morning with the two long-lived hotel macaws, Napoleon and Joseph. MIFM

15

A Tumble of Ideas

Even as Miller and Hiram Chittenden shook hands in greeting, both had the road on Mount Rubidoux in mind, but beyond that, their thoughts went off in different directions. Miller talked leisure, urging Chittenden to rest and recuperate, confidently asserting, "I can predict that you will not be here long before you will begin to throw out spontaneously the very suggestions and advice I want to receive from you."[1] He quite misread Chittenden. The civil engineer would make his own decisions about what was needed rather than offer what Miller thought he wanted to hear.

Early on his first morning, the brisk last day of February 1906, the dignified, scholarly, and, above all, task-oriented Chittenden met the city engineer and his survey crew on the mountain. In ten days he'd finished the road survey, engaged the topographical map maker, and presented his optimistic report and his modest bill for $250, his professional fee. The Huntington Park Association board accepted his plan, and Chittenden traveled north to continue his distinguished service in Seattle with the US Army Corps of Engineers. Miller admired Chittenden's smooth professional efficiency. Actual road construction, however, tried his patience by dragging on longer than promised, soured with arguments, though redeemed by coming in below budget.[2]

The now accessible hill became an open-air opera house for Miller's enactment of several kinds of dramas, each, I believe, affirming his personal need for *firstness* and for a responsive audience.[3] This impulse included adding symbols and commemorative mysticism, something that would continue most of his life. The appraisal of a friend rang true: "He hopes for better things and believes better things can be brought about. He is a live wire—a dreamer—a doer—a thinker—a planner—an idealist and a practicalist all combined."[4]

This amalgam began to appear on the mountain in 1907 in a decorated, wide place in the road with tons of heavy chains and two or three cannons, slightly at odds with Miller's growing peace advocacy. The place became Fort Chittenden,[5] the first such personal monument in Riverside, even though Chittenden stayed so briefly. More would come. A flagpole erected beside the cannons drew hundreds to a windy ceremony for Washington's Birthday.[6] The flag went up, and vocal and band music framed a "memorable little address" of some four hundred words by the diminutive Jacob Riis.[7] In his guttural voice, Riis symbolized the 1771 arrival of San Gabriel Mission as the arrival of the cross, the 1848 arrival of John C. Fremont as the era of the flag, with the two together bringing mercy and liberty with the obligation on all to sustain progress and national brotherhood. These were Miller's idioms—he habitually told his speakers what he wanted said. Close-by Riis as he spoke was the construction site for a huge cross,[8] Miller's next mountaintop adornment.

Two months later, the drama unfolded in two more acts. The afternoon erection of a large wood cross preceded an evening banquet at the inn to launch the good-roads movement for Southern California. This was an incongruous combination as each drew its own specific audience. At this distance, the day seems like an unintended and innocent farce, heightened as each of the leading actors headed off in his own direction as the audiences mingled.

Miller believed the cross on the mountain should honor mission founder Junipero Serra, a person then little known and unconnected with Riverside's past. Even so, Miller needed suitable ceremony. He invited Roman Catholic Thomas Conaty, the bishop of Monterey and Los Angeles, to "direct," doing so with trepidation lest Protestant and Catholic sensitivities become roiled.

On the mountain Bishop Conaty presided, splendid in ecclesiastical vestments of purple and white, crosier and miter adding solemn theater. Beside him waited what might be seen as an opera chorus—silent black-robed friars and a single Franciscan in brown. Conaty prayed, sprinkled the cross, and unveiled a large plaque inscribed, "Fra. Serra, 1713–1784. Dedicated April 26, 1907, by Rt. Rev. Thomas James Conaty, Bishop of Monterey and Los Angeles, in the presence of many people."[9] With that done, he abandoned the script to give what amounted to his justification for the Catholic presence, the claims of the cross, and the ecumenical service he had provided. Miller's earlier trepidations about Protestant and Catholic sensitivities were likely justified.[10]

In the evening, guests at the inn included those for whom good roads was primary. Others at table had come for the dedication of the cross, devoid of passion for the good-roads movement. Again Miller had coached his speakers to speak his lines, but they didn't do so. The principal speaker, Reverend E. E. Goff of the Congregational Church, abandoned Miller's "cram" instructions and praised Henry Huntington, for whom the mountain park was named. Without Huntington, said Goff, Miller's hopes would remain in the air.[11] Bishop Conaty, extempory again, simply ignored the good-roads theme to praise again the good church and the good Junipero Serra. Miller headed off to bed early as this, the second of his two-act, daylong opera began. He'd spent so much nervous energy planning the day and assigning everyone's part, he said, that the emotional strain had worn him down.[12]

How might Riverside see all this, Miller's first large and physical venture outside the hotel? He could be seen as doing private deeds for public benefit: a road up the hill, decorations along the way, and the promise of even better roads. Further, the flag high on the hill, the cross, and the cannons brought easily absorbed symbolism to enrich community ceremonials, adding icons to other rituals—Washington's Birthday, July 4, and Lincoln observance. But few local residents cared or even knew about Padre Junipero Serra or the Franciscan missions or how they might be linked to Riverside or Rubidoux. Some recognition might be appropriate for Juan Bautista de Anza's 1774 arrival or Jedediah Smith's in 1826, if known. But why have a visiting bishop, with his flotilla of friars, promoting his church and its stalwart? Why not have Protestant clergy take the lead at both events in a Protestant town? If they had minds to do so, Miller, his guests, and his neighbors all had something to ponder.[13]

We know nothing about how Miller's family understood the day, but we do know that he habitually shared intimately with Isabella and by turns shared his anxieties, his moralizing, and his protective benevolence with the extended family. The Hardenbergs needed and received a reserve fund.[14] He arranged an extended absence for an alcoholic in-law.[15] He found institutional respite and paid the bills for a sister-in-law debilitated by "nerves."[16] Two nephews had unsolicited avuncular guidance as they stumbled briefly in the youthful mazes of school and work.[17] Often directive and even controlling, Miller sent uncalled-for advice to Alice and her husband, Frank Richardson, as they opened the summer season at the luxurious Tahoe Tavern in Northern California.[18] When Alice took legitimate umbrage, Miller sent a derisive reply, saying if she were "a thorough-bred Christian Scientist," she would ignore everything that gave pain.[19] Miller moralized and grumbled, more in anger than grief, at the suicide of his popular steward Alexis Bjornsen in mid-1906.[20] With that death, Isabella's usual resilience shattered into severe depression, slow in recovery.[21] Here Miller was again acting as he had in his youth—moralizing, lacking the warmth that might have grown within his long partnership with Bjornsen. It is a small wonder then, that his biographer should describe him as "this violent personality"—influential and powerful, often unrestrained and passionate.[22]

Tragedy doubled a month after Bjornsen's death when Frank Richardson, still at Lake Tahoe, suffered a succession of heart attacks. He mended, moved south to Los Angeles, relapsed,[23] improved impressively, and then died suddenly. All underestimated the seriousness of his illness;[24] none anticipated a sudden death. A September 2 telegram brought Frank alone from Arizona to the funeral at the Mission Inn, a simple, Christian Science service read by two friends to a very small group. Miller returned the next day to Allis and the depressed Isabella at the Grand Canyon.[25] The bereaved wife, Alice, found consolation in her Christian Science faith as she went north again to the Tahoe Tavern. Her son, Stanley, at twenty, would live in and out of the emotional mists that children know with the loss a parent.

For Miller, the death of his brother-in-law remained unmentioned in any of his letters, then or later. His brief, solitary return to the obsequies strikes me as another instance of him avoiding evidences of mortality. These were trying times indeed, in which the Mission Inn had, with appalling suddenness, lost a favorite majordomo of twenty-five years and a highly regarded manager,[26] both lives torn without warning from the fabric of the family. Isabella's depression ebbed slowly. She returned home from the East improved[27] but far from robust.

The arrival home from Washington began dramatic flourishes by Miller in person and in the local newspapers. Yosemite almost filled his horizons, about to take every ounce of strength, he said, and every dollar of cash.[28] Much of that cash, he'd been told, would come from the railroads.[29] As to the style for his northern hotel, Miller wanted architect Myron Hunt of Los Angeles to use a rugged rough-stone exterior to match the Yosemite Valley site he'd already chosen. The next year, 1907, in Europe, he'd search out the best examples of such buildings in Scandinavia and Scotland. The three-column report in the *Daily Press* surrounded a new photograph of the Master of the Inn. The text reviewed earlier negotiations and displayed all his letters of recommendation and a transcription of Roosevelt's note to Interior Secretary Hitchcock. In his note, Roosevelt had underlined the words, "if proper," regarding granting Miller's request. In the newspaper, Miller omitted this cautionary reservation, scarcely accidental given the underlining in the original.

Miller was betting against failure. He described Yosemite and the hotel there as his reward for all his years of effort, picturing it as his greatest work and imagining what he would want to do to best make it his monument.[30] But such was not to be: more years of effort beckoned; rewards lay much nearer to home. The hotel that is now remembered as his greatest work, then only partly imagined, would continue to evolve; his monuments would endure in Riverside, though only briefly linked to his name in the public mind.

Although President Roosevelt's note spoke confidence, Miller knew that the politics were uncertain. Washington bureaucracies served their own interests as the Yosemite Park status mutated among private, state, and federal jurisdictions. To complicate matters, Miller insisted on acreage and lease terms different from the usual. Also in the mix were the existing Yosemite hotels, which were resisting the threatening change. Miller visited the park and solicited knowledge from fellow hoteliers, readily hearing opinions, advice, and congratulations.³¹ Whatever the public hoopla about the assurance of a "million dollar hotel" and the seemingly interminable negotiations, Miller's private letters only occasionally showed uncertainty about how to move ahead. Yosemite became a reference point: as his monument, as the anchor of his imagined chain of hotels stretching south, and as a given reason for doing or not doing many other things.³²

On May 23, 1907, the Millers, Frank, Isabella and Allis, boarded the SS *Hellig Olav* in New York for Scandinavia and other European destinations.³³ Miller's preoccupation with Yosemite and his proneness to travel sickness did nothing to deter him.³⁴ Travel at the family's own pace, with easy days of ocean travel before and after, could be a healing pilgrimage for all, especially Isabella. Together, they would find ideas and artifacts in Europe³⁵ while savoring relief from the trying and busy years since the opening of the New Glenwood.

A series of notes to the local papers before the departure in May reassured readers and financial backers that Miller had planned carefully, set out a credible itinerary, and had specific goals. Letters to railroad-management friends, similarly reassuring, sought advice about sources of pewter and copper, the location of stone buildings, even of stag-handled cutlery.³⁶

At home, Alice Richardson returned to Tahoe alone to manage the season there. Frank's younger brother, Ed, took over management at the Mission Inn and directed financial settlements of Miller's numerous loans and mortgages. He'd supervise maintenance during the three-month absence,³⁷ relying on a long list of wear-and-tear items and design weaknesses from basement to roof. Miller had appended his usual cautions about contractor or staff carelessness and ignorance.³⁸

Surviving family correspondence, as it often does, opens small windows on family opinions of each other and reveals the writers. Perhaps the changed roles the European travel brought on added stimulus. Miller wrote about Alice's contrariness. He thought her determined to manage alone in Tahoe against his wishes. He was snide: perhaps she was better off without "the two Franks" to advise her. Alice responded to Miller without resentment, whatever his condescension. Miller thought Isabella equally independent, like Alice unable to take advice, though ready enough to accept full responsibility.[39] Ed, for his part, treated his brother, Frank, lightheartedly, seeing him as foolishly generous in giving free rooms to scores of people, irresponsible in buying up carloads of decorative "junk," and partial in the treatment of his staff. Ed thought Frank far too indulgent, for example, of his new secretary, Marion Louise Clark. (As he left, Miller had sent her off for two weeks at the Hotel del Coronado and later to Lake Tahoe.) "All she thinks about," Ed wrote to the traveling Miller, "is getting through with her work and having a good time."[40] Neither Frank nor Isabella disagreed or disliked those habits, as would soon be evidenced. Frank's older sister, Emma, herself traveling and away from the rest of the family in these months, was outside the exchange of letters.

The family arrived in Norway, traveled to Scotland, Germany, the Rhine, Paris, and London—their itinerary different in each report.[41] Miller gathered bric-a-brac and decorations but not in the usual sense of seeking superior examples with the eye of the connoisseur. He purchased in large quantities bronzes, copper items, wood carvings, pewter, ancient weapons, carved birds and animals, and at least one piece of furniture with the date 1728 carved into it. His bell and cross collections grew as he traveled, costing $554.10 when he tallied it all for his December journal.[42] A gift bell from Allis in Rome had launched him on a hobby that eventually gave the Mission Inn a collection of at least five hundred bells in his lifetime, growing later

A Tumble of Ideas

to one of the largest then in the United States and certainly the most heterogeneous.[43]

At sometime while in Europe, Miller attended one or more sessions of the Hague Peace Conference. He mentioned the visit in letters[44] but said nothing later. Perhaps the agenda, spelling out the rules of war and war crimes in the hope of control, did not fit his thinking. He rejected such a beginning point: he began with and talked only of peace, bluntly resisting war as the subject or context for even preliminary discussions. War, in his view, was an absolute evil—a decidedly minority position in those years when "big stick" diplomacy grew in popularity among the many who talked peace.[45]

But however abundant his gathered artifacts, and although he had seen "crude, primitive buildings" in Europe, he found neither the architecture nor many furnishings or decorations that he wanted for Yosemite.[46] But there was a tumble of ideas.

The family arrived home and was warmly received.[47] When Miller talked about the trip, he described hotels, tourism in Europe, and roads. The grand mountain scenery, picturesque old castles, and beautiful resorts of Scotland, Scandinavia, and Switzerland passed in just as many words. Paris? A disappointment. Berlin? A fine city. Venice? At night as enchanting as in the pictures, but not in the daylight. Faint praise indeed. Something of the youthful traveler of 1874, preoccupied with getting to California, seems to have endured in the fifty-year-old hotelier, at least when he talked publicly about the journey. But his sociability and his habits of garrulous daily dialogue with family, guests, and business associates must have drawn him while traveling into a more varied experience than he shared with the newspapers. Charles Lummis of the Landmarks Club, for one, heard much more—details of the $7,000 spent on the trip, Miller's assessments of what he had seen and purchased, and especially a bulging grab bag of ideas about city organization, roads, and hotels, even though Miller found no architecture to match the Yosemite Valley.[48]

☙

All three Millers picked up again with hotel and hometown routines as if they had been away for just a day.[49] Miller tackled piles of letters, dictating late into the night to the efficient and fun-loving Miss Clark.[50] His letters were almost always brief, generous, and well composed, all typed on the buff-brown Mission Inn letterhead paper using a monastic brown typewriter ribbon.[51] They came from the "Master of the Mission Inn." Miller depended heavily on his secretary, Marion Clark. She had impressive skills based on a strong academic high-school record, two years at the Riverside Business College, and two years of office experience. She was excellently prepared to "get her work done." Ed thought she liked fun. Isabella and Frank drew her increasingly into their confidence and affection.

16

Much Sweetness of Character

By 1908 Miller agitated for action to combat the local effects of economic depression. Many in Riverside were losing their jobs, and transients came to town in numbers reminiscent of 1884. Few of the needy were turned away at kitchen doors, but few found work or even attractive prospects.[1] He and others had softened their attitudes about the use of city funds for private relief, influenced by Progressive reforms, although fears of socialism often reared a vague but restraining presence. As before, church groups talked; the Chamber of Commerce planned, and city trustees pondered.

Miller now moderated his robust confidence in private initiative to approve public funding for private distress. Contrarian that he was, he sent the mayor his check for twenty-five dollars, evidence, he said, that he would not try to dodge any personal obligation. He also offered the trustees a consultation with a "level-headed" socialist manufacturer, Nelson O. Nelson, ready to talk about bringing a private, cooperative business to Riverside for longer-term unemployment relief.[2] The trustees went silent, timid with any kind of "socialism" at a time of "red" scares and also chary about "manufacturing," cooperative or otherwise, in their comfortably residential and tourist town with its monoculture agricultural base.[3]

༄

Miller also had new projects. Among the tumble of ideas Miller explored with Lummis on returning from Europe was their mutual interest in doing something for Native Americans. He'd kept informed on changing opinions at the annual Lake Mohonk Conferences of the Friends of the Indian, and he'd read national journals and heard local lectures. Riverside had its antagonistic opinions—beliefs pro and con about Indians' gradual disappearance, their conversion to Christianity, the majority culture's obligation to redress a scandalous past, and about absorption into the majority culture. Miller had an Indian conference in mind, something bigger than Riverside, intended for scholars and advocates knowledgeable on the many issues stirring nationally. He dismissed what he'd seen elsewhere as trivial, even condescending: the "Indian Days" with feather-decked Indians on parade, crafts on display, and native costumes, drums, and dances. He wrote his hopes to several authorities. The consensus in response: "Yes, but not now."[4] Miller would wait, but he would not be put off.

Within months the "not now" became "now" at the hands of Federal Indian Commissioner Albert K. Smiley of Redlands and the Mohonk Mountain House, joined by Charles M. Loring and C. E. Rumsey, both capitalists in Riverside. Together, the three put form and content onto Miller's idea. They set the date for the first such conference in California for April 27, 28, and 29, 1908. Miller stood aside while those who were qualified to manage a convention, influence attendance, and wrestle in public with divisive issues about the American Indian took charge.

David Starr Jordan, president of Stanford University, would take the chair. Fully a third of the 150 attendees were themselves Native American tribal and district leaders. They stayed at the hotel, active in scheduled presentations and discussions. Among the others attending there were at least half a dozen college presidents, as well as Charles Lummis of the Landmarks Club, California bishop Thomas Conaty, and invited visitors from the Midwest. The chosen participants had a Californian view on Native Americans, "no eastern Indianpholists [sic] with fine-spun theories and a woeful lack of insight and information, but men who have lived with Indians, who know something of their mental processes and capabilities."[5]

The conference was not all sweetness and light among the participants, but the resolution of appreciation to Isabella, Allis, and Alice Richardson spoke of harmony, with its Indian baskets "of love" and, for Miller, a tiepin.[6] Charles Lummis, of the Landmarks Club, editor of *Out West* magazine, librarian at the Los Angeles Public Library, and a voice widely heard on behalf of Native Americans, reported Miller's public spirit as heroic, the presence of David Starr Jordan as notable, and the discussions as common sense on issues of merit.[7]

Isabella had been active in the conference, but she had not been well since the return from Europe. Before and after the conference, the family sought healing for her through rest at various times—in a small, rural sanitarium near San Diego, for a few days in San Francisco in January and then in Yosemite, and in a brief respite in the hot springs in Paso Robles.[8] But relaxation away from home did not bring recovery. In his anxiety about her, Miller quietly consulted the noted Los Angeles physician and Riverside County ranch owner John Randolph Haynes, MD.[9] Haynes confirmed Miller's worst suspicions, a bleak prospect indeed with no hope offered of effective treatment or of Isabella's long survival.[10]

Still seeking her comfort, the family started for Yosemite in June, but even before arrival in Los Angeles, Isabella's slight stamina ebbed away, so much so that she took to bed at her sister-in-law Emma Newman's home with a physician's care. As she gained strength slowly, she sent Allis off to summer in Minnesota, hopeful that her own strength would continue to build but yet uncertain. She shared her anxiety with her sister, Rose Hardenberg, about not wanting to be separated from Allis, adding, "I should want her closest to me at the end."[11]

It was not to be. Her recovery slowed. Frank sensed the need to gather the family. Allis responded, boarding the train in Minneapolis to return in response to Miller's telegram: "Mama is glad you're coming. Not strong."[12] But even before this first telegram reached her en route, Isabella was dead.[13] The death certificate gave "Uraemia," kidney failure, as the cause of death on July 21, 1908.[14]

Miller hurried north to meet Allis, his progress and hers further telegraphed back and forth by Miller's railroad friends to assure their meeting in Salt Lake City, where Allis first learned of her loss. In grief, father and daughter traveled back to Riverside.

A private ceremony, arranged and attended only by family and hotel staff, departed from the customary public rituals and dolorous funereal themes. A warmly personal eulogy of Isabella's life and beliefs replaced the usually read service; in the hotel parlor flowers completely obscured the casket, all under a large floral bell, as had been at her wedding. The music affirmed the inspiration of nature and divinely inspired kindness to others as the means of perfection here below. All this, undoubtedly arranged between Frank and Isabella many months before, departed far from Victorian beliefs in life as a toilsome preparation through suffering for bliss beyond.

City offices, stores, and businesses closed at the time of the funeral, interrupting Riverside's long practice of late shopping. As the sun set on Friday, July 24, the cortege drove to the Evergreen Cemetery, the pallbearers four family members, Miller's trusted assistant Frank O'Kelly, and Quong Quang, the hotel's longtime cook. There at the cemetery, in a bow to convention, a read committal accompanied the lowering of the casket as hotel employees heaped flowers all around:[15] "Inasmuch as the Lord has seen fit to take unto Himself our beloved sister, Isabella Hardenberg Miller…"

Tributes to Isabella arrived for months. Many came from persons having only briefly known her but moved to admiration by her quiet dignity.[16] The *Los Angeles Times* eulogized the "woman of much sweetness of character";[17] the city trustees self-consciously memorialized her passing, taking care to identify her as the first woman to be recognized in this way.[18] Miller's unlikely friend, the secular and skeptical Elbert Hubbard, leader in the arts and crafts movement, published a memorial in his newly launched magazine, *The Fra*, calling it "Note the Passing of a Great Soul." Isabella, he wrote, distinguished herself in efficiency and general intellect, one who "planned, executed, invented, encouraged, accomplished." Without the usual trappings of office, she controlled a small army of workers and disciplined them without tyranny. Hubbard contrasted her habitual gentleness with her adamant will. "The Glenwood Mission Inn is her creation," he said. Her husband was mature and generous enough, he thought, not to block her plans, which she carried out with "the impressive seriousness of a superior person."[19] Hubbard's sketch of Isabella presented her as the incarnation of disciplined bourgeois virtue.

Several assessed both husband and wife in their condolences, suggesting the harmony of her directing and his complete reliance.[20] Many agreed with one who wrote, "The beauty and charm of the Glenwood was in great part an unconscious expression of…Mrs. Miller's nature."[21] Miller himself had praised Isabella often in saying, as an example, that all his virtues were in his wife's name.[22] One eulogist surpassed even that: "Mrs. Miller's greatest work…[was in] the making of a man. Riverside's first citizen is her handiwork." Sensing nuances of what that implied, he added, "This is no disparagement of Frank Miller for he himself quite frankly confesses the artisan and that he does this is his own chief element of greatness."[23]

Assessments of Miller in his grief varied widely. One wrote that his courage, force, and determination had risen intact above an almost insurmountable challenge[24] of bereavement. Another praised his "self control...his worshipful, tender, reverent love."[25] Another, equally acquainted, noted an absence of fortitude, an opinion shared, he thought, even by Allis.[26] Another friend encouraged the family, through Miller's brother, Ed, to "do everything possible so that Mr. Miller may be able to bear *without breakdown* this the greatest loss of his life." Miller's nephew wrote, "I hope that you will be able to *manfully carry your great burden*."[27] Some saw no grief, only strength, calmness, and resilience of spirit. His biographer knew Miller's character had large dimensions, seeing a volatile, tempestuous temperament,[28] one quite able to accommodate expression that some saw as resilience and stoicism while others feared emotional collapse. If nothing else, this kaleidoscope of opinions confirms a complex personality and a variety of deeply concerned friends.

Allis, at twenty-six, drew more closely to her father than before, traveling with him and more fully sharing in planning for the inn and its program. Unwitting friends may have added to her burden by urging her to sustain Miller. He for his part sensed her continuing anguish and asked Sarah Seger, Isabella's older sister, to write something that might offer help to Allis. Sarah, herself grieved, had mingled doubts and uncertainty; she was able at best to assure Allis of her mother's love and that Isabella's loss was "for the best."[29] Allis might have wondered how her mother's death, or any mother's death, could be "for the best."

Many years later, Miller told of falling into despair after Isabella's death. He became passive, he said, unable to follow any normal routine, and almost completely lacking motivation[30]—signs we could interpret now as transient depression, not unusual following severe loss. Even at the funeral, his sister Emma noticed his stooping, rounded shoulders, so different from his usual energetic posture. She had urged Allis to confront him with a picture of himself that might help him brace up.[31] She made no connection between stooping shoulders and a sorrowing heart in her letter.

Recovery from depression came not from seeing his picture or the passage of time or even from the divine comfort that so many, in sympathy, had wished for him. What helped most came in a friend's forthright rebuke. David Starr Jordan delivered "rough talk" rather than "kind sympathy" when Miller visited him in Palo Alto. Jordan directed Miller to do as countless others had done in similar circumstances: to get moving on his obligations and opportunities. Their long friendship and Jordan's own early double loss of his wife and daughter provided a strong mutuality. However unexpected, Jordan's abrupt common sense, itself an affirmation of confidence, stirred Miller back into action. Jordan's salutary rebuke marked the beginning of renewed motivation and a return to earlier routines recast now in single life.[32]

Allis, ever caring, encouraged afternoon relaxation in reading, placing his magazines correctly and closing out afternoon sunshine in his suite, tasks she delegated on occasions to Marion Clark, Miller's secretary.[33] John Burroughs, the grandly bearded nature essayist and advocate of conservation, wrote out "Waiting," his poem of tranquil acceptance, for Miller,[34] thinly veiled advice under the circumstances. Carrie Jacobs Bond, the songwriter, did much the same by giving the Master of the Inn tranquil lines for use about the hotel.[35]

Some observers saw nothing of any passivity but saw unceasing activity. His public record of that year and 1909 reveal impressive public service. He transformed his hopes for a civic center into specific plans, setting them out as viewed from the corner of Orange and Seventh: the Carnegie Library, the already built Christian Science and Unitarian Universalist churches, and his choice of sites for the YMCA, a town hall, the Congregational Church, a new post office, and, possibly, a "club building" or two. "I believe I have it lined up so it will go through," he wrote.[36] His impulse came from reading and conversation, a quest for civic beauty, and a broad knowledge of current city planning and beautification. He already shared the Progressive vision that embraced the good-roads, garden-cities, civic-centers, and city-beautiful movements. He had seen the microcosm of the Chicago Exposition of 1893 and believed Riverside deserved the best.[37]

Miller reached among organized labor and the Socialist Party for local support in his mired-down good-roads ambitions. These were not his usual political bedfellows.[38] He worked tirelessly to assure inclusion of provisions guarding fiscal honesty in the State Highways Act of 1909. Miller knew his state politicians, convinced that in the unamended act they saw plums for the plucking.[39] During debate and after the act became law, Sacramento newspapers singled him out as the preeminent activist and for his promoting legislative safeguards against corruption.[40]

In Riverside his choice of a site for the new Riverside Post Office bested nine others to become the federal choice. The location opposite the Carnegie Library and adjacent to the inn augured well for his civic-center plans. Others endorsed his efforts: the *Los Angeles Times* wrote positively about the post office in the wider context of "Mission Architecture."[41]

༄

Progressivism in the nation surged in the years after the election of Theodore Roosevelt in 1901.[42] As its influence strengthened in California, Miller thought about his Republicanism. His Progressive Republican shoe pinched increasingly. He did not oppose privilege in politics. He had no animus against the lords of capitalism. He had no personal brief for curbing big business. He was not antirailroad; he opposed women's suffrage, legislative initiative, referendum, and recall. In fact, he championed no reform causes that came with the Progressive territory. These differences with the party denied him a seat on the platform with the county Republican elite when aspiring governor Hiram Johnson came to town campaigning in October 1910.[43]

Miller appears to have uncomfortably accepted the Progressive notion that racial segregation provided at least two benefits: a better way to forestall social conflict that probably could not otherwise be stopped and an acceptable social matrix within which change could emerge to suit the Progressive vision of society.[44] His mind-set fit most easily with his early years—a pre–Civil War pattern of individualism, agrarianism, and the small, rural community. His Riverside was in some ways still the colony of his youth, shielded from industrialization, rampant immigration, and urban blight and flourishing quite without a large or complex population of blue and gray collars, all these bêtes noires that energized Progressives.

Perhaps theses opinions prevented a bid for elected office; he was of an independent mind. On the other hand, he knew enough people and had traded enough favors and brought home enough trophies, political and otherwise, to support candidacy. He had the time and income enough. At the same time, he knew the weave of compromise and corruption that covered the legislative body. As for the electorate, his experience in canal construction and at the tin mine and in the community had revealed the common man as too common. His legislative and commissioner experiences of 1891 and 1893 had chastened him. Much later he wrote, "I cannot think of one thing that the people ever did toward the creation of the city of Riverside or the County of Riverside..."[45]

Moreover, with maturity he'd looked inside and decided he'd found his place in life. His sense of *firstness* and his independence in action as the Master of the Inn deterred him from joining the political fray as one of the elected. He sought influence without office, achievement for himself and his community without the obligation of sustained teamwork in the elected community.

Even so, a rocket shot skyward in the *Los Angeles Times* in 1910, lighting up the name of Frank A. Miller for US senator.[46] Enthusiastic talk about him and another Riversider glowed briefly then sputtered out. It was flattering, of course, but not life changing. At fifty-three, he knew that he would not fit easily in the ruck of politicians as merely one of the legislative crowd.

※

The winter-season holidays after Isabella's death only increased the pain of the family's loss. Christmas and New Year had always been such festive family times at the inn.[47] Now "the house that was once so cheery would be still and drear."[48] Knowing their own loneliness, Allis and her father readily accepted an invitation to spend two weeks in the sparkling, new Hotel Raymond in Pasadena, taking in the New Year parade with their hosts.[49] They left town quietly after cameo appearances at the Mission Inn staff Christmas party.[50]

Miller's life after Isabella's death hints at a personal spiritual pilgrimage that had already begun. The unorthodox funeral service for Isabella bypassed Victorian and denominational conventions. And his dedication of a cross and a plaque for Junipero Serra claimed neither institutional loyalty nor historical validity. His planned addition to the hotel would include his own chosen icons—an emphatically ecclesiastical design, with an organ called a cathedral organ, a tiny, splendid Saint Cecilia chapel, and stained-glass windows, one of which depicted Isabella as Saint Cecilia. In this catalog I see more than merely the addition of new spaces and a succession of events or a reach for community prosperity. Miller was loosening but not severing his ties to institutional religion, reaching toward his own sacred places and practices. These all might be seen as physical expressions of what his academic friend David Starr Jordan would call his moral philosophy. But in his bereavement, privately at first then more publicly, Miller wrestled with disturbing affairs of the heart.

PART THREE:

The Return of Laughter

17

Propinquity Does It

Six months after Isabella's passing, DeWitt Vermilye Hutchings, a bland-faced, youthful winter guest from Colorado Springs, arrived at the inn.[1] By the end of the season in May 1909, he had been drawn into the affairs of the hotel and family enough for him to go with Alice Richardson and the inn staff to run the summer season at Tahoe Tavern in northern California.[2] His departure north with them drew more than usual newspaper mention and space, a tacit public recognition of his identity with the inn family.[3]

In those months DeWitt and Allis found more than propinquity, sharing much in common. Both had been in Europe, he to travel, she for the year in Rome. She had graduated from the selective Marlborough School; he was Ivy League from Lawrence and Princeton. Allis, at twenty-seven, radiated the charm of young maturity and social grace. He was single and thirty, an eastern exotic among the older, married guests. Perhaps most important, he was there, in the hotel, and helpful enough to merit a staff berth at Tahoe.

If Miller gave thought to it, DeWitt's arrival in Riverside without any clear direction in his life at age thirty and the nubile Allis's presence at the hotel nearly mirrored his own vocational drifting period and Isabella's arrival in Riverside years before. Miller saw enough potential in this dignified newcomer to invite him in 1909 to "Come and help us express the importance of hospitality."[4] The door opened on the rest of DeWitt's life.

Early one Monday morning in September, DeWitt and Allis stood by Frank and Isabella's twenty-fifth wedding anniversary windows for a short wedding ceremony.[5] She was radiant in her traveling gown and holding red carnations and ferns. Few expected to hear that Allis and DeWitt Hutchings had married. The younger society set of the city was amazed. Nothing fit their expectations: not the absence of prior announcement, not the day or the time of day, not the place, and not the sparse ceremony attended by only Frank Miller of the family. The arrangements excluded all and defied explanation. Most expected a grand affair in the best Mission Inn style with Glenwood floral abundance, sumptuous banquet, and dancing into the night.

Later explanations sound weak: The scant ceremony showed respect for the traditional two-year mourning period following Isabella's death. DeWitt had urgent eastern business, hence an earlier than expected wedding date. But even at the time, nothing fit convincingly. Indeed, five months earlier on Mount Rubidoux, Allis was photographed at a public event in a bold plaid dress and sported a suitably Tyrolean bonnet, hardly mourning garb at all.[6] DeWitt stood nearby in his best Sunday black.[7] Besides, the fully extended, formal, two-year periods of grief in Riverside were more honored in the breach than in the observance. DeWitt's business commitments in the East didn't seem to press. The couple spent two weeks in Salt Lake City before going leisurely across the continent to return home two months later. Few could see urgency for business or otherwise. These were merely reasons of convenience rather than good reasons for the unexpected, unusually private, Monday morning wedding.

Belated souvenirs, wedding announcements with small portraits of Allis and DeWitt, brought a curious message, presumably in Miller's voice: "Welcome to the daughter of the Inn, Allis, and her good man DeWitt."[8] Did Allis Miller, for all her twenty-seven years a resident in Riverside, really need a welcome? Or an introduction? And there was no mention of her much admired parents in the souvenir. Perhaps the more recently arrived Hutchings needed a public welcome, but calling him "her good man" lacked something of Miller's usual bonhomie, particularly considering he was introducing a new son-in-law, a new family member. Who wrote the text? Did the words fit the current social usages for wedding announcements? I think not but see instead a loving father's ambivalence about his only child's marriage, shadowed by his own recent loss. He faced the distancing marriage of his daughter and only child, inadvertently perhaps offering a less than wholehearted acceptance to the man who had come between them, a common enough response of many fathers but not often expressed so clumsily.

On Easter morning 1909, before DeWitt and the others went north to the Tahoe Tavern, Miller initiated an Easter sunrise service on Mount Rubidoux.[9] His stimulus seems to have come first from the visiting garrulous Jacob Riis. On a Palm Sunday visit, Riis had talked with emotion about "the beauty of the mountain and [the] religious and mystic atmosphere" of the place.[10] He suggested pilgrimages to honor the mission founders and later urged Christmas carol singing on the breezy summit.[11] This fit Miller's notions of symbol and ceremony on the mountain and his ecclesiastical bent. But why wait until Christmas? Miller seized the warmer Easter Sunday just days away for a simple nondenominational hilltop ceremony at sunrise.[12] He; Allis, there to play the portable organ; DeWitt; Miller's secretary; and about two hundred others gathered in the darkness long before daybreak. Pilgrim-like they climbed to the cross, once there doing little more than singing one or two Easter hymns and repeating the Our Father,[13] elated by the rising sun. The unusual thing about this impulsive Easter observance was that it caught the public mind, becoming a community ritual attracting increasing crowds year after year and even bringing Riverside a special touch of sober fame.[14] Other observances that Miller initiated on the mountain would scarcely outlive him, but the Easter morning service has persisted.

Miller himself put the sunrise service among his foremost achievements, claiming a first for Riverside and the nation.[15] He even made it an imperative for the town. "Dear Zona," he said as a summary of recollections for his biographer, Zona Gale, "I would say that it is more important for Riverside to learn to continue and to value the Sunrise pilgrimage, much more than to put over the Civic Center if both can't be done."[16] And that is just about what happened.

Shortly after Easter the *Daily Press* published details of a hotel addition.[17] Miller and Benton had worked through a transformation of design from a "monolith" to a cloister, as it was called.[18] Architectural features from several missions formed the exterior. A Spanish baronial hall below street level comprised the interior public space. Guest rooms rose for two floors above. In appearance and decoration, the Cloister differed from the original Mission Wing primarily because Miller now sought a physical presentation through specific architectural gatherings to induce the spirit of the missions. He set aside a stricter mission-revival style to adopt an eclectic style with emphatic ecclesiastical references and decoration. He worked his growing aesthetic around what he could profitably use, from his perception of guests' enjoyment and what he thought would beautify Riverside. And he included a glowing memorial tribute to Isabella as Saint Cecilia in stained glass.

Construction watchers who saw large excavations along Orange Street to Sixth Street in June 1909 also saw Miller squiring over the workmen almost every day. He'd been cheated before on construction, he thought.[19] His new, close supervision with his symbolic yardstick in his hand[20] signaled his intention to measure payment against progress. His secretary, Marion Clark, probably went with him, notebook in hand to record his instructions. What is certain is that they declared their commitment in love to each other during that month, an event memorable for both.[21]

With Isabella's death Miller had come to rely more and more on Allis and, in the office, on his secretary, Marion Clark, who continued with the smooth, executive efficiency Isabella had praised.[22] Whatever Ed thought of her love of fun, Frank and Isabella thought she worked as if she was one of the family.[23] In a year-end gift, Miller had sedately inscribed a book flyleaf: "Dear Marion, You are one that is mighty helpful in running this Mission Inn. Frank A. Miller, January 1, 1909."[24]

But even before the book gift, his feelings of "mighty helpful" and hers had soared toward mutual love, feelings that could not remain hidden. Close to them, Allis and DeWitt were reaching tentatively toward each other in romance. In a letter Allis asked Marion to arrange some personal items for Miller, details that she usually cared for, adding, "I'm sure you'll be good to him." Folded discreetly within the letter on a tiny square of the same writing paper, she had written, "I want you to know that I love you very much and that I hope you can make father happy some day."[25]

Miller traced an emotional maze through paths of elation, guilt, and anxiety. The joy of new love conflicted with the lingering deep affection for his lost Isabella, driving him to pour out his disturbing passions to his out-of-town adviser, Rev. E. F. Goff, business manager at Pomona College in Claremont. The way Miller liked to remember it, Goff had "put [him] in his place pretty quickly, saying, 'Frank Miller, are you daring to be ashamed of loving that girl? You should be proud and humble and very grateful—for I think she is foolish enough to feel as you do,'"[26] something Miller already knew all too well. As he put it, "I had not got out of the nervous condition of [Isabella's] loss before I found I was loving Marion," and he was racked by guilt over it.[27]

Goff recommended a time apart: college in the East for Marion. Marion refused: "I <u>can't</u> [emphasis in the original] go away and leave you and I don't think it would do me any good." Their compromise: she'd enroll at Pomona College in the fall of 1909.[28] The college near home shielded them from public talk, a separation honoring Isabella's name to satisfy "some people." Neither Marion nor Frank liked the separation, then or later; in fact, within days Miller wrote pleadingly, "Dear One, Loved One, I love you. Can you forgive me some day for sending you away?"[29]

The year at Pomona brought social and academic success for Marion. Miller visited when he could, going riding with Marion, and she returned to Riverside often.[30] But Goff's persistent urging prevailed: in September 1910, Marion left Riverside for the Dwight School for Girls in Englewood, New Jersey. The homes of DeWitt Hutchings's parents and grandparents lay within easy walking distance from the Dwight School,[31] more than a coincidence, I believe, in her choice among eastern schools.

Even as Marion arrived in New Jersey, Miller fired off a telegram of love and longing,[32] the start of what would become three months of almost daily exchanges. They shared the rich language of lovers' conspiracies, with endearing phrases and tokens exchanged, matching one another almost letter for letter.

Miller made no secret of his love, advising friends in Riverside of his intention to marry. Opinions varied. Some shared his delight.[33] Some spoke harsh pessimism. "I think your plans for the future together cannot result happily for either of you," one wrote to Marion, "but that must be your affair." Others shared Jacob Riis's view: "Do you listen, both of you, to the heart too, and all will be well." Miller's sister Emma cautioned, warning Miller that Marion's frail health needed care if she were to become a mother. The robust, horse-riding, outdoor-loving Marion may have wondered about that assessment.[34]

The course of mature love and separation from Marion, with its yearning daily letters, did not interrupt Miller's hotel building, but he was concerned about the failing health of Marion's father, Charles B. Clark. There was well-based fear that he may not live to see his daughter married as covertly planned for the summer of 1911.

A month after Marion traveled to the Dwight School in 1909, President William Howard Taft provided the big event of Miller's checkered year as president of the Chamber of Commerce.[35] Taft's afternoon and evening in town and at the inn were not without hitches, but generosity and tolerance smoothed the way, and by ten o'clock, when President Taft left, he had paraded the streets, unveiled a plaque on Mount Rubidoux, been wined and dined at the inn, and sat in the huge chair much larger than he deserved.[36]

A year after construction began, Miller still had yet much to add to the Cloister Wing. Most guest rooms were unfinished and unfurnished. The Music Room lacked its sculptured mission-related saints' windows;[37] the tiny Saint Cecilia Chapel off the Music Room needed its velvet and gold treasures. Organ specialists worked carefully, assembling the organ in its cavernous alcove, but awaited the pipes. Nothing daunted, Miller scheduled a November 1909 lecture about mission Indians as a formal opening event of his still unfinished Music Room. This miscellany of lecture, music, and dance[38] put the Music Room into the hotel program. A Peace Conference scheduled for early 1911 in a completed room would tap into the widespread peace talk of the period and provide a more influential opening event. Miller's vague plans took shape in other capable hands, the date set for February 27, 1911. He insisted on a brilliant organ recital to open the conference.[39]

Few disagreed with a guest whose convoluted praise claimed that the hotel had become "a spot without seeing which no self-respecting tourist can look himself in the face."[40] What was to be seen of the Cloister and Music Room that might allow the self-respecting tourist to face himself?[41] Much suggested an ecclesiastical atmosphere: stained-glass windows with friars and nuns and Frank's beloved Isabella, now as Saint Cecilia at an organ.[42] The heraldic and religious motifs, sculptured saints, high-backed choir benches, and dark-stained wood succeeded all too well in eliciting references to church. Miller began to suspect that he had missed his original aim of creating an aristocratic Spanish Baroque great hall.

Outside, visitors saw a Sixth Street facade for all the world like a thousand church fronts scattered through Spain and Latin America: domed towers framing a semicircular pediment. Along Orange Street they'd see more church-like construction—five flying buttresses arched over the sidewalk and a pilastered wall imitative of Mission San Gabriel.

Other additions confirmed new directions: a rooftop tennis court, a basement cloister walk displaying religious artifacts, a "Garden of the Bells" hung with some of the growing bell collection, and a room housing his cross collection. Miller's new offices and living quarters moved him away from the ground-level comings and goings of guests. Alice likewise moved into new third-floor quarters. Both needed retreats to privacy, given their very public lives at the hotel and, especially for Miller, in the town.

The whole construction turned its back on almost all then-current trends in hotel and church architecture. It reached to the Spanish past and Miller's growing inclination toward the symbolic and ceremonial, and in the prominent triptych above the stage, he enshrined his devotion to Isabella.

Much about the new Cloister Wing raised public eyebrows: Isabella as a saint in stained glass, below-grade floor levels, the absence of fixed seating, a visitors' gallery on only one side of the room, and a dining room hidden under the floor. Some objected to a softly lit sign with the words, "Please Do Not Applaud"; others disliked the blue-tinted stage lighting, the many saints set in niches, and the excavated passageways, quickly named catacombs. Were the chancel-like upper stage and glowing stained-glass altarpiece appropriate? The tiny, gilded Saint Cecelia Chapel, resplendent with religious artifacts and a gathered silk ceiling, evoked awe and questions.[43] Miller's far departure from local expectations created immediate opportunity for continuing comment at home and in magazines and journals beyond Riverside and his lifetime.

Some of this comment lacked understanding or thought. Some of it remarked only on the novelty of a strongly ecclesiastical motif. Others obliquely suggested influence by priests and church dignitaries.[44] One local comment in verse, however, had an edge of undisguised nastiness, calling Miller a "bold untamed fanatic" with a "tyrant hand" in the town. This rhymed meanness stood unique before or after.[45] But it *was* published as the Cloister neared completion. The doggerel could only wound Miller, his family, and friends. He overlooked it then and later. The youth lived on in the adult; he still acted on the belief that "my kind of boy was pretty scarce," still willing to stand by the consequences of his intuitions, even if that meant standing apart.

Whatever the mixed reception, Miller could say with satisfaction, "It happened to come out right, some way";[46] his inn was a unique structure in Riverside and the West.[47] He had a new theater, not intended as a church but as a Spanish baronial hall, the imagined scene of grand Iberian aristocratic living, and he was the Spanish grandee. The room and its program gave new definition to the inn for the community and guests alike and would do so until challenged by another addition about a decade later.[48]

By December the Music Room organ pipes had not arrived from W. W. Kimball Company in Chicago. Miller went from concern to anxiety. A fully voiced organ was essential for the performances already scheduled with a distinguished organist for early 1911.[49] He would go to Chicago to supervise the shipping of everything needed for completion.

That was the story he gave out for his departure for Chicago, the journey in fact a convenient smoke screen for something quite different. A lot more was afoot than packing and shipping organ pipes.[50]

Miller slipped quietly out of town by train days before his announced departure of Wednesday the seventh. On that day he arrived not in Chicago, where the organ builder did business, but at the Dwight School in New Jersey. There, with a huge tray of chocolates presented for her fellow students, he and Marion met, appropriately chaperoned.

Early the next morning, on December 8, Dwight School student faces watched through frosted windowpanes as Marion Clark and her chaperone climbed into the sleigh that would take them to the train and together on to the Buckingham Hotel in Manhattan. There, at four thirty that afternoon, Marion married her prince charming, who had come to carry her off to his castle in California. Prince Charming, indeed. At the school there had been rumors, of course: the fifty young women in the boarding school had few secrets, especially about the romance of this somewhat older student, so gregarious and involved.

The daily letters, even telegrams, could scarcely be hidden; the several shopping trips to Altman's in New York City and an overheard phone call by Marion reserving a hotel bridal suite were proof positive. The thrill of that morning departure stayed fresh for over forty years with at least one of the watchers; the recollection even then, she said, made her heart beat just a little faster.[51]

"Frank Miller Weds in New York City," and "Frank Miller Takes a Wife."[52] These newspaper headlines caught and surprised many a reader the next morning in the *Riverside Morning Enterprise* and the *Los Angeles Times*.

18

Big, Jovial, and Genial

The mere formality of Marion's marriage to Frank did not bring easy acceptance in the family or with a host of others. Both Marion and Frank had foreseen this. They had talked about it and written to each other about it, well aware of the barriers to her acceptance and knocks to Miller's reputation but resolute in their confidence and resourcefulness.[1] One observer, biographer Zona Gale, knew the Miller women—sisters, wife, daughter, sisters-in-law, close friends—seeing among them what most women know of the usual mixture of warmth and jealousy, trust and suspicion. In her opinion, family harmony came only as the result of "adhesion"—individual devotion to the Master of the Inn, who melded each of these categorically different women in his energetic ambience.[2] Marion had changed roles; adjustment came slowly.

Gale wrote about Marion: "Her light gray hair smoothly coifed, her gray eyes intent, her left hand filled with papers, she moves through corridors and courts like a symbol of both balance and swift flight. The head a little bent, the eyes intent as on some inner calculation, but the smile ready and unremote, she is like some fragment of the days when marbles expressed women: grave, absorbed, integrating action with some ultimate, and accessory to a central theme to which they themselves momently contribute. Miraculously practical, she is the classic pattern, detail-conscious, but handling details with moral energy." Far from diminishing Miller's creative reach, said another when a new project arose, "it was she who took hold of the dream and worked out its possible application; interviewing artists, wrote to authorities for their opinions, to artists for designs, to craftsmen for estimates. She received no credit for the finished product and apparently expected none."[3]

She did not need to be told then or later of the confused feelings, the tension, or the gossip. "To have him marry his secretary," she said, "that didn't please everybody. But they didn't tell me that," she said, adding, "I don't think any of them were happy about the marriage." Marion explained that any family fortunate enough to harbor the Master of the Inn should not to be too deeply blamed for distrusting a woman who could hardly be anything other than filled with designs on him.[4] Miller himself felt that only Allis and Jose Seger, Isabella's younger sister, seemed to understand him.[5] He prompted a would-be biographer years later to "say nice things about Marion," an unnecessary caution if all were sweetness and light.[6]

Miller's male friends rallied, reported tersely in the *Daily Press*: "A few close friends of Frank A. Miller gave a luncheon yesterday at the Glenwood in honor of that gentleman."[7] This was the only published notice of the couple's return to Riverside; arriving winter guests had more said about them than that.[8] Perhaps Miller wanted brevity.[9] He and, no doubt, Marion had weathered more than they wanted of solicited and unsolicited advice, warnings gratuitously pointing out his dishonor of Isabella and making accusations that he betrayed his "finer instincts" and yielded to the blandishments of sensuality.[10] He wanted to keep fresh the friendships that seemed to be threatened by his marriage. Rose Hardenberg, Isabella's sister, for instance, announced the end of their friendship. Miller responded with calm, if naïve and illogical, assurances that their friendship could be the same as always, even stronger, because of his continued love for Isabella and his new love for Marion.[11] To others, "Dear Friends" and "Dear Family," he sent an explanatory letter seeking to reassure, offering his reasons for marriage and claiming his love for Marion as the best reason of all.

Even though for months the Riverside papers said nothing about Marion, habits, civility, and sociability blended to allow growing recognition of her in new roles as wife and mistress of the inn. She welcomed a steady stream of nieces and nephews visiting during the holiday season. A small newspaper note reported a rooftop reception, naming "Mrs. Frank A. Miller" among those present. Warm, embracing informality spread even further with a springtime evening picnic on Mount Rubidoux. As the full Easter moon rose, Frank and Marion sat with friends on Indian rugs and sang along with a banjo and toasted marshmallows.

Miller had found again the full happiness he sought in his private life. The few personal letters and cards that survive from their married years glow with affection, intimate personal details, and promises of lovers' exchanges. In his reminiscences, Miller, understandably full of his own story, nevertheless gave unstinted recognition to Marion, "a spiritual miracle," she the core of supportive inspiration, the one who put laughter back into his life and kept it there.[12]

Marion carried much of the in-house planning for the February Peace Conference; Miller had more than enough to do. The Cloister, Music Room, and many of the upper-floor hotel rooms remained near completion. Technicians arrived to install about two thousand pipes and voice the organ, knowing they had barely six weeks before the opening recital.[13] The chosen guest recitalist was John Jasper McClellan, the Salt Lake Tabernacle organist.

This Peace Conference of February 1911, as the Indian conference in 1908, would succeed from others' strengths, this including the Carnegie Peace Foundation. The invited luminary participants addressed themselves to the two chosen national issues as themes: "Civic Life" and "The Peace Ideal."[14] Their deliberations went out on the press wires, including summarized speeches by David Starr Jordan, the conference chair, and observations and lectures by Charles W. Fairbanks, former vice-president of the United States, and by James A. McDonald, editor of the *Toronto (Canada) Gazette.*

"The Peace Ideal" especially engaged Miller. His own early convictions for peace had several sharpening influences, among them the Second Peace Conference of the Hague Conventions in 1907, David Starr Jordan's 1907 *The Human Harvest*, and the Smileys' Mohonk Conferences on Arbitration, annual since 1895, which kept the focus on law in place of war.[15] Miller habitually read Lyman Abbott's peace-promoting publication, *The Outlook*, and loyally invoked his mother's presumed Quaker principles and his father's rejection of war.[16] Logically and emotionally, he rejected the use of destructive means to achieve constructive ends.

Miller intended second blessings from the Peace Conference. Locally the event led to organizing a local peace society.[17] Additionally, he used the conference to initiate new directions for the hotel, specifically an increase in the intellectual and cultural programming at the inn. Lectures by visiting speakers or resident guests were added to the Sunday Evensong services. Dance enthusiasts could glide over the parquetry floor weekly and on special occasions.[18] Weeknights not otherwise scheduled would accommodate speakers of Miller's choosing. All this fitted his belief that true hospitality included nurture for mind and body. The new Music Room made these redefinitions possible and visible, providing benefits to hotel and community.

Two "Civic Life" conference themes reached deeply into Miller's business and personal life.[19] The women's suffrage issue and labor relations swirled about him, but to neither could he bring much of his adaptive pragmatism. He opposed both, holding on to attitudes learned early about men and women, masters and servants, seeming to be unmoved by social changes that for many could not be resisted.[20] Indeed, notable suffrage reformers, women and men, attended his Peace Conference, every one of them outspoken on the issue. He thought he saw the most wisdom in his influential friend Jacob Riis's widely published and elegant rejection of women's suffrage urging the greater moral force of women if in the home and delegating their political voices.[21] Later an interviewer described him as a benign "patriarch and dictator" at home and in Riverside.[22] Very much later he concluded he'd been wrong on both issues,[23] but by then his influence was slight and his opinion interested only himself.

Soon after the conference, California's hoteliers' worst fears materialized in state legislation limiting women's workdays to eight hours.[24] All employers of women, not just the hotel owners, puzzled over how to live within the new law. Miller championed leaving things the way they were. He claimed a satisfied staff, content with longer hours. His resident employees, he said, enjoyed steam-heated rooms with baths, a parlor, a piano, and like comforts; they were entirely satisfied with conditions and could hardly be induced to make a change. To have them leave the inn would be "little short of heart breaking."[25] He spoke with a genuinely fatherly feeling.

Willing to test his convictions in court, he provided a case: his cooperative head waitress reported overwork for nine hours daily over two months. The court imposed fifty dollars or thirty days. Appeals to the superior court and the state supreme court proved unavailing. The US Supreme Court offered no relief. Local papers told the town, "Miller Loses in High Court," when in February 1915, it affirmed the California Supreme Court ruling, ending almost four years of litigation.[26]

As the lead for the hotel fraternity in this dispute, Miller was far from being simply their front man. His own paternalist convictions ran deep, reflected, for example, in his adopting the title "Master of the Inn." He and many of his generation had accepted the gospel of work from a thousand sermons, read it in every self-help book, and passed it on as a bastion against mischief.[27] But he grew some in this as in other convictions, moving from the reactionary to something more benign. His paternalism, which resisted any organized action by his employees, conceded at least their equal claims on organized efforts. He also moved further away from earlier individualism to an acceptance of some government regulation. But even this late blooming struggled in one calling himself Master of the Inn and referring to his wife as "the wife" and "Girl,"[28] in this quite out of step with much of the community.

Almost as soon as the court case began, with its slow ascent to the US Supreme Court, the Millers set off for Europe. The Hutchingses were already on their way.[29] Frank and Marion's plans emerged less directly: the newspaper first announced their visit to San Francisco, and then in headlines they were off "To Study Life in Spain." Soon dispatches arrived of their progress in Europe as "Riversiders Are Abroad."[30]

As lovers they had yearned to go away together, but there was more than just fulfillment of yearning in this trip.[31] He had aimed to make the Music Room a Spanish baronial hall but already had heard too many comments about the Music Room as a church. He and Marion would spend time in Spain looking for ideas. What they saw of villas, mansions, and castles convinced him fully that his Music Room "was a mistake as far as it being regarded as a Spanish thing. Everybody in Spain who had anything [had] an art gallery or some effort of that kind."[32] He arrived home determined to align himself with the "everybody...who had anything"—he'd have a gallery "or some effort of that kind." Interestingly the architectural ideas for the Spanish art gallery he'd build matured in detail in New York, not in Seville.

But in addition, in Spain he found an abundance of artifacts, oddments, and bric-a-brac—what his brother, Ed, called "junk." Added to all that he grasped what became other *idées fixes*: one, the desirability of patios throughout the hotel and the other an obsession to replicate in Riverside the huge, ancient Giralda Tower of Seville. One he would achieve; the other would elude his grasp like a will o' the wisp.

Two stories Miller enjoyed telling on his return from Spain delineate his acquisitive strategies in buying artifacts. His recommended dealer in Spain flatly refused to negotiate on price. The frugal Miller conspired with Marion to tease cooperation from him. The couple bought elsewhere and at the end of each shopping day carried their purchases home in full view of the reluctant dealer's shop. The stubborn merchant relented, unwilling to have business pass him by. Miller wanted iron; the dealer found iron—old iron and more iron and older iron. The Millers bought and bought again, unable to resist loveliness revealed in rusted metal.[33] The *Los Angeles Times* reported $40,000 spent on decorations during the European trip; the Riverside paper counted 342 iron objects.[34] The two gleaners in Spain filled two railway cars.

A treasure arrived home months after everything else; the object and its acquisition lodged it securely into the folklore of the inn. As Miller told it, he and Marion traveled through London en route home. There, two old bells in a founder's yard took his eye: one a Japanese bell and another with what he thought were Spanish inscriptions. He bought them both, received a bill of sale on each, and then took a rubbing of the Spanish inscriptions for translation at the British Museum. Later the dealer flatly refused delivery of the Spanish bell. Confrontations followed; demands escalated; and accusations of double-dealing flew, and then came threats of lawsuits, even Miller's threat of international consular action to enforce the sale. His obstinacy, said a knowledgeable friend, was that of the very great, and his temper matched it. He displayed stubbornness, shrewdness, and a hot temper in the confrontational demands and refusals that followed.[35] Later, sentimental admirers and the Master of the Inn himself glossed over any such behavior but loved the story.

The roadblock to delivery of the bell to Miller lay with British Museum staff, who cast covetous eyes on it, wanting it for their own. They asked the seller to cancel the sale to the American so as to make a donation to them. The irate Miller, however, pressed even more vigorously on the US consul and implored his longtime acquaintance Wilson Crewdson, an English director of the English-owned Riverside Trust Company and annual visitor to the inn from England for many years, for assistance.[36] These two prevailed within the glacial English bureaucracy, shipping the bell to Miller months after he left England.[37] The bell was indeed old and Spanish, its inscriptions dating it to 1247—what appeared to be the oldest dated Christian bell.[38]

༄

"It appears," one of the Riverside newspaper reporters wrote, "that somewhere in his journeying through Spain Mr. Miller discovered the magical spring of youth which Ponce de Leon looked for in vain, for ten years seem to have rolled from his shoulders as big, jovial and genial he leaned back in his desk chair to talk over his trip." All this was evidence enough of the return of laughter to Miller's life.

This journey added nothing for Yosemite but yielded all and more than he had been seeking in visual and material expressions of the atmosphere for the inn. "I'm always seeing visions, of course," he told the reporters. "Some people think I've dreamed enough, don't they. But let me tell you, some day we are going to have this inner patio the best part of the hotel." The reporters scribbled their notes for lively stories. They knew now that demolition on Sixth Street would make way for a Spanish/Moorish addition, where Miller would house a center for Spanish art and enclose the patio.³⁹ Just a year later, his "art gallery or some effort of that kind" began to emerge with all its implications for satisfying Miller's self-definition.

Something about the Giralda Tower, seen in Seville, kept Miller's imagination captive for the rest of his life. This three-hundred-foot-high bell tower rose erect and elegant above the largest church in Spain, priapic almost, a potent symbol of Moorish and Catholic history. Its setting in mixed architectural styles, with niches and arches for bells, viewing alcoves, gargoyles, and a citrus-tree-filled patio—all these attracted Miller and, in small or large, reappeared at the Mission Inn over the next decades.⁴⁰ This Moorish and Catholic structure provided Miller's only long-term recorded vision for the inn. Over many years, one sketch after another pictured the tower thrusting up in various locations around the hotel, one ideal site after another chosen then rejected, bequeathed to his grandson.

In buying paintings, objets d'art, and even bric-a-brac, Miller's criteria of acceptance ran simpler than those of either a collector or savant. *Firstness* seems to have helped: he sought and acquired the first church bell in Agua Mansa, a tiny, early Spanish village upriver from Riverside. He did the same with Riverside's first school bell, the first local streetcar bell, the first electric streetcar bell, and the bell from the first Santa Fe Railroad engine to enter Riverside. The crosses and the bells were organized at others' hands, carefully written up in booklets published at the inn.⁴¹ A collector guest quite colorfully described all the rest of the decoration as a clashing discord and a mad, artistic jumble displayed in halls and passages and under arches and beside stairways.⁴²

Among the discord and jumble, the bells, swelled in numbers by the returning Hutchings, had special significance, becoming a small, personal universe. They provided a gentle pun on Isabella's name and memory. Their mission symbolism remained strong, even though the collection took in strange bell-like objects lacking any mission allusions. He could hardly have missed novelist Edmund Mitchell's use of the Mission Inn's bell ringing as a redemptive force in *The Captain and His Soul* (originally titled *The Call of the Bells*).[43] Miller's own view of life embraced the conviction of Mitchell's main character: "the certainty of a revelation that by loving-kindness and mutual helpfulness among the individuals of the world, humanity was being swept on and on in irresistible evolution toward universal good and ever-abiding happiness."[44]

19

A Play, a Hotel, and a Gallery

As early as 1909, Miller wanted a dramatic play for the inn, something he later called the Oberammergau of America.[1] With the Music Room in mind as the venue, he had offered $1,000 for a script set in early California and its missions and about Franciscans and Indians to "depict the life of the happy time before the gringos came and the missions began to crumble to ruins." The local press lauded the idea as "the most ambitious and startlingly original that has so far had conception in Mr. Miller's fertile brain." Miller's ideas, said the reporter, in some way seemed to find "the men of power who reduced them to practical form and left them unveiled ultimately as resplendent realities."[2] And that's just what happened to this idea, but not as might have been expected.

Miller chose *Los Angeles Times* writer John Steven McGroarty,[3] contracting with him for a completed script by October 1, 1909.[4] McGroarty dawdled. Miller waited. Eight months later, Miller bypassed McGroarty to contract a New York theatrical impresario, Gustav Froleman, to produce the Oberammergau of America for the courtyard of the inn, with six hundred Indians provided as actors playing principal roles in the California mission story.[5] McGroarty jolted into action. As told in family anecdotes, Miller kept McGroarty on task by installing him as a guest at the inn for a month or more.[6]

I suspect that the publicity and the talkative Miller alerted local "men of power" to an opportunity too good to miss.[7] They included McGroarty's employer, Harrison Gray Otis of the *Los Angeles Times*, Henry E. Huntington, Catholic Bishop Thomas Conaty, and Charles Lummis of the Landmarks Club. Together they had the makings of collaboration: a performance place under the walls of the San Gabriel Mission and streetcar lines to bring audiences—hordes of tourists and school children, and they saw the potential for profit and an ideological interest. The play, to McGroarty's script, opened in San Gabriel in 1912, hugely successful. The story wrapped priests, soldiers, Native Americans, and all the uncomfortable past in veils of optimistic myth. In doing so, it became a canon of Californian history for almost two decades.

Miller lost his play to its new location and sponsors. He convinced a friend that he had merely fostered it with his left hand while he went on to something else.[8] But that seems too blithe an explanation for so grand a conception, something he had imagined over at least three years and lost. The generous thoughts likely combined with his admiration for the men of power and his common-sense acceptance of their ability to produce the play closer to his ideal than he could. For his own Mission Inn theatrical presentation, Miller contented himself with an annual costumed pastiche of the New Testament nativity theme, with seasonal songs and robed Franciscan friars performing in the Music Room, entertaining staff, their families, and his hotel guests. He played Junipero Serra; Marion was the usher.

For all his nonchalance in losing the mission play, the conception fell well within his often repeated maxims. "What we need is a vision," Miller said, "and so few can visualize things for themselves and to my mind the more beautiful and splendidly done the thing is, the more surely it will reach the soul of those who should be reached, and make them know there is something more than just the material in life."⁹ Here lay his creative tension points: the material and the spiritual, especially beauty. He saw himself among the few possessing the capacity and the gift of imagination that provided vision for the mind and the spirit as well as the body.¹⁰ He envisioned missions restored, not in adobe and sacred icons or priestly ministry or even in the play, but in quiet expressions of hospitality redolent of missions imagined. His was a vision of a better present and future. Later he'd have a text inscribed above the hotel's Spanish Patio, where it remains: "Where there is no vision the people perish." The youth, unsure of his life's direction, who longed for money to care for his mother and bring him social acceptance, had matured into a richer personality, one called poet and visionary.

Two of Miller's other endeavors began to resolve, one toward failure, the other toward success. The resort hotel in Yosemite would never be built, but the realized Spanish Gallery would put Miller, at least for himself, among those "that amount to something."

Even before his marriage in 1910, Miller despaired of Yosemite success. Legislators had invited him to federal hearings related to his interests. He declined. "Personally I do not want to appear [at the hearings] in this matter," he wrote to the secretary of the interior. "I tried to do this Yosemite act once and failed, and I had hoped to have no publicity…with this effort until I knew that it is going to go."¹¹ What Miller wanted to make it "go" included a twenty-year lease (rather than the usual renewable five-year term) and more than the stipulated five acres for the building site. He would accept no less. And therein lay the contention; his insistence on these significant factors led to failure.

But even so, opportunity came toward him.¹² In October 1912, Secretary of the Interior Walter L. Fisher dined at the inn,[13] a carefully planned meeting anticipating rising action. Fisher liked Miller and made no secret of his willingness to back the Yosemite hotel project. H. W. Childs, Washington insider, superintendent at Yellowstone, and Miller's adviser, knew the visit was happening. He telegrammed and wrote to Miller, "The thing is all lined up now and you must go after it with an ax."[14] Fisher agreed, writing to Miller almost immediately after arrival back in Washington: "It is my very earnest desire that there shall be erected at once in the Yosemite Valley a suitable hotel..."[15]

Optimism surged, and Miller relented of his reluctance to budge. Frank and Marion arrived in Washington ten days later. Miller talked details; the department listened and summarized it all, including the secretary's approval.[16] But the sticking points remained: the lease could be only ten years; it could not be more without congressional approval. But continued expectations of success propelled Miller to Yosemite with a building contractor and architect.[17] Together, the three walked the snowy valley near the existing Sentinel Hotel, chose a site, and fully measured and marked out the shape of the new hotel's foundations with driven stakes connected by strong strings.

In this kaleidoscope of hope amid discouragement, Miller gathered prices on hotel crockery, fuel oil, furniture and furnishings, plumbing fixtures, and lumber. His friend and adviser H. W. Childs in Yellowstone Park encouraged him: "Cheer up! Be calm! And be a sport! You plucked off a plum but up to the present haven't got *all* you want but you got pretty near everything and have no kick coming."[18] But Miller did have a kick, and he did want it all—that was the whole point of the seemingly interminable negotiations.

Knowing this and knowing Riverside and Miller, his friend Charles Loring roundly advised against Yosemite in 1913. Miller was ignoring costs, Loring wrote, and should confront competition locally, not in Yosemite. "The greatest asset at the Glenwood is Frank Miller," he wrote, "and if he is not in evidence to the tourists...as he used to be, the business will fall off." Ever benign, Loring reminded his younger friend that "nearly all your friends who love you as I do regret that you are taking this great burden upon yourself when the prospect of success in their opinion is very questionable."[19]

During these months Miller clearly had more than Yosemite on his mind. On a mid-February morning in 1913, readers of the *Daily Press* were taken aback:

> *Glenwood Gets Ready for Mexican Invasion.*
>
> *With a revolution in Mexico City and likely to break out on the border between the United States and Mexico, Master Frank Miller of the Glenwood Mission Inn is taking no chances, but means to protect his hotel and guests from an attack by Mexican invaders.*
>
> *In the court of the hotel near the adobe he has planted a Maxim automatic machine gun, which is set facing the Seventh Street entrance of the court. If an attack were to be made the Seventh Street side of the hotel would offer the least resistance and for this reason Mr. Miller has stationed a Maxim at the very entrance of the drive and also one on the roof of the adobe.*
>
> *The automatic guns are attracting considerable attention and hundreds who look at them wonder what reason Mr. Miller has for buying them unless he fears an invasion.*[20]

No recorded explanations appeared—then or ever.

⚘

Over the next two years, Yosemite hotel negotiations took on a complexity speeded by telegrams, slowed by regular mails, and compounded by Miller's habits of adding ideas as he went along and undulating with the economy. The core issue was the length of the lease. Miller hired a very effective lobbyist,[21] but opponents of change in the park persisted.[22] Even the weather conspired against him. When severe frosts in 1912 ruined Riverside's citrus crops, Miller's local backers could not make good on investment promises. His early major financial supporters, the Southern Pacific and the Santa Fe Railroads, offered one promise after another, and then they too withdrew their support. Miller confirmed his fears that "right down in their hearts neither of the two great roads [were] willing to cooperate."[23]

Collapse came softly, at first with a broad hint from Miller's Washington lobbyist and then with word that other Washington contacts wanted a comprehensive overview of the situation. The lobbyist asked Miller in mid-January 1914 for "as much truthful data as I can get [from you] on…good faith and losses."[24] We might wonder about the language. Responding, Miller admitted frankly that he could not go ahead with his plans,[25] confirming the end of this lengthy drama by a letter and telegram sent directly to the Department of the Interior. In June, Riverside papers announced, "Yosemite Valley Hotel Abandoned."[26]

In previous years, when his energies for Yosemite surged for the last time, Miller had written a long history of his efforts, concluding, "up to date I have never been connected with any project that I have not pulled through and made a success of."[27] What's important here is not so much the accuracy or inaccuracy of his claim of complete success. He was convinced of his own habitual ability to meet and overcome challenges, to manage through to success, and, in that way, to realize in material expressions the ideas that sprang from his active imagination. When late in life he summoned up memories of successes and failures, Yosemite had disappeared from all recall.

※

On that sudden 1912 trip to Washington to talk Yosemite with the Department of the Interior, Marion and Frank also went to New York and sought help from the Hispanic Society of America on the planned Spanish Wing addition. To the couple's great surprise, Archer Huntington himself, the founder, opened the closed gallery for their private consultation, spending a day with them.[28] Miller had a barrage of questions. Huntington responded. Together, they measured wherever needed as Marion busily scribbled notes. Miller laid bare his aspirations to Huntington and his feeling that his Music Room was a mistake as far as being regarded as Spanish. In Spain, he told Huntington, everybody who amounted to anything had an art gallery or something like it. Now he needed help to achieve that for himself. Their talk also included ideas about involving a membership art society as a supporting organization and Huntington's willingness to help in due course with an exhibit of distinguished Spanish paintings. Huntington gave freely, also offering the adage, "A business founded on a historical background with a religious color will last as long as anything." This became Miller's mantra.[29] He and Marion left New York well satisfied, working together in close partnership on details for the gallery and its program.[30]

Four months later, demolition began on Sixth Street, abutting the Cloister Wing, to clear space for the Spanish Art Gallery.[31] In the same months, Myron Hunt, who was part of the Yosemite planning, prepared the drawings for the addition and its patio.[32] A local architect of growing popularity, G. Stanley Wilson, designed a small, protective canopy to build over the new Sixth Street entrance.[33] His appointment, something of a

November afterthought by Miller, began more than eighteen years of professional association that brought into being some of the Mission Inn's most flamboyant architecture.

The Spanish Art Gallery and patio, Miller's affirmations of his amounting to something, opened in December 1914, ready with an exhibition of fine paintings on New Year's Eve. The vast and elegant room soared to the billowing ceiling of gilded canvas slung into widely spaced cables thirty feet above the floor.[34] Gilded and varnished chests, coffers, lecterns, and paschal candlesticks decorated the floor under heraldic standards and tapestries on the walls, all in the spirit of aristocratic Iberia.[35] Here indeed was spatial and decorative grandeur for the Spanish cultural distinction Miller sought but believed he had forfeited to the ecclesiastical in the Music Room.

The design thoroughly satisfied Miller's desire to grasp as his own what he'd seen in Spain. By its appearance, the addition also expressed his evolving appreciation for arts and culture and displayed his own growing collection of paintings, many of them of religious subjects. Other hotels, though none in Riverside, displayed objets d'art in rooms designed for that and other uses, but none, at least in California, combined a gallery and exhibition program on the scale that Miller initiated on the opening. That uniqueness extended with the later organization of the Spanish Art Society in 1916 and enlarged with the 1928 addition of floors above the gallery where artists' and authors' names identified suites under towering terracotta pinnacles.

But the whole enterprise embraced much more than self-aggrandizement for Miller and evidence of his aesthetic growth. Notable authors, lecturers, painters, actors, and musicians, occasional visitors before, now came more often. In addition, the other added spaces—a new bakery, a brightly tiled new kitchen, food service in the court, and an enlarged dining room—prepared for the surge of guests expected in 1915 for the Panama–California Exposition in San Diego and the Panama–Pacific Exposition in San Francisco.[36] Guests would dine while served by waitresses in white uniforms and short yellow jackets hung with tiny bells, everyone under heraldic devices, flags, and assorted Spanish and medieval artifacts.

On August 1, 1914, World War I had begun, shattering Miller's hopes for international reconciliation but intensifying his devotion to peace and advocacy. Miller became a delegate in Los Angeles to select national peace-commission members en route to Europe.[37] He joined volubly in planning and guiding a city-wide peace rally for mid-September, campaigning for a Peace Day march up Rubidoux[38] but settling instead to be included in a Fairmont Park event sponsored by the city.[39] Immediate local reactions to war in Europe favored isolationism and peace by negotiation, but also cautioned, "Hold on to Your Hay," in anticipation of Europe's need for US food and fodder.[40] Newspapers published daily front-page dispatches of military, diplomatic, and civilian turmoil at home and overseas. But the war was far away, coming closer only at second hand: a local student returned after arduous travel from Berlin; Marcella Craft, Riverside's esteemed opera star, arrived home from years in Munich.[41] Washington Gladden, an orator of renown, visited at Miller's invitation. His first sermon in the Congregational pulpit, "The Futility of Force,"[42] drew solid agreement from Miller and others who listened in the pews of their new Congregational church; they too advocated the weapons of truth and love. Little did they suspect that with equal passion, and from the same pulpit, they would soon be urged to renounce their peaceful convictions and embrace not just the utility but also the purported morality of force.

If local residents wondered why Miller would invite someone such as Gladden, a man of contentious views, they might consider Miller's openness to ideological and racial sentiments in the roster of others he invited to speak or visit. There was Liberal Democrat William Randolph Hearst in 1913[43] and the ever-skeptical Elbert Hubbard, Miller's "ungodly friend,"[44] and Booker T. Washington came to the hotel at Miller's personal invitation.[45] On Washington's death about a year later in 1915, Miller convened a memorial service at the inn, open to all to honor his memory and his achievements.[46] Lyman Abbott, who had married Frank and Marion in 1910, came in 1914. He preached vigorously, proclaiming his mission to stamp out ignorance and evil. He publicly targeted Christian Science as a weed in the gardens of life.[47] Did he choose an easy target, knowing the unpopularity of the religion in Riverside in earlier years? More personally, did he know and ignore the close association his hosts had with the local congregation: Miller's mother, sisters, brothers-in-law, and a nephew and a niece all worshipped as Scientists. Certainly those who sat near Marion and Frank in the Congregational sanctuary as Abbot held forth must have felt discomfort, even for the speaker.

The year that Miller crowded with building at the hotel and events in the Yosemite drama ended in gala fashion. He opened the sumptuous Saint Cecilia's Chapel in the Music Room on Saint Cecilia's Day, November 22, 1914, in a thinly veiled homage to Isabella.[48] A few weeks later, he and Marion and two guests witnessed the first wedding in that gilded intimacy.[49] Christmas brought seasonal joy in special song services in the Music Room, with an especially tall, gaily lit Christmas tree on the stage and a brilliance of lighted palms in the new Patio of the Fountain.[50] Frank and Marion went on foot to the Watch Night service at the Congregational Church, finding the gentle strength of optimism in Tennyson's poem "Ring Out Wild Bells." At midnight, the service ended, and the Millers, wrapped up against the brisk night air, walked home to the inn where all-night merriment, dancing, and card parties welcomed the New Year.

20

Peace, Race, and Ceremony

When World War I began in 1914, public sentiment in Riverside favored staying well clear of European entanglement, strongly in favor of a negotiated peace. But within six months, talk of US preparedness surfaced.[1] Even so, although pro-war attitudes hardened year by year, in most ways the usual flow of community life continued unchanged until the United States' declaration of war in 1917.

Miller, however, stuck resolutely to peace. He arranged a visit by David Starr Jordan, an ardent pacifist who came fresh from Europe in 1914. Jordan drew the largest crowd ever for a visiting speaker and also breathed new life into the largely defunct Riverside chapter of the American Peace Society, where Miller was elected president.[2] Jordan came again the next year as the national mood heated toward US involvement. His forthright ethical and practical rejection of war brought applause, unusual in the Congregational Church or in any church in those years. But elsewhere in town a bellicose meeting shouted fiery condemnations on peace organizations and endorsed wartime restrictions.

Miller's steadfast convictions of the moral superiority of peace were widely known. His views were complex.

Hard-edged pacifism seems to have not commended itself to him as any more constructive of peace than controlled militarism; he never accepted the simplistic and widely touted propaganda of a war to end wars. Fanaticism, whether of sentiment or dogma, had slight place in his personality. He rarely ever talked about war, whether to deplore, control, or abolish. Whenever talk turned to armed national and international conflict, he talked of peace—achieving it and sustaining it.

For Miller these were prosperous, productive years. Bumper harvests of his favorite crop—tourists—came with the Panama–California Exposition in San Diego, 1915–1917, and with the long-awaited Panama–Pacific International Exposition in San Francisco in 1915. For June 1915 alone, he reported a thousand more guests in the Mission Inn than in the previous year, and many months lay ahead until the expositions closed.[3] Even then, late-arriving visitors lingered on in the California winter sunshine. Whatever Miller's disappointment over not having a hotel in Yosemite, all the effort toward the Spanish Wing with its extra rooms, art gallery, outdoor dining, and sparkling, new kitchen were more than rewarded by overflowing patronage. Indeed, these and the next ten years would be the inn's most prosperous, with annually increasing patronage.

Soon after Easter, Miller visited San Francisco and the exposition for eight days, thriving on the excitement. He preached to all about the "most wonderful show the world has ever seen," enthusiastically urging a visit, even if doing so meant wearing old clothes for the next ten years.[4] In May he went north again, on this visit affably convincing several distinguished individuals to visit the inn as his guests, sure that in Riverside they could advance his and their own causes. His persuasion and the inn's reputation must have been considerable, because Riverside had little else to attract some of those who came—a distinguished West Coast city planner,[5] a soprano concert soloist who stayed several years,[6] and General G. W. Goethals, famous supervising engineer of the Panama Canal.[7] Ida Tarbell, the investigative journalist nationally known for her 1904 exposé, *The History of the Standard Oil Company*, came and came again.[8] He convinced Rose V. S. Berry, author of the exposition's official guidebook and docent at the exposition's Palace of Fine Arts, to hang his year-end exhibit in the Spanish Art Gallery.[9] The popular, nationally known organist and composer Edwin H. Lemare came "for an indefinite stay" following his appearances at the exposition.[10] The Music Room organ and willing audiences awaited him.

From the closed exposition, a railroad car crammed with Miller's gatherings went south to the Mission Inn: Chinese bells, antique structural columns, ecclesiastical banners, twenty angels in relief, "ancient relics," and twenty thousand red clay tiles.[11] One huge item arrived separately in San Bernardino, allowing him a moment of swaggering enjoyment, then vanished, drained of interest, enthusiasm, and attention. The huge item came in fourteen cars, which contained a complete pueblo Native American village—life-sized, with plaster, wood, and sandstone blocks. Miller and his colleagues were convinced that the village would be the biggest thing ever for tourists if installed as a permanent attraction on Fairmount Hill beside Riverside's main park. A welcoming banquet announced its arrival. Then the village vanished. Months then years went by, and nothing happened: no plans, no museum, and no village, then or ever. Not every project Miller hatched succeeded or even left a trail of record.

Something that did endure, however, was a painting at the exposition that spoke deeply to Miller, a large canvas, *California Alps*, by California artist William Keith. Miller had seen it earlier, while hopes for his Yosemite hotel still burned bright, and later purchased it, hanging it prominently at the inn, where it remains now in the hotel lobby. "It reminded me better than anything else could," he wrote, "of the dreams and plans and the love of Yosemite which I formed during my many visits there."[12] The comment is a rare glimpse into Miller's enlarging aesthetic and his lingering attachment to even frustrated hopes.

~

In another matter, Miller's acquisitive utilitarian interests proved politically divisive. He needed a parking lot, coveting an unused block across the street from the hotel. The city council blocked his petition for almost a year in a running exchange that raised council-member hackles and elicited wild accusations. Lacking approval, Miller went ahead, cutting the street curbs for easy auto access and assuming the absence of any legal restraint.[13] Raucous council objections followed; warm words became hot, and tempers flared. A council member urged Miller's prosecution; another publicly assailed the "One man ring running the town."[14]

The frequency, persistence, and novelty of Miller's buzzes could easily rattle council members wanting bureaucratic tranquility.[15] But he lacked the unfettered influence and, especially, the power to run the town. More accurately, he was one of a handful that exerted influence in varied directions, often having "strenuous differences" among themselves.[16] In this instance, as the political pot boiled so nastily toward an election year, Frank and Marion traveled east for seven weeks, leaving the council members to their own devices.

During the hassling and while they were away, the tides of popular support flowed for them stronger than they knew. Soon after their return from the East, almost six hundred people gathered to honor them,[17] the timing linked conveniently to the forty-fifth anniversary of the Miller family's arrival in Riverside in October 1874. At the event Miller accepted a gold watch and chain, assuring all, as he often did, that coming home was the best part of the trip. He prophesied better times and urged burying the hatchet for the best interests of the community. Few could miss his allusion to the earlier acrimonious parking-lot exchanges, his own contentions with the city council, and the then-raging election fever.[18]

At a smaller, more private "little party," one guest thought the praise given Miller then and earlier was formula driven and superficial, saying "that the men who spoke did not know Frank Miller in his innermost soul." He reminded the guests of Miller's unnoticed care for the down-and-out, his aid to the needy in such gestures as salary boosts for the meanly paid local clergy. The editor of the *Enterprise* keenly remembered "the profound mutuality" of this occasion with its tears and "lumps in the throat which persistently refused to be downed."[19] Miller later said that the comments spoke of his deepest values, the finer things he stood for.[20] There is usually more to people than meets the eye, and in this episode of Miller's complex life, the speaker had glimpsed the integrity that Miller had struggled to express in his youthful diaries, still precious to him and now active in his maturity: "to do good, and make others happy."

Not everything about Miller's initiatives made for easy acceptance. He had in mind, for instance, a series of arches along the Seventh Street sidewalk, stretching from the inn five blocks to the train depot. He wanted to make the project one for his Spanish Art Society. The combination misfired. The society began in great style, a tour de force of organization, suggesting Marion's efficient hand. Miller had everything already arranged;[21] the members needed only to enjoy it. Two days of gala events inaugurated the society—a lecture series, a dinner, demonstrations of Spanish dancing, a society dance, and a private exhibition preview of rare and precious paintings for the privileged few.[22]

There were other notable exhibits and a mission-themed parade float that won a silver award in the Pasadena Rose

Parade.[23] Even with so promising a beginning, the society itself wilted. Somewhere there lurked a worm of atrophy. Perhaps Miller did too much for the society; perhaps membership alone gave all the distinction his members wanted; perhaps fund raising for sidewalk arches didn't mix with art appreciation. For his part, within the glow of the society Miller began to accumulate a collection of artwork, some of them California *plein air*[24] and including several Russian paintings, William Keith's *California Alps* and Vasili Verestchagin's *Come on Boys*, or, as it is more familiarly known, *The Charge Up San Juan Hill*,[25] both of the latter still prominent in the hotel. The society would revive only briefly, but the collection of paintings would grow, one in particular inspiring a most distinguished architectural feature in the last addition to the inn.

In its five years of existence, the mountaintop Easter service had been claimed "for our people" by the community, woven tightly into the Easter fabric of other church musical performances, Polo Club meetings, special art exhibits, and spring bargains in the stores.[26] For Miller the mountaintop service provided moments of rapture that obscured his concern with the mundane—auto and foot traffic blocking the threading road and the newspaper and other vendors hawking wares. He overlooked the disjointed singing that lacked vocal or instrumental leadership and the guidance of printed words.[27] Miller believed that the event "was so fundamental that it would take care of itself."[28] It didn't. That annual temple of his delight needed cleansing.

Aroused to all this by a friend's rebuke, Miller took over directing the planning. Not leaving well enough alone with better management that threw out the vendors, the ever-theatrical Miller cobbled in more embellishments—lighting the cross from a distant point and inviting the opera singer Marcella Craft and the songwriter Carrie Jacobs Bond to perform.[29] His agile mind soared to propose a Greek theater on the mountain, with fixed seating at fifty cents. Enthusiasm for this wilted at protests over public funds being spent for private benefit on the private mountain.[30] Miller's later suggestion of a Greek temple as a war memorial on the mountain also failed. His noble talk about a "miniature Parthenon crowning our acropolis," housing memorials to the fallen, a statue of Christ, war relics, and bronze tablets,[31] did, however, keep alive the appropriateness of some form of memorial to peace and wartime sacrifices. Miller would be heard.

As Miller weighed his patriotic obligations in wartime years, he served on and hosted the executive committee of the local chapter of the Red Cross Society. He turned the adobe over to the busy society volunteers.[32] He sold war bonds[33] and led in food conservation in the hotel and with grow-your-own campaigns.[34] When in November 1917 the United States and Japan signed the Lansing-Ishii Agreement, seen as a harbinger of peace, Miller gathered about fifty Japanese and a dozen local businessmen at the inn,[35] using the banquet also as a blatant repudiation of local sentiment that contested the purchase by the Haradas, a local Japanese family, of a home on Lemon Street.

The Harada children, as citizens born in the United States, had taken the title to the house; the parents, as aliens, could not do so. Hostility toward the purchase and the presence of the family in the Anglo neighborhood led to the case of *The People of the State of California v. Jukichi Harada et al.*, resolved in superior court in 1918 in favor of the Haradas. But for Miller and his like-minded townsfolk,[36] opposition to the purchase and the ensuing court proceedings gave them opportunities to publicly signal not only their support for the family and other Japanese residents[37] but also their notions of the open society they saw Riverside to be.

Miller's opinions on racial matters were never in doubt then or later, nor were they unique to him in Riverside. He acted from no finespun ideology. His hiring practices provide one mirror. Among his three hundred employees, one observer saw Japanese, Chinese, Europeans, African Americans, Mexicans, Americans, and American Indians.[38] Eyebrows rose in a town of clear social and ethnic divisions when Miller hosted Booker T. Washington's visit in 1914, the two of them photographed for a postal card together on Mount Rubidoux. The next year Miller arranged an interracial memorial service for Washington in his Music Room, he and Marion attending and leading guided tours of the hotel.[39] In January of the next year, he rescued four Panama–Pacific Exposition Mexican artisans off the road, abandoned by the Mexican exhibitors when the exposition closed.[40] Miller gathered them in, housed them, and employed them at demonstrating their crafts—pottery, lace making, jewelry making—as they earned enough to travel home at the end of the tourist season in May.

Diversity unaided rarely brings community.[41] Miller's practices at the hotel appear to have been organized comfortably around the conventions of gender, race, and work of his time: male Anglo and Chinese cooks (there were few, if any, Chinese women in Riverside), single Anglo women as waitresses, male Japanese waiters, single, white housemaids, and Mexicans and Native Americans in back-of-the-house tasks, invisible there to the public and the public record, as in any fine hotel. Miller measured his own acceptance of people by merit and character far more than by ethnic background, though all the while respectful of community strictures. His independence of mind and a resilient contrarian streak allowed neither a crusade against social and ethnic divisions nor disregard of the proprieties of the time. As Master of the Mission Inn, he presided over casting his performers, stage-managing with timely graciousness shared among his wife Marion, his sister Alice, and the Hutchingses.

The weapons of modern warfare came to Riverside's borders, and Miller, for all his peace loving, was more active than most in bringing them and profited most of all in keeping them there. The narrative stretched over two years. In 1917 prospect of an army air base in Southern California ignited fierce competition from San Diego to Los Angeles. Riverside's Chamber of Commerce, Miller at full strength, set off in hot pursuit of the prize, offering as a site a small but operational civilian airfield in Moreno Valley, some eight miles east. Competition raged; influence peddling and string pulling flourished. Riverside took the prize, duly confirmed early in 1918, and celebrated at a dinner in the month of March. Arrangements provided that federal purchase of a mile square of property could follow an interim rental at a dollar a year.

In the scrambling competition for the prize, Miller's diligence reached far beyond his entertainment of federal visitors coming to inspect the Moreno Valley site. He adopted a trio of shrewd tactics: he compiled persuasive weather and topological statistics for the winning proposal in 1918; he purchased, for twenty dollars, two half sections of land within the rented property; third, he personally paid part of the subsidized rental until June 1919. When the government bought, just a few months after Miller's own purchase, he sold his land to the government. His selling price was $64,000.[42] What he thought about his armaments related to profit making and helping bring the newest weapons of war to the edge of the city remains unrecorded. How did he reconcile his peace advocacy while offering a home to the US Army Air Service and harvesting a financial windfall for himself and Marion?

One clue to his thinking came from a friend who thought Miller "bewildered" by the war; if so, Miller was not alone. Many Americans who deeply honored those who served and sacrificed found themselves adrift among such turns of event as President Wilsons's reversals, fickle public opinion around patriotism and fanaticism, and the Protestant clergy's retreat from the morality of peace to justification of war. They found little relief for their helplessness in the face of profiteering at home and the carnage of trench warfare. In those circumstances, Miller could well have been shaken in his reliance on instincts for peace and sentiment, as some suggested.[43] However, such opinions seem to disregard much evidence, all too facile to describe his complex personality.

But he did find rational and public expression of patriotism in service with the Red Cross, war-bond sales, and food-conservation efforts. For him, and many at this time, patriotism confronted conscience; convictions resisted obligation, but no grand resolutions surfaced. Conversational admission of bewilderment does not certify the absence of thought. Miller wrestled with personal and national values, unresolved perhaps, though anything but mired in sentiment.[44] All this considered, the March Field episode revealed little bewilderment: he was all foresight and business, wartime business. And on the face of it, as mere observers after the fact, we may see hypocrisy.

Miller prepared theatrically for the war's end, intending a flag-bedecked Armistice observance on Rubidoux, something patterned on the Easter service. But storms threatened, canceling his first attempt, and the influenza epidemic stopped his second. In November 1919, however, he nervously launched his production. More than a year before, while planning, he wrote to a friend: "I cannot tell you how happy your [supportive] letter of May 23rd has made me. Sometimes I wonder if I am well balanced, so few approve of what I often think important to do, and your desire to want to help me to do this thing, although not a Riversider, satisfies me that I am not crazy in thinking that if this [Armistice] service can be properly handled or evolved into the beautiful and wonderful thing that it can be and ought to be, that it will bless everybody in this part of the world."[45]

His liturgical, wind-whipped event invoked hopes for friendly relations among former combatants. The next year an even-shorter ceremony carefully avoided denominational bias.[46] In 1921 Miller, who could seldom leave simple alone, expanded the program to include a costumed and metaphorical peace pageant with a Prince of Peace gathering children at the foot of the cross. Then came spectacular fireworks from the mountaintop, an evening banquet at the inn, and songs from Puccini, Del Rigeo, and Leoncavallo in honor of Italy.[47]

In these events Miller would educate his town, often a reluctant pupil. The community was called to a more generous international outlook that found many uncomfortable. For most in the town, these often solemn mountaintop Armistice observances were far less attractive on a public holiday than a parade, sports, a picnic in the park, or an evening of dancing.[48] Of the mountaintop Armistices nothing now remains. They disappeared from the mountain with the founder.

21

A Gorgeous Creation

Frank and Marion went east, leaving town the morning after he sold his March Field land to the federal government in 1919. In Tomah, Wisconsin,[1] they hurried about the village, Miller greeting his few remaining old acquaintances and praising the old and new landmarks alike.

They arrived back in California in mid-August 1919, spending a day or two at their all-but-finished beach house, "Mariona," in Laguna.[2] This house was set on rock foundations over the ocean and rambled on for several levels with irregularly shaped rooms, balconies, and separated apartments that assured privacy and ocean views. Construction on the first phase ended in 1920; later additions in the Miller style of piecemeal building continued until 1929. He named the villa for Marion, her name alone on the deed a testimony to his profound love and of her central place in its design and construction.

Miller told a biographer that she "took hold of the dream and worked out all the possible application[s]; interviewed the artists, wrote the authorities for their opinion[s], to artists for designs, to craftsmen for estimates. She received no credit for the finished product, and apparently expected none."[3] A longtime observer confirmed the closeness of their relationship, calling Marion "an essential partner in the Inn. She had always been essential to its success and welfare. She is the constant companion of Mr. Miller in all his rest hours, many of which are spent at Arch Beach in the family cottage and she is also his constant confidant and advisor in all his business matters."[4] The villa was hers in law and in love, an expression of Miller's affection and a prudent provision in their separate estates, especially wise for a twice-married man.[5] Granting all this, Miller was unlikely to fully resign involvement with the project.

The impulse to build new things, change plans, and add to buildings, evident in all his enterprises throughout life, seemed to spring up continuously in Miller, the Laguna villa unlikely a departure. His admitted reliance on imagination and intuition—"dreaming dreams" as he himself said—and his occasional confessions of self-doubt suggest a note of uncertainty, even insecurity. They give the impression of an inner restlessness, even anxiety, seeking relief through change, adaptations, and new perspectives conjured up as he went along. The preeminent example was correcting what he believed to be false steps in the Music Room that failed to capture the Spanish grandeur he sought.[6] Whatever this mix, his restless energy, fertile imagination, persistence, and willingness to get advice carried him.

In November 1919 Miller announced more construction at the Mission Inn: his intention was for a permanent three-story brick-and-concrete building across Sixth Street from the hotel. He'd use it to accommodate the hotel services, with rooms for female employees on the upper floors.[7] A knowledgeable writer, however, thought that the completion of the Spanish Wing, with the Gallery, had fulfilled Miller's dreams. In his opinion, the Gallery and the floors above it, designed by architect Myron Hunt, "welded poetry with history, fact with fiction in one memorial structure," bringing Miller's ideal to full realization.⁸ Other writers echoed the same high regard for the completeness of the hotel as it stood, a goal achieved. High praise indeed, but it overlooked Miller's almost compulsive persistence in building. Even more dramatic additions would appear. In a compact space, Asian and Spanish baroque designs would encompass office space, public rooms, elegant guest rooms, an innovative spiral staircase, and a breathtaking medieval chapel. Even then, Miller was still cherishing his unfulfilled dream of the Giralda Tower.

By 1920 the Miller family could look back on over forty-five years in Riverside and a long list of achievements. Miller's visible success had been likened to a spreading tree, wide and generous in influence.⁹ This tree cast a benign shade, attractive enough to all the family, though not all stayed under it. Yet some family members may have seen themselves obscured by its shade, their comings and goings and public service only dimly noticed. Frank's oldest sister, Emma, married to G. O. Newman, lived a few miles away in Riverside for over twenty years but busied herself independently from the inn before moving to Los Angeles. Newman's own direct association in the hotel, except as family, ended even as Frank bought out all the interests in 1880. His sister Alice Richardson became the hotel manager when widowed in 1906, her personality radiating a golden charm that "made a fool feel wise."¹⁰ A favorite family comment had it that people came to the inn to meet Frank Miller, but they came back because of Alice Richardson. She, of all the family, dispelled any shade that Frank's visibility may have cast in her direction. His brother, Edward, seven years younger than Frank, grew up in Riverside, finding his identity in the town as much as at the inn.¹¹ But he stayed close to Miller's call, acting as manager at the inn on several occasions and directing the desk for at least two years.[12] Frank's daughter, Allis, the daughter of the inn, spent her whole life there, as did DeWitt Hutchings after they married.

In all these family members Miller had irreplaceable assets, something he recognized, even though Henry Huntington thought it necessary to remind him of their importance to his success.[13] They provided a managing team. He could visit around and politick about town and travel throughout the state and across the nation. He could follow his enthusiasms on his own schedule, a rare luxury indeed among businessmen and his hotel-keeping colleagues. And whatever his generosity to the family, he was still Master of the Inn, an individualist, a genial loner and contrarian, a first boy who reigned, even though he did not always rule. In his end-of-life reminiscences, he acknowledged that dependence on his family, warmly naming his daughter and two wives as most essential to his success.[14]

Son-in-law DeWitt Hutchings wanted more than being under Miller: he sought direct management at the hotel. He had limited opportunities to do so. The matrimonial door had not brought the share in hospitality that Miller gave as an invitation.[15] Even before he married, the inn group held together by Miller was composed of members who had well-protected turfs: Isabella, Alice Richardson,[16] the longtime majordomo Bjornsen, and Marion Clark. Her return as Miller's wife and partner closed any power gaps that might have been hoped for. His daughter, Allis, all but replaced the deceased Isabella, sharing with Hutchings but unlikely to resign influence to her husband. The next tier of organization—hostess, housekeeper, steward, chief clerk, and even the head doorman and porter—knew the lines of authority and protected their smaller fiefdoms.

Though not satisfied, Hutchings was not idle, filling necessary support roles[17] in the Sunday services, at Easter, in the hotel social program, in community interests, in the Tahoe summer team, and, in second place to Francis

Borton, as curator of artifacts, eventually becoming the editor of several mainstay inn publications.[18] But for all this, even with his signature in correspondence above the title "Assistant Manager," his managerial role at the Mission Inn remained slight. That bothered him at a time when he wanted to hone his "business experience and judgment"[19] if he was to become more active with Allis in future, a role foreshadowed by Miller's indifferent health at sixty-five years of age.

An opportunity in management had come during the 1919–1920 winter. He grasped it, with success. The Broadwater Hotel, a shuttered, grandiose railway resort hotel a few miles outside Helena, Montana, would reopen for summer tourists.[20] Optimism in Helena soared. "With good management of the hotel," the planners said, "there would be no such thing as fail."[21] H. W. Childs, concessionaire of Yellowstone hotels and Miller's Yosemite adviser, received carte blanche in selecting a manager for the hotel.[22] Childs invited Hutchings to Helena and welcomed him in temperatures between thirty and forty degrees. Hutchings looked around, made beguiling speeches with a wildly chamber-of-commerce ring, and even offered to invest in the hotel himself if he should become manager. A report headlined him: "Tourist Expert Tells How to Lure 'Em, Hold 'Em." When he left, town locals predicted his return; the prospects were "the biggest thing for Helena in years."[23] The group made its offer; DeWitt accepted. Here was the opportunity he sought, set in a new location, the employment neatly bounded by a beginning and an ending date. He'd be well out from the shade of the Miller tree and away from Riverside's ever-inquiring local newspapers. In Montana he could be his own man.

Hutchings arrived on May 15, 1920, in a somewhat warmer Helena. He arrived with his group of experienced staff from the Mission Inn and four Berkeley students—a man each for piano, saxophone, drums, and string bass,[24] all key people in the success he was to have. Guests began arriving. By June 21 the hotel was fully booked, even before the dinner and dance that officially marked the season's beginning.

From then until late September, Hutchings programmed all the diversions expected for hotel summer pleasure—dances, the latest steps demonstrated and taught by the college men; swimming in the mineral pools; swimming races; visiting entertainers; convention groups; overnighters; and a choice for guests of hotel-room or tent lodging.

On schedule after breakfast on Monday, September 20, the Broadwater closed for the season. The Mission Inn staff boarded the train, and the orchestra began its long trek back to Berkeley. Hutchings reported the season "only partially successful" from his point of view. Even so, the Broadwater owners were encouraged enough to schedule reopening in 1921, voting to invite Hutchings back, commending his management, and noting his popularity with transient guests and with the people of Helena, hundreds of whom he had met in a business and a social way.[25] But many years would pass and more dissatisfaction would surface before Hutchings could put into practice the management expertise that brought success to his Helena summer. Not until three years after Miller's death would he come formally into his own in the hotel hierarchy.

For several months after Hutchings returned from Montana he and Miller looked ahead to a visit in Mexico. They put the lure of travel and the prospects of gathering artifacts ahead of any fears about bandits or revolutionaries to travel south with a Los Angeles Chamber of Commerce group in late November 1920. The recently victorious President Alvaro Obregon's government invited them and over a thousand others in the interests of increased travel, trade, and good relations. While there, abundant hospitality surrounded the visitors with receptions and visits to the theater, the opera, bullfights, architectural sites, and what the Riverside papers called the "aesthetic lives of the people." The visitors occasionally saw torn-up railway tracks and burned-out buildings, stark reminders of the recent revolution.[26]

Miller and Hutchings mixed their pleasures, attending the planned hospitality and going off together to haunt art and antique shops. On these jaunts, they passed beautiful old churches, city palaces, and country villas. In the shops, filled with never-ending sources of delight, they purchased freely for shipment through El Paso to the Mission Inn. DeWitt described their finds, mentioning especially a double-barred cross with the date 1794, a sculptured stone madonna and child, and a number of structural columns that Miller later built into the inn.[27] The elaborate Giralda-like towers on the Cathedral of Mexico and the Nun's Church of Regina Coeli confronted Miller and Hutchings as they passed around Mexico City, confirming images not only of the tower that haunted Miller's mind but also the baroque richness of the Spanish heritage. His architectural extravagances born in Spain grew among what can only have looked like unrestrained indulgences in Mexican baroque church architecture and furnishings.

A dealer in Mexico, Margaret Crane, then, or soon after, offered Miller an altarpiece from a private chapel in Guanajuato, some four hundred miles north of Mexico City. Their correspondence flowed back and forth for months following his return to California. The dealer had seen the piece, so she knew something of what she offered; Miller remained nervous about buying sight unseen from an untried dealer in a troubled country,[28] but he consented to the purchase. Crane had to chivy Mexican artisans and civil servants through mazes of negotiations and labyrinths of bureaucracy and bribes. In Guanajuato, she watched as the huge altarpiece was taken apart—its frame, sculptured saints, and gilded columns crated in straw. At intervals she signed sheaves of papers and collected bureaucratic stamp imprints. Assuring a safe journey north by rail to the border and El Paso was an act of faith.

Miller had seen similar altarpieces but had no basis for knowing prices or exact details of what he was buying. In his uncertainty, and facing the asking price of $5,800, he questioned almost everything: Crane's aesthetic judgment, her ability to manage the export, and even the accuracy of the names she gave some of the pieces. She admitted vagueness about the names: "I'm not a good Catholic." But her dealer's sense correctly gauged the depth of his desire, understood Miller's tightfistedness, and appreciated his valid apprehension of risk.

In May 1921, Miller agreed to Crane's offer in an uncharacteristically clear and brief letter. He deposited two-thirds of the payment in an El Paso bank, promising the balance when the altarpiece arrived safely in the United States. She, however, wanted payment on arrival across the border from El Paso in Juarez, Mexico. They haggled. In what seems to me an ironic resolution, all the goods, in a single railroad car, crossed the border into Texas while they argued. Twelve days later the boxcar arrived in Riverside.

The eighteenth-century baroque altarpiece or reredos, packed in stable straw, arrived in several crates. Family tradition told of bullet holes in some of the cases, the work of foiled bandits, they said. Others said that straw stable sweepings were chosen to foil thieves, who'd be deterred by the stink. Still other stories had the gold-leaf-covered saints smeared with mud to disguise their appearance. Good stories, they sustain the aura of hazards and cunning so fitting for the arrival of the spectacular purchase from a country still in economic and social turmoil. Whatever the stories, the brilliance and detail of the altarpiece itself beggared any myth. Twenty-five feet tall and sixteen feet wide (another opinion said thirty-five feet high and eighteen feet wide),[29] the gold-leaf-covered carved wood assembly, jointed and pinned without screws or nails as was common, displayed nine—some said twelve—figures, many almost life-size, gathered around the Holy Family and surmounted by the Trinity. This reredos came from a private chapel in Guanajuato, Mexico, the wealthy silver-mining owners having fallen on less prosperous times over a generation or two. They had retained the central figure of the altarpiece, the Virgin, but from cold necessity had offered their treasure for sale.[30]

The undiminished eighteenth-century gilding shone in the August sunshine as piece by piece the sculptured saints, columns carved in a style called *estipite*, richly decorated panels, and supporting pieces came to view. Miller bubbled with enthusiasm as he viewed what he'd bought. All anxiety evaporated in praise for the object, its history, and the distinguished Mexican mining family, even the carpenter who had dismantled and packed it with such care.[31] His letter to Margaret Crane effused his thanks for what he called the "gorgeous creation."[32] Having seen it in its magnificence, Miller promptly announced his intention to place it in a chapel to be built in his Giralda Tower. In the meantime, he'd install it in the Spanish Art Gallery high above the floor at one end of the room. There it stayed for ten years.[33] For whatever reason—lack of knowledge or Protestant habit—the whole structure, correctly an altarpiece, reredos, or retablo, became "an altar" in the press and ever after in public awareness.

The installation of the gilded masterpiece, unique in Riverside and rare in Southern California, gave Miller one of his four most impressive artifacts. The other pieces—a huge Chinese bell, eight Tiffany glass windows, and a pair of sculpted bronze doors—though equally imposing, were each as different as impressive. Several years would pass before all entered his life, each linked to small personal dramas. In the meantime, the altarpiece graced a remote wall in the Spanish Art Gallery, a gorgeous creation even there with its splendor muted in the subdued light.

22

Hospitals and Egotism

The unusually prosperous years after the war brought changes of pace and pattern to Riverside.[1] More local banks prospered, and new families moved to town. Cheaper and faster transocean travel competed with railroads for tourist dollars. The auto, the streetcars, and interurban railways dominated popular transportation. By 1922 no less than six companies brought tour groups to Riverside daily, each tour complete with a "rubber-neck orator" who unfolded glories of the town and inn unknown until heard from the guide.[2] The inn could report serving 1,100 guests on a Sunday.[3] More convention groups chose the Mission Inn.[4] Hundreds motoring to Banning viewed the early spring almond blossoms after a stop off at a Riverside hotel.[5] But on their next outing, they might bypass the inn completely to visit resorts in Palm Springs or drive in the mountains or gather at a beach town.[6] Humbler accommodations in car camps sprang up, fitted to smaller purses and egalitarian tastes. Miller's favorite crop—the tourist crop—was changing.

For Miller and the inn, these would be banner years of prosperity, the family busier than ever.[7] Miller kept up his involvement in local and state politics for local benefit, the city-beautiful movement, and good roads. He represented Riverside on the Los Angeles Chamber of Commerce discussions about the highway connecting Los Angeles with Phoenix, Arizona,[8] bent on assuring a route through Riverside, what is now California Highway 60.

Miller listened in Riverside to visiting city planners who offered paths to prosperous futures. One urged making Riverside an "ideal place," expressive of the town's individuality.[9] Responding, locals got up a series of advertisements boosting Riverside as "The place where town and country meet," naming poultry raising, citrus production, truck gardening, fruit growing, and marketing facilities. Here was a pattern change toward an expanded agricultural, social, and economic base, moving away from the earlier reliance on citrus orchards and tourists as the basic crops. The consciousness of town identity and the search for a competitive edge went on and would continue for many years, as was true for many growing cities.[10] No consensus emerged about planning or a destination for Riverside. Strongly held differences separated those seeking an expanded worker population for small industries and those who would retain the citrus-and-tourist economy.

Miller occasionally recorded his vision for Riverside's future but more often pressed for specific individual projects. One, on which for years Miller bided his time, was the memorial for those who served in World War I, something that honored sacrifice and promoted peace. His mountaintop amphitheater and the Greek temple suggestions both fell into neglect. Then in 1919, under a *Press* headline of "Another Plan for Memorial," the unnamed mother of a returned soldier suggested a hall or auditorium as an appropriate community statement. Her suggestion described a building very like what eventually appeared on the corner of Seventh and Lemon Streets with a main auditorium, a basement, and other rooms, as well as a garden at street level and another on the roof.[11] This all matched ideas Miller had shared, though he despaired of the memorial ever being built. The published letter, whatever its source, had enough appeal to stimulate the appointment of a town committee, with Miller a member.

But any movement toward action lagged. There was no lack of loyalty to servicemen, but two city-hall bond-issue proposals took priority over any memorial in 1920 and 1921 and failed.[12] Furthermore, disenchantment about the war had surfaced. The promised new era of internationalism had not appeared. Added to that, a sediment of guilt about war had been joined by a growing awareness that business interest, not high moral principles, drew the United States into the war.[13] A US Senate investigation of the topic continued into the 1930s.[14] Riverside's war memorial waited; Miller had hope but little faith.

Sometime about 1920, Riverside had focused on its need for a better hospital. National changes in institutional health were comprehensive, embracing constituencies in patient expectations, physician training, medical science, nurse training, costs, hospital architecture, and management. In Riverside the inadequate Doctors' Hospital competed for middle-class patronage with hospitals in Pasadena and Los Angeles; the resort-like Loma Linda Sanitarium twenty-five miles away served select patrons and the county hospital served indigents, too *déclassé* for the upwardly mobile. Having a hospital to occupy a place "between the high priced sanatorium and the community institution" gained widespread acceptance.[15]

The hospital being proposed was a departure from the ordinary. It would be managed not by physicians but by a community board of directors "chosen from men and women outside the medical profession." It would support a close relationship with a nurse-training program at the community college. That program would emphasize academic and clinical training far superior to what existed in the local Doctors' Hospital. The *Los Angeles Times* editors watched with interest, seeing Riverside's efforts as "an example...of doing the right thing in the right way."[16]

Miller joined enthusiastically in the community-hospital proposal, adding his idiosyncratic view that organized churches had an obligation to participate in support. "Religious people go off to Asia and Africa and build hospitals," he said. "Why isn't it the work of the churches to minister to the sick at home? Jesus did it. But only the Catholics and the Adventists are known across the land for their hospitals. What's the matter with the rest of us? We're falling down!"[17] There was little doubt that Miller had not only humanitarian but also the financial support of the hospital in mind. That in itself was a caution to the clergy, whatever their own humanitarian impulses. Miller's pleas failed to convince—of the thirty-two churches only five actively worked in support of the hospital.[18]

Miller and others wanting solid public support for their community hospital knew they must speak with the authority of current knowledge. They moved carefully and successfully, the community hospital opening after about four years. Fund-raising as the first order of business began in 1920, and in about six months they had raised half of the $250,000 needed. Miller became almost completely immersed. "I have never tried to do anything that seemed so necessary or that my heart was so much in," he wrote. He knew the uphill struggle in raising the $250,000 needed but radiated cautious optimism. This was the first ever community-wide campaign, and in his private judgment "teamwork [was] something the community [did] not know how to do."[19] Miller's own unexpected $25,000 gift to the campaign brought a planning committee to its feet, infusing a new urgency. A few days later, in 1921, by a twist of fate, the twenty-eight-year-old Doctors' Hospital partially burned,[20] another imperative for something new, better, and different.

Miller added even more drama by having his resident artist paint a huge banner crowded with sentimental symbolism: "In Humanity's Service—Riverside" displayed a sweet-faced angel of mercy in the garb of a Red Cross nurse holding a chalice marked "LIFE" and standing at a door marked "Community Service"; behind her a shrine-like niche held a crucifix and another cross inscribed IHS. The more than life-sized banner offered something for almost everyone in its blend of religion, health care, and community service.[21]

Given his habit of getting advice from the experts, Miller readily joined with some local physicians seeking wider knowledge about significant changes in medical education, hospital practice, and architecture.[22] The group talked with the director of the Southern Pacific Railroad's extensive hospital system and with Los Angeles architect Myron Hunt. Local interests weighed in: clergy wanted denominational and hospital harmony; businessmen wanted economy; the local cement company and Southern Sierra Electric wanted to assure their interest in health care for employees, each making $10,000 contributions.[23] While traveling, Miller sent word of an anonymous $10,000 gift for the hospital, conditional on a local match.[24] The Newman family offered an attractively priced five-acre site on Fourteenth Street, readily accepted for the new hospital.[25]

Community hospital matters and personal health issues took Frank and Marion to the Midwest in April 1923. During their travels, the Millers went to inquire about hospitals in Chicago, Milwaukee, Detroit, Rochester, New York City, Boston, and Toronto. Frank and Marion kept detailed records that were later typed by Marion into a long narrative of warmly personal comments, with observations about hotel service and opinions from some of the nation's leading innovators in hospitals, nursing, and management. All the advisers urged hospital management by "a business mind" on "strictly business principles." Most specifically, they warned against management by physicians.[26] Where asked, most recommended a two-year nurse-training course to allow specialty training to follow.[27] The widely informed Charles Mayo of the Mayo Clinic and George Edgar Vincent of the Rockefeller Foundation both suggested a female administrator as their preferred choice for the size of the Riverside Community Hospital. Such would conserve Riverside's budget[28] and combine a nurse's point of view with administrative expertise.

Frank and Marion had a personal agenda at the Mayo Clinic in Rochester, Minnesota. Miller stayed there for fifteen days consulting with Dr. Charles Mayo, "because of my nervous condition." He said little about that on return home, but two years later he confided his chagrin to Henry E. Huntington. "It seems pitiful," he wrote, "that at 68 I have got to quit." The cause identified by Dr. Charles Mayo, the distinguished surgeon, was that Miller as "a country boy living long in a small town [had] as a consequence a bump of egotism that I think nothing can be done unless I do it."[29] Mayo had rebuked Miller's obsessive work habits, springing, he thought, from Miller's need to be central to everything. In the argot of the day, Mayo called it "Egotism," a Freudian concept that gained indiscriminate use in professional and everyday speech. Whatever the language used, the real challenge for Miller's tranquility lay in his need to balance activity and rest, requiring a change in his lifestyle.

While Frank and Marion visited in hospitals in New York, an invitation to visit came from Louis Comfort Tiffany, a 1915 guest at the inn.[30] This reacquaintance led to the spectacular acquisition of eight Tiffany windows for the hotel, another of Miller's quartet of spectaculars. The visit began in tension, because at their 1915 parting, both were in high dudgeon over Miller's refusal to sell Tiffany a huge Chinese bell, another of his spectaculars. One of Miller's would-be biographers heard the story from Miller. Their exchange ended as Tiffany told Miller to go to hell, and Miller, claiming the host's obligation, said only, "If you were not my guest I might have some wishes for you, Sir!"

In New York Tiffany pressed eight spectacular church windows on him, wanting them to "go into a setting where they will belong" and not to "a crank evangelist from Los Angeles." Miller, who himself pressed for bargains, habitually said even he blushed at remembering the meager and unrecorded price Tiffany asked.[31] The magnificent Tiffany windows with the gilded Rayas altarpiece from Mexico furnished and defined a chapel Miller would build, his last and most extraordinary addition to the inn.

Back in Riverside from his travels, Miller took up again his enthusiasms for the hospital, the city hall, and the memorial auditorium. An intimate who knew his health welcomed him back, saying, "Now that you've beaten the Doctors [Mayo] as far as going to the hospital is concerned [I] trust that you will be feeling as good as new before a great while."[32]

Feeling as good as new would have been too much to expect, but he brought on all his available vigor to his interests, especially with nurse training, something he saw as professionally and economically crucial to the hospital's success. "One of the outstanding things that appeals to me," he said to the planning group, "is the shortage of nurses, and we lack intelligence if we don't realize it. We are not civilized if we have to pay from $14 to $16 a day for nurses in a city like Riverside."[33] That daily rate went to "special" nurses, certificated and qualified by two or three years training, who attended to individual patients in the Doctors' Hospital and on in homes. Hospitals as employers avoided the expense of these licensed nurses, depending on unpaid student trainees for the drudgery of housekeeping and bedside care. Whatever Miller meant in 1922 about being civilized in Riverside, his efforts would see to it that the proposed community-hospital nurse-training program would become a college program under professional nurse supervision. Trainees, free from housekeeping, would learn clinical procedures and bedside care. Miller's views of nurse education and roles prevailed but not until after the new hospital opened.

Miller's support of the hospital fit into his habitual philanthropy, a practice that began in his boyhood church offerings recorded in his early diaries. A compilation of his gifts to charity from the records of three typical years, 1923 through 1925, list a steady pattern of donations. He usually gave $100 and to a diversity of organizations,[34] no one organization having special priority.[35]

❧

Gradually Miller began to act on his understanding of what "egotism" meant to his family, friends, and perhaps the Mayos and what he himself called his "nerves." He tried with some success not to "dip into these outside things," like Chamber of Commerce discussions about bringing industries to Riverside. But he just couldn't help giving advice on a familiar topic.[36] He'd experienced no change of heart, still opposing industries; so he merely rebuked the chamber for impotence and indecision.[37] Egotistical or not, he endorsed wholeheartedly the visiting speaker who a month later praised the inn as "something far more important than any industrial plant [Riverside] might secure. Nothing," said the visitor, "can equal the wonders and glory of your Mission Inn with its atmosphere of the early Californians."[38]

Miller reduced his metes and bounds, declining several directorships on statewide and regional boards. His usual refusal included some version of "my health and my work are such that I cannot take it on."[39] These decisions were problematic for one so used to consulting widely, expressing freely, and going his own way and at his own considerable speed. Little in this suggested retirement, however. Still energetic in his late sixties, he still traveled, planned new building projects, kept up a steady and extensive correspondence, and made his presence felt and his voice heard in the town—and he relaxed often by the sea in the company of his much-loved Marion.

He had been in the public eye for more than forty years. Photographs reveal the slight stooping of age, suits of an older cut that fit less well, and a more than ample girth. Lines etched his face, framed in jowls. His gaze in photographs is often distant, with a suggestion of impatience, his posture posed. He moved more slowly, and fatigue came more readily; the years were showing.

Appropriately, recognition and honors began to come his way more often, each fully reported in the local papers. He presented graduation diplomas at the Sherman Institute;[40] the Laguna Chamber of Commerce gave him life membership with a simple ceremony;[41] the Riverside Chamber of Commerce, not to be outdone by Laguna, presented a "scroll of commendation" endorsed by the principal community associations;[42] his hotel colleagues praised his virtues and his hotel in *Hotel Management* under the title "The Spirit of True Hospitality";[43] Japanese businessmen met to honor him in Calexico on the Mexican border;[44] and the Sons of Saint George, an association of British-born residents in the United States, honored Miller's "kindly spirit" in his honoring of British war dead on Mount Rubidoux.[45]

On the twentieth anniversary of the hotel, about two hundred gathered at the Mission Inn. The guests brought "their tokens of love and esteem and good wishes and laid them before Frank A. Miller, Master of the Mission Inn." They feasted together on lobster cocktail, bouillon, baked spring chicken, new potatoes *rissolet* and garden peas, with tutti-frutti as a sundae desert. The simple menu delighted the select group of influentials. By their own admission, they were often at odds with one another "in religion, in politics, in the administration of civic affairs" and "strenuously differing" with Miller. But all affirmed "the value of a manly man." The consensus credited Miller with more influence on progress in Riverside than any other person, a view the *Press* editor summarized in presenting Miller as the "idealist, the builder, the humanitarian, the friend and their neighbor." When the chorus of praise paused, Miller spoke briefly, approving the recognition and accepting a commemorative book and a large photograph of himself aged "about twenty." The next day the newspaper printed a more recent photograph showing his seasoned face, his abundant hair swept back and high on his head, his gaze steady, mildly expectant, and focused far off, with his mouth firmly, noncommittally between frown and smile.[46]

With recognition and honor came other less welcome reminders of mortality, at times brutally sudden and close. The city librarian succumbed quickly to successive paralytic strokes.[47] A month later, longtime champion of Riverside beautification Ethan Allen Chase died. Within weeks Miller's own brother-in-law G. O. Newman, a year younger than Miller, collapsed and died as he left his home.[48] A month later, in early January, Mayor L. V. W. Brown died in a grisly auto accident.[49] Just two months later, Miller's own younger brother, Ed, died in Riverside after two years of infirmity.[50] These all were people of Miller's world—family, friends, and lifetime associates. Their passing left him and their loved ones bereft and grieving.

Making good on his intentions to moderate his pace, he and Marion drove again to Laguna as soon as winter guests began to check out in May, staying a full week beside the sea.[51] A few months later, he and Marion, with another couple, sailed for Hawaii, where their plans and the hospitality of friends would fill six relaxing weeks.[52]

23

Go on a Long Sea Voyage

Miller's first Hawaiian vacation paid large dividends. Friends seeing him even several months later told him and each other how well he looked.[1] More than just looking well, he felt better and planned to stay that way. He'd said so earlier: he emphatically did not want to quit his busy pace. He'd take the Hawaiian respite, wanting good health—getting well,[2] not beginning a life in retirement.

At home again, Miller juggled continuing interests: Armistice Day (which would flee indoors from stormy weather), the community hospital, and the twin passions—city beautiful and the civic center. The latter spread wide, including a city hall, locating and defining a memorial auditorium, moving the YMCA off his hotel block to a new site, and supporting a YWCA. Energetic public opinion now gave this cluster of interests fresh support so that people now asked questions: what specifically was planned, and how would they be asked for support—with donations or would there be increased taxes?

Well aware of this freshening interest in the prosperous times of 1925, Miller seized an opportunity for one of his favorite themes, the city beautiful. He staged a press conference on the roof of the Cloister Wing. There he protested the removal of thirty-year-old trees near property owned by his wife Marion's family and beside the extensive citrus orchards that reached for miles, all the way to and around Arlington to the west. He blustered into improbability, threatening to close the inn when Riverside had cut down its bounty of trees.

He knew better. There was no reckless tree felling. Infested, diseased, and overgrown trees were being cut and biological controls sought, something as a Chamber of Commerce director he'd heard talked about.[3] His querulous rooftop performance ignored the facts and the larger frame. That wider focus, so adroitly avoided, rose from differing visions for the kind of town Riverside should be. Even as he held forth, the Chamber of Commerce and the realty board were responding, not only to pests gnawing into the town's principal economy, but also by courting industries—makers of clay products, small-parts manufacturing, and a bottling company.[4] Everyone knew that industries would compete with home builders and citrus growers for building sites and skyline. In addition, a continued increase of blue-overall workers would alter the demographic balance that had attracted earlier residents.

Miller never wanted an industrial town or a worker component in the local economy. What he had in mind, as he phrased it later, was "a community that depends upon the luxuries, oranges and tourists for the major part of its existence." His civic center would provide the institutional and architectural core. Even so, he wondered whether these "luxuries" could support the community he favored. But he persisted in his belief that it could be made to pay,[5] reassured, no doubt, of postwar prosperity in an already solid community.[6]

Even so, unplanned development could be threatening as he thought about the *firstness* Riverside had achieved—a gold medal first for citrus ahead of Florida, "the first polo team, the first double drive in Magnolia Avenue, the first Christian Science Church, the first Junior College building, the first Citrus Experimental Station, the first Mission hotel, the first library school, the first Sunrise service on the American continent..."[7] None of these suggested "industries." For Miller, Riverside's manifest destiny was as a residential and educational center, and he said so to the end of his life, even adding this view to a codicil to his will.

Miller found an alluring fictional description of his kind of town when he read *Walled Towns* by Ralph Cram, a nationally distinguished architect. "Salvation is to be found," Cram wrote, "in the restoration of all things of small human units, the testing of all things by value not bulk and the acceptance once more of the philosophy of sacramentalism."[8] Cram meant devotion to the spirit of community. Crafting material, not industrial production, conferred grace. Necessary spiritual benefit to individuals and society came from living within an ideal social organization, something closer to medieval times than to contemporary America. Cram's beguilingly attractive utopia took Miller's mind. He yearned for something ideal for Riverside and believed that such might be within reach. The introspective Miller seemed to have found in Cram's book a vision of what might be and a reminder of his lonely hopes, his adult dream deferred.[9] He'd not turn the clock back but move into a future avoiding the blight and blemishes that seemed to go with urban growth.

As the community-hospital board shouldered fund raising, Miller stirred interest into activity on the soldiers' memorial. He offered a building site. The city council argued about cost—$150,000. Inactivity followed. Moreover, Miller's stipulations weren't popular: he wanted an "educational" building that included museum space, an art gallery, and programs to promote peace. Others had their own ideas. Veterans, for their part, just wanted their own clubhouse. Some voters were cool to the educational inclusions. Others pointed to the gallery spaces already serving the town. Voters had twice rejected such proposals as Miller's—in 1920 and 1921. In this instance Miller read his opposition correctly, "convinced," he wrote, "that it is going to be impossible to work out any national [sic] educational memorial." Even his offer of paying half the bill, he said, "cut no ice" with the opposition. Friends with their ears even closer to the ground agreed.[10] Two months of council passivity became two years.

Not only that, but the public interest veered to having a new town hall. Miller's adaptable mind thought he might use the moment to move his own ideas ahead. Accordingly, he offered inducements of property as building sites, adding a sweetening of $5,000 toward the YWCA and an American Legion building if the city-hall bond issue passed. This did cut some ice: the package was thought to be worth $45,000. The editor of the *Press*, after publicly washing his hands of loyalty to Miller, gave impetus to the proposal, commending Miller's offer as a rare opportunity for the voters to do something they ought to do anyway. Support the bond issue, he wrote, and "anchor this $45,000 gift that will virtually guarantee the success of two other valuable city improvements."[11]

If he chose to do it, Miller could stand at his own front door at Orange and Seventh Streets and visualize the new city hall across the street, a solid addition to his civic-center hopes. And that's just what came about. For six months, he and S. C. Evans each carried water on both shoulders to bring success to the project. Voters approved it. Construction began in January 1924 on the corner of Seventh and Orange, across from the Mission Inn, just as Miller had imagined. The compact structure with its handsome Spanish entrance pleased everyone. Miller's praise for the architecture and its harmonious fit with nearby buildings reflected his sense of progress with the civic center.[12]

Mayor Evans moved into his new office. His own agenda for the next six months offered nothing as relaxing as the

Asian vacation the Millers had planned. The mayor needed more successful bond issues in November to finance city water and fire services and the much-delayed and variously defined memorial auditorium. Voters, he thought, might readily give a high priority to their water and fire services, even with tax increases. But the memorial auditorium was doubtful. Whatever its prestige and attraction for conventions, it needed a lure to draw voter approval. Evans wanted to announce his bond proposals in June.

By June the Millers would be traveling, taking the recommended long sea voyage that would further assure the Master of the Inn's health.[13] They would be away about six months, taking the holiday Miller felt he had coming to him.[14] He and Marion would visit Hawaii on the eve of the initial meetings of the Institute of Pacific Affairs in June. From there, details of travel were in the care of the Japanese American Association in Japan.[15] One result of the visit would be strengthened bonds between Miller and Japan, something already physically visible at the Mission Inn and something that would be heard from Miller for the rest of his life, even in increasingly difficult times. His pace might become more sedate, but his intensity in this widely unpopular cause of improving relations between the United States and Japan would lose nothing of its urgency.

Mayor Evans remembered that the strategic card from the successful city-hall campaign included Miller's conditional 1923 commitment of sites and money for the auditorium, the YMCA, and the YWCA if a city-hall bond issue passed. Evans sat daily in the evidence of the successful city-hall vote. He knew Miller's plans, heard about his resignations from one thing after another, and was aware of the planned six-month absence and his capacity for changes of mind. Evans also knew that the memorial auditorium had captured Miller's heart and that although water and fire stood lower in Miller's priorities, he could not oppose them. Could Evans play his card so that a deal with Miller on convergent interests might move all three items to approval at the polls? He seemed to think so.

He met with Miller to explore common interests. Miller stipulated that the auditorium must cost at least $200,000 and that building must begin "within a year," presumably a year after the passage of the bond measure. The auditorium was to have a courtyard and fountain on Lemon Street and architecture emphasizing "National and California patriotism and the ideal of world-wide peace." Evans committed to presenting the $200,000 bond issue for water, fire, and the auditorium to the voters "if and only if" Miller would deed land to the city with clear title and all structures removed, forswear withdrawal from the agreement or adding encumbrances, and authorize not only Evans but also the title company to announce all this. Miller felt no coercion and promptly filed all the necessary papers with the Riverside Title Company.[16] Evans prudently suggested they put their agreements in writing. Miller agreed. Their signatures on May 21, 1925, bound them both personally. Miller later explained why he signed so readily: at the time of his agreement with Evans, he said, he fully expected that voters would again utterly reject any bond proposal tied to an auditorium.[17] Evans and Miller were betting against each other.

One day after Evans and Miller signed, the town's heavy lifters added their own hedges on both of them to assure perpetual use of the memorial auditorium for the intended purposes and considerations of veteran interests. They then promptly leaked all the details to the *Daily Press*.[18]

❧

Miller's well-laid Asian travel plans included $75,000 in letters of credit to buy materials and furnishings for a "Japanese temple" and tearoom at the inn—something he'd neglected, he said, even though he had a long interest in things Japanese.[19]

He had written ahead, also, to two former Chinese cooks at the inn, sharing with them his wish to meet in good fellowship while he visited either Shanghai or Hong Kong. Political unrest prohibited these meetings of old friends.[20]

Among the flood of letters he wrote on the eve of departure, Miller described his health in several ways. In one letter he said, "everything I do seems to tire me." In another he said, "I am going away from Riverside in a rather depressed or disturbed condition." He called it "nervousness" in the context of naming difficulties with his self-composure and ability to throw off worry. He mentioned "a bump of egotism." Even his own thinking, he said, became unclear to him on occasions, but his oft-repeated resolve included turning over a new leaf, so he could "quit worrying about so many outside things."[21] None of this offers us the kind of diagnostic clarity we might want or gives the "egotism" label credibility as the underlying cause for his fatigue, depression, anxiety, and unstable emotions. But in the absence of organic causes, all of these symptoms might benefit from rest and relaxation with his loved wife and sister in Asia, a place that had such an attraction for him.

The traveling group left Riverside late in May: Frank and Marion; Marion's sister-in-law and brother, Mr. and Mrs. John Standish Clark; and Alice Richardson. In Hawaii Miller's name did not appear among the delegates to the Institute of Pacific Affairs, even though any one of his friends who were delegates could have nominated him for immediate acceptance as a guest. He had opportunity, however, to enjoy time on the beach and swim while in Honolulu[22] and, during the two weeks of their stay, to meet and talk with notable institute delegates, including Ray Lyman Wilbur, president of Stanford University; Frank C. Atherton, Hawaiian industrialist and the institute's keynote speaker; and William G. Hall, director of the Honolulu YMCA.

At the inn, the guest register bulged with crowds of convention visitors, day-trippers, and, on one weekend, some twelve hundred guests passing through. The roster of weddings continued steadily throughout June and July in the Music Room, in the tiny but luxurious Saint Cecilia Chapel, beside the organ, in front of the memorial windows, and, weather permitting, on Mount Rubidoux, with the receptions at the inn.[23] Allis managed operations. DeWitt packed his own bags and headed east for three months.[24] All summer long the bond-issue proponents hustled for approval at the polls. Their ambition beggared anything seen in Riverside before, and it even went beyond the Miller and Evans pact: $200,000 for the auditorium, $300,000 for city water, and an "undisclosed amount" for fire prevention and the operation of the department.[25] Even opponents must have been surprised at the vote that swept all to victory by wide margins. Such triumphs, said the supporters, were certain signs of Riverside's Progressive qualities.[26] No one who wrote to the Millers shared the surprising news.

The Millers arrived in Yokohama, met there with considerable ceremony by an official delegation and taken almost immediately to a resort hotel in Hakoni for a week.[27] The local America-Japan Society, a cultural relations association, arranged details of their extensive itineraries.[28] This included a speaking appointment for Miller at a society luncheon where Prince Tokogawa, the society patron, praised Miller's peace interests, his stature in Riverside, and the depth of his commitment to amity between their countries. For his response, Miller jumped boldly into his views of American foreign policy related to the League of Nations and the Japanese Exclusion Act of 1924. He then called up his own version of an "America First" ideology, advising *firstness* in things of the spirit—ideals, principles, and character. All of them, he said, if applied, led "into the New Jerusalem where wars shall be no more." Just what his translator made of the sensitive political content, the concepts, and the Biblical allusions for his Japanese-speaking listeners was not recorded, but *The Japan Advertiser*, an English language newspaper, carried its own report.[29]

Another Tokyo paper, *The Japan Times and Mail*, interviewed Miller about his hotel and hotels in general, reporting his "smilingly impatient" comments. He disliked noise in the halls, shady interiors, and standardized appearance. His hotel, he said, came about as an idea growing over two generations, not as a sudden inspiration by any one person. He thought the size of Riverside and its location in a rather monotonous orange-grove section of the state didn't give him the best environment for the inn. He had compensated, however, by making the inn a pleasure to manage and a joy to come back to, offering as it did "luxurious comfort, restfulness and austerity." Hotels, like individuals, were most often remembered, he thought, if they had striking characteristics.[30]

Frank and Marion traveled widely in Japan, went to Hong Kong and Shanghai for several weeks in September, and then went on to the Philippine Islands. Alice Richardson went her own way after Japan.[31] Exactly where the couple went, what they saw, and what their impressions were are lost now, if ever recorded. What they bought of Asian items to create an Asian-like space at home followed them to Riverside many months later in a miscellany of crates and boxes.[32] They sailed home via Vancouver, British Columbia, to Riverside, an arrival Miller declared (as he so often did) to be "the best part of going away."

His greatest surprise upon arrival was hearing that the bond issue had passed. "I had taken it for granted," he said, "that they would be defeated, as I had not heard to the contrary."[33] His Los Angeles friend General M. H. Sherman liked the voting outcome a great deal: Miller had "captured the 'works,'" he said. "Even Mr. [S. C.] Evans, who sometimes did not do just as he should, seems to be working in harmony with you for the good of Riverside."[34]

Miller's friends had another surprise for him, a stone tower and bridge built on Mount Rubidoux to honor his community service. This footbridge of rough granite arched some twenty feet over the road up the mountain, serving a seldom used path that crossed the road. A bulky, slightly Moorish minaret tower, housing a bell and topped by a tiny cross, stood at the bridge's uphill end.[35]

Whatever his resolves to go at a slower pace, Miller had no time for inactivity between arrival home and the bridge-and-tower dedication set for December 1925.

24

The Things We Believe In

In December Marion and Frank joined a large crowd of well-wishers for the mountainside dedication of the tower and bridge. The buffeting cold wind was only part of Miller's discomfort. His emotions swirled among feelings of elation at the personal honor, temptations to hubris, and, as a man often misunderstood in his community, surprise at the terse accuracy of the words on the plaque:

> Peace with justice for all men.
> Anno Domini 1925.
> This bridge is built by
> Neighbors and friends of
> Frank Augustus Miller
> In recognition of his
> Constant labor in the
> Promotion of civic beauty
> Community righteousness
> And world peace.

Everyone strained to listen through gusty interruptions as the voluble John Steven McGroarty and the profound David

Starr Jordan each held forth on Miller's own topics—Christian obligations to neighborliness and international peace. His emotions allowed him only the briefest response: "We love this bridge and peace monument," he said. "It is a wonderful and beautiful thing. It symbolizes the things we believe in. I am grateful from the bottom of my heart." He added brief thanks to the Japanese men whose friendship honored him with their unsolicited plantings below the bridge, the grace of friendship.[1]

Miller spent the next few days in bed, worried that something serious ailed him, aware that he wanted to preserve the fragile benefits of the long ocean voyages. He lightheartedly quipped to visitors about his headaches and a swelled head and later commented that the recognition might make him lose his equilibrium.[2] Privately he unburdened himself with tears when he spoke of the honor he saw in the bridge and tower, the spontaneous gifts of the Japanese garden, and the music provided by the José Arias group, their personal tribute so generously offered on Mount Rubidoux. His illness persisted, slowly ebbing by mid-January.[3]

Publicly Miller linked the tower and bridge to his wish for Japanese-American amity, convinced that with a just understanding of the Japanese, the people of the United States would revise their impressions of Nippon as warlike. In his condemnation of the Japanese Exclusion Act of 1924, he described it as an affront by the United States to Japanese pride and justice, something that overlooked Japanese peacefulness.[4] He aptly named the national symbols of Great Britain, the United States, and Japan: "They are respectively the Lion, the Eagle, and the Sun. Draw your own conclusions." This conviction never left him; his passion for better United States–Japan relations fluctuated little. Even in small gestures, such as dressing in Japanese robes for photographs, he expressed his beliefs. Whether or not he knew the social significance the Japanese assigned to dress or how they regarded foreigners adopting their garments, costume provided his theatrical affirmation of respect through adopted identity.

In 1926 he combined hospitality and a direct statement of these values at a dinner for two hundred Japanese American parents and children. They met to view displays of the arts and artifacts brought from their ancestral home. In addition Miller had a Japanese tea garden built, courteously complimented as "a very good attempt" by visiting Japanese architect Henry Yamaguchi, whom he knew from his Asian travels. Miller hastened to assure Yamaguchi that the garden and a display room called Fuji Kan served only for the time being and for only some of his Asian art, not as a substitute for "the big building that I am preparing to build."[5] Details of that "big building," with its Asian-like architecture, would emerge as Miller and local architect G. Stanley Wilson talked and sketched in a new and close partnership of client and architect.

Travel in Asia and especially in Japan had given new urgency and sharper focus to the peace interests Miller had cultivated for years. On one occasion he claimed that his whole Asian visit was aimed at East-West relations,[6] an emphasis that overlooked the sheer physical necessity of recuperative rest he faced for several years previously. After that visit, his peace-related correspondence expanded to include letters to and from a wide national range of persons and organizations—the Rockefeller Foundation, the World Alliance for International Friendship Through the Churches, and the Institute of International Relations of Los Angeles, as well as Jewish and Catholic organizations committed to peace.[7] He had become known nationally, and certainly in Japan, as a peace advocate with an unwavering focus on Japan.

The narrowing of his peace interests reflected the Asian visit and also other shared experiences and opinions. He had loyally supported the local Harada family in their court case. Wilson Crewdson, an early and annual visitor, collector of Japanese wood-block prints, and author of *Japan Our Ally*,[8] talked knowledgeably during visits. David Starr Jordan of Stanford University, who had also spent time in Japan, exerted continuing influence.

Miller shared with many a belief that the movies influenced morals and behavior, a concern that placed the medium on social-reform agendas.[9] Full of optimism for stronger Japanese-American relations in 1925, Miller, on impulse, wrote to Cecil B. De Mille, the movie mogul, urging production of a film to restore the old friendship between Japan and the United States, something that might stem the "Red radicalism" threatening Asia. De Mille replied courteously, but no film was forthcoming.[10] Miller also wrote to John D. Rockefeller in appreciation for Rockefeller's underwriting much of the cost of the Hawaii meetings of the Institute for Pacific Relations in 1925. He implored him to use his considerable ability to turn events toward a more amicable United States–Japan relationship, something neither politicians nor missionaries could do, Miller believed.[11]

Miller's influence and shared convictions created a local organization, the Riverside Peace Committee of Fifty. He took charge of its community relations; DeWitt and Allis Hutchings joined as founding members. In his wish to build support and give a cohesive statement to the committee, Miller suggested the "America First" creed from Woodrow Wilson's presidential campaign of 1915. It was so broad, he said, that everyone could work within its principles. Those who took the time to read the statement saw its emphatically isolationist notion of strict neutrality.[12] Regardless, *Tidings*, the Southern California Roman Catholic weekly, embraced Miller's beliefs, noted his warm patriotism, and cleared him of any suggestion of propaganda or of being willing to sacrifice the national honor. For him, the magazine reassured its readers, peace began between persons within a community founded on toleration and understanding. Miller hoped, readers were told, that eventually there might be peace among the nations through the spread of the gospel of goodwill among men.[13]

Another who shared that view was Rufus von KleinSmid of the University of Southern California. Shortly after his appointment to the presidency in 1921,[14] he joined his interests in international relations with Miller's periodic meetings, a continuation of which survives in Riverside after over ninety years. Their planning throughout 1926 led to the first of continuing annual four- or five-day meetings at the Mission Inn, beginning in December of that year. Selected participants heard lectures and participated in round-table discussions on assigned topics. Evening sessions included invited local residents and guests at the hotel. Such informed discussion among the knowledgeable and influential and the absence of activism or robust calls to action fit easily into Miller's definition for the town cultural life and served KleinSmid's ambitions for serious consideration of international issues.[15]

For a man limiting his activity, Miller carried an impressive, self-selected portfolio. In addition to his continuing activities in promoting peace, he found ways to promote civic beauty, getting his version of the much-delayed Giralda Tower sketched on paper for the first time that year. Another project was completed, the equally sluggish development of a pocket park between the railroad tracks at the depots—a welcome removal of trackside windblown trash, discarded wooden ties, old iron, and a shack or two. Miller also reminded the public of the planning afoot to enlarge the Spanish Wing at the hotel, particularly in the Gallery.[16]

The addition of the memorial auditorium that had been assured by C. S. Evans's successful bond issue would provide another unit in the expanding civic center. Miller willingly lent every encouragement to the planners while keeping his oar of influence in the wider waters of public discussion. He adjusted his spiel to his audience. With voters he praised their love for Riverside; with civic leaders and veterans, he honored the men who went to fight in the World War; for the culturally sensitive, he projected cultural enrichment through art and music at the auditorium;[17] and to the Santa Fe Railroad administration, he noted the supportive influence of the local Santa Fe agent.[18] He pictured the finished auditorium as an endorsement of moral courage and the spiritual insight so necessary to a healthy community.[19] To others he endorsed the moral influence of architecture in school architecture.[20] He wooed Methodists by backing his imperatives with a gift to their building fund: "Beauty and genuineness in permanent construction better reflects Christ's philosophy," he told them, leaving them to make the connection he saw.[21] At least in the years since Benton had introduced him to the mission style, Miller had come to believe that buildings molded the arts and culture, themselves potent in forming ethical values and expressing civic priorities. Buildings could become, in fact, civic righteousness expressed in concrete.

He applied these same values more widely to the town, as his advice about the auditorium and elsewhere revealed. His primary locale of advocacy, however, lay at and close to the Mission Inn, and in this perspective we might understand the continual building at the inn as his own quest for metaphysical and physical value. At the inn he saw the dynamic core of his influence and achievement, more so than his persistence in city-wide planning, suburban development, or domestic architecture. Even his opposition to industries could flex to accommodate them if they were well off at a distance and preferably downwind, as in the case of the Portland cement plant.[22] Buildings served more than a merely utilitarian purpose. He regarded architecture as a vehicle of virtue.

୨୦

After the illnesses in the early weeks of 1926, Miller successfully preserved his stamina, in part by avoiding boards and committees, refusing several new appointments and resigning from others.²³ Even his political activity shrank. "I am taking no active part in political work" he wrote in July 1926, thus excusing himself from advising and cajoling. Yet as the year-end approached, his old political know-how easily netted him enough local supporters to make him a member of the Republican County Central Committee.²⁴ There are resignations, and then there are resignations.

Miller rejoined the hospital board, valued there for his acquaintance with major figures in American hospitals and his knowledge of corporate organization gained from his visits around the country. He focused on future financial viability;²⁵ he probably wanted to keep alive his church-hospital notions. He stayed well clear of contentious administrative matters and, interestingly, took up the cause of nurse education. He and Board Chairman Sellack brought to Riverside a national expert on nursing, Carolyn E. Gray, recently chairman of the Education Committee of the National League of Nurses. Miller wanted her advice on a management plan to link the School of Nursing at the junior college with the hospital. In mid-May 1926, Gray spent several days in Riverside. Her point of view in a detailed report about administrative options to safeguard the financial and professional integrity of both the hospital and school largely influenced the direction of both. "A community hospital is such a new development in our democracy," Gray wrote, "that there is little or no precedent to guide such a pioneering as you are attempting": a nonprofit hospital, governed by a nonprofessional board, supported by a volunteer association of member donors, and affiliated with the junior college.²⁶

For Miller, being cast in the role of pioneer flattered rather than deterred his "first boy" energies. He had walked new paths before—in his grocery store, in the architecture and decoration of his hotel, in his second marriage, and in his positive attitude toward Japan. Taking a road less traveled did not deter him often, especially when prestigious professional expertise such as Gray's saw a way ahead.

∽

In the first planning meeting for the annual international relations conferences with KleinSmid, Miller named Japan as the central focus for the sessions and named the strategy he favored. The international future, he said, lay with Japan and the United States. "The only way we can unite in this effort," he continued, "is to apply the Christ philosophy. It is only in that spirit we can unite and accomplish what is necessary."[27] Miller was blending his concern for world peace with his companion value, civic righteousness. As for its place in the annual institute, or even the centrality of Japanese–United States relations, that was up to KleinSmid, who appears to have set the agendas, named the annual chairmen, and invited almost all participants. He scheduled nothing related to a Christ philosophy; however, he understood it and included merely a lonely pair of Christian missionary topics.[28]

What are we to understand of Miller's "Christ philosophy"? He could speak almost cryptically, I believe, because at the time what he meant was readily recognized, even in the increasingly secular world of the 1920s. His compressed formula included virtue as an individual and an institutional trait, belief in peace among nations a result of the New Testament gospel of good will among men, and communities committed to toleration and understanding.[29] A prayer shared by Miller and Marion, carried typewritten in his wallet, spoke the same idiom in childlike simplicity: "Teach us to live and work for Jesus sake." His daily devotions echoed the same theme, comprising one or two Bible verses, a short rhyme, and an equally short homily, all from *Daily Strength for Daily Needs*.[30] Miller's quest for civic righteousness extended to a formal memorandum, his plan for permanent peace among national governments through appointment of national ministers of peace.[31] Whatever its formality, it was at base the same theme.

Miller's philosophy shared much with the papal encyclical of 1922, "On the Peace of Christ in His Kingdom." An institutional rather than personal statement of the Christ philosophy, it's true. He and Marion attended a reading of the encyclical in the local Saint Francis de Sales Church, missing their habitual attendance at the Congregational Church watch-night service at year-end in 1926 to do so.[32] In the encyclical, Miller heard the authoritative ideas on which his hopes rested: the necessity of religious values as the basis of social and political life and the Christianizing of all aspects of increasingly secular societies.

The "Jesus way" he heard in the encyclical and the values it espoused had reached Riverside much earlier in popular religious books, swelled by Charles M. Sheldon's 1897 best seller, *In His Steps: What Would Jesus Do?* The book ran in serial in the Riverside papers. Sheldon's novel made the title question a rule of conduct and described the sometimes highly disruptive effects as several of the novel's characters attempted to act out what they thought Jesus's actions might have been in their urban circumstances. Miller also strongly approved of Walter Russell Bowie's widely popular book *The Inescapable Christ*,[33] impressed enough from his reading in 1927 to write directly to the author for eighty-three copies, at a discount, for distribution to schools and public libraries.[34] Bowie preached an almost mystical cultivation of the presence of Christ in the believer's life as the inner guide to private and public behavior. Miller appears to have distilled his phrase "Christ philosophy" from Sheldon's provocative novel and Bowie's devotional writing, foundations for daily living (though hardly international affairs).

Equally influential, the opinions elegantly written by David Starr Jordan in his *Religion of a Sensible American*, spoke Miller's beliefs: "To believe [in the religion of Jesus] is to have faith in the universe, in man, and in all the forces inside and outside ourselves which shall make for righteousness...We may strive then toward a religion which shall not be collective alone, but personal; not the religion of a time or a state, but of man; not one of creed or of ceremony nor of emotion, nor primarily of the intellect, but a religion of faith and cheer, of love and action, of trust in the realities of nature and in the reality of the spirit, a faith that the universe is in the hands of perfect wisdom and that in our way we may be at one with it, striving toward abounding life and helping our brother organisms as we meet them to struggle toward all good things."[35]

These views threw Miller on his own resources of conscience and motivation, a subjective delight to his independence perhaps, whatever the burden of decision making that followed. He had early declared himself an independent spirit, willing to fight his own battles, seeing himself as a rare kind of personality. He was convinced that success would follow application of his philosophy: other tactics would fail. Politicians, Miller thought, defeated their own purposes through their "political clap-trap business."[36] Clergy, especially Protestant clergy, compromised themselves in allowing the eagle to perch prominently on the pulpit. Christian missions and missionaries elicited no greater confidence in their work in non-Christian countries.[37] The efforts of international bodies seemed to have withered, meshed in bureaucracy and nationalism. He put no stock in corporate and associational means to social improvement. However sketchy in details and whatever the skepticism he met, Miller throughout his life forged a personal, spiritual dynamic to organize his world. He relied little on existing institutional forms, especially in religion. "When it comes to denominations I don't know what I am or what I believe," he was remembered as saying. "But there isn't any other light than the Prince of Peace."[38] Observing the application of his personal persuasion led to the words on the bridge and tower: "Promotion of civic beauty, community righteousness and world peace."

25

Peace Plans and Straws in the Wind

In 1926 at his November Armistice observance on Mount Rubidoux, Miller wanted to deliver a strong teaching statement urging international peace and brotherhood.[1] What better way to do so than by having wartime enemies join hands in reconciliation? He would have representatives of two ancient combatants, France and Germany, clasp hands in amity amid billowing national flags, the music of national anthems, and a tableau symbolizing peace. Moreover, Germany had been admitted to the League of Nations, an even wider gesture of reconciliation. The message would be clear and effective, or so Miller believed. He misjudged.

Tension arose almost as planning began. DeWitt Hutchings knew better than the overeager Miller that local feelings would balk at any inclusion of Germany. In his reluctance, he labeled Germany's national anthem *nux vomica* (a powerful emetic), repulsive to veterans and civilians alike. Memories of World War I atrocities stayed too fresh,[2] and the carefully cultivated wartime propaganda remained effective. Locally the League of Nations had few supporters, Germany even fewer. But Miller would not be swayed. He forged ahead, insensitive or ignorant of local feelings, determined to educate the groundlings, saying as much in a letter to Harry Chandler of the *Los Angeles Times*.[3] It was wishful thinking.

Local veterans wanted none of it, needing all of Hutchings's persuasive powers to convince them even to appear.[4] Then the invited national representatives began a ballet of reluctance. Eventually a language professor from Redlands University carried the burden for France, and a member of the German Club of Los Angeles represented the Fatherland.[5] With the scales of protocol in this delicate balance, the two men shook hands on the mountain after each made clear his national differences, polar from the other.[6] National anthems followed: for France, its impassioned calls to the colors; for Germany, its blunt statement of dominance. Then came a saccharine allegory of peace in which Prince of Peace consoled Bereaved Mother as Children of the Nations were gathered to the cross and blessed, and all sang "Abide With Me."[7] Even at that time that hymn was an emotional set piece for funerals. Reports of the whole event were guarded.

Whether or not chastened by these 1926 faux pas, Miller gave Hutchings a larger role in guiding the next year's Armistice program. But even then, in spite of advertising, the release of doves, and the skirl of a bagpipe band,[8] attendance shrank noticeably, as it did again the next year. The causes of decline probably lay outside the 1926 assault on local loyalties. Miller's Armistice observances went beyond fife-and-drum patriotism to the language of internationalism, challenging assumptions and narrow loyalties and urging acceptance of national friendships with strong ethical imperatives. Popular response often sets what becomes the official agenda. To avoid competition with the city events, Miller's committee moved their programs to the Sundays nearest November 11,[9] a tidy blending of symbolic religion and patriotism, an exemplar of civic religion. The mountaintop ceremony claimed no enduring place in the public mind and disappeared immediately after Miller's death in 1935.

Peace Plans and Straws in the Wind

☙

The collaborative annual Institute of International Relations proved more durable.[10] The self-promotional KleinSmid named himself chancellor, firmly in charge, choosing an annual chairman and inviting notables from across the nation. Fifty-five participants came to the first conclave in December 1926; three times that number came in the years following. Evening lectures, the only part open to the public, met in the Music Room,[11] to which Miller invited local school administrators, teachers, and high-school students. The collaboration of the president of the University of Southern California and Master of the Inn seemed perfect: Miller habitually looked to others to carry his initiatives toward completion, always the generous host; KleinSmid thrived on being the titular and visible leader of impressive attendees.[12]

What did those attending the institute see as the seventy-year-old Frank A. Miller met them or sat with them in round-table discussions and in casual settings? His greetings were always warm and accepting, his smiles ready and genial, his initiative in conversation prompt, sometimes surprising.[13] They saw a man of average height, already noticeably corpulent. He dressed in dark, three-piece suits of conservative cut, the jacket, often unbuttoned, a little longer and looser than the current shorter, trimmer styles. A light-colored jacket signaled his leisure hours. His preference in shirts favored fashions of a decade earlier, with detachable, severely starched stand-up collars and a loosely knotted "poet's" cravat, usually in a dark color. His lapel held the distinctive emblem of the Loyal Legion, commemorative for him of his father's Civil War service. Perhaps he carried his increasingly necessary knobby walking cane. His abundant, bushy hair, well streaked with white, rose brushed back, unparted and unrestrained, something distinctive among his peers who wore their hair short, parted, and often fashionably controlled with lightly perfumed pomades or oils. From behind rimless glasses his deep-set eyes looked out, sometimes with interest, sometimes questioning, but always benign. The shallow lines and wrinkles on his oval face told little of intermittent illnesses or of his inner feelings.

Miller reflected on his motivations after the institute in 1926. He placed himself as sharing in stellar company and years later said to his daughter, Allis, with his usual candor, "There is nothing that your father ever has done in Riverside for which others do not deserve more credit than he,"[14] a generous tribute appropriate to his collaboration with KleinSmid. There were others: he adopted David Starr Jordan's strategy of educating toward peace; he used convening as did Albert Case Smiley of the Mohonk Mountain House. Miller weighed his own role. "All I can do is to provide the place for the meeting," he said, "and entertain all those that take part in it as my personal guests."[15] He was a man of independent disposition in many things, yearning for achievement yet sensing his dependence on others. The praise he received might have stirred honest recognition. "I have been just as weak," he said, "in craving for recognition or appreciation...as any other fellow."[16]

Recognition that many might welcome came early in 1927, a time for distribution of political plums, as his name floated across the country as the next US senator from California.[17] The Riverside paper and the *New York Times* doubted that Miller would leave the Mission Inn, even temporarily. Even so, Miller could savor the widespread publicity and praise, especially his being called the embodiment of the Southern California spirit. He performed, it was said, as "a vigorous 'spieler,'" in a region where "spieling" (giving persuasive, lengthy speeches) was "an old but universal profession."[18] The papers were right; he would not leave the inn or Riverside.

He complained that other unsought approval was a burden. He recognized personal obligation, but he felt loaded down "with the projects of the community they want to put over."[19] Community demands could not help but come his way: he was visible, available, energetic, and possessed imagination and persuasive skills in civic matters. Even though slowing with age and illness, he wanted to know what was afoot and to choose his part in it.

☙

Miller doggedly kept his campaign for including a museum and gallery in the municipal auditorium alive during the seventeen months after the approving popular vote,[20] a delay that merely forecast others to come.[21] Miller complicated life for the supervising architect G. Stanley Wilson by getting him started on plans for a hotel dormitory annex on Sixth Street.[22] Construction there also lagged, complicated by cost overruns, heated disagreements, inactivity, and, at times, confusion all round at the auditorium.

The ribbon cutting on March 14, 1929,[23] at the auditorium did not include Miller. He may have chosen to be elsewhere or taken a place on the sidelines. The architecture and landscaping pleased him well enough, and the location fit his civic center. Perhaps he was unwell or piqued from the ten years of delays between proposal and completion or the neglect of his museum and gallery notions. He had wanted a richer symbolism, something more than rentable space for conventions, high-school graduations, or, as he said, "American Legion prize fights and jazz dancing."[24] Most, however, found pride in the completion of the imposing structure.[25]

Miller's notions on the civic center rested on solid ground. He had seen and learned about the city beautiful in 1893 at the World's Columbia Exposition and in the widely publicized redevelopment of Washington, DC, in 1907. In Riverside Miller assigned his topic to resident artist W. C. Tanner: "The Fine Art of City Planning."[26] He shared the moral perspectives of his friends Jacob Riis of New York and Jane Addams of Hull House in Chicago: city beautification would rid urban centers of unhealthful slums, reduce crime and disease, and encourage more elevated living.

Riverside lacked spreading slums, rampant crime, and slumlords.²⁷ But the city-beautiful movement spoke to other concerns, vital to Riverside, such as aesthetically planned street alignment; traffic control for safety and flow; zoning for residential, commercial, and industrial uses; building construction standards; and equitable distribution of utility services. For Miller, the city beautiful lay within the Mile Square and close to the hotel.²⁸ The purpose was attracting tourists, though he acknowledged that general economic benefit must follow. For some reason, in the thirties he came to believe that Riverside's dependence on citrus and tourists, "luxuries," he called them, made agreement on a formal civic center unlikely.²⁹ He already knew that most businessmen were cool to the city-beautiful movement. Perhaps the influential citrus growers, living among their orchards, felt the same. His fellow hotel and restaurant owners might view the movement as an expensive nonattraction that offered little to short-term guests, day-trippers, weekenders, and couples bent on marrying. In the twenties, Riverside seemed to like the way the town had turned out, just as it was.

Two deaths in 1927 touched Miller closely, grim reminders of mortality. In May the frail Henry E. Huntington died in Philadelphia. Frank and Marion attended the funeral at Huntington's mansion in San Marino, California, where he was buried quietly in a remote part of his estate.

Just when Huntington and Miller first met is uncertain, but their acquaintance strengthened as Huntington influenced politicians in Sacramento and San Bernardino to get the Riverside county division in 1893. He supported Miller's local street-railway ventures and later purchased the whole operation. He financed the New Glenwood in 1902 while Miller mortgaged everything he had as surety on the loans. Miller remembered Huntington as clearheaded, although at times too demanding.[30] Some later recollections described their association as very close, even as Miller's "first great friendship."[31] This appears to be something more than the record allows of this long, strongly supportive business relationship, touched by mild subservience on Miller's part and quite lacking the social and more intimate aspects we usually look for in friendships, great or otherwise.

Only rare hints of informality broke through between "Mr. Huntington" from Miller and only an isolated "Dear Miller" or "My Dear Frank" from Huntington. Miller readily and repeatedly spoke with unstinted admiration for Huntington's assistance. In a touching gesture (that he tried to keep anonymous), Miller sent roses to Huntington's office for many months and then sent gifts of oranges from the tree planted by Theodore Roosevelt and two deer for the park on Huntington's estate.[32] He kept photographs of Henry E. Huntington and Collis P. Huntington hung in his office for more than thirty years. In their last exchange of letters, Miller repeated the thanks he had shared often before: "Please remember how grateful I am for all that you did for me in the early days and continually." He offered the solace of rest in the splendid Alhambra Mirador suite high above the Cloister Wing. Huntington accepted, writing that he'd come: "When I feel it is possible, not for the Spanish room but to be with you a while," warm courtesies between two aging entrepreneurs.[33]

Later that year, on a quiet Saturday afternoon in mid-September, architect Arthur B. Benton, sixty-nine, died at his home in Los Angeles's Echo Park.[34] He had been confined to his bed much of the year, unable to give attention to Riverside's lagging memorial auditorium or the affairs of his office. For almost forty years, he had been among the leaders in developing the regional style known as mission and active in restoration of the originals, Mission San Juan Capistrano particularly. Later observers would come to identify the first unit of the Mission Inn, the New Glenwood of 1903, as the best expression of the mission style he and others had developed. Since 1894 his

Riverside commissions included the Indian school in Perris, the Church of Christ, Scientist a block away from the Glenwood, the New Glenwood, some private homes, the Cloister addition to the inn, the Peace Tower and Bridge on Mount Rubidoux, parts of the Spanish Wing, and his final project in the city, the memorial auditorium. He and Miller worked well together. Miller's enthusiasms, occasional impatience, and penchant for making alterations seem not to have disrupted their productive relationship—Benton grasping Miller's often vague intentions to give them concrete expression.[35]

DeWitt Hutchings and former mayor Horace Porter each wrote tributes to Benton, mentioning particularly Benton's superior qualities of mind and sentiment, his thoughtful insights into the spirit of the missions, and his winsome personality. Hutchings thought, "No one could be more unselfish, devoted to ideals, generous of his time and unsparing of his energies than was Mr. Benton," who gave more attention to art than to financial gain.[36]

The published eulogies have nothing from Miller—no words of reminiscence, affection, praise, or bereavement, even after their more than thirty years of collaboration. He and Benton were often together, intellectually intimate on matters of design and architecture; in these matters, Benton was closer to Miller than anyone else. The luck of their meeting and their combined skills largely explained much of Miller's success with buildings. Later, as Miller gathered up threads of memory for his biographer in his beach home, itself designed for him by Benton and Marion, the name did not come to his mind, an absence that surprises. Was there envy, even resentment suppressed under a shell of silence, a sense that his visions took on form and substance only on Benton's fertile drafting table, realized better there than Miller himself could? Perhaps genuine grief took him again into stoic silence as with the passing of his parents and Isabella and his younger brother, Ed.

Signs of change in hotel patronage began to appear in the prosperous years of the twenties. Early in the decade, summer and winter tourism surpassed each previous year; these were years of growth in the city's population, property valuation, and bank clearances.[37] But in 1927 Miller's eye for detail caught an unwelcome trend in that thermometer of the hotel economy: the daily room count. By his own analysis, patronage for several months revealed a decline in long-term and short-term guests. Indeed, the house stayed largely vacant most of the time. He wanted Allis or DeWitt, or both, to give their opinions: why did most of the business come only from lunch and dinner, especially with nine tour agencies directing tourists toward the inn?

They had already thought about what pulled people to "this out-of-the-way spot" and how long guests stayed. The whole character of the inn, they said, favored looking, lunching, and leaving. The appeal of noon organ concerts waned after one or two hearings; after dinner at six until eight nothing was offered except bed until the morning. And, they noted, "The place is always kept dark."[38] Apparently the inn had become an object of regard, a place to visit, much like a shrine—not a magnetic center of culture, entertainment, or enveloping hospitality beckoning long stays in peace and rest. The new mobility and a new restlessness had brought new patterns to the tourist crop. Autos dominated the middle classes in work and recreation, and an extensive Red Car interurban railroad service radiated from Los Angeles. A different Southern California had emerged with a desert and mountain holiday culture and increased living and recreation in beach towns.

Allis and DeWitt did not lack for ideas. They suggested later dinners, more light in the Music Room, and leaving the Curio Shop open for thirty minutes after the evening events. They also recommended scheduled entertainment Monday through Thursday evenings. They suggested photographic slide shows, readings, talks on popular topics, and showing movies—a whole new opportunity, they thought.[39] Whether their changes were introduced or not, the decline continued into the new season. Miller labeled 1928 "the first year since the hotel opened [with the exception during the war] that business has not increased from year to year."[40] Surprisingly, even on this slow downgrade the inn continued to show a profit and sustain a credit rating strong enough to support borrowing on the building projects Miller undertook then and into the 1930s.[41]

In 1927 Miller and the Hutchingses could see only straws in the economic wind, coded indicators, their full meaning hidden. If in the prosperous years of the early and midtwenties Miller ever seriously doubted continued prosperity for the city and, more specifically, for the hotel, he failed to write it down. Given the declines, the chosen defense was frugality: deferred maintenance and a reduced staff. Even so, planning what the inn and the town must have to "bring out its best," he continued to say, was "more fun than any other fun."[42]

PART FOUR:
No Currents of Despair

26

Medals, Minarets, and Flying Buttresses

Planning to bring out the best for Riverside and the inn meant action as well as fun for Miller. He knew the wider currents of city planning, and in 1915 his enthusiasm brought a nationally known planning advocate to Riverside. Locals, however, were not even ready to plan, much less act.[1] Years later, in 1926 and 1927, his still-strong advocacy backed Sacramento legislation that at first authorized planning and, the next year, mandated city master plans.[2] Local opinion had changed. Riverside now took the lead in California by appointing its own planning commission and inviting the nationally known planner Charles H. Cheney to visit.[3] Cheney came, consulted, and visited widely then drew up his recommendations.[4] But neither Cheney's recommendations nor Miller's own separate initiative for pergolas along Seventh Street met with local approval. Cheney, a visitor, could be ignored; Miller's poor health robbed him of thrust.

Local businesses and professional people resisted city planning; the pergolas just stirred up protest all along Seventh Street. The newspaper appealed to readers' better natures to dissolve local prejudices and personal differences in a glow of cooperation and harmony. Local prosperity, he said, was the goal.[5] But the majority was content with existing arrangements that protected comfortable property ownership and real-estate covenants based on race and ordinances locating certain industries. Miller lacked his former driving energy. "At present and for some time to come," he wrote in 1930, "my activities along both social and business lines have been curtailed on account of recent illness." And writing to another person on the same day, he wrote, "My health does not permit me to [any] longer take an active part in Community work." Perhaps this was so, but he had infected others with his hopes: Mayor Joseph Long's year-end forecast for the city included reference to a civic center as part of the "Municipal Program." He talked of property acquisitions, an open plaza fronting the existing library, and a museum building based on sketches already in hand from the planning commission.[6] Miller took some comfort from this.

His dwindling community involvement did not shrink his case for amity with Japan, often done through hospitality enacted with theatrical flair such as dressing in a kimono to greet Japanese visitors. He spoke passionately of the United States and Japan as sister nations: "We are still one in our desire for a good life for our nation and for our children. How could we ruin our common life by the madness of war? And [war] about what? In the name not only of humanity but of common sense let's be friends forever."[7] Miller was usually a careful observer and a determined optimist.

He painted Japan as an especially worthy economic ally for the United States. And he offered optimism beyond economics. "The greatest thing of all," he said, "is that there is no nation on earth more likely to remain sympathetic through all the stress that comes at times. The only people who in five or six hundred years have not killed a ruler. A people whose great religion is

Shintoism, the worship of ancestors. A people who, as no other on earth, make so much of the home. A people who are cleanly, industrious and kindly. A people who may be snuffed out or perverted if they do not have the right kind of cooperation." The threats to snuff out Japan, as Miller saw it, came from China and Russia, the first guided by what he called a confused view of life and the other given to barbarity, Communism, and force. Japan in contrast, he said, embraced love as a force.[8]

He must have known of Japan's precipitous rise to international status through military supremacy over Russia and China, so evident to all. I wonder whether a very realistic awareness of Japan's imperialistic goals led Miller to consciously reject all such topics and speak only of peace and friendship.

His was a foreign policy based in free trade and international friendship, even then out of step with the era of "big stick" diplomacy, tariffs, and the emergence of a fiscal-military state. His offbeat view led to his being labeled a Bolshevist, a radical, and a Red, and, of course, to accusations of being unpatriotic.[9]

His Japanese friends at home and in Japan were well aware of their own need for islands of sympathetic advocacy in the United States. They valued the stalwart they had in Frank Miller. But in Riverside the majority did not admire or endorse Miller's love of Japan or his foreign policy. Most measured the range of his influence poorly, surprised in 1928 when the Japanese court announced Miller's inclusion in the emperor's coronation honors. He was to be decorated with the Order of the Rising Sun at the Mission Inn.[10]

On a March evening in 1929, an official delegation of Japanese consular representatives, hotelkeepers, and railroad officials gathered to dine at the inn following the investiture. Before the banquet, in a quiet suite far above the active centers of the hotel, Miller and Marion stood in Japanese costume with the formally dressed official Japanese representatives. All listened to the reading of the emperor's citation and saw Miller receive the inscribed scroll. Presentation of the medal signifying the Order of the Rising Sun completed the investiture.[11] A small banquet in the underground Spanish Refectario followed, with few Riverside guests invited.

At the banquet, Miller had DeWitt Hutchings read his formal acceptance. It began with respectful appreciation to the Japanese consul, the national government, and the new emperor, Hirohito, who had bestowed the honor. "I know of no reason why I should be so honored," Hutchings read from Miller's text, "except that on account of my admiration for Japan I have been trying to express the simple everyday and basic sentiment of friendship and neighborliness to Japanese whenever the occasion offered." Here was Miller's credo on international relations, his motivations, and the directions of his activism. "The world will go forward," he emphasized, "only as we honor distinct and national characteristics, and as we understand that each person and each people contributes of its own special worth to the beautiful painting of the whole."

Miller's text reminded his hearers that Japan had been "most humbly sitting at the feet of the west as student," leading the West to "think of itself as peculiarly constituted to be the teacher, and as possessing exclusively the knowledge worth learning." No so, he thought. The West had much to learn from the Orient if it was going to attain its own highest possibilities. His prepared script ended with an invocation: "Let us each one be humble, respecting and accrediting the thoughts and ways of others; and let us be loving, for without such simple things as friendships and loving thoughts and sympathetic contacts the world falls apart and is a barren place."[12]

The official photograph of the occasion revealed the seventy-two-year-old honoree, appropriately sober faced and weary, though patient as the photographer did his work. Marion, his wife, sits beside him, calm and composed. Both had dressed in kimonos.

Later that same year, local Japanese honored Miller, presenting a medal and honoring his peace endeavors with a large, flowering cherry branch, symbolic of mutual regard.[13] In another ceremony of recognition and in what were called elegant ceremonies, Miller became an *Officier d'Academie* at the hands of the Los Angeles consul general of France. The handsome medal on a purple ribbon affirmed Miller's significant contributions to arts, culture, and international understanding.[14] Just weeks earlier in 1930, at the graduation ceremonies of the University of Southern California, he received an honorary master of arts degree from the hands of President Rufus von KleinSmid. For him that day took on an added glow from being there with his friends US Secretary of the Interior Ray Lyman Wilbur and musician Carrie Jacobs Bond; they were all hooded together.[15]

The editor of Riverside's newspaper soared with optimistic predictions of prosperity for 1930, though cautious about expected rainfall.[16] The rainfall, however, proved to be about the usual amount and stayed that way over the next five years. What the editor did not factor in, however, was the already tumbling collapse of the financial world that began in September and October of 1929. That turbulence had not yet shaken a Riverside still living in the spell of the prosperous twenties. Miller was of the same mind, still experiencing no crippling decline in what had been twenty-five years of hotel prosperity and about six years of continuous construction on Sixth Street.[17] For now he could overlook the skimpy room counts. Miller and his architect G. Stanley Wilson, with his gifted assistant Peter Weber, had ambitious plans that would bring the Sixth Street and Main Street parts of the hotel together. The hotel would then completely enclose the city block, built out to the sidewalk on three sides.

Planning these additions energized his imagination in his years of physical decline. His friend Harry Chandler of the *Los Angeles Times* commented, "No matter whether you are sick or well you are everlastingly on the job."[18] Chandler might have mentioned also Miller's steady optimism. But Miller needed to calculate costs carefully, despite his robust standing with the banks. Looking ahead, he became a board member of the Los Angeles–based California Standard Finance Corporation, investing over $50,000 with it. Almost in the same breath, he discussed his hope of a large building loan from the corporation, a request dryly thought a bit premature by a corporate executive.[19]

A January 1930 headline confirmed what Miller's creative mind had worked at over the preceding two years: "Addition to Mission Inn Outstanding Architecture."[20] The real news was what drew the comment of "outstanding": a complex grand section in steel and poured concrete, unmatched elsewhere in the hotel or the city.

At the time of the announcement, Miller was at his beach house. Most years he and Marion stayed there for a week or two at New Year; this year Miller was bedfast at the Mariona for almost six weeks.[21] His illness isolated him from almost everything, including what would be the most spectacular building project of his career. The unidentified illness not only kept him confined but robbed him of bodily vigor and even of a sense of satisfaction in the little he could do. He confessed an unwelcome observation: "The further I get away from my work the sooner I get well."[22] He wanted to have it both ways—to be well and to immerse himself in his work at the hotel.

At the Mission Inn, Miller's street-level renters felt the pinch of increasingly hard times. Some left; some sent Miller partial monthly rents, begging indulgence.[23] The two railway booking offices closed their hotel service,[24] leaving a forlorn emptiness. In the county and city, unemployment and delinquent tax lists grew. The city reduced its workweek by a half day and wages by 5 percent. All overtime vanished.[25] Unemployed men found work on previously deferred city projects until the money ran out; the Red Cross and church groups distributed food then clothing, reporting six hundred families in need in January

1933.[26] Miller, still preferring private initiative to public welfare, hired at least ninety local unemployed men for construction on the "mammoth block of concrete," as the newspaper called the latest addition.[27] In a more personal gesture, he hired a distressed former vocal soloist, reminiscing with pleasure about her singing. The warmth of his letter, with its inclusion of opinion and commentary far beyond the business at hand, must have reassured her of friendly acceptance in a time of need.[28]

Miller's planning with architects Weber and Wilson produced innovations unlike anything elsewhere in the hotel. These embraced a splendid chapel, itself a breathtaking contrast in size and mood with the gemlike Saint Cecelia Chapel in the Music Room. Great novelty also surrounded a six-floor circular office building with an interior spiral, open stairway and a two-level Oriental court with an adjoining three-level Asian public room called Ho O Kan. Flying buttresses spanned the Main Street sidewalk to match those on Orange Street.[29] These diverse additions joined ingeniously with each other and the existing halls, walls, and doorways. The subtlety delighted visitors as they passed through vaulted corridors, in and out of patios, along gentle changes of floor level, and up or down a dizzyingly narrow spiral stairway. With the completion of the whole five-story addition, with its rich facade of arches, balconied windows, flying buttresses, and arcades, the hotel block became fully enclosed. For the Master of the Mission Inn, if he cared to think of it this way, it completed a personal walled town within which to express the spirit of his hospitality.

The Rotunda office building, with a central spiral stairway open to the sky, had origins in Miller's life and thought, especially related to a painting in the Spanish Art Gallery that depicted somberly garbed priests in a monastic courtyard with a curved staircase.[30] Miller's instruction to Wilson had been clear: "I want this picture embodied in steel and concrete. I want the romance, the charm of that painting put into a modern office building."[31] In saying so, one of his only two recorded comments about paintings, Miller revealed something of his aesthetic. He wished to do more than combine the utilitarian and the symbolic, to go beyond the visually attractive and the useful. He sought to translate what he understood as "romance" and "charm," narrative and intellectual content, from canvas to the finished Rotunda.

The Saint Francis Chapel and its contiguous Galeria beckoned weddings. Many hotels offered wedding suites, but no hotel and, indeed, few churches, boasted such a richly ecclesiastical setting as Miller offered. He had the chapel built around the Tiffany windows and the Rayas family altarpiece—that "gorgeous creation" he had acquired in 1920. Visitors entered the interior through doors of grandiose proportions set in a Spanish Rococo facade. In the dim light only the gilded altarpiece could be seen in the distant apse, rising resplendent to the ceiling. Medieval choir stalls backed by carved, life-sized facial profiles of twenty-six saints lined the empty nave. More than a dozen representations of Saint Francis hung on the walls between and beyond the six magnificent Tiffany windows. All spoke of the enclosed ecclesiastical life. The chapel affirmed Miller's intellectual and sentimental identity with traditions of emphatic religious color, all far more elaborate, embellished, and symbolic than anything in his Protestant roots. However much the chapel diluted his early institutional-religion ties, it affirmed diligence in acquisition, growth in appreciation, and a greater clarity of intention than in any previous addition to the hotel.

Similarly, the Rotunda Internacional rejected cubes of commercial space in name, form, and in its welcoming, curved interior spaces. Miller decorated the curved, open interior with encoded names of Spanish explorers, missions, and their padres in banister ironwork, adding glazed-tile crests and coats of arms from Europe and the Americas. Visitors might easily overlook these decorations, not recognizing them as blended tokens of Miller's selective internationalism, his wholehearted peace advocacy, and his attachment to the spirit of California's Spanish past.

A similar blend of use and symbol expressing intensely held values suffused the Court of the Orient, with its Asian-like architecture and adjoining Ho O Kan. That three-level public Asian-style room housed, among other artifacts, a huge Buddha, carved narrative transoms, a water-spewing dragon, and fanciful lanterns. For all their personal significance to Miller, Ho O Kan, the Court of the Orient, the Rotunda, and the Saint Francis Chapel were rentable spaces, hardheaded responses to the deepening economic depression and the huge debt Miller had taken on, which some said was as much as a million dollars.[32]

Sometime during the construction of the Rotunda Internacional, Miller began long conversations with a biographer. The result was an eighty-page, typewritten manuscript.[33] Just what Miller had in mind and what he and the author shared remain uncertain. All we have is the manuscript that the family decided not to publish, because, they said, it lacked details of Miller's achievements,[34] as indeed it does. Eighty pages could scarcely contain the man.

His own later comments suggest that the family had little enthusiasm for a biography of any kind.[35] So his biographic intentions waited. Whatever his occasional protests of humility, the first boy born in Tomah, Wisconsin, who became the Master of the Mission Inn, saw himself as a fit subject for biography. His only supporters, he said, were his chief doorman and the beloved Marion. She rescued the rejected typewritten manuscript, preserving it among her own memorabilia.[36]

Marion and Frank together watched progress on the construction every time they returned to visit the inn after lengthening stays in Laguna. On all earlier additions he had been constantly on the jobsite, planning as the building went on, making changes as ideas took hold, and freely contradicting plans and specifications already on paper. With this project, however, involvement became difficult; much of the project's thrill fell victim to illness. Marion remembered that "For such a long time he could only think of the things he wanted to do and that ought to be done, but he had not the strength to do or to see that they were done right."[37] But for all that, the completed building convinced writers that it surpassed everything else in interest and that it gathered the spirit of the inn in richer concentration than before, offering a logical conclusion to what they saw as an evolving idea.[38] Miller rested.

27

Advancing Years

Old love glowed briefly in a poignant reunion for the seventy-five-year-old Miller. In 1875 his youthful sweetheart Mattie Weed had married Adolph Schulz in Tomah, moving several years later to Porterville in central California. A widow since 1916, Mattie came to Ontario near Riverside for the 1932 annual gathering of former Tomah residents, who called themselves Tomafornians. Miller knew about the group but had not attended.[1] This year, however, the celebrated cartoonist from Tomah, George H. King, creator of the popular *Gasoline Alley* comic strip, visited Ontario. This lured Miller, who, with Marion and her mother, went there, meeting Mattie—perhaps unexpectedly. He and Marion had seen Adolph and Mattie Schulz many years before in Tomah, and Miller talked often with Marion about Mattie, young love lingering in memory.[2] Ever hospitable, Miller invited all the assembled Tomafornians to Riverside, entertaining them at a splendid tea in the Atrio beside the Saint Francis Chapel after a Music Room organ concert. A watchful newspaper reporter caught the special attentions Miller showed to Mattie Schulz, "a very close friend," and her companion Mamie Runkle Hollister, a girl playmate from Miller's mud-pie age, he said. These were the only visitors named in the newspaper description of the day.³ Did the youthful lovers find opportunity for quiet moments together, reliving conversationally, in mature propriety, their passionate adolescent years? "What a day we had," Marion wrote later, always discrete.⁴

※

During the 1932 Olympics in Los Angeles, a Japanese equestrian forfeited what looked like certain victory by withdrawing during an event to spare his horse. Miller read about it, seeing nobility and drama. He began immediately soliciting funds for commemorative plaques at the Coliseum in Los Angeles and another on Mount Rubidoux.⁵ A state visit by Japanese royalty two years later provided the ideal moment for unveiling the local plaque. The royal couple arrived enveloped in an official entourage and high security. Miller's careful choreography carried the prince and princess from "Banzais" at the Santa Ana River Bridge to the Presidential Lounge in the Mission Inn. There they met Miller, Marion, and the family, all appropriately dressed in Japanese robes and Miller wearing his Order of the Rising Sun. Lunch followed, the cool Saint Francis Atrio offering some relief from the August heat. On Mount Rubidoux, the Japanese prince unveiled the plaque that memorialized the rider, Colonel Kido, "who heard the low voice of mercy, not the loud acclaim of glory." The *Los Angeles Times* noted the Riverside unveiling, commenting, "The little candle of [Miller's] good deed can still shed its rays a long way in this naughty world."⁶

The candlelighter had been in Riverside fifty or more years, ample time for others to take his measure. One astute observer wrote, "I found that Riverside is known because of the Mission Inn but the Mission Inn was known because of Frank Miller and Alice Richardson." Many in the business and cultural community agreed, willingly proclaiming him "First Citizen" when the bridge and tower on Mount Rubidoux were dedicated.⁷

Advancing Years

Miller's age even then—he was sixty-eight in 1925—and his failing health may have given urgency to adding laurels on one so prominent, this man of affairs known so widely. Of course there were others in Riverside who merited and received recognition but none so frequently or over so long a period.

His admirers were diverse. He and the Boy Scouts shared mutual admiration: he chose them to light the way of Easter pilgrims on Mount Rubidoux, and they made him chairman for the day—all praise and no responsibilities—when service clubs boosted scouting.[8] The *Daily Press* took the occasion of his birthday in 1931 to print a large photograph and its compliments.[9] The next year the local Daughters of the American Revolution honored him on Washington's Birthday.[10] Rotary twice declared him one of Riverside's first citizens, distinguished for his persistence in spite of opposition. The Lions Club, not to be left behind, turned hospitality's tables, arranging to be guests of his hotel while, in fact, making their banquet a special honor for a surprised Miller. In 1933, the Chamber of Commerce, in which Miller held office for many years, awarded him its Pioneer's Medal.[11]

Peace advocates across the country knew Miller as one of their own. Fred B. Smith, an internationally traveled speaker, came to talk in Riverside about the "World Outlook for Peace and War." His hearty praise in his 1929 publication, *Must We Have War?*, described Miller as his chosen example of what individuals could do to promote peace.[12]

Others praised his ready sympathy and kindness. Some commented in wonder at his unfailing fountain of fresh ideas; he always had some new agenda for others to pursue. There were persistent critics, but even from them praise could at times run down like a flood, moving Miller deeply and making his public response difficult.[13] On most occasions of praise he spoke a few self-deprecating words, laced always with appreciation for generous friends. With the passing years he became more comfortable with spoken recognition, but applause gave him acute physical discomfort, at times drawing a muttered,

"Quit it, please! I am no opera."[14] Certainly he was not operatically comic or tragic, although his talent for the dramatic impressed many. In a reflective moment he admitted that the gracious words of friends were "the things that keep me out of bed."[15]

Japanese honors continued. In 1933 Japanese naval officers brought him lines from the imperial pen: "Vast spaces of untilled noble sea/Lying serene in the morning sun/Would that all nations of the world might be/ Like you forever peaceful and at one." Among those hearing the lines read on their arrival were Colonel (later General) H. H. Arnold and Major (later General and Chief of Staff) Carl Spatz, both from March Field.[16] They, and the Japanese naval officers dining with them that day, would take on their much less serene assignments in a few disruptive years.

That same year Miller and President Franklin D. Roosevelt both received gifts of large, highly decorated Japanese battledores, ceremonial items from a Japanese cultural exhibit in Chicago. Miller received his gift at Mariona. Photographed afterward at his entry gate, he stood hatless, holding the gold-and-silk symbol, his abundant hair now almost white, his face lean and jowly, his posture revealing all his years. His suit fit poorly; his cane waited conveniently near. An observer thought his visible aging of less consequence than the aura of high-mindedness he radiated.[17]

Miller himself needed no added reminders of his mortality. He echoed a friend's complaint: "The only mournful thing about [the passage of time] is that in the place I helped [establish] and where I used to know everybody I am almost a stranger."[18] He knew also that his family sensed his decline. "They are all worrying more or less about me," he wrote, "thinking I should let up on the work, and I am trying mighty hard to do it."[19]

Even more somber reminders of life's frailty came with the daily papers, often with the headline, "Pioneer Passes." Miller knew them all and mourned them all, every death poignant: Henry E. Huntington and Arthur B. Benton in 1927; Francis Borton, poet and his curator of artifacts, in 1928;[20] Marion's brother Benjamin F. Clark, age forty-one, in 1930.[21] Fifty years of shared ideas ended with the death the next year of David Starr Jordan. Friend General M. H. Sherman died in 1932. They had worried together over the Arcadia Hotel in Santa Monica and later, as old men do, commiserated sedately on dominoes and intimate details of their illnesses.[22] And there were others. That year six more in his circle answered the call, as the current phrase had it, an *annus horribilis* indeed for Miller.[23] Rose Hardenberg, Isabella's sister, passed away March 1935, but not before a small pearl of understanding had grown from old antagonisms over Miller's marriage to Marion Clark. Rose reached out in a verse called "Old Friendship": "Beautiful and rich is old friendship/Where light has lingered intimate and long/That asks no longer deeds of gallantry/Or any deed at all—save that the friend shall be/Alive and breathing somewhere, like a song."[24]

Miller attended funerals when he could, walking unsteadily the slow paths as honorary pallbearer,[25] easing his own grief in private tears, comforted always in the strong love Marion gave so unstintingly.

The Depression deepened into the thirties, bringing hard times to the Mission Inn. Miller cast around for money-makers, especially as his storefront renters struggled with payments or moved out. He wanted a beauty operator to join his barbershop, an in-house chiropodist to complement his treatment rooms with their water and massage therapy based on the redoubtable John Harvey Kellogg's Battle Creek Sanitarium in Michigan.[26] He made reductions: Alice trimmed her kitchen staff from twenty-four to fourteen over three years. Individual paychecks shrank by almost 13 percent.[27] Fifty-eight returning house staff came to an enlarged hotel for the 1933–1934 season, their number down from nearly one hundred. Added help would be hired on a daily or an event basis.[28] At Miller's request Stanley Richardson, Alice's son with experience in hotel management, surveyed the inn to advise him "as to what phases of economy and increased cooperation might be possible."[29] Miller and everyone else hoped for better days, and the 1934 and 1935 seasons did show a slight improvement, but two-thirds of the rooms remained empty for months. Even the optimistic Miller could see only small gains ahead,[30] slight improvements but not recovery.

There must have been satisfaction for Miller in seeing others who were willing to advance the causes close to his heart. But he felt unease in letting go after a lifetime of being out in front, fulfilling his *firstness* and being the Master of the Inn. Occasionally his ambivalence came through. In politics his mantle of leadership had passed fully to others, but in spite of himself, when approached he confessed, "I am not active in politics but think I can help in working [this particular] matter out."[31] He kept political contacts at least warm through his political legman, Michael Westerfield, a relative and local printer, working him locally and to Sacramento.[32] Miller's condemnation helped send a candidate to political oblivion.[33] He canvassed his choice for Republican leadership in California[34] and boosted presidential candidate Herbert Hoover and all Republicans at the Riverside Colored Citizens Club.[35] However much he saw himself out of the political fray, he still merited a brief personal visit from California's acting governor Frank Merriam shortly before the 1934 election.[36] Even so he wrote plaintively about the anxiety he felt in quitting.[37]

His interest in sustaining the dialog for peace and international relations had found a champion in Rufus von KleinSmid,[38] who all but satisfied Miller's wishes for a strong voice on world affairs. And even though KleinSmid kept a tight rein of control, Miller never hesitated to bring in his own speakers: a Father Augustine of San Francisco and suffragist Carrie Chapman Catt in 1933 and ex-president of Mexico Ortiz Rubio in 1934. Rubio, all flourish and bluster, came in an armored car to check on the inn, returning a few days later to speak.[39]

Miller's long crusade for good roads found new focus in his committee memberships for the transcontinental Highway 60 from Banning west toward Los Angeles. He weighed in, his credentials good since supporting the 1928 opening of a new bridge on the Colorado River.[40] Advocates of two routes competed; tensions mounted; aspersions and denials flew. Miller spun all the advantages of his route through Riverside, describing it as shorter and cheaper, a boost for local employment, a revenue source for and from roadside business, and a benefit to the Los Angeles Metropolitan Water District as it built an aqueduct from the Colorado River to the city. Frail as he was, he lobbied all across the county, aided impressively by Harry Chandler and the Automobile Association in Los Angeles. Success came in 1933. Then in grand gestures, as though he had been the sole mover, Miller sprinkled praise and assigned credit, generous with some earlier opponents. To his steady supporter Harry Chandler, he telegraphed, "Harry! Harry! Blessings on you for what the Highway Commission did."[41]

Miller's excitement during the road campaign was dulled because Marion was ill. His concern mounted from June through September, her physician insisting that she continue to rest quietly, not even permitting her the auto ride to Mariona. But by October she had recovered enough to travel to Phoenix and on to Globe, Arizona, where she recuperated in "sunshine and clean air" while Miller briefly attended meetings of the successful Highway 60 Association.[42] They stayed on for almost three weeks after the meetings, wined and dined by friends.

Marion thrived in the desert sunshine and brisk evening temperatures and equally from being away from tensions at the inn. Their hosts graciously accommodated her, alert also to Miller's need for his knobby cane, easily aware that his earlier jaunty pace had slowed to a less confident gait.[43]

※

For Miller there was always time for small generosities. He offered hospitable consultation and assistance to many—the director of the National Council of Jews and Christians[44] and the Japanese Buddhist archabbot, who visited with a small entourage of robed priests. He and Miller ate together and lingered long in conversation. Miller entertained two Japanese scholars who were visiting Pomona College.[45] When he heard that Lyman Beecher Stowe, biographer of Booker T. Washington, would speak at the Congregational Church, Miller organized a Beecher reunion, enrolling author Hamlin Garland (already at the inn) as a special guest and inviting Charlotte Perkins Gilman, great-granddaughter of Lyman Beecher, as guest of honor.[46]

As his social and political world shrank, Miller's physical world also became smaller. There were no more transcontinental railroad journeys or even hurried trips to San Francisco and Sacramento. Travel in a comfortable Pullman tired him, making a visit to the Century of Progress fair in Chicago impossible.[47] But one journey could not be denied, regardless of age, infirmity, or family cautions. In the spring of 1934, with a small group, he went to Victorville in the high desert northeast of Riverside. There, with little fanfare, they all boarded the first Union Pacific streamliner train, a shining two-car marvel. Miller rode into history in a vastly changed railroad era—quiet, steady travel a world away from those sooty, grinding rides in Wisconsin or across the continent. The air-conditioned streamliners, capable of 110 miles an hour, were to dominate rail travel east and west until the 1950s. In that 1934 ride, Miller's years of train journeys ended in the quiet luxury of that symbol of railroad achievement. In air-conditioned comfort, he moved smoothly across the desert and down the long grade of the Cajon Pass to Riverside and a crowd of five thousand people.[48] Travel that began for him and his family nearly sixty years before in the first years of transcontinental railroads had carried him now onto the new pinnacle of passenger rail travel. What vignettes of memory must have come to mind: riding freight trains in wintry Wisconsin, the piano playing in the Carlin House, days of rail travel across the continent to San Francisco. Railways had defined his world. This was not so for Allis and DeWitt Hutchings. They had joined the aviation world, becoming known as the Flying Hutchings and, at the inn, custodians of the Famous Fliers Wall just outside Miller's Saint Francis Chapel. The good Saint Francis, patron of Mission Inn hospitality, had become Saint Francis, patron saint of birds and birdmen.[49]

Inquiries about the inn and its origins came often. Miller sent one of these to DeWitt Hutchings with his bold, steady handwriting: "Help her in any way you can. Let me see it."[50] DeWitt wrote about the way the hotel had "grown as we worked out the thought of paying tribute the Missions, to picturing the Spanish days, to a business founded on history and art, to the connection between European and Asian art on our West Coast, and to the need of international understanding and friendship among all peoples," all taking place over fifty-eight years.[51] In a separate letter to the same person, he looked deeper. The Master of the Inn had succeeded, Hutchings wrote, because of his many wonderful friendships. Further, Miller and his sister combined their management talents with their artistic, even poetic, sense in offering service that blended interest and personal emphasis. Both had inexhaustible energy; Miller especially possessed a mind that never rested. The singular focus on international peace had brought him new friendships, new associations, and new fame. Overall, Hutchings thought the enterprise "a moderate success."[52] Had he written in the midtwenties, he might have used a richer adjective, but by 1935 the Depression had changed all that.

The memory-evoking streamliner ride may have drawn Miller back to thoughts of his biography. There were other prompts: the earlier, rejected biography with Ida Dorothy Cottrell, requests that came for life summaries, and Hamlin Garland staying at the inn for weeks writing his own memoirs. Quite as likely, his new tenant in the Rotunda, attorney William G. Irving, suggested the prudence of a review of end-of-life plans.[53] Their consultation added a codicil to Miller's will about who was to manage the inn when he was gone. This done and witnessed on March 22, 1935, he was ready to talk with a professional writer about how he wanted himself remembered.

28

Master No More

When Marion and Frank went to the beach house early in 1935, he had his memoirs in mind. The first effort at biography had pleased no one. For this second effort, Zona Gale had come from Wisconsin planning an indefinite stay.[1] Miller had pleaded with her to come, offering expenses but only vague allusions to what he had in mind. His long letters to her shared his doubts about the wisdom of what he was undertaking for Riverside and claimed that there was "not a friend on earth with the vision and sympathetic understanding of what I am trying to do that you possess." Most important, he told her, she, Marion, and "little Billy" (Herbert, the head porter) were practically the only family members sympathetic with what he wanted.

Even the newspapers, he complained to Gale, were continually against him[2]—not true, of course—he had more newspaper comment than almost any other Riversider, though more sparse now because of his frequent absences and infrequent local involvement. He confessed to her that he was "wobbling" in his business life, aware that his way of doing things may no longer fit a changed world.[3] But away from all that, beside the sea, he'd find quiet and rest, even though his slower movements made for an arduous climb down to the tiny beach and pool. But his clear mind drove his body more than his few visitors to the seaside villa expected.[4]

Gale's Pulitzer Prize–winning status gave her the skill and stature that attracted Miller, as did their shared interests in social, political, and philosophical matters. As they talked at the beach in March and April, Marion took it all down in her facile shorthand for Gale, who would write at her home in Portage, Wisconsin. This was to be her first and only venture into biography. Miller would not live to see the publication of her efforts, *Frank Miller of Mission Inn*.[5]

Miller began with his *firstness*—"I was the first boy born in Tomah, Wisconsin, in 1857."[6] He talked about his life chronologically, easily veering off into thoughts about what might have influenced his own and others' behavior, the causes and motivations. As often happens in recollections, he sacrificed many details but clearly had wondered about why he and others did the things they did. Sometimes he invoked maxims—"You get what you give"—explaining his hotel success. He mentioned mystical influences, "forces beyond our control,"[7] and the places of significant others in his life—his father, Henry E. Huntington, Elbert Hubbard, and even the biblical Moses. He recognized some motivations as internal, describing his awareness of immediate opportunity or of his moral responsibility. He buttressed some of his actions or obligations with claims of "the law of nature."[8]

Love, his ethical mooring for many years now, became a recurrent theme as he talked—the need for it, its transformative power, and its historic importance. As a youth he had reflected on his commitment to love and respect for the Bible. Love and respect for friends were the makings of "a man of men."[9] His advice to his grandson, Frank Miller Hutchings, rehearsed another maxim, one attributed to Aristotle about learning to love by loving. He had included the same wisdom in a letter attempting reconciliation with Rose Hardenberg when she disapproved of his marrying Marion in 1910.[10] Now with

Gale and Marion, as he reminisced he seemed to be bracing his own convictions: "We have got to believe in something—we've got to love as some philosopher said. If this force to believe and love is not used, and it is not by this present generation, I cannot help but feel that the future is a very dark one." He was convinced that "love is a force that clarifies our minds and strengthens us and it pays [original emphasis]," in family life, in the workplace, and in the national economy.[11] This love emphasis, spoken of as brotherly kindness in other settings, embraced the Christ philosophy he spoke of as also the basis for success in international relations.[12]

Miller reflected on his own personal needs: "I guess I needed recognition and affection as much as anyone."[13] He wondered about the role of mere chance and coincidence. Might the Easter services, for example, have been mere coincidence arising from nothing more than whatever brought Jacob Riis to Riverside and took Miller up the mountain a few days later? Perhaps these events connected as cause and effect only in the convenience of retrospect?[14] In other events he placed himself in charge or as a partner, calling himself "a factor." He asked Gale not to present him as "too long headed,"[15] or as being insightful and exceptionally wise, reluctant to claim for himself what many in the town had long recognized as his innovative turn of mind, restless advocacy, and yen for reward-driven achievement.

As he talked, Miller's catalog of internal, external, personal, and mystical motivations cropped up in an unexamined miscellany. They reflected not only his inquiring mind but also his times. His generation came to maturity in the post–Civil War years of industrialism, immigration, urbanization, and economic fluctuation—five years up and five years down, some said. They lacked much of the sure foundation claimed by their parents, whose own values and outlook, though fractured by the Civil War, stayed largely intact. The parents' generation could "worship and was sure."[16] Their children, Miller among them, confronted increasingly severe economic fluctuations, a muddled evolutionary scientism, and then, in their maturity, the disenchantments of World War I, with its broken promises and greedy materialism. Earlier appeals to God's will, noble patriotism, obligation, and loyalty to the right—come what may—had dissolved for many into a flaccid pragmatism or raw greed. Later scholars would describe the confrontation of modernists and antimodernists and the resulting social discomfort. In Riverside Miller thought he had seen a "surge of radicalism and unbelief so tremendous."[17] In the absence of solid guides to behavior, matters of cause and effect lost objective bonds; the personal and social world might be accounted for in any one of a number of ways—as internally or externally driven, the consequence of psychological, economic, or social impulses, even forces beyond our control. Miller's reminiscences revealed just such a kaleidoscope. But with the range of his explanations, he brought his own generally conservative ethical principles to bear as guides to behavior. His youthful claims of independence of mind stayed with him.

Marion and Frank returned to Riverside in early April where he was admitted to the hospital for diagnostic work. That provoked inquiry. When asked, Marion described it tersely to a well-wisher as "examination and treatment,"[18] too vague, I believe, to reassure his friends that the prospects were benign. This, added to his long absences from town and his frail presence when he did return, could only heighten concern.

When Easter came on April 21, 1935, Miller was not on the mountain in his usual place among the notable guests.[19] He had attended every sunrise service since the first. If on this day he followed his preferences, he walked the short distance from his rooms to the quietness of the Saint Francis Atrio as the sun came up. He loved the moving shadows on the masonry, the strong perfume of the lilies brought in for the week, and the gentle splash of water in the fountain. Seeing all this, he told a friend, he became part of some medieval and walled city in a time before life and haste had formed a partnership. It stood for memory, he said, with all of memory's clinging chains of love and tenderness, bright and full of hope, like Easter morning, with nothing of sadness or regret,[20] no currents of despair.

Shortly after Easter he and Marion returned to Mariona and his memoirs. He felt some nagging anxiety, a worm of doubt among the fruits of success. At least one worry had been laid aside when Harry Chandler had assured him that the Easter service offered a legitimate vehicle for spiritual values and, for that reason, was something worth doing.[21] Miller remained uncertain about the annual Institute of World Affairs, however.[22] In fact, by the time he asked, both of these events had passed beyond his control—the Easter service already a community ceremony and the institute lodged firmly with KleinSmid.

But Miller continued worrying. Gale appears to have kept asking for more details about his role in city incorporation, county formation, the Indian school, the Carnegie Library, and the memorial auditorium, as well as his internationalism and Japan's virtues as an ally of the United States. In each of these he could place himself as a "factor" and said so, implying his own role while readily including the essential roles filled by others, many of whom he named. He mentioned men of power and influence, those to whom he gave deference. To the common people, he gave short shrift. "Your belief in the dear people is much deeper and stronger than mine," he wrote for Gale. "I cannot think of any one thing that the people ever did toward the creation of the City of Riverside or the county of Riverside"—except that they talked, yelled, and clamored for political office.[23] Here the *firstness* of Riverside's first citizen is revealed in a new light, at least for us at this distance.

Early in May 1935 Marion and Frank returned quietly to Riverside, the reminiscences as complete as he could make them. He'd add no more. His arrival home went unremarked in the papers, but word of mouth kept his friends and the business community aware. They knew he fared poorly. And though they wished for recovery, they feared otherwise, writing their eulogies against the inevitable.

༃

Miller's passions for the civic center and an elite college on the slopes of Rubidoux had both languished. Locally his ardor for Japan proved too much against the grain of popular opinion for anyone to adopt. Even the Asian decoration at the inn dwindled before December 7, 1941, replaced in the Court of the Orient by a nightclub in the trendy island mode, with faux palms, fishnets, glass floats, and bamboo poles. The long-delayed three-hundred-foot-high Giralda Tower, not shoehorned into the five-story 1931 Rotunda Internacional, remained on Miller's mind, willed to Frank Miller Hutchings, his grandson.

In long conversations with his daughter, Allis, and in a letter, of which only a fragment survives, he advised her on control of the governing board that she was to direct. He named those he had appointed and potential trustees and briefly etched their strengths. Naturally enough in conversations and a letter like this, he reflected on his life. He rehearsed for her his belief that his own success came from following Archer Huntington's advice about business based on history and colored by religion. He endorsed his habit of seeking advice from knowledgeable friends. More credit should go to them than to him for his accomplishments, he thought. He weighed the benefits to business from friendship, deciding it helped greatly. He regretted leaving her so many burdens, perhaps thinking of the huge indebtedness from his last addition to the hotel and its repayment in financially difficult times.[24]

Well-advanced cancer at times engulfed him in waves of abdominal agony, managed daily by a physician friend.[25] Marion attended him constantly in his Sky Room above the Cloister Wing. Alice was in and out; DeWitt and Allis visited and brought occasional business items to him. Other family members came often; others visited with requests for advice or endorsement of their causes, all generously received.[26] A visitor remembered him in bed—"wan and worn, but his eyes were as bright, his spirit as strong, and his mind as clear as ever"[27]—dictating replies to some correspondence but leaving most for others.

Of independent disposition to the end, Miller planned his funeral services in detail.[28] He fixed the place and the time of day; he named pallbearers and named his street-railway motormen and conductors as honorary pallbearers. He named the small group who might attend the funeral in the Saint Francis Chapel. He chose the music, arranged who should speak and who should assist, and wrote the sparse details for his grave marker. Even to the last, Miller showed his contrarian streak, choosing among funereal conventions to suit his own preferences: a funeral within his own walled town and officiants directed by his scripting. Only at the interment would he include the conventional committal, presided over by a pastor of the Congregational Church: "In as much as it has seemed good to Our Heavenly Father to call unto himself our brother Frank Augustus Miller…"

With details settled, uncertainties of mind seemed resolved into satisfaction with all he had done—his only regret that he could not do more.[29] At times he had not easily found words to describe himself, relying on others and on material expressions to make clearer his feelings about hospitality or peace or what Riverside might become or what religion meant. For all his volubility, there was such a poverty of mere words in the service of his thoughts. He had searched for the generous spirit of the missions, what he imagined as the essence of exemplary hospitality in the vaguely remembered time of the Franciscans. He had preserved as symbols some solid walls of the old adobe behind a glass panel—Isabella's idea really—displaying the blocks for all to see their honesty, praised by Roosevelt.[30] So many hotels were mere shells filled with the hubbub of business and pleasure, lacking the embrace of spirit, mind, and body that lay at the heart of his tavern. The Mission Inn offered quiet and service—these revealed of his character just as much as his flamboyance in architecture, his decorative enthusiasms, and his oration.

As May became June, he needed his physician more often for relief from pain; the rising summer temperatures added nothing to his comfort. For a few days he seemed more comfortable, comfortable enough to speak in his rooms with peace activists protesting the US Navy maneuvers in the Pacific.[31] He may not have known that even as he so willingly signed their protest, Japan invaded China from Manchuria, driving south on Tientsin.[32]

His vitality ebbed slowly over the next week, even as his enthusiasm buoyed those around him.[33] In the half hour after midnight on Saturday, June 15, his life ended as Marion and Allis stood at his side.

On Monday the cool retreat of the Saint Francis Chapel took on an added solemnity as his casket was brought in. Family and staff moved quietly, adding flowers that filled the choir benches lining the aisle and spilled out into the Atrio and under the arcaded ambulatory. Within, the Master of the Mission Inn lay, "in state," at rest in his own chapel. The obsequies were brief and of Miller's own composition. A college president from a distant town read a short scripture; a businessman from Los Angeles spoke the eulogy. From the distant Music Room, the voice of an operatic soprano sang about daily obligations to serve others and a hymn. Intense emotion swelled among the family, the few guests, and the hotel staff as DeWitt Hutchings invoked the pathos of the final lines of Carrie Jacobs Bond's "Perfect Day":[34]

> Well, this is the end of a perfect day,
> Near the end of the journey too,

> But it leaves a thought that is large and strong
> And a wish that is kind and true;
> For memory has painted this perfect day
> With colors that never fade,
> And we find at the end of a perfect day
> The soul of a friend we've made.

Inn bells tolled in funereal strokes; the central business district went silent. The procession moved in Sabbath quiet from his inn to the family plot in the Evergreen Cemetery.[35] On the simple granite stone laid flat on the earth was only his name: "Frank Augustus Miller."

Epilogue

How was Frank Augustus Miller remembered when the flood of eulogies subsided and the voluminous tributes in the local papers had been carefully folded away for future rereading or neglect?

From Los Angeles there came almost immediately talk about a heroic monument, a "statue in marble or bronze in a public square, to bear at its base a suitable tribute to its subject's contributions of his home city and country."[1] That idea faded. But in September a commemorative service on Mount Rubidoux drew crowds to hear praise and massed choirs.[2] The same month newspaper readers learned that a small contingent of Japanese veterans had stood silently in tribute beside his grave as a Boy Scout bugler played taps.[3] On Miller's birthday a year later, the *Los Angeles Times* summed up his legacy in a title: "What He Gave was His Monument."[4] Later that summer an unnamed prominence in the San Jacinto Mountains became Miller Peak.[5]

Miller's biography, *Frank Miller of Mission Inn*, appeared in 1938, tepidly reviewed as constantly edging too close on sentimentality and as failing to reveal the inner man as biographies are expected to do. Even so, the family ordered more than 650 copies, and a second printing followed in 1939.[6] DeWitt Hutchings found the book disappointing, because, he said, Gale failed to "show [Miller's] mental and philosophical development clearly enough." He wanted a "more vivid description of his dynamic personality and its compelling power—and better picturing of how his ideas advanced and broadened." Hutchings wrote as much to Harry Chandler, whose reply was soothing, saying that all a biographer could do, especially with as complex a person as Miller, was write personal impressions.[7] (Chandler knew better.) Hutchings was right: almost all who wrote about Miller relied on admiring enumeration, taking little account of the man in his time, the development of his personality, or even what the architectural and decorative sequences of the inn might suggest. Almost everyone writing since then has also skirted the inner man and certainly his "mental and philosophical development," and been most comfortable rehearsing quirks, catalogs, and chronologies or describing the Mission Inn.

Sunset on June 18, 1935, the day of Miller's funeral, may well have been the end of a perfect day for the inn itself, as De Witt had recited in the Saint Francis Chapel.[8] The halcyon days of the inn would continue to fade, interrupted in the feverishly plebian patronage of the war years. The town's citrus economy, once dominated by wealthy growers and almost-as-wealthy packers, merged into corporate interests as citrus plantings made a slow geographic migration to California's Central Valley. The earlier social and economic interest from elite and financial Los Angeles looked elsewhere, especially to the San Fernando Valley and the Los Angeles West Side. The infusions of Los Angeles capital that launched so much in Riverside all but disappeared. The thrust for innovation, city vision, and elite patronage that Miller radiated disappeared with him. What did endure was the inn and the city buildings, so much the result of Miller's long presence.

Epilogue

At the hotel the family remembered Miller. They struggled with grief and followed the daily round, keenly aware of the loss of the Master of the Inn and of new, unsought roles and changed relationships among themselves.

His bereaved widow, Marion Clark Miller, served on the board of directors as Miller had specified, living between the Mission Inn and Mariona, her home at Laguna Beach. Other directors bought out her interest in a lump-sum settlement. She sold Mariona in 1941 and then lived with a companion in Riverside, rarely visiting the inn. "It's so changed," she said, "the spirit of the place—it's a different sort of place. I don't know what will finally become of it."[9] She died in 1972, her obituary in the local and Los Angeles papers making no mention of a quarter-century long marriage to Frank A. Miller and her essential role in the success of the inn.[10] Affectionately, she accumulated her memorabilia for care by her own family.[11]

Allis Hardenberg Hutchings, who came to use the name Allis Miller Hutchings, became president of the seven-member board, sharing the day-to-day management with DeWitt, her husband, and Alice Richardson. She began writing about the hotel's collections of dolls, bells, crosses, wedding rings, and aeronautical items for hobby and travel magazines, publishing more than fifty articles in the forties. She died at the inn in October 1952, a notable community member.[12]

DeWitt Hutchings, excluded from the Master of the Inn's will and from the hotel's management, traveled following Miller's death and promptly resigned from the Easter service committee after the 1936 observance. He'd likely had enough of reading or reciting van Dyke's poem in the chilly dawn—he had done it so many times.[13] Three years after Miller's death he did become a board member, at last formally sharing in the hotel's management. In 1951, because of his and Allis's failing health, the hotel was leased to the Fairmont Hotel Company, although he and Allis stayed on. He found interests in many county and state committees and in local charities. He died four months after Allis on February 15, 1953, at age seventy-two.[14]

Frank Miller Hutchings, Miller's grandson, had been charged with management responsibilities by the Master of the Inn's will. The dying wish of his grandfather was that he build the long-delayed Giralda Tower, a task that remains unfulfilled. He served on the board, and he left Riverside for military service and later to live in Newport Beach. More than any other family member, he researched ancestry and genealogy and accumulated the large collection of family and hotel records now preserved archivally.[15]

Alice Richardson turned seventy-five the year Frank died. She continued as a reassuring, if increasingly demanding, presence, delegating more and more from her threatened domain with the arrival of the manager. She resigned in 1936,[16] after acting as the grand lady and consummate manager of the inn for fifty or more years. She died there in 1938.[17]

Miller's grandchildren—Frank, Helen, and Isabella Hutchings—had grown up at the inn. They continued to live and assist there until the war years when Frank entered the army. Helen married and moved away, and Isabella married, remaining in Riverside.

Frank's younger brother, Edward, had died in 1922; his wife, Emma Tompkins Miller, lived on in her Sixth Street apartment until 1952, survived by three children, Donald, Albert, and Emma—Mrs. Fred Forquer.[18] Frank's oldest sister, Emma, had lived with her husband, G. O. Newman, in Los Angeles from 1905 until her death in 1925. She visited often in the earlier years, less so with the passing of time. She was the only Miller child that was never an employee at the inn. Her husband, G. O. Newman, had died in 1923.[19]

Twenty years after Miller's death, a local writer talked to a score of residents about him. What she heard abounded in the trivial—he wore a white shawl; a parrot rode on his shoulder; he greeted guests wearing a monk's robe and sandals—or the shallow—he, with two others, ruled Riverside; he was a determined dreamer; he was a vibrant, compelling person.[20] Perhaps what earlier appeared in strong contrasts during his

Epilogue

lifetime had, with the years, blended into a comfortable gray vagueness, punctuated by the isolated, the odd, and the exceptional. Even so, his hand had been in so many enduring projects in the city, and over so many years, that the easy absence of his name is surprising. Perhaps, as the writer said, and as many of Miller's contemporaries knew, he was not an easy read: his novel proposals burst out unexpectedly and without end, but the inner currents rarely surfaced. And his generation had all but passed by the mid-1930s.

In 2009 a new middle school was named for him, the first public memorial in a city he had done so much to define. By that year, and since the refurbished Mission Inn reopened in 1998, twenty thousand or more guests tour each year, hearing Miller's name as they follow tour guides through the hotel, easily forgetting his name amid the beguiling decorations, the minarets and flying buttresses, and the radiance of the Saint Francis Chapel.

What remains, however, is the hotel, filling a city block, still a place beyond expectation within and without, still giving definition and distinction to Riverside beyond everything else. In restoration, it still speaks to those who listen of a vibrant personality who presided over almost every detail in three decades of imagining and building. His youthful conviction, sustained over a lifetime, proved true: his kind of boy was pretty scarce.[21] Even his antagonists agreed. As all must be, he was of his times and of his place, but much more than that, he was a man in mind and spirit unlike the rest.

In 1907 Miller received as a gift a colorful and noisy macaw, brilliant in blue and yellow plumage, promptly named Napoleon. The bird lived his days at the hotel, daily roaming cage free in the Garden of the Birds and often on Miller's arm or shoulder. In July 1956 Napoleon died at his perch in the Garden of the Birds, full of years and, some said, grieving over changes at the hotel. So passed a last vibrant link with the Master of the Inn's presence and, indeed, with an era in Riverside. Few noted the bird's passing or, if they did, they were puzzled why longtime employees and a few guests might see meaning in the death of a parrot.[22]

FINIS

Acknowledgments

From the first days of this project I have had an abundance of help and encouragement. Joan Hall and Vincent Moses offered their insights even as the subject was being chosen. Archivists and librarians came enthusiastically to my aid with all their accumulated skills. Those most frequently called upon in Riverside were Steven Spiller of the Mission Inn Foundation Museum and Kevin Halloran of the Riverside Metropolitan Museum. Both brought to my notice documents and photographs almost without number, most previously unstudied. From these archivists and from the equally generous Steve Lech, local historian who made his extensive post card collection available I received permission to publish all the illustrations used. The jacket portrait is published by permission of the Mission Inn Foundation and Museum and the Historic Mission Inn Corporation, Kelly and Duane Roberts. My indebtedness to them all is great.

Jim Hofer who presides over the Robert Fitch Archives of the Riverside County recorder office provided essential records from unsuspected places. Bill Abney of Inland Printworks was unfailingly helpful and cheerful with solutions when confronted by my computer illiteracy. At the Riverside Public Library, Ruth McCormick, Dominique McCafferty, and William Swafford in the Local History Resource Center and Kathy Korn and Cathy Nguyn, presiding over the interlibrary loan service, and the La Sierra Branch staff filled my many requests expertly. Kitty Simmons, director at the La Sierra University Library in Riverside, California, provided microfilm-reading equipment in a quiet room, and David Ramos kept the arrival and departure of some fifty years of on-loan newspaper microfilm as constant and reliable as he could.

Rev. Jane Quandt and archivist Mike Hammer of First Congregational Church Riverside opened essential records of Miller family religious affiliation. Kim Walters and Manola Madrid at the Braun Research Library of the Southwest Museum in Los Angeles kept Charles Lummis resources coming my way under ideal circumstances. William O. Hendricks and Jill Thrasher of the Sherman Garden and Library, Corona del Mar, California, guided me through the General Moses H. Sherman and Miller family correspondence. The Yosemite National Park archives provided "Old Central Files Collection 180, Frank A. Miller," with details of Miller's failed 1912–1914 attempts to build a hotel in the park. Hannah Crooks and Joanne Cullen Ringstrom generously shared their recollections of Marion Clark Miller and letters from the jewel-like family archives, now the Jane Cullen Clark Collection at the Mission Inn Foundation Museum, that added factual richness to the narrative and delight to the research process. Patrick J. Rafferty shared generously from his named collection at the Bancroft Library. Francis J. Weber, archivist at the San Fernando Mission, gave access to the Miller correspondence with Bishop Thomas Conaty. Jennifer Goldman of the Huntington Library, Art Collections, and Botanical Gardens in San Marino provided document copies and guidance from the Huntington and Miller correspondence.

A travel grant from the John Randolph Haynes Foundation through the Southern California Historical Society assisted in a week of indispensable research at the California State Library in Sacramento. The Wisconsin State Historical Library, Madison, Wisconsin, provided several days of richly productive mining for state and local Wisconsin history; the church

Acknowledgments

secretary of the United Methodist Church in Tomah, Wisconsin, offered unrestricted access to what amounted to "boxes in the attic," recording the earliest Miller association with the church in Tomah, Wisconsin, from 1856 until 1874. Jarrod Roll, at his exemplary Monroe County History Room, Sparta, Wisconsin, arranged a most productive visit. Several days in the Millers' hometown of Tomah, Wisconsin, allowed me to view the skylines, walk the meadows and marshes, and trace the streets in a topography little changed in over a century—rare privileges for a biographer.

No less welcoming and helpful were Amanda Gustin of the Mary Baker Eddy Library in Boston; Megan Halsband at the Library of Congress in Washington, DC; Josie Hartsough at the Dwight-Englewood School in New Jersey; Brenna Lissoway of the Yosemite Park Foundation; Carrie Marsh, the special collections librarian of the Honnold-Mudd Libraries at the Claremont Colleges in Claremont, California; Christina Rice in the history section of the Los Angeles Public Library; and Jennifer Whitlock of the Architecture and Design Collection at the University Art Museum in Santa Barbara, California.

Equally valuable guidance, though on shorter visits, came from reference librarians at the Laguna Beach Public Library in Laguna Beach, California; the Norman Feldheym Public Library California Room in San Bernardino, California; the Ontario Public Library in Ontario, California; the Pasadena Public Library California Room in Pasadena, California; the Smiley Library in Redlands, California; the Tomah Area Historical Society Archives and Museum in Tomah, Wisconsin; and the Victorville Public Library in Victorville, California.

Several people read all or part of the manuscript. These included Jerry Gordon, Kevin Halloran, Steve Lech, and Walter P. Parks, all of whom brought to my aid their detailed knowledge of Riverside, California, and the Mission Inn in particular. All offered valuable comments to improve the narrative; I usually took their advice. John Briggs of the University of California, Riverside and William Deverell of the Huntington-USC Institute on California and the West, distinguished scholars both, aided more than they knew and perhaps more often than they expected. Much merit came from these reviewers; I alone am responsible for the defects.

Although biographers live almost alone with their subjects, fresh, personal relations emerge, and older acquaintances are immeasurably enriched over the years of research and writing. For me, those that merit special mention include: Larry Burgess of the Smiley Library in Redlands, California; Toby Burrows, with ready and profound literary characterizations of the inn and its personalities; Blaine Rawdon and Clint Marr, patient mentors in things architectural. Bill Abney shared generously from his technical knowledge and stylistic elegance. Peter N. Weber shared freely the architectural renderings made by his father, Peter Weber, for the Rotunda addition of the Mission Inn. Yumi Yamaguchi, granddaughter of Miller's 1925 hotel host in Japan, interpreted to me the hotel experience and other aspects of Miller's admiration for Japan.

Miller family descendants and relatives provided insights and expressed interest, some through oral histories already in the Riverside Metropolitan Museum collections and others through correspondence and conversation. Notable help came from Hallett Newman, sixth-generation descendant of Emma Miller Newman and G. O. Newman. Bruce Richardson and Allan Richardson, grandsons of Edward E. Miller, added to the richness of the narrative.

All authors are indebted to those who have gone the way before, and in that company, especially relevant to this biography, are Zona Gale's *Frank Miller of Mission Inn* and Esther Klotz's two publications, *Riverside and the Day the Bank Broke* and *Mission Inn: Its History and Artifacts.* Joan Hall's volumes, *Through the Doors of the Mission Inn*, yielded ready narratives of the nearly rich and almost-famous visitors; Steven Lech's several publications and his huge collection of postcards were useful. His *Along the Old Roads*, especially chapters 14 through 16, is indispensible to anyone researching the arrival of county status to what became Riverside County. Thomas Patterson's *Colony for California* spans the history of Riverside with a newspaper reporter's ease in narrative. James Brown and James Boyd, writing from firsthand knowledge and compiling autobiographical sketches in their 1922 publication, *History of San Bernardino and Riverside Counties*, provide eyewitness accounts of a vanished world. *Anecdotes of Mount Rubidoux and Frank Miller, Her Promoter*, by Glen Wenzel, assures a detailed chronology and copious illustrations of that site of Miller's ceremony-making impulses.

Lawrence Arthur Cremin and Garrett Mattingly, though remote in time, were always near.

Abbreviations

Manuscripts and Manuscript Collections

A500-190	Frank Miller Hutchings Collection, Riverside Metropolitan Museum
Braun	Braun Research Library, Los Angeles, California
Huntington	The Huntington Library, Art Collections, and Botanical Gardens, San Marino, California
JCCC	The Jane Cullen Clark Collection at the Mission Inn Foundation and Museum Archives, Riverside, California
MHS	Moses H. Sherman Collection, Sherman Gardens and Library, Corona del Mar, California
MIFMA	Mission Inn Foundation and Museum Archives, Riverside, California
Notes	Item number 86.8.22, "Notes For an Autobiography[sic] Dictated at Laguna Beach." Jane Clark Cullen Collection, Mission Inn Foundation and Museum
RPL	Local History Resource Center, Riverside Public Library, Riverside, California
ZGC	Zona Gale Collection, at Mission Inn Foundation Museum Archives

Newspapers

LAE	*Los Angeles Examiner*
LAT	*Los Angeles Times*
MM	*Morning Mission*
RDP	*Riverside Daily Press*
RME	*Riverside Morning Enterprise*
RP	*Riverside Press*
RN	*Riverside News*
RPH	*Riverside Press and Horticulturalist*
RPE	*Riverside Press Enterprise*
SBG	*San Bernardino Gazette*

Names

AMH	Allis Miller Hutchings, wife of DeWitt Hutchings, only child of Frank and Isabella Miller
DH	DeWitt Vermilye Hutchings, husband of Allis Miller, son-in-law of Frank A. Miller
FAM	Frank A. Miller
HEH	Henry E. Huntington
IHM	Isabella (Bell) Hardenberg Miller, first wife of Frank A. Miller
MCM	Marion Clark Miller, second wife of Frank A. Miller

Chapter Notes

Preface
1. Esther Klotz, *The Mission Inn: Its History and Artifacts* (Corona, California: UBS Printing Group, 1981). Thomas Patterson, *A Colony for California* (Riverside, California: Riverside Museum Press, 1996).
2. Frank Miller Diary, March 18, 1877, Mission Inn Foundation Museum Archives, Mission Inn Museum, Riverside, California.

Chapter One: Going West
1. Frank A. Miller Diaries (hereafter Diaries), January through November 1874, Mission Inn Foundation Museum Archives, Mission Inn Museum, Riverside, California; Frank A. Miller, "Notes For an Autobiography Dictated at Laguna Beach [California] March 1935, by Frank Miller," typescript, 1, (hereafter Notes, MIFMA), Zona Gale Collection 90.16.122.2, Mission Inn Foundation Museum Archives, Mission Inn Museum, Riverside, California. See also Patricia Kelly Hall and Steven Ruggles, "Restless in the Midst of Their Prosperity, New Evidence on Internal Migration of Americans, 1860–2000," Department of History and Minnesota Population Center, Minneapolis, Minnesota, June 2004 (Minneapolis, Minnesota: University of Minnesota, 2004). This chapter was based on the above sources.

2. Notes, 2, MIFMA.

3. "Combined CPRR and UPRR Train Schedules," International Railway and Steamship Guide (Montreal P.Q.: Chisholm, 1880). cpr.org/Museum/indes.html. Better emigrant cars included four passenger-seat alcoves of facing seats that made down into berths almost forty inches wide and almost six feet long—a close fit at any time. These had replaced earlier slatted benches lining the sides of the cars, one tier above another, the lower as seats and the upper hinged downward to provide cots, depending on the time of day and the number of passengers. The newer cars could be entered from either end, with an aisle lengthwise, lit by three hanging lamps fueled by kerosene or lamp oil and heated by a potbellied stove near the ladies' saloon. The stove provided highly localized heating, a convenient cooktop, and the most frequent source of destructive fires that would readily destroy the wood cars. A gentlemen's saloon and a ladies' saloon were at the ends of the car, small, closet-like spaces, each with a galvanized handbasin and overhead tank of water. Waste of every kind went out onto the tracks through a convenient hole in the floor under a drop-chute toilet in each saloon. Emigrant trains moved more slowly than the daily expresses. According to schedules, the Millers' outbound from Omaha would cover 291 miles to North Platte, Nebraska, in the first twenty-four hours, a slow twelve miles an hour even without unscheduled delays. In the same period, the express could expect to gobble up 496 miles, arriving close to Cheyenne, Wyoming, but even then the average speed was about twenty miles an hour.

4. For none of these migraine episodes, whether in the past or in the future, did Frank Miller mention the usual warnings of onset or speculate about causes. He noted their duration—usually less than twenty-four hours, seldom their intensity.

5. Notes, 2, MIFMA.

6. No hotel or boardinghouse called Brobling House (or a similar name) is listed in any contemporary San Francisco or

Chapter Notes

Oakland city directory. Miller's often phonetic spelling may confuse what was, in fact, the name of a family home.

7. *San Francisco Daily Evening Bulletin* 39: 9, October 17, 1874.

8. John Haskell Kemble, *The Panama Route, 1848–1869* (Berkeley: University of California Press, 1943), 71, 148–149, 152–153. Shipboard conditions may have improved somewhat since 1869.

9. Doyce B. Nunis, *Women in the Life of Southern California* (Los Angeles: Historical Society of Southern California, 1996), 166. Most visitors found Los Angeles disagreeably vulgar and untidy. A visitor coming two years later saw Spanish women in black shawls and Chinese men in blue blouses, wearing pigtails, in an otherwise commonplace little city with streets full of reckless hardcases and swarthy, old Californios, scenes disappointing her expectations of something better.

10. John Brown and James Boyd, *History of San Bernardino and Riverside Counties* (San Bernardino: Western Historical Association, 1922). Chapters 1, 2, 11, and 37 contain Boyd's reflections on the early years. He arrived in the colony in 1873, spent the rest of his life there, and died in 1923.

11. Charles Nordoff, *California: A Book for Travelers and Settlers* (New York: Harper and Brothers, 1873), 146, 148; Brown and Boyd, *History*, 1: 358–359.

Chapter Two: Seventeen Years in a Frontier Village

1. Notes, 2, MIFMA. All details of Frank's life in this chapter are based on his unpublished diaries for the years 1871, 1872, 1873, and 1874. Other sources were used as cited.

2. Notes, 2, MIFMA. Frontier village mothers ruled in the home and in the kitchen garden; the outdoors belonged to the men. Frank took over the garden from his mother and made a tidy profit selling vegetables in the village. Housecleaning, his mother's domain, involved Emma and Alice as they grew. Summer dust, winter slush, and tracked-in mud in any season would be scoured, usually twice each week, while on the knees

with a bucket and scrubbing brush and an array of brooms, brushes, and even scrapers. Bed making and room tidying were likely part of Frank's assignment, at least for his own space. Emma, joined later by Alice, prepared meals, served, and cleaned up, all under a careful mother's close supervision.

3. Diaries, 1871, several entries May, June, and July.

4. *Tomah Journal*, January 1, May 1, 1869; Jerry Apps, *One Room Country Schools: History and Recollections from Wisconsin* (Amherst, Wisconsin: Amherst Press, 1996), 20; J. W. Stearns, *The Columbian History of Education: Wisconsin* (Milwaukee, Wisconsin: State Committee on Educational Exhibit for Wisconsin, 1893), 48. See also annual reports of the Wisconsin Department of Public Instruction.

5. Zona Gale, *Frank Miller of Mission Inn* (hereafter Gale, *Miller*) (New York: Appleton-Century, 1938), 9.

6. First United Methodist Church Collection, Tomah, Wisconsin; First United Methodist Church, Butts Avenue, Tomah, Wisconsin; Alice McCaul Hayward,*The Story ofTomah* (Tomah, Wisconsin: Journal Printing Company, 1955), 13.

7. Gale, *Miller*, 2, affirms the Millers' interest in California, based on her firsthand knowledge; Willis J. Abbot, "Chicago Newspapers and Their Makers," *Review of Reviews* 11: 6 (June, 1895). Just which editions of the books Miller read in these years cannot be established with any certainty. The Twain volume was not named; Turnbull's *Indian Wars* remains obscure; *Jane Eyre* appeared in so many editions that no certainty is possible; Scott's *Marmion* appeared in many editions following its publication in 1809, as did Charles Dickens's *Dombey and Son* in 1848. Publication dates nearest to the years of Miller's reading suggest the following as probable: LaFayette C. Baker, *History of the Secret Service* (Philadelphia: Baker 1867); J. M. Bailey, *Life in Danbury* (Boston: Shepard and Hill, 1873); J. O. Choules, *Young Americans Abroad or Vacations in Europe* (Boston: Gould and Lincoln 1852); Edward Eggelston, *End of the World* (New York: Judd, 1872); Edward Eggleston, *Mystery*

of Metropolisville (New York: Orange Judd, 1873); J. T. Headley, *The Great Rebellion, a History of the Civil War in the United States*, 2 volumes (Hartford, Connecticut: American, 1866); Thomas E. Hill, *Hill's Manual of Social and Business Forms* (Chicago: Warren, 1875); J. McD. Leavitt, *The American Cardinal* (New York: Dodd Mead, 1871); William Matthews, *Getting on in the World* (Chicago: Griggs, 1872); Walter Scott, *The Lady of the Lake* (Boston: Little Brown, 1853); W. H Seward, *Travels Around the World* (New York: Appleton, 1873); W. J. Snelling, *West of the Mississippi* (Boston: Gray and Brown, 1830); Johann D. Wyss, *Swiss Family Robinson* (London: Nelson, 1871).

8. Diaries, September 4, 1874.

9. Increase Cook, *The American Orator* (Boston: The Intelligencer, 1828). First published 1818 and many times thereafter; which edition Miller purchased is not known.

10. Diaries, January 21, 1871.

11. Diaries, February 1, 1872; Elmer Holmes, *History of Riverside County with Biographical Sketches* (Los Angeles: Historical Record, 1912), 333.

12. *Tomah Journal*, December 23, 1871.

13. Diaries, December 23, 1871; December 16, 1872.

14. *Sparta Herald*, February 22, 1874; Diaries, March 23, 1975.

15. Notes, 1, MIFMA; FAM to Mary N. Shepard, March 31, 1932, Thomas Patterson File, "John W. North." Riverside Metropolitan Museum (hereafter RMM).

16. Notes, 1, MIFMA.

17. Diaries, November through December 26, 1872.

18. Diaries, August 1, 1873.

19. Diaries, January 28 through November 11, 1873.

20. See, for example, *RDP* February 22, 1922, when he's honored by townspeople in Riverside.

21. Diaries, January 21, February 5, October 27, March 3, June 30, July 14, November 27, 1872; March 3, 1873; January 5, May 31, 1874.

22. Diaries, March 27, 1873.

23. *RE*, May 23, 1932; *RDP*, May 23, 1932; Frank A. Miller's 1873 diary, Found Box 77, 1990.16.75, MIFMA. Handwritten notation in a partial transcription of this diary.

24. See, for example, the inscription on the tower bridge and tower of 1925, chapter 25.

25. Diaries, April through July 1873.

26. Notes, 2, MIFMA. Diaries, July 2–21, 1873; November 2–11, 1872.

27. Diaries, January 5–April 22, 1874.

28. *Tomah Journal*, August 15, 1874. Diaries, August 3–7, 10–12, 1874.

29. "Taxes for 1873," memorandum in Diaries, 1874; Monroe County Plat Book Map 1877; Miller C. C. Oakdale/ Tomah Township 17 Range 1 Section 7 in Real Property Records, Monroe County Wisconsin Records Office. Sparta, Wisconsin; Richards, 343 et seq.; Hayward, *Story of Tomah*, 11–15. Diaries, May 29, 1871.

30. *RDP*, March 10, 1934.

Chapter Three: Almost Like Starting Over

1. See, for example, *RDP* April 17, 1914, and *RDP*, April 28, 1927. Reminiscences differ.

2. *RDP*, April 30, 1915.

3. *RDP*, April 30, 1915. Brown and Boyd, *History*, 1: 434.

4. Jane Cullen Clark Collection, 86.8.22: 1, 2, 3, Mission Inn Foundation and Museum, (hereafter JCCC 86.8.22, MIFMA). This is what the unnamed typescript is identified as.

5. Diaries, October 28, 1874. Brown and Boyd, *History*, 1: 212, 220, 221.

6. Merlin Stonehouse, *John Wesley North and the Reform Frontier* (Minneapolis: University of Minnesota, 1965), 225–227.

7. See Lisbeth Haas, *Conquest and Historical Identities in California, 1796–1936* (Berkeley: University of California, 1995).

8. Brown and Boyd, *History*, 434.

9. Emma Miller to W. R. Cross, November 23, 1874, in Zona Gale Collection 90.16.110.1, MIFMA.

10. Diaries, November 2, 1874; Patterson, *Colony*, 63.

11. See Roy L. Haglund, *One Hundred Years of Masonry, 1879–1979* (Riverside: Evergreen Lodge, 1979), 6, 8, 11, 12, 63.

12. Notes, 2, MIFMA.

13. S. B. 405, Statutes of California, Twentieth Session, 1873–74, chapter 516, 751.

14. Folders 2, 4, 8, Riverside Public School Records Series V LHRC RPL.

15. Notes, 1, 13, 19, 27, MIFMA.

16. Diaries, 1873, 1874.

17. "Newman, Gustavus Olivio" in *Press Reference Library, Notables of the West* (New York: International News Service, 1915), 2: 366.

18. Diaries, July 29, 1875; Emma and Newman married at 7:30 a.m. on July 29.

19. Diaries, November, December 1874. FAM to "Dear Friend," November 27, 1874; Emma Miller to Mr. and Mrs. W. H. Cross, November 23, 23, December 21, 1874. Zona Gale Collection, 90.16.96, MIFMA; G. A. Zentmyer (ed.), *The Lighted Cross, The First Hundred Years of Riverside's First Church, 1872–1972* (Riverside, California: First Congregational Church, 1972), 20.

20. Diaries, November 2–December 31, 1874.

21. Diaries, December 20, 1874.

22. Diaries, November, December 1874. Diary entries about Mattie Weed and letters received, expected, and sent are frequently mentioned in November, almost daily through December 1874.

23. Diaries, December 31, 1874.

Chapter Four: Going I Don't Know Where

1. Diaries, June 28, 1875.

2. Diaries, January 16, 1875.

3. Diaries, Januaty 7, 1875.

4. Diaries, January 9, 1875.
5. Diaries, February 20, August 23, September 25, 1875.
6. Diaries, February 9, 1875.
7. Thomas E. Hill, *Hill's Manual of Social and Business Forms: A Guide to Correct Writing* (Boston: Hill Standard Books, 1875).
8. San Bernardino Deed Book R, 485. San Bernardino County Archives, San Bernardino, California.
9. Diaries, July 1, 1875.
10. Diaries, March 9, November 22, 28, December 9, 1876.
11. Notes, 2, MIFMA; JCCC, 86.8.22, 17, MIFMA. No floor plans survive of the original Glenwood, but photographs and isolated comments indicate adode construction on the lower floor of at least three large rooms, one with a large, open fireplace. The kitchen and service areas appear to have been at the back, even detached. The upper floors, framed in wood, provided about a dozen rooms, those on the third floor with dormer windows.
12. Untitled manuscript, Jane Cullen Clark Collection, 86.8.22: 7, Found Box 7, Zona Gale Collection, MIFMA (hereafter, JCCC, 86.8.22).
13. "How I Made Adobe Bricks," Brown and Boyd, *History*, 2: 640–642. The article describes how adobe blocks are made. A close reading reveals no personal claim of Miller's actually making the adobe blocks. James Boyd, the author, had contracted in 1875 to level the lot in preparation for building. His 1922 reminiscence, forty-seven years after the event and after having read Miller's "How I Made Adobe Bricks," was written as his direct observation, "Frank, now Master of the Inn, without his shoes treading clay to make bricks." Brown and Boyd, *History*, 2: 675. I accept the diary record of the youthful laborer writing at the time rather than the later memory of the contractor. Notes, 7, 8, MIFMA; Gale, *Miller*, 20, 27, 29; *RDP*, June 28, 1913.
14. Emma Miller to Mr. and Mrs. Cross, December 14, 1874, 90.16.110, Zona Gale Collection, MIFMA.
15. Diaries, December 21, 26, 1876.

Chapter Notes

16. Diaries, October 19–November 1, 1875.
17. Diaries, October 22, 1875
18. Diaries, October 26–November 1, 1875.
19. JCCC, 86.8.22: 13, 14, MIFMA; Gale, *Miller,* 21, 22.
20. FAM to Rev. W. H. Cross, October 1, 1876, Correspondence, 1 C 1, A500-190.
21. Diaries, December 27, 1875.
22. JCCC, 86.8.22: 16, MIFMA. A shallow, vertical slit is made in the host, and a carefully selected and prepared bud on a sliver of freshly cut bark is set into the slit and bound up until growth occurs. Because the receiving stock usually stood less than three feet high, the "budder" crouched or knelt, a tiring position requiring repeated standing and crouching while performing delicate movements with the knife, bud, and binding tape.
23. Nearly fifty years later, a biographical essay recorded a story about his eyestrain from budding that put him in the hospital for weeks in San Francisco until he recovered. Nothing in the other available records of the 1870s or in later records supports this.
24. Diaries, February 28, 1877. Frank's account keeping appears irregularly in Memorandum pages of his diaries.
25. Diaries, December 21, 1876.
26. Diaries, March 27, 1876.
27. Diaries, April 17, May 15, August 1, December 15, 1875.
28. Diaries, December 1875–March 1876; Emma Miller to W. R. Cross, November 23, 1874, 90.16.110.1 Zona Gale Collection, MIFMA; *RDP,* November 11, 1922; Diaries, October 21, 1876; "Samuel C. Evans" in Brown and Boyd, *History,* 1: 657; Lewis J. Holmes, *Riverside Directory 1889* (Riverside, California: Daily Press, 1889), LHRC RPL; "Newspaper Abstracts: Births, Deaths and Marriages 1887, 1882, 1892," typescript (Riverside, California: Riverside Genealogical Society, 1976); "1880 Federal Census: Riverside California," typescript (Riverside, California: Riverside Genealogical Society, 1976), LHRC RPL. The baseball team had provided

little close bonding for Frank, who young or old, usually radiated affability. The other team members who played baseball with him were friends to a degree, some for very many years, but none close. He may have sensed economic or social barriers or differences of political party loyalties. Frank himself was a committed Republican. Education also brought separation as some team members went off to college. Most of them arrived in Riverside about the same time as he did; many moved away, with almost half gone from Riverside a decade later.

29. Diaries, August 22, 23, 1876.
30. Diaries, March 25, August 22, 23, 1875.
31. *Tomah Journal*, December 30, 1876.
32. Diaries, January 12, 1877.
33. Diaries, March 12, 1876.
34. *RN*, June 3, 10, 1876.
35. Frank Miller had come to maturity before any high school served Tomah youth. Compulsory education for all youths, whether in Wisconsin or in California, lay in the future; even then the laws led far in advance of compliance. College attendance depended on family wealth. His two years of concentrated schooling in Tomah, 1872–1873 and 1873–1874, would have qualified him for admission to a teacher-education college of the preparatory departments of several California colleges. The family's migration across the country did provide economic strains calling for earning hands.
36. Diaries, March 10, 1875; *Diaries*, November 8, 11, 18, 1875. *RN*, December 4, 1875. Diaries, February 20, 1877.

Chapter Five: So Here Goes for Business

1. Family correspondence and publications use various forms of Miss Hardenberg's name: Isabella, Bell, and Belle. In direct quotations I use whatever the document specifies; at other times I use her given name, Isabella, the form chosen by Zona Gale in her biography of Frank A. Miller. She knew the family better than anyone, and I take her choice as appropriate,

confirmed by other sources, which present her as the quintessence of Victorian bourgeois virtue.

2. Diaries, December 3, 1876.
3. Diaries, June 8, 1877.
4. Diaries, July 11, 1877.
5. Diaries, September 5, October 29, 1877.
6. Diaries, October 7, 17, 20, 1877.
7. Diaries, flyleaf, 1877–1878.
8. Diaries, September 23, 1877. The diary entry implies three days spent with Huntington in Anaheim, Tustin, and Santa Ana.
9. Diaries, November 23, 25, 1877.
10. Diaries, January 1, 18, 1877.
11. Diaries, January 27, 1878.
12. C. C. Miller to Dear Wife. November 9, 1877. Notes about C. C. and Mary Ann Miller, II C 2, A500-190.
13. A. K. Sandoval-Strausz, *Hotel: An American History* (New Haven, Connecticut: Yale, 2007). See especially the author's typology of hotels beginning on page 81.
14. Diaries, January 21, May 12, September 14, November 24, 1877.
15. Notices appeared regularly; see *RDP*, 1878 and 1879.
16. C. C. Miller to Dear Wife, November 9, 1877, Notes about C. C. and Mary Ann Miller, II C 2, A500-190.
17. Diaries, February 19, 1878. Fueled on robust fare, the laborers working under Frank's experienced eye dug the canal three feet deep with sloping sides. It was four feet wide at the bottom and several miles long.
18. Diaries, January 17, March 9, 1878.
19. Notes, 6, 7, MIFMA.
20. Diaries, April 28, 1878.
21. Isabella Hardenberg to Dear Sisters, March 20, 21, May 20, 1878, Family Correspondence, 1877–1891, II C 3, A500-190. Isabella rode outside all the way, sitting high up beside the driver, prudent for a single woman traveling alone on a crowded coach, although an uncomfortable perch on

a hard, padded cushion with no backrest and only bent iron seat dividers as handholds. The journey beyond Ventura led at times along the beach, terrifying her so that she avoided looking left or right, determined only to hold on. All physical discomfort from the journey easily disappeared, however, in the warmth of her welcome and the balmy airs of her new home at "Sea Side Hill" in Santa Barbara with her cousin Alice, herself a teacher, and her husband, Peter S. Brinkerhoff. See Roelif C. Brinkerhoff, *Supplement to the Family of Joris Dirksen Brinkerhoff, 1628* (Riverside, California: the author, 1902), 13–16.

22. *RP*, August 17, 1878.

23. *RP*, August 17, 24, December 7, 1878; Gale, *Miller*, 66.

24. *RP*, December 13, 1878; May 3, June 28, 1879; Mrs. F. Daniels Battles (compiler) *Diary of Two Decades* (Riverside, California: the compiler, 1967), 24.

25. Another diary begun in 1887 rapidly raveled out in the first weeks to scattered appointments and then to blank pages.

26. The only hint that there were other diaries came much later in a reference by a biographer to an 1884 diary. See Gale, *Miller*, 37. Thorough searches in Riverside and Wisconsin produced nothing; the possibility remains of other diaries in family archives or shoe boxes in attics or that have been lost.

27. *RP*, September 21, 1878. On the ground floor it added a guest dining room, an office, and a kitchen that would replace the original kitchen. A "row of chambers" filled the upper floor, every room opening onto a long balcony on both sides of the building, so typical of settler hotels. A large cellar gave storage space. The homelike appearance of the original building, with its dormer upper windows, had given way to a more conventional hotel design.

28. *RP*, September 21, 1878.

29. Emma Newman to T. C. Hunt, October 2, 1876, Eliza Cross Correspondence 1874–1876, I C I, A500-190.

30. Diaries, November 7, 1877.

31. A dated balance sheet shows investments by Frank and others of $1,531. See single sheet in Family Correspondence 1878–1891, July 17, 1879, II C 3, A500-190; Wallace Elliot, *History of San Bernardino and San Diego Counties* (Riverside, California: Museum Press, 1965), 108. A reprinting from 1883.

32. *RP*, November 23, 1878.

33. *RPE*, July 1, 2007.

34. Joan H. Hall, *Pursuing Eden* (Riverside, California: Highgrove Press, 2010), 5, 8, 10.

35. Ronald J. Baker, *Serving Through Partnership* (Riverside, California: Riverside City and County Public Library, 1988), 2.

36. *RP*, July 6, 1878. *RDP*, June 28, 1929.

37. He had known a Red Front Store in Tomah, possibly an inspiration.

38. *RP*, November 23, December 20, 1879; *Tomah (Wisconsin) Journal*, March 20, 1869. The Red Front Store in Tomah opened when Miller was eleven years old. In so small a village, its distinction would have been well known to Frank, who was so often the family shopper.

39. *RP*, December 6, 20, 1879.

40. Notes, 2, MIFMA.

41. *RPH*, April 17, 1880.

42. *McKenney's Pacific Coast Directory, 1880–81* (San Francisco: L. M. McKenny, 1881), 500; Campbell J. Gibson and Emily Lennon, *Historical Census Populations of Counties, Places, Towns and Cities of California 1850–1990* (Washington, DC: US Bureau of the Census, 1999). Other local village centers included Anaheim, population about two thousand; San Bernardino, population about one thousand five hundred; Pomona, with few more than three hundred; San Gabriel, the old mission town, with a population of about seven hundred; and Pasadena, with slightly fewer than four hundred. For a detailed narrative and chronology, see Steven Lech, *Along the Old Roads* (Riverside, California: the author, 2004).

43. *RPH*, January 31, 1880.

Chapter Six: Like a Duck to Water
1. *RPH*, February 14, 1880.
2. *RP*, July 6 1876; *RPH*, April 24, 1880; "Newman, Gustavus Olivio," *Press Reference Library, Notables of the West*, 366. The wheels of bureaucracy had begun to turn toward G. O. Newman's appointment almost two years earlier. The appointment moved him back into civil engineering for the rest of his life, though he and Emma stayed in Riverside almost twenty more years before moving to Los Angeles.
3. *RPH*, April 24, 1880; "Newman, Gustavus Olivio," *Press Reference Library, Notables of the West*, 366; San Bernardino Deed Book 21, 79, San Bernardino County Archives, San Bernardino, California; Gale, *Miller*, 58; Klotz, *Mission Inn*, 5; *RPH*, February 7, 1880.
4. Brown and Boyd, *History*, 1: 513.
5. Alice Richardson to Zona Gale, January 8, 1938, Zona Gale Collection, 90.16.81, MIFMA.
6. *RPH*, June 12, 1880.
7. Larry Burgess, *The Smileys* (Redlands, California: Moore Historical, 1991), 13. Even Albert K. Smiley, the eminently successful patrician proprietor of the Mohonk Mountain House in New York's Catskills, reported hotel keeping as a little less than respectable.
8. See, for example, *RDP*, October 29, 1914.
9. *RPH*, April 10, 1881.
10. Miller signed an autograph book: "Lone Rock May 18, 1881 Frank A. Miller." Internal evidence suggests that the book was Gertrude Hardenberg Stewart's, although it is now identified in archives as Rose Hardenberg Autograph Book, II D 2, A500-190.
11. *Tomah Journal*, May 7, 1881.
12. *SBG*, December 24, 1892, reprinted in *RDP*, December 26, 1892.
13. *RDP*, July 2, 1881.
14. Joan Hall, *Through the Doors of the Mission Inn* (Riverside, California: Highgrove Press, 2000), 2: 13.

15. In her two volumes, Joan Hall chronicles eighty-five notables who visited the inn.

16. *RPH*, July 2, 1881.

17. These large Glenwood notices with an engraving of the Seventh Street facade of the hotel appeared first in *RPH* on December 18, 1880.

18. *RDP*, May 14, 1931. Steve Lech, *Resorts of Riverside County* (San Francisco: Arcadia, 2008), 12. In the late 1880s the Anchorage, a small, canal-side private resort, would be similarly placed in park and garden surroundings.

19. *RPH*, December 17, 1881.

20. *RPH*, July 24, 1880.

21. *RPH*, July 30, October 2, 1886.

22. *RPH*, August 27, 1881.

23. *RDP*, August 27, 1881.

24. *RPH*, July 16, 1881.

25. *RPH*, February 18, March 4, July 1, November 17, 1882.

26. Steve Lech, *Riverside's Mission Inn* (San Francisco: Arcadia, 2008). This source has many illustrations.

27. *RPH*, September 30, December 9, 1882.

28. *RDP*, May 14, 1931. This was Cuttle's comment: "The Glenwood had already [by 1881] earned an enviable reputation for its hospitality."

29. *RPH*, January 13, October 13, 1883.

30. *Los Angeles Times*, November 2, 1882, reprinted in *RPH*, November 4, 1882.

31. *RPH*, March 18, 1882; *RPH*, April 20, 1882; A500-190.

32. *RPH*, October 8, 1881; January 7, March 18, June 17, September 2, 1882.

33. Emma Miller to W. R. Cross, November 23, 1874. Zona Gale Collection 90.16.110.1, MIFMA. His Republicanism stemmed mostly from his family and Wisconsin, leading to Protestant evangelical views, Union loyalties, temperance advocacy, and strict observance of the Sabbath. Miller had early declared himself a staunch, active Republican, saying as much as soon as the family arrived in Riverside.

34. *RPH*, April 16, June 14, 1884.

35. Miller always refused to accept tubercular guests or residents. See FAM to Charles D. Fagar, MD, February 14, 1905, Letter Book 5, I H 5, A500-190.

36. *RPH*, April 5, 12, 1884, from the *Los Angeles Express*; Walter H. Case, *History of Long Beach* (Chicago: S. J. Clarke, 1927), I: 98–99.

37. *RDP*, February 27, 1901.

38. *RPH*, April 7, 1884. The hotel attracted a growing number of guests staying a month or more to escape winter's chill elsewhere. They traveled west in the increasingly popular tour groups organized by tour companies or the railroads. Businessmen and commercial travelers whose territory included Riverside knew that Glenwood rates were slightly higher than other Riverside hotels, but they enjoyed the family welcome, quality of service, and a common table, something Miller catered especially to them, because he valued their return patronage. Even twenty years later, when Miller built a new hotel, he provided a welcoming banquet for several hundred of "the boys"—the commercial travelers—because of their value to him as patrons and promoters of his business and the town. The mutual benefit of the hotel and town also influenced almost continual improvements at the hotel. He added to the landscaping; the guest program grew, with horseback rides into the hills and along the river, rugged walks for the hardy up comfortably rounded Mount Rubidoux, buggy rides through orange groves heavy with ripening fruit between November and March, and the winter contemplation of snow-covered mountains, comfortably distant. When rain kept guests indoors, Manager Alice Miller and an Assistant Manager Frank W. Richardson arranged games, impromptu plays, talks by the guests themselves, and, on one occasion, a mock trial of Miller on the charge of running a disorderly house. The guest judges, lawyers, and ready wits in residence carried out the proceedings with great élan, finding him guilty as charged and imposing an immediate fine of cigars

to all gentlemen guests. The next month, hotel guests staged another "dramatic entertainment." Later two short plays, *A Nice Piece of Business* and *Box and Cox*—a longtime favorite one-act comic farce by Arthur Sullivan—starred staff and family members.

Chapter Seven: For Sale at a Bargain

1. The 1880s brought a notable boom in prosperity to California. Many thousands of immigrants and land-buying hopefuls came west, but only a few of them came to Riverside while real-estate boosters hawked the virtues of nearby Colton, Redlands, Moreno, and a dozen other places existing only as words in the boosters' brochures and on sales sheets. There were cheap rail fares, free lunches, and always a gaggle of smooth-talking agents making commissions on sales, largely short in duration and long on hope. There were valid sales, of course, and increasing numbers of settlers. In Riverside, the population of 1880, 1,358, grew to 4,583 by 1890; in the same years San Bernardino's population grew from 1,673 to 4,012. Such growth had consequences not only for land sales but also for population density and particularly the visibility and influence of the pioneers as they came to call themselves—settlers who had arrived before 1875. More people meant fewer direct acquaintances. By my calculations, pioneers in 1880 knew one in every two people they met on the streets; by 1890 only one of eight shared the memory or motivations of those early years. Sensing this, perhaps, a Pioneer Society was organized in June 1889. The population figures are from *FAQ: What was the Population?* LHRC, RPL; Joan Hall, "Riverside' Historical Societies Centennial," *Journal of the Riverside Historical Society*, 7 (February 2003) 1–6. See also Glenn Dumke, *The Boom of the Eighties* (San Marino: Huntington, 1945).

2. *RPH*, June 1885.

3. *RPH*, December 13, 1884; James Turner, "The Boom Period, 1880–1910" in *History of Roller Skating* (Lincoln,

Nebraska: Roller Skating Rink Operators Association of America, 1975); *RPH*, March 1, 1884; June 13, 1885. These Orange Street additions, especially roller-skating, caught a wave of popularity as respectably middle-class recreations, something that would continue for about twenty-five years. The skating took place in elaborate buildings and included a sedate pastime with its own clothing and rituals, accompanied by live music.

4. Diaries, 1887; *RDP*, March 5, 1887; *RDP*, July 2, 6, 1887; *RDP*, January 11, 12, 1888.

5. *RDP*, December 21, 1886; February 2, 1887.

6. A. K. Sandorval-Strausz, *Hotel* (New Haven, Connecticut: Yale, 2007), 95, 112.

7. *RDP*, December 21, 1886.

8. http://hts.org/ASNCTimeline.pdf; Heather Menninger and Mervin Acebo, "A Century of Transportation in the San Bernardino Valley" (Claremont, California: AMMA, 2001), 15–18.

9. This was a retrospective judgment. See *RDP*, February 27, 1901.

10. C. C. Miller to Mary, Emma, Ed, and Ally, February 12, 1883, Notes about C. C. and Mary Ann 1880–1895, II C 2, A500-190.

11. Hindsight suggests that the history of Riverside would be vastly different had a buyer, in fact, come forward to purchase the Glenwood.

12. Diaries, January 2 through June 24, 1887. Among the steady succession of sales with gradually rising prices for land, Riverside had one spectacular land sale in July 1887. Those attending were treated to brass band music and were sheltered under shade tents and offered an abundant lunch. After the meal and the obligatory oratory, all eighty-five lots on offer sold, purchased by local residents. Some said this village picnic and auction launched Riverside's land boom, but a survey of previous years shows not a boom but steadily rising land values and construction of new homes and business buildings.

Certainly the sale of so many lots on one day brought a brief, giddy acceleration.

13. Diaries, 1887. The tabulation appears in the Memorandum section toward the back of the diary.

14. Glenwood Misc. Advertising, III E 2, A500-190; Sandorval-Strausz, *Hotel*, 87–92, 112–120, 89–90, 98–299.

15. Diaries, January through March 1887; Charles B. Sumner, *The Story of Pomona College* (Boston: Pilgrim Press, 1914), 64; *RDP*, February 21, 1887.

16. *RDP*, July 30, October 2, 1886.

17. Mary Wells in Lech, *Roads*, 708–709. For unblushing local self-adulation see Lech, *Roads*, 710. Lech's chapters 14, 15, and 16 provide the definitive narrative and analysis of Riverside County separation from San Bernardino. Riverside's incorporation in 1883 brought the county direct control of a schedule of local matters, including water and alcohol, taking the control away from the county administration in San Bernardino. Many agreed that local wishes to control water and alcohol fueled passions and the process. With the change to incorporated status, those elected as trustees were all men quite untried in city management, more wedded to advancing their own private prosperity than to public administration. Issues large and small came to them, some personal and others more neutral but affecting exciting divisive responses. Issues presented included permissions to build, business licenses, street conditions, trees in public places, sewage disposal, the irrigation runoff in the streets, and all forms of transportation from railroads to buggies and bicycles.

18. Patterson, *Colony*, 162, 172–174.

19. *RDP*, February 9, 11, April 29, May 11, June 16, 1887.

20. *RDP*, February 2, 9, 17, June 16, 1887.

21. Diaries, 1887; MIFMA.

22. *RDP*, November 26, 1887; December 10, 1888.

23. *RDP*, November 26, December 10, 1888. *Diaries*, January 2, 10, May 6, 24, June 25, July 5, 11, 16, 23, November 26, 1887.

24. Esther Klotz, *Riverside and the Day the Bank Broke* (Riverside, California: Rubidoux Press, 1972), 14, 15; Patterson, *Colony*, 172, 173. Revival efforts failed; the local bank that had loaned heavily for the project itself slowly tottered into collapse over five years.

25. *RDP*, January 9, April 23, December 11, October 8, 10, 1887; May 26, September 27, 1888; June 25, 1889; Patterson, *Colony*, 172, 232.

26. All information about the Miller family's association with the First Church of Christ, Scientist comes from three sources: Earl C. Ward, *A Goodly Heritage* (Riverside, California: First Church of Christ Scientist, 1973, 2000); a typewritten copy of a letter, Mary Ann Clark Miller to unknown, September 1895, in the Mary Baker Eddy Collection, ORM Field Collection, S-35, 011, 836. Mary Baker Eddy Library, Boston, MA; and from personal correspondence between the author and the Mary Baker Eddy Library. The absence of date, addressee, and salutation and the discrepancy in dates between Mary Ann Clark Miller's death in mid-August and the September date of the copied letter may be accounted for by clerical error at the time of transcription. The letter states that it was intended for "readers of the Journal," a reference to *The Christian Science Journal*, first published in 1888. There are no doubts about Mary Ann Miller as the author, the date of her death, or the authenticity of the letter. Newspaper reports of the criminal trial for manslaughter of a Mrs. V. B. Ward, a Christian Science practitioner, contain testimony for the defense by G. O. Newman. *RDP*, February 3, 4, 5, 1892; *(San Bernardino, California) Weekly Times Index*, February 5, 12, 1892.

27. I found no reference to Mary Ann Miller's Quaker beliefs anywhere except in Miller's reminiscences in 1935. Gale wrote of Mary Ann Miller: "she was of Quaker ancestry" and that there are no records of this or other details of her life. Gale, *Miller*, 177. I believe Gale relied, without further inquiry, on what she had been told by Miller. Other details of Mary Ann Miller's life have been found; however, none confirm a Quaker connection.

28. *RDP*, November 5, December 2, 1892.

29. Notes, 1, 27, MIFMA.

30. *RDP*, February 27–April 11, September 15, 26, November 15, 1888. A regular column in the *Press* (a politic inclusion by the editor) reported WCTU meetings, visits by regional and national advocates, and summaries of their presentations. In 1888 passions rose, accusations flew, conspiracies were suspected, and youthful morals were thought to be in grave danger at the hands of those who opposed desiccation. On Election Day April 9, the Baptist ladies met to pray all day for the outcome, which, as it turned out, favored their petitions but by only forty votes among 858, revealing a community chasm beyond bridging then or ever. The dry victors shot off guns in the streets, lit bonfires, waved flags, and rang bells, stimulated by their own heady brew of ideology and success. But the issue didn't rest; it was never left alone by the Women's Christian Temperance Union, whose members stirred continuously, providing meanspirited comments about lapses of enforcement or practices in other towns and opposing any appearance of "wine on hotel tables."

31. Notes, 27, MIFMA; FAM to H. Waldo Foster, February 27, 1905, Letter Book 5, I H 5, A500-190. See Lech, *Roads*, 810, 811, for the text of the Riverside County Ordinance of 1893 allowing sales in hotels having more than twenty rooms.

32. Notes, 27, MIFMA.

33. *RDP*, April 12, 1888.

34. H. H. Monroe, "Looking Backward" in *RDP*, January 8, 1926.

35. Douglas Gilbert, *American Vaudeville: Its Life and Times* (New York: Dover, 1968), 149; *RDP*, May 4, 1888.

36. *RDP*, October 26, 1886; February 14, 1887; January 7, April 4, October 2, 1888.

37. *RDP*, October 26, 1886; February 14, 1887; January 7, October 2, November 20, 1888; Notes, 20, MIFMA.

38. *RDP*, December 28, 1889.

39. *RDP*, April 19, 1890.

40. *RDP*, March 13, 14, 1889.

41. *RDP*, January 2, 8, 1890; Ralph Freud, "Frank A. Miller, Theater Manager," *Southern California Quarterly*, 41: 1, 10; Marshall Duell, "Frank Miller and the International Expositions," (master's thesis, University of California Riverside, 1987), 19; Benjamin McArthur, *Actors and American Culture, 1880-1920* (Philadelphia: Temple University 1984); *San Bernardino Times Index*, January 9, 1890.

42. *San Bernardino Times Index*, January 9, 1880.

Chapter Eight: Telegraph in Cipher

1. See McArthur, *Actors and American Culture*; Edward A. Berlin, *Ragtime: A Musical and Cultural History* (Berkeley, California: University of California Press, 1980); John E. DiMeglio, *Vaudeville, U.S.A.* (Bowling Green, Ohio: Bowling Green University Popular Press, 1973).

2. FAM to Manager, KMT Radio, April 17, 1934; Easter Sunrise Services 1934-1935, VI A 19, A500-190.

3. For effect he inflated his role from manager to theater builder and lengthened his theater management career.

4. Notes, 19, MIFMA.

5. James Horsburgh to FAM, November 7, 1891, Correspondence Concerning "Temescal Tin," 1891, 1 C 3, A500-190.

6. *RDP*, February 15, 1892.

7. *RDP*, January 13, 1892.

8. *RDP*, February 8, 1890. The smaller and far-from-elegant Lawrence Theater on Eighth Street competed only obliquely with the opera house.

9. *RDP*, January 13, 1892.

10. See Patterson, *Colony*, 19, reprint of the broadside *A Colony for California*, paragraph 4. "Whatever would advance the prosperity of Riverside would benefit me too." Brown and Boyd, *History* I, 303.

11. Ellery Irving Garfield, *Knights Templar Tactics and Drill* (Detroit, Michigan: E. B. Smith, 1871), 128; *RPH*, February 11, 15, June 7, 1890.

12. JCCC 86.8.22: 6, 7, 8, MIFMA.

13. FAM to Frank Miller Hutchings, June 25, 1933, Correspondence 1933, I B 18, A500-190. He painted a similar picture in his reminiscences to a would-be biographer. See JCCC 86.8.22: 6, MIFMA.

14. For local and legislative details of the protracted process of county division, the definitive discussion is in Lech, *Roads*, chapters 14, 15, 16, on which much of this is based.

15. Lech, *Roads*, 530ff provides a detailed review.

16. Folder V B 7, Advertisements 1890ff, Riverside City and County, A500-190.

17. *Los Angeles Examiner*, March 21, 1891.

18. Unidentified newspaper clipping, Political Scrapbook, 28, Subseries V B, A500-190.

19. *RDP*, March 28, 1891.

20. *RDP*, June 16, 1890.

21. W. H. Mills to FAM, June 27, 1892, Large Record Book, 102, Subseries V B, A500-190.

22. *RDP*, October 6, 1892.

23. "San Bernardino County," *Los Angeles Times*, February 11, 1893. A few weeks later Isabella and local Senator H. M. Streeter's wife joined their husbands in Sacramento, knowing that their men would be away until the session ended with the bill either passed and signed or defeated again. *Los Angeles Times*, February 11, 1893.

24. James R. Mills to FAM, February 16, 1893, Large Record Book Riverside City and County, Subseries V B, A500-190.

25. Bradley Morse to FAM, February 26, March 5, 1893, Riverside City and County History, V B 7, A500-190.

26. Large Record Book, Riverside City and County History, Subseries V B 7, A500-190. Some encrypted messages and code-word lists survive and are pasted into the above source.

27. T. C. Hunt to FAM, February 10, 1893, Large Record Book Riverside City and County, Subseries V B 7, A500-190.

28. Bradford Morse to FAM, February 26, 1893; Bradford Morse to FAM, March 7, 1893, Large Record Book, Subseries V B 7, A500-190.

29. *Los Angeles Tribune*, January 28, February 27, 1893.

30. *RDP*, January 25, 1890.

31. *RDP*, January 25, February 1, June 21, 1890.

32. Notes, 4, 24, MIFMA.

33. Telegram: FAM to IHM, February 14, 1893; V B 8, A500-190; Notes, 4, MIFMA.

34. *RDP*, February 25, March 8, 13, 1893; *Los Angeles Times*, March 13, 1893.

35. *Los Angeles Times*, February 27, 1893.

36. *Riverside Reflex*, March 18, 1893; *RDP*, March 15, 16, 1893.

37. Notes, 24, MIFMA.

38. Lech, *Roads*, 785ff. His only other political appointment, as a trustee of the Southern California Hospital for the Insane and Inebriates in San Bernardino (later known as Patton State Hospital), extended two years.

39. For them the tasks were all new, but they had statutory guidance and a helpful consultant from the earlier formed Orange County as they assigned administrative district and precinct boundaries; identified judicial, school, and other district lines; certified the eligibility of candidates; and drew up the ballots, among a multitude of other tasks.

40. *RDP*, December 24, 1892. The handsome certificate of appointment is in the Large Record Book, Riverside City and County History, V B 7, A500-190.

41. Notes, 29, MIFMA; *RDP*, March 16, 1893. The equally disgusted editor of the *Press and Horticulturalist* flayed in print those who, having never lifted a finger or given a penny, came clamoring for preferment, qualified only by their gall in demanding offices for themselves or their families.

42. B. A. Worthington to FAM, January 31, 1894, 1 A 1, A500-190; *RDP*, May 14, 1893; Frank Norris, *The Octopus* (New York: New American Library, 1964); William Deverell,

Railway Crossing: California and the Railroad, 1850–1910 (Berkeley: University of California, 1994). Riverside had no railroad land controversy, and citrus growers wanted to move their fruit to distant and profitable markets. After all, one good turn does deserve another. The prospect of competitive freight rates and excursion fares to special events attracted widely.

43. *Riverside Reflex*, March 18, 1893.

44. James Horsburgh to FAM. November 7, 1891, Folder 1 C 3, Correspondence about Temescal Mine, 1891–1899, A500-190; *RDP*, February 11, 15, 1892.

45. The temptation still attracts current commentators.

46. Lech, *Roads*, 611ff.

47. *RDP*, June 5, 1893.

Chapter Nine: Influence Without Office

1. *Los Angeles Times*, February 11, 1893.

2. *RDP*, February 10, 11, 21, 1893.

3. A. D. Noyes, *Forty Years of American Finance* (New York: Putnam 1898, 1909), 222.

4. *RDP*, April 11, August 1, 5, 18, 30, 1893.

5. Klotz, *Bank*, 32–37; *RDP*, June 19, 1893. The paper announced the bank's "uncertain future."

6. *Riverside County Directory 1901* (Riverside, California: Weed and Payne, 1901), 19.

7. *RDP*, November 23, 24, December 5, 1893.

8. *RDP*, December 5, 11, 17, August 1, 14, 22, 1893; Marshall Duell, "Frank Miller and the International Expositions" (master's thesis, University of California Riverside, California, 1987), 26. Duell sees great influence on Miller from this visit. Two artists whose work he enjoyed on this trip were William Keith, who lived from 1838–1911, and Henry Chapman Ford, who lived from 1828–1894.

9. Biography Frank and Isabella Miller Photographs, IV A 14, A500-190.

10. *RDP*, May 15, 1895.

11. See Sarah W. Tracy, *Alcoholism in America* (Philadelphia: Johns Hopkins University Press, 2005).

12. *RPH*, November 15, 16, December 26, 27, 1892.

13. *RPH*, October 17, 1891; *61st Annual Report, Commissioner of Indian Affairs* (Washington, DC: Government Printing Office, 1892), 60; Lech, *Roads*, 370.

14. Notes, 24, MIFMA; Gale, *Miller*, 85, 86.

15. Trustees' meetings were monthly, sometimes more frequent.

16. *RDP*, February 22, 1900; Patterson, *Colony*, 301. Patterson demolished the durable lunch-pail myth in 1970.

17. FAM to James C. Needham, April 3, 1899, Correspondence 1899 through June 1889, I A 2, A500-190.

18. George A. Knight to FAM, January 14, 1895, Correspondence, I A 1. A500-190.

19. *RDP*, May 16, June 8, 1896.

20. *New York Times*, June 20, 1896; *Boston Sunday Journal*, July 19, 1896.

21. *RDP*, August 17, 1896; FAM to Edward Stanwood, August 12, 1896, I A 1, A500-190.

22. *RDP*, August 17, 1896.

23. *RPH*, August 22, 1893. The panels measured forty inches by six inches.

24. *RDP*, December 6, 9, 1893.

25. *RDP*, December 17, 1893.

26. *RPH*, December 19, 1893; January 8, 11, 1894.

27. *RPH*, December 23, 1893; January 1, 6, 1894.

28. The tensions of individualism and corporatism are well presented in Michael McGerr's *A Fierce Discontent* as characteristic of the Progressive period, 1870 through 1920. Michael McGerr, *A Fierce Discontent* (New York: Oxford, 2003).

29. *RPH*, December 6, 9, 15, 16, 1893; *Los Angeles Daily Journal*, January 21, March 29, 1894. The Free Labor Bureau, several years in existence but previously torpid, registered and employed close to thirty men within days. Costs were never argued, because the county that year would close its

books debt-free with $87,236 in hand, unassigned; deposits in Riverside banks in the same year ran $30,000 more than in the previous year. A financial reckoning after three months revealed a better than break-even balance for the city and cost savings for the county as the number of arrests declined.

30. Anti-Chinese and anti-Japanese feelings persisted throughout Miller's life. See Brown and Boyd, *History*, II: 637, 652 for Boyd's most starry-eyed reminiscence from 1922.

31. See *RE*, July 22, 1908, regarding the description of Isabella's interest in employees in the obituary published for her.

32. *Los Angeles Express*, December 16, 17, 1893. The protesters sought to increase wages beyond the current monthly wage of $12.50, board, room, and advanced fares for travel to Riverside.

33. Duell, *Expositions*, assigns an important role to the World's Columbia Exposition in influencing Miller toward his "first class" hotel.

34. *RDP*, March 27, 1894; *Los Angeles Daily Herald*, March 29, 1894.

35. John Crawley to FAM, May 7, 1894; Walter Raymond to FAM, May 14, 1894, General Correspondence 1887–1898, 1 A 1, A500-190.

36. *RDP*, May 22, 31, June 1, 1894. The hotel drew national attention in *Harper's Magazine* in March 1894.

37. *RDP*, March 27, 1894.

38. *RDP*, March 31, April 29, May 3, 1894.

39. Walter Raymond to FAM, May 14, 1894, General Correspondence 1887-1898, I A 1, A500-190.

40. FAM to John Hamilton Gilmore, quoted in *San Francisco Chronicle*, July 15, 1894.

41. George W. May, *Charles E. Duryea Automaker* (Chillicothe, Illinois: River Beach Publishing 1996).

42. FAM to Frank Miller Hutchings, June 25, 1933, Correspondence 1933, I B 18, A500-190.

43. "Crossed the River," *RDP*, August 16, 17, 24, 27, 1895. See also the folder Notes About C. C. and Mary Ann 1880–1895, II C 2, A500-190. The other paper, the *Daily Enterprise*, told a little more about Mary Ann Miller, giving her place of birth as Cincinnati, Ohio, the first Miller residence at the corner of Mulberry and Seventh, and a brief description of the colony in 1874, when she and the family arrived.

44. Brown and Boyd, *History*, 3: 143.

45. *RDP*, August 19, 24, 1895.

46. Notes, 6, 19, 24, 27, MIFMA.

47. *RDP*, November 14, 1896.

48. *RDP* and *RE*, July 6 through August 27, 1897.

Chapter Ten: Wide-Ranging Enterprises

1. *RDP*, November 17, 1897.

2. Luther A. Ingersoll, *Ingersoll's Century History, Santa Monica Bay Cities* (Los Angeles: printed by author, 1908), 196. Hollis P. Huntington in New York and Henry E. Huntington, both directly active in the Pacific Improvement Company, had encouraged Miller in his hotel hopes and supported streetcar plans. General M. H. Sherman and E. P. Peters, both of the Pasadena and Pacific Railroad, sent day-tripping passengers on their streetcars to and from this most popular beach resort.

3. Richard Orsi, *Sunset Limited* (Berkeley: University of California, 2005), n.61, 483.

4. *RDP*, July 19, 21, 24, 31, 1898; *Los Angeles Times*, August 9, 1898.

5. FAM to F. S. Douty, December 30, 1899, Correspondence 1899, October–December, I A 4, A500-190. The exchanges were on November 12, 15, 17, December 13, 30, (possibly not sent) 1899; FAM to HEH, December 30, 1899, Correspondence 1899, October–December, I A 4, A500-190.

6. *RDP*, March 10, 1900.

7. FAM to K. C. Wells, September 17, 1903, Letter Book 3, 1 H 3, A500-190. In Claremont and Santa Monica there were indeed forces beyond Miller's control. Buyers were repelled

in Claremont by the stony, scrubby alluvial fans, and Santa Monica was in transition socially and economically, being outpaced by immediate neighbors. The Arcadia Hotel closed, briefly reopened as a military academy, and then was demolished in 1904.

8. *RDP*, June 8, 1898. The school had been announced locally in 1890. A site many miles from Riverside was chosen in 1891; students enrolled in 1892, and by the time Miller went off to Santa Monica in 1898, it had become well known in the region.

9. *RDP*, November 28, December 6, 1890; *RDP*, October 11, 1899; Brown and Boyd, *History*, 1: 16, 569f; Lech, *Roads*, 370, 405n; Jean Keller, *Empty Beds* (Ann Arbor, Michigan: University of Michigan, 2002), 1–5.

10. Commissioner of Indian Affairs, *60th Annual Report of the Commissioner of Indian Affairs to the Secretary of the Interior* (Washington, DC: US Government, 1891), 224.

11. *RDP*, October 17, 1891; Commissioner of Indian Affairs, *61st Annual Report*, (Washington, DC: US Government, 1892), 60; Lech, *Roads*, 365–371.

12. Riverside attitudes in the 1890s spanned the range characteristic of the period. A survey article of wider scope with solid bibliography on the topic is Eugene F. Provenzo and Gary N. McCloskey, "Catholic and Federal Education in the 19th Century: Opposed Colonial Models," *Journal of American Indian Education*, 21: 1 (October 1981); Lech, *Roads*, 365–371, describes Perris up to 1893.

13. Commissioner of Indian Affairs, *61st Annual Report*, 49. With suggestions of relocation or a second school, aspirants surfaced overnight. Father Antonio Ubach in San Diego, threatened by loss of federal money for his sectarian schools, found support from former US Congressman William W. Bowers and Adolph Claus Spreckles, the sugar baron. San Bernardino solicited support from the Santa Fe Railroad and Albert K. Smiley, a federal Indian commissioner. Redlands made no secret of its conviction that Smiley, who donated the town library, had "also the means of giving [the town] two other things that

Redlands wanted, the City Park and the Indian school." FAM to HEH, January 23, 1899, Correspondence H. E. Huntington, 1899–1907, I E 15, A500-190. Miller saw the Redlands bid as formidable opposition indeed, because of the combination of the Santa Fe Railroad's political clout and Smiley's magisterial knowledge of Indian education backed by his heavy political pull in Washington as an Indian commissioner. Another antagonist, the crusty General Harrison Gray Otis of the *Los Angeles Times*, wanted the school for Los Angeles. His editor at the *Times*, Harry Chandler, wanted the school to stay in Perris, where he and his family held property investments. Whatever the differences between employer and employee, both Otis and Chandler joined a Washington lobbying melee opposing Riverside.

14. Nathan Gonzales, "Riverside, Tourism and the Indian: Frank Miller and the Creation of Sherman Institute," *Southern California Quarterly* 84: 3/4, (2002), 193–222. Gonzales offers a narrow interpretation of Miller's role in the arrival of an Indian school in Riverside.

15. FAM to S. A. Mellice, January 11, 1899, Indian School, I A 2, A5000-190.

16. *RDP*, February 27, 1901. For a concise technical and historical record of the Riverside and Arlington railroad and all other local ventures, see: R&A, Electric Railroad Historical Association, http://www.erha.org/index.html.

17. *RDP*, October 1, 1898; *Los Angeles Times*, 1898; *RDP*, October 6, 10, November 25, 1896. *RDP*, December 9, 1895; September and December 1896; October 1897; April 1898; February and May 1903. In the interim between 1888 and 1896, loans from Glenwood income and mortgaged property kept the company afloat through the economic downturn until recovery in 1898. During these years, the R&A further assured deficits by absorbing the two competing streetcar operations, pushing for new routes, installing standard-gauge tracks, and, in 1896, proposing electrification of its system and plans for a recreational park near the end of the line in Arlington. Equally

important, the R&A, through secretary Miller's efforts, had developed a sympathetic interest from Henry E. Huntington of the Southern Pacific Railway, who visited Riverside several times after his crucial role in assuring county division for Riverside in 1893 and construction of the S. P. passenger and freight line through Riverside in 1895. For Schermerhorn loans, see Documents-Mortgages Records I–XII, A500-190.

18. *RDP*, June 21, 1898.

19. *RDP*, October 2, 1900.

20. The pace of streetcar electrification, however, outran any hope that the trustees could solve their own electricity problems before the R&A crews strung the last overhead cable that would drain off large amounts of unreliable power. When the editor of *RDP* wrote "discouragement beset him on every side," some of it came from one or two trustees, but there were construction problems with the slow arrival of ties, cables, connecting plates, transformers, and generators. *RDP*, January 24, 1899.

21. "R&A," Electric Railroad History Association, 3; *RDP*, April 11, 1899.

22. *RDP*, February 27, 1901.

23. Earlier, in 1875, San Francisco money joined newcomer Samuel Carey Evans's money to open the large Hartshorne Tract; Charles M. Loring brought Minnesota money to build the opera house in 1880; Albert S. White's New York money had funded his large real-estate holdings and guaranteed countless notes to finance local development. Loans (probably not so widely known) from Pauline Schermerhorn of Los Angeles underwrote Miller's several annual Glenwood refurbishings and his street railways; a San Francisco German fraternal society loan had built the Rowell Hotel. On the Hartshorne Tract, see Brown and Boyd, *History*, 1: 365; on Charles Loring, see Hall, *Doors*, 1: 11; on Albert S. White's loans, see *Notes*, 4; the Schermerhorn loans are documented in Documents-Mortgages Records II and III, Documents Notes Records, A500-190. On the San Francisco German Savings and Loan Company, see also *RDP*, December 7, 1897.

24. Klotz, *Bank*, 13, 15. Understandably, Miller and everyone else wanted investments that suited their tastes and hopes for Riverside, but not if they had to live with the Santa Fe Railroad maintenance shops, a sugar-beet processing plant, or a glass factory. No one, local or elsewhere, came forward to invest in the languishing city hospital. In this context, the lagging pace of electrification and Miller's persistent applications for more electrification and more new routes were irritants and threats.

25. FAM to the Board of Trustees, Riverside, California; *RDP*, February 27, 1901.

26. Notes, 6, 19, 23, 24, 25, 28, 29, MIFMA.

27. Suspicious minds created the notion of Miller's collusion with the Santa Fe Railroad, but his channel to Southern Pacific financing was solid fact. Henry Huntington provided series of $10,000 loans to R&A during electrification, whether known in Riverside or not. These short-term loans in themselves gave Huntington no legal ownership, but over the next five years, his interest evolved from loans to purchases of stock and transfers of bonds in 1903, hence an effective control of the whole operation. In the spring of 1903, ownership of the Riverside and Arlington transferred to the Los Angeles Interurban Railway Company. By that time the local players' roles had changed: Miller had recognized this and gave large amounts of the management to others, rewarding all his crews with, among other things, a gift membership in the YMCA. Huntington had sold his interest in the Southern Pacific, determined to make the smaller, interurban lines succeed; he had personally negotiated a franchise in Riverside for a Riverside to Corona line, doing so in the lunch break of a trustee meeting, political smoothness of a high order. There had been other changes. Hostile trustees had either left office or had a conversion experience; the R&A crews had greater skill in operations and management; and a multitude of small problems yielded to experience, thus quieting most public complaints about operations.

28. *RDP*, March 5, 6, 14, 21, 28, 30, 1901.

29. *RDP*, March 20, 1901.

30. See for example correspondence between Huntington or his assistant B. A. Worthington and Miller, January 3, February 20, April 8, 17, 26, May 9, November 14, 1899. Railroad Correspondence 1899, 1 G 1, 1 G 2, and 1 G 3, A500-190; Marie Liebert, *Observations* (Arlington, California: Teresa Gordon, 1982), 124–125.

31. FAM to E. Randolph, March 31, 1904; April 1, 1904; April–June, 1904; March–June 1909, Railroad Correspondence, 1 G 8–1 G 30, A500-190.

32. *RE*, November 2, 1902; *RDP*, November 1, 3, 1902; #10– FAM to HEH, November 5, 1902, The Huntington Collection, The Huntington Library, San Marino, California.

33. *RDP*, January 24, 1899. FAM to HEH, December 19, 1903, Railroad Correspondence, I G 6, A500-190, FMHC, RMM.

34. R&A, Electric Railroad History Association, 8; Liebert, *Observations*, 124–125.

35. John G. North Esq. to FAM, June 28, 1902; FAM to HEH, September 2, 1902; FAM to J. A. Muir, April 16, 1903, The Henry Huntington Collection, The Huntington Library, San Marino, California; FAM to HEH, December 19, 1905, Letter Book 7, I H 7, A500-190.

36. Notes, 23, MIFMA.

Chapter Eleven: Practically a Gift to Riverside

1. Notes, 1, 24, MIFMA; Brown and Boyd, *History*, 1: 514.

2. Each of these is discussed elsewhere.

3. C. W. Barton, "Riverside's New Indian School," *Sunset* 7: 3 (October 1901), 153–156.

4. *RDP*, June 25, 1900.

5. Some recent, local writers have attributed a narrow, exploitive motivation to Miller, saying that he wanted an Indian presence at the inn as a part of his recreation of California missions or their ethos. I find this focus simplistic in that, among other things, it ignores what we know of Miller's complexity, our knowledge of human motivation as almost always

multifaceted, and the physical evidence Miller left us in the variety of architecture and decoration at the Mission Inn, little, indeed, of it suggesting a desire to recreate the California mission life.

6. *RDP*, August 31, 1900.

7. CPH to FAM, February 18, 1899, Correspondence 1899 I, January–June, I A 2, A500-190.

8. J. C. Needham to FAM, November 29, 1898, Correspondence 1887–1898, 1 A 1, A500-190.

9. *RDP*, January 8, March 6, 1900.

10. *RDP*, April 16, 1900.

11. Riverside City Property Ownership Book 4 1892–1895, Robert J. Fitch Archives, Riverside County Records.

12. Elmer W. Holmes, *History of Riverside County California with Biographical Sketches* Record, 389; *RDP*, February 11, 1903. An even larger corps of supporters included US Senators George Clement Perkins and Thomas R. Bard, US Congressman James C. Needham, and Captain A. C. Tonner of the Indian Service. Local supporters volunteered and gave money. When Tonner visited Riverside in 1903, he had the "largely determinative" billing for locating the school in Riverside and the choice of site, both effusions of the moment but nowhere contested.

13. *RDP*, September 24, 1900.

14. Notes, 4–5, MIFMA.

15. *Arlington Times*, February 28, 1940.

16. Office of Indian Affairs, *Report of the Superintendent of Indian Schools 1903* (Washington, DC: US Government, 1903), 5.

17. *Citrograph (Redlands, California)*, February 14, 1903.

18. Documents of Incorporation, Box 3 of 3, Mission Inn, RMM Ephemera, RMM.

19. For the FAM correspondence to and from the attorneys Cochran and Williams Esq. of Los Angeles and for the mortgage documentation from March through July 1898, see Letters, Folder 1, 11, and Documents, Mission Inn, Local

History MIFM; Paulina Schermahorn to FAM, July 24, 1899, Paulina Schermerhorn, 1 A 2, A500-190.

20. C. M. Loring to FAM, December 11, 1898, C. M. Loring Correspondence, I A 1, A500-190.

21. *RDP*, December 24, 1898.

22. FAM to Alice Richardson, May 4, 1907, Correspondence with Richardson Family, II C 10, A500-190.

23. Frank's younger brother, Edward Easton Miller (1864–1922), gets little mention in the Miller archives and only occasional mention in the newspapers.

24. "Marlborough Don'ts," Odds and Ends, I BG 30, A500-190. See also Allis Miller Literature II D 4, A500-190; Miscellaneous Papers 1878–1900, II C 6, A500-190.

25. FAM to J. A. Muir, May 17, 1899, Correspondence January–June 1899, I A 2, A500-190; *RDP*, in various places, 1884–1899.

26. FAM to J. M. F. Murphy, September 10, 1902, Letter Book, 1 I H 1, A500-190.

27. FAM to J. C. Carter, September 26, 28, 1899, Correspondence July–September 1899, I A 3, A500-190.

28. William P. Penn to FAM, August 24, 1899; FAM to William P. Penn, August 26, 1899; FAM to Governor Henry Gage, Colonel D. M. Burns, Congressman J. C. Needham, Senator G. C. Perkins, August 26, 1899, Correspondence July–September 1899, I A 3, A500-190.

29. Memorandum, FAM to J. A. Muir, August 1899, Correspondence July–September 1899, I A 3, A500-190.

30. FAM to W. A. Purrington, November 18, 1899, Correspondence October–December 1899, I A 4, A500-190.

31. Karen J. Weitz, "Arthur B. Benton," in Robert Winter (ed.) *Toward a Simpler Way of Life* (Berkley: University of California. 1997), 191–200; "Makers of Los Angeles: Benton, Arthur B." *Out West*, 30 (April 1909).

32. Lummis Journals, Saturday June 3, 1916, 16, Ms. 1.2.217, Braun Research Library, Southwest Museum, Los Angeles, California.

33. Brown and Boyd, *History*, 2: 693. The steady rise of George Reynolds, local department-store merchant, had allowed his bold gesture in building an impressive new business block, the first downtown construction in several depressed years. Patterson calls Reynolds a "genius," perhaps for his financial acumen and spectacular success in introducing his department store to Riverside. Patterson, *Colony*, 383.

34. HEH to FAM, February 28, 1902, HEH Correspondence 1902, Pacific Electric Railway, 1 E 17, A500-190, FMHC, RMM.

35. *RDP*, March 21, 1902.

36. *RDP*, July 31, August 14, September 1, 1902.

37. *RDP*, March 24, 25, 26, 1902; April 2, 11, 23, 1902.

38. *RDP*, April 23, 1902.

39. FAM to J. A. Muir, June 9, 1903, Correspondence HEH, (financial) 1903, I E 18, A500-190.

40. Correspondence Henry E. Huntington (financial), 1902, I E 16, A500-190. Though undated, this envelope fits best into the known chronology at this point.

Chapter Twelve: In Clear Over My Head

1. The drafts added up to $124,000, although a January 23, 1903, letter summarized the amounts as $120,971.72, and other letters reveal Miller's less than accurate accounting. But with the $25,000 pledged locally, Miller was near to his specified amount.

2. FAM to J. J. Byrne, October 31, 1902, Letter Book 1, 1 H 1, A500-190.

3. FAM to HEH, May 1, 1903, Letter Book 2, 1 H 2, A500-190; June 17, 1903, Correspondence HEH Financial 1903–1904, 1 E 18, A500-190. Miller's commitment and Huntington's response narrowly staved off the imposition of liens due on July 3.

4. FAM to Frank Wheeler, October 4, 1933, Correspondence 1933, 1 B 18, A500-190. Notes, 6, MIFMA. Wheeler was a realtor in Claremont, an associate from Miller's Palomares Hotel involvement and Claremont land sales.

5. HEH to FAM, February 13, 1901, The Henry Huntington Collection, The Huntington Library, San Marino, California; *RDP*, May 13, 1903; HEH to A. D. Schindler, April 9, 1905, Correspondence HEH 1899–1907, 1 E 15, A500-190; *RDP*, February 21, 1911.

6. HEH to FAM, April 2, 1904; March 17, 1905, Correspondence Henry E. Huntington 1899–1907, I E 15, A500-190.

7. For publications illustrating the hotel buildings and interiors, see Steve Lech and Kim Jarrell Johnson, *Riverside's Mission Inn* (San Francisco: Arcadia, 2006); for the Mission Inn as restored in 1993, see Barbara Moore (ed.) *Historic Mission Inn* (Riverside, California: Friends of the Mission Inn, 2nd ed., 2009).

8. Marshall Duell, *Expositions*, on California fairs, 57f, on the Chicago fair, 31–37; Norman Bolotin and Christine Laing, *World's Columbia Exposition* (Champaign, Illinois: University of Illinois, 2002), 34.

9. Karen Weitze, "Arthur B. Benton," in Winter (ed.), *Simpler Way* (2007), 162.

10. Benton and his fellow architects, in search of a characteristic regional architecture, did not try to imitate the mission padres' choice of form or materials, even though Benton particularly was active in mission restoration, especially San Juan Capistrano. In mission revival they sought the spirit as inspiration, believing, said Benton, that "ideality and adaptation to environment and fundamental architectural virtues under some conditions [are] more important than architectural correctness and the niceties of perfected construction" (Arthur B. Benton, "California Mission and its Influence Upon Pacific Coast Architecture," in *Architect and Engineer of California,* 24, February 1911, 36). Benton, and Miller for that matter, would scoff at the notion that California lacked a history. Both knew of the historic presence of Native Americans in the West long before the arrival of mission padres. Benton always referred in his writing and public lectures to the Spanish heritage of California and respect for local materials.

11. *RDP*, October 24, 1894.

12. *Land of Sunshine*, 4: 3 (February, 1896).

13. Benton, "California Mission," 36.

14. FAM to Wilcox and Rose, December 1, 1902, Letter Book 1, 1 H 1, A500-190. There are no descriptions of construction progress; the Riverside Metropolitan Museum archives have a few photographs. What follows is conflated from newspaper and correspondence comments about the process at the Glenwood and other buildings in Riverside in the period.

15. FAM to Albert Smiley, August 25, 1902, Letter Book 1, 1 H 1, A500-190.

16. *RDP*, August 16, 1902.

17. Letters to W. R. Dexter, C. C. Desmond, William Bradford, Sanborn Vail, October 6, 1902, Letter Book 1, 1 H 1, A500-190.

18. Letters sent between August 23 and September 20, 1902, Letter Book 1, 1 H 1, A500-190.

19. FAM to C. C. Wainwright, September 1, 1902, Letter Book 1, 1 H 1, A500-190.

20. FAM to E. H. Burnham, November 6; FAM to A. B. Benton, November 8, December 1, 1902, Letter Book 1, 1 H 1, A500-190.

21. FAM to R. H. Ingram, September 22, 1902, Letter Book 1, 1 H 1, A500-190.

22. FAM to T. T. Porteus Esq., October 24, 1902, Letter Book 1, 1 H 1, A500-190.

23. FAM to H. Jevne, October 16, 1902, Letter Book 1, 1 H 1, A500-190.

24. FAM to Riverside County Board of Supervisors, September 10, 1902, Letter Book 1, 1 H 1, A500-190.

25. FAM to "Dear Minerva," September 17, 1902, Letter Book 1, 1 H 1, A500-190.

26. FAM to Paul Smith and A. K. Smiley, September 25, 1902, Letter Book 1, 1 H 1, A500-190.

27. The YMCA building on Main Street remained for many years.

28. FAM to Norman Pierce, October 27, 1902, Letter Book 1, 1 H 1, A500-190.

29. FAM to A. S. Garvetson, October 6, 1902, Letter Book 1, 1 H 1, A500-190.

30. *RDP*, October 16, November 25, 1902; May 13, 1905.

31. *RDP*, November 25, 1902.

32. *RDP*, October 16, 1902.

33. Oliver Wendell Holmes, "The Chambered Nautilus," first published in 1857.

34. *RDP*, December 10, 30, 1902.

Chapter Thirteen: Frank Is Proud of His Hotel

1. *RDP*, December 26, 1903; Charles Leech Diary, January 16, 1903, LHRC, RPL.

2. FAM to Elbert Hubbard, May 16, 1905, Letter Book 5, 1 H 5, A500-190.

3. *RDP*, January 23, 1903.

4. *RDP*, February 14, 21, 1903.

5. *RDP*, March 21, 1903.

6. *RDP*, May 13, 1903.

7. The commercial travelers were members of the Commercial Travelers Associations of Los Angeles and of San Francisco and of the Pacific Coast Commercial Travelers Association. From the earliest years of the old Glenwood, he offered them display rooms and preferential rates, to the annoyance of some of Miller's competitors. They ate together at a large round table, paid $3.00 a day "for a cozy room and board," and, as Miller's son-in-law said later, "had as an extra dividend the friendship of Frank Miller." FAM to H. C. Judell, October 5, 1903, Letter Book 3, I H 3, A500-190.

8. *RDP*, October 23, 1903.

9. *RDP*, October 26, 1903.

10. *RDP*, October 17, 1902.

11. *RDP*, January 23, 1903.

12. *RDP*, March 9, 1903.

13. Conflated from Letter Book 3, 1 H 3, A500-190.

14. *RDP*, February 10, 1903.

15. *RDP*, February 9, 1903; Joan H. Hall, *Doors*, 1: 82–83. Hall has written sketches of ninety-five distinguished visitors, publishing them in two volumes titled *Through the Doors of the Mission Inn*, (Riverside, California: Highgrove Press, 1996, 2000).

16. Harold Simondson, *Zona Gale* (New York: Twayne 1962), 28, 96.

17. Hall, *Doors*, 2: 63.

18. *RDP*, March 7, 1903.

19. FAM to E. H. Rose, April 9, 1903, Letter Book 3, 1 H 2, A500-190.

20. FAM to E. P. Clarke, March 27, April 7, 1903, Letter Book 2, 1 H 2, A500-190.

21. *RDP*, January 8, 1903; Brown and Boyd, *History*, 1: 290.

22. Joan H. Hall, "Riverside's Historical Societies' Centennial," *Riverside Historical Society Journal* (February 2003) 7, 1–6.

23. FAM to CL, May 1, 1903, Letter Book 2, 1 H 2, A500-190.

24. *RDP*, December 23, 1902; *RDP*, May 7, 1903.

25. FAM to HEH, May 10, 1903, Correspondence 1899 through June 1903, Letter Book 2, I H 2, A500-190. This was the second presidential visit, Benjamin Harrison having come to Riverside in 1891.

26. *Picturesque Riverside*, Presentation Portfolio, Braun Research Library, Southwest Museum, Los Angeles, California.

27. *RDP*, May 8, 1903.

28. Roosevelt frequently took white wine at dinner, enjoyed a flute or two of champagne at banquets, and sipped mint juleps—three ounces of bourbon whiskey over crushed ice garnished with a sprig of mint leaves, all in a tall glass—at the White House during the oppressive Washington summers of his presidency. Edmund Morris, *Colonel Roosevelt* (New York: Random House, 2010), 183.

29. Klotz, *Mission Inn*, 16. Klotz cites an unnamed oral source.

30. FAM to ABB, May 9, 1903, Letter Book 2, 1 H 2, A500-190.
31. Hall, *Doors*, 1: 39.
32. Jeffrey Limerick, et al., *America's Grand Resort Hotels* (New York: Pantheon, 1979), 5.
33. *RDP*, May 9, 1903.
34. David Starr Jordan to FAM, February 14, 1905, Correspondence David Starr Jordan 1905–1931, I E 21, A500-190.
35. FAM to T. C. Hunt, March 18, April 18, 1903, Letter Book 2, I H 2, A500-190.
36. FAM to T. C. Hunt, March 18, 1903, Letter Book 2, 1 H 2, A500-190.
37. FAM to E. P. Johnson, March 24, 1903, Letter Book 4, 1 H 4, A500-190; FAM to T. C. Hunt, April 19, 1903, Letter Book 2, I H 2, A500-190.
38. Paul Gleye, *The Architecture of Los Angeles* (Los Angeles: 1981), 82, 90; Karen Weitz, "Arthur B. Benton," in Robert Winter (ed.), *Toward a Simpler Way of Life: The Arts and Crafts Architects of California*, 191–200.
39. *RDP*, March 1, 1903.
40. FAM to A. S. Garvetson, October 6, 1902, Letter Book 1, I H 1, A500-190; *RDP*, January 23, 1903; *RE*, February 25, 1903; *RDP*, July 17, 1905, quoting the *Pueblo (Colorado) Chieftain*. Guests could choose rooms from among a variety of styles. The East Wing on the ground floor offered interconnected suites entered either from under the pergola in the entry court or from Orange Street. Guests assigned to first- or second-floor rooms could ride an elevator conveniently to the left of the desk. Long central halls with rooms on either side were a familiar hotel style, not different in the New Glenwood except for their carpeted quietness. Many rooms, however, though quite similar in the plans in dimensions of twelve feet by eighteen feet, differed from each other in small but noticeable ways: many had small balconies outside large windows; many, but not all, had fireplaces; a few had split floor levels. All, however, had large windows overlooking either a street or the interior

courtyard, floor mats on plain, polished linoleum, mission or arts-and-crafts furniture, plaster walls finished in light colors, and white bed linens and covers. The effect, as nearly as photographs reveal, was one of sunshine and airiness. On arrival guests would find fresh flowers, probably a basket of oranges, and a printed card of welcome or exhortation. Rooms above the second floor, less prestigious because of the distance from the ground-floor services, were no less characteristic of the inn but were just as open to sunshine and fresh air and were possibly even quieter than those below.

41. Notes, 1, MIFMA. There were other architecturally mission-style hotels in California, New Mexico, and Florida.

42. FAM to ABB, June 27, 29, 1903, Letter Book 2, 1 H 2, A500-190.

43. Although there is no specific document of acceptance in the archives, the correspondence implies a resolution by means of arbitration. See FAM to Mr. Haupt, December 15, 1903, Letter Book 2, I H 2, A500-190; FAM to Wilcox and Rose, Contractors, January 12, 1904; FAM to W. G. Hutchinson, January 14, 1904, Letter Book 3, I H 3; FAM to HEH, December 5, 1903, Letter Book 3, I H 3, A500-190; FAM to Wilcox and Rose, January 2–14, 1904, Letter Hook 3, 1 H 1, A500-190.

44. FAM to Dr. Lewis Thorpe, April 14, 1903; FAM to HEH, July 23, 1903, both Letter Book 2, I H 2, A500-190; FAM to C. F. O'Kelly, September 3, 1903; FAM to E. F. Goff, September 6, 1903; FAM to J. Stuart McConnochie, September 9, 1903; FAM to Grace Nicholson, September 10, 1903, all Letter Book 3, I H 3, A500-190. Isabella was reading him Sarah Platt McLean Greene, *Winslow Plain* (New York: Harper and Brothers, 1902), a best seller of lingering love.

45. FAM to Alice Brinkerhoff, October 19, 1903, Letter Book 3, I H 3, A500-190; FAM to Alice Brinkerhoff, December 23, 1904, Letter Book 4, I H 4, A500-190.

46. FAM to R. F. Brinkerhoff, October 14, 1903, Letter Book 3, I H 3, A500-190.

47. FAM to G. W. James, December 8, 1904; FAM to Norman Pierce, December 12, 1904, Letter Book 4, 1 H 4, A500-190; Notes, 3, MIFMA.

48. FAM to Yale Town Lock Co., November 17, 1902, Letter Book 1, 1 H 1, A500-190.

49. Thomas J. Conaty to FAM, September 15, 1904, Letter Book 4, 1 H 4, A500-190. Miller's recollection is otherwise unconfirmed. A churchman would more likely consider the Latin cross a strongly religious symbol associated with the crucifixion of Jesus, hence sacrilegious in a secular use, not "irreligious."

50. FAM to John G. North, April 9, 1903, Letter Book 2, 1 H 2, A500-190; FAM to Shreve and Co., to Montgomery Bros., March 5, 1906, Letter Book 7, I H 7, A500-190.

51. Maurice Hodgen, "The Romance of the Rain Cross," *Journal of the Riverside Historical Society*, 9 (February 2005), 17–35.

52. Notes, 7, 8, MIFMA.

53. Allis Hutchings, *Francisciana*, Art Catalogs Mission Inn, 3 F 20, A500-190.

Chapter Fourteen: A Trying and Busy Time

1. *RDP*, May 21, 1903.

2. FAM to P. W. Olsen, June 4, 1903, Letter Book 2, I H 2, A500-190.

3. Patterson, *Colony*, 250–253; Notes, 1–5, MIFMA. One story that Miller told made the hilltop the site of his own mystical change of attitudes from youthful rebelliousness to constructive determination for his life in Riverside.

4. *RDP*, June 16, 18, 1903.

5. *RDP*, June 21, 1903.

6. *RDP*, June 26, July 3, August 3, 10, 1903.

7. *RDP*, October 7, 9, 13, 29, November 14, 1903.

8. *RDP*, September 20, 1904.

9. FAM to George Perkins, September 15, 1904; FAM to Paul Morton, September 20, 1904, Letter Book 4, I H 4, A500-190; *RDP*, September 30, 1904; Allis Miller European Trip No.

1, 1904, II D 7, A500-190; Allis Miller to FAM, September 19, 1904, Allis Miller European Trip No. 1 1904, II D 7, A500-190.

10. FAM to T. C. Hunt, August 5, 1904; FAM to HEH, August 10, September 13, 1904, Letter Book 4, I H 4, A500-190.

11. FAM to Dr. McKenzie, September 8, 1904, Letter Book 4, I H 4, A500-190; FAM to C. M. Loring, May 16, 1905, Letter Book 5, I H 5, A500-190.

12. FAM to HEH, August 10, September 13, 1904; FAM to C. M. Loring, October 11, 1904, Letter Book 4, I H 4, A500-190.

13. FAM to HEH, August 10, 1904, Letter Book 4, I H 4, A500-190.

14. Miller's undated proposal, is titled: "———College. A School for the higher education of women. Why would such a school be established and located in Riverside?" Department of Manuscripts, The Henry E. Huntington Library and Art Gallery, San Marion, California. Miller first mentioned the college to Huntington in an August 14, 1904, letter. Thereafter, *RDP* reported discussions in Los Angeles (*RDP*, March 15, April 15, 1905). Miller contacted the Rockefeller Foundation and asked Charles Loring to contact the Carnegie Foundation (FAM to Charles Loring, May 16, 1905, Letter Book 5, I H 5, A500-190). Miller traveled east to solicit financing from unidentified capitalists (FAM to R. L. Kinnear, January 9, 1906, Letter Book 6, I H 6, A500-190) then looked to Edward Hyatt as California superintendent of schools to deliver.

15. Allis Miller to FAM, November 9, 1904, Subseries II B. Allis Miller/Hutchings, A500-190.

16. *RDP*, March 15, August 11, 1905. Miller's colleagues in the Chamber of Commerce remembered his interest years later, directing a Lutheran representative to him in 1921when that denomination considered a college location in Riverside. See Riverside Chamber of Commerce, Board of Directors' Minutes, July 6, 1921. And although nothing came of their exchanges, Miller remained the man to see about colleges in Riverside. On the Marienfeld Open Air School for Boys near Riverside, a school Miller had helped

with land purchase, see Correspondence Henderson/Herrin 1908, I C 13, A500-190. And Miller's interest in a college for Riverside surfaced again almost twenty years later when he urged an air academy for March Field. FAM to Hon. Samuel Shortridge, May 26, 1927, Correspondence 1927, April–June FAM, I B 11, A500-190. This letter urges the appointment to the California air command of an officer sympathetic to the local interest.

17. See Klotz, *Bank*, especially chapters 11, 12, 13; Patterson, *Colony*, 346f.

18. *RDP*, March 22, 1904.

19. *RDP*, August 20, 1904; FAM to C. M. Loring, August 29, 1904, Letter Book 4, 1 H 4, A500-190.

20. Letter Book 5, 1 H 5, February 15–February 27, 1905, A500-190.

21. FAM to Gov. George H. Pardee, June 6, 1904, Pardee, George C. Papers 1871–1968, C-B400, BANC-MSS Box 48, Bancroft Library; FAM to Gov. George Pardee, March 3, 1905, Pardee, George C. Papers 1871–1968, C-B400, BANC-MSS Box 48, Bancroft Library.

22. FAM to Walter Parker, July 29, 1904, Letter Book 4, 1 H 4, A500-190.

23. FAM to A. J. Scott, August 1, 1904, Letter Book 4, 1 H 4, A500-190; FAM to Miguel Estudillo, February 25, 1905, Letter Book 5, 1 H 5, A500-190.

24. FAM to W. H. Herron, April 13, 1905, Letter Book 5, 1 H 5, A500-190; *RDP*, March 7, 1905; Patterson, *Colony*, 329.

25. *RDP*, July 27, 1905; FAM to C. M. Loring, March 5, August 10, 1906, Letter Book 7, 1 H 7, A500-190; FAM to ABB, August 14, 21, 1905, Letter Book 6, I H 6, A500-190.

26. *RDP*, July 31, 1905; August 16, 1905; January 9, 1906.

27. FAM to F. O. Johnson, December 21, 1905, Letter Book 6, 1 H 6, A500-190.

28. FAM to I. G. Thye, October 3, 1905, Letter Book 6, 1 H 6; FAM to C. M. Loring, October 19, 1905; FAM to Matthew [no last name], August 15, 1905, Letter Book 8, 1 H 8, A500-190.

29. Le Roy (ed.), *Chittenden*, 36. Chittenden knew Riverside and the Glenwood from an 1896 visit.

30. FAM to Frank Wiggins, March 1, 1905; May 29, 1905, Letter Book 5, 1 H 5, A500-190.

31. *RDP*, September 30, October 23, November 24, 1905.

32. *RDP*, October 11, 1905.

33. FAM to HEH, November 8, 1905, Letter Book 7, 1 H 7, A500-190.

34. FAM to HEH, November 9, 1905, Letter Book 7, 1 H 7, A500-190.

35. E. E. Calvin to C. S. Fee, October 21, 1905; J. Horsburg to C. S. Fee, October 26, 1905; J. Horsburg to FAM, October 27, 1905, Pacific Electric Railway October–December 1905, 1 G 15, A500-190. Details of the Miller/Evans rivalry are as obscure now as the motivations that fueled it. The mountain already belonged to the Evans family that dominated Riverside Land and Water Company, and they might have sold it to their own syndicate of which Pliny Evans was a member. The Huntington Park Association, which would formalize Miller's interests in corporate form, moved only slowly toward formation. Did Pliny Evans as a director, for his part, have office but lack the control to sway a board majority in the water company? Were the Evans brothers, Samuel and Pliny, making Miller and his friends sing for their supper? Did Miller mean that he would, indeed, quit and be satisfied if Huntington advised it? Perhaps the city trustees slowed the process, balking at the strings of repurchase Evans attached to his offer but agreeable to more Huntington finance for the city.

36. C. W. Barton to John G. North, November 25, 1905, Letter Book 7, I H 7, A500-190.

37. *RDP*, December 14, 1905.

38. Miller had also left town after tense competition with Reynolds over the new hotel and earlier, after his failed hotel-courthouse proposal, perhaps glad each time to be away from the aftermath of conflict.

39. FAM to Gustav Stickley, June 30, 1905, Letter Book 6, 1 H 6, A500-190; FAM to C. M. Loring, August 10, 1905, Letter Book

8, 1 H 8, A500-190; FAM to C. M. Loring, November 18, 1906, Correspondence Charles M. Loring 1906, 1 C 15, A500-190.

40. Charles M. Loring to FAM, April 24, 26, August 11, 1906, Correspondence Chas. M. Loring, I C 5, A500-190.

41. FAM to Sen. Frank Flint, October 24, 1905, Letter Book 8, 1 H 8, A500-190.

42. Richard Orsi, *Sunset Limited* (Berkeley, California: University of California Press, 2005), 205.

43. Notes, 10, MIFMA. The letters, dated November 25, 1905, are filed in Correspondence 1 A 7, A500-190.

44. Notes, 10, 11, MIFMA.

45. FAM to Sen. F. P. Flint, February 24, 1906, Letter Book 8, I H 8, A500-190.

46. FAM to C. M. Loring, January 6, 1906; FAM to C. M. Loring, February 18, 1906, Letter Book 7, I H 7, A500-190.

47. Hall, *Doors*, 2: 58–62; *RDP*, March 13, 1906.

48. FAM to C. M. Loring, February 28, 1906, Letter Book 7, 1 H 7, A500-190.

Chapter Fifteen: A Tumble of Ideas

1. FAM to H. M. Chittenden, December 29, 1905, Letter Book 7, 1 H 7, A500-190.

2. Wenzel, *Anecdotes*, 30, 31. This source gives a detailed chronology.

3. Notes, 3, MIFMA. Miller recognized this in his life. Speaking specifically about his need for appreciation from hotel guests, but more widely applicable, I believe, he said, "I expect I have been just as weak in the craving for recognition in that way as any other fellow, but it has led me to run a hotel in a creditable way." And, he might have added, to achieve a great deal more. (Notes, 3.)

4. John S. McGroarty, "A Free-hand Sketch of a Man and a Mission," *The West Coast Magazine*, August 1913, 21.

5. *RE*, February 6, 23, 1907; *RDP*, February 6, 1907.

6. *RDP*, February 23, 1907.

7. Edmund Morris, *Colonel Roosevelt* (New York: Random House, 2011), 275. Jacob Riis arranged Miller's introduction

to Theodore Roosevelt in Washington. He was well known for his popular lectures and his books *The Making of an American* (1901*)* and *How the Other Half Lives* (1890).

8. *RDP*, February 23, 1907; Wenzel, *Anecdotes*, 55, 56. For the complete evolution of this process, see Wenzel, *Anecdotes*, in "Ceremonies, Events and People" and "Ceremonies, Events and People II."

9. Wenzel, *Anecdotes*, 58.

10. FAM to Bishop Thomas Conaty, March 30, 1907, Letter Number 1468, Archdiocese Center, Archdiocese of Los Angeles, San Fernando California; Notes, 7, MIFMA.

11. *RDP*, April 27, 1907.

12. J. R. Gabbert, "Tribute to a Visionary" in *Arizona Highways* (November 1936).

13. *RDP*, April 22, 27, 1907; FAM to Bishop Thomas Conaty, March 20, 1907, Letter 1468, Archival Center, Archdiocese of Los Angeles. The letter reports the decline of doubts, not their removal. In a later letter, FAM revealed his continuing tension about the Catholic/Protestant balance. See FAM to Henry L. Graham, [no date], To Henry L. Graham and Other Helpful Friends, Mission Inn Scrapbook 224, undated 1914, III H, A500-190. Effective historic preservation and restoration for the crumbling Franciscan missions is a recent, twentieth-century interest, years ahead of Miller's time, whatever the commendable beginning efforts of Charles Lummis, the Landmarks Club, Arthur B. Benton, and successive bishops. See Edna Kimbro, *California Missions: History, Art and Preservation* (Los Angeles: Getty, 2009.) And Junipero Serra remained unknown to many until the California public-school curriculum mandated the study of California missions in the fourth grades.

14. FAM to Sister Rose [Hardenberg], October 22, 1904, Letter Book 4, I H 4, A500-190; FAM to Sarah Seger, April 18, 22, 1906, Correspondence 1906, I A 9, A500-190; FAM to Rose Hardenberg, April 18, 22, 1906, Correspondence 1906, I A 9, A500-190; Myrtle Hardenberg Miller, *The Hardenberg Family: A Genealogical Compilation* (New York: American Historical

Company, 1958), 206–212. The Hardenberg sisters who came to Riverside were Henrietta, Rose, Isabella, Sarah Jane, and Maria.

15. FAM to Sarah Seger, April 22, 1906, Correspondence 1906, I A 9, A500-190; FAM to C. L. Pardee, June 2, 1906, Correspondence 1906, I A 11, A500-190.

16. FAM to Josephine Seger, January 3, 1907, Miller Family Correspondence 1907–1908, II C 11, A500-190. The institutional name later changed to Patton State Hospital in San Bernardino.

17. FAM to George Pearson, July 10, 1906, Correspondence 1906, I A 12, A500-190; Letters to and from Alice Richardson, between FAM and Stanley Richardson, Miller Family Correspondence 1907–1908, II C 11, A500-190.

18. *Truckee (California) Republican*, May 31, 1905; May 9, 1906.

19. FAM to Alice Richardson, May 8, 12, 19, 1906, Correspondence Richardson Family 1906–07, II C 10, A500-190.

20. *RE*, May 19, 22, 1906.

21. FAM to G. W. Wilder, May 23, 1906; FAM to Miss McCormick, May 31, 1906, Correspondence 1906, 1 A 10, A500-190; FAM to C. M. Loring, May 23, 1906, Correspondence Chas. M. Loring 1906, 1 C 15, A500-190; FAM to T. C. Hunt, June 1, 1906, Correspondence 1906, 1 A 11, A500-190.

22. Gale, *Miller*, 126.

23. *RDP*, June 18, 1906.

24. Stanley Richardson to FAM, June 10, 1906 (telegram); FAM to Duncan McDuffie, June 20, 1906; Alice Richardson to FAM, August 23, 1906; FAM to Alice Richardson, August 24, 1906; FAM to Alice Richardson, August 28, 1906, Correspondence Richardson Family 1906–1907, II C 10, A500-190.

25. *RDP*, September 3, 1906.

26. *RDP*, September 3, 1906.

27. FAM to Clarence Barton, July 14, 1906, Correspondence Clarence Barton 1906, I C 8, A500-190; FAM to J. J. Byrne, August 24, 1906, Correspondence 1906, I A 13, A500-190.

28. *RDP*, October 16, 1906; FAM to J. M. Dodge, November 23, 1906, Correspondence 1906, September–October, I A 13, A500-190.

29. FAM to Ed E. Miller, October 12, 1906, Correspondence 1906, October–December, I A 13, A500-190.

30. FAM to Louis Titus, August 26, 1906, Correspondence 1906, I A 13, A500-190; C. W. Barton to Charles M. Loring, November 10, 1906, Correspondence Charles M. Loring 1906, I C 15, A500-190.

31. FAM to C. W. Barton, August 7, 1906, Correspondence W. Barton at Glenwood, II C 8, A500-190; *RDP*, December 12, 1906; *RE*, December 14, 1906.

32. The Yosemite correspondence is almost all contained in Subseries I C, A500-190 in folders 6 through 30. See also Carson and Arnold to FAM, March 22, 1906, Correspondence 1906, I A 8; Charles F. Eaton to FAM (telegram), January 28, 1907; FAM to Charles F. Eaton (telegram), January 29, 1908, Correspondence 1907, I A 13, A500-190.

33. *RDP*, May 23, 1907.

34. *RDP*, May 23, 1907; FAM to T. C. Hunt, May 4, 1907, Yosemite 1907–09, I C 27, A500-190.

35. *RDP*, May 4, 9, 1907.

36. FAM to E. S. Williams, May 6, 1907; FAM to E. P. Ripley, May 7, 1907; FAM to John A. Thayer, May 10, 1907, Correspondence 1907 May, I A 19, A500-190.

37. FAM to C. M. Loring, May 15, 1907, Correspondence Chas M. Loring 1907–08, I A 19, A500-190.

38. FAM to William L. Slaughter, May 13, 1907; William Henry to FAM, May 15, 1907, Correspondence 1907, I A 19, A500-190.

39. FAM to T. C. Peck, May 14, 1907, Correspondence T. C. Peck 1906–1907, I E 23, A500-190.

40. FAM to Alice Richardson, May 4, 1907, Correspondence Richardson Family 1906–07, II C 10, A500-190; A. Thompson to FAM, May 10, 1907, Correspondence 1907, I A 19, A500-190; *RDP*, June 3, September 4, 1907; FAM to E. E. Miller, May

16, 1907, Correspondence 1907, I A 19, A500-190; E. E. Miller to FAM, May 25, Correspondence 1907, I B 29, A500-190; E. E. Miller to FAM, August 28, 1907, Miller Family Correspondence 1907–08, II C 11, A500-190.

41. *RDP*, August 7, 1907; Wilson Crewdson to FAM, September 6, 16, 1907, Miller Family Correspondence 1907–1908, II C 11, A500-190. In London they visited Wilson Crewdson, one of the directors of the Riverside Trust Company and an annual visitor at the inn. Miller searched in London for tapestries, Crewdson assuring him that antique tapestries would be easier to find, somewhat uncertain why Miller wanted modern items.

42. Journal 1907–1922, FB 106 F2000 1869, MIFMA. Surging interest in things old and European and Asian combined with a strong dollar led many Americans to buy heavily in these years.

43. Francis Borton, *Bells and Crosses of the Mission Inn* (Riverside, California: Mission Inn, 1916) described the numbered bells for interested visitors viewing the items widely scattered through the inn. Satis Narrona Coleman, "The Miller Bell Collection," *Bells, Their History, Legends, Making and Uses* (New York: Greenwood, 1971), 395ff; Articles About the Bell Collection, Manuscripts I 1 A, A500-190. On arrival in the United States, Miller's purchases filled a railroad car, with everything put into storage in Riverside in anticipation of the Yosemite hotel.

44. FAM to G. Kelljberg, November 12, 1907; FAM to T. D. Reynolds, November 13, 1907; Correspondence 1907 November, I A 22, A500-190.

45. Gale, *Miller*, 147–148; Fred B. Smith, *Must We Have War?* (New York: Harpers, 1929). Smith's praise of Miller appears on pages 316 and 317.

46. Rolf Newman to FAM, December 4, 1906; FAM to Rolf Newman, January 7, 1907, Miller Family Correspondence 1907–1908, II C 11, A500-190; FAM to Gen. M. H. Sherman, October 30, 1907, Correspondence M. H. Sherman 1908, I E 24, A500-190.

47. *RDP*, October 5, 21, 1907.

48. Charles Lummis Journal, October 31, 1907, MS 1.2.58, Braun Research Library, Southwest Museum.

49. *RDP*, October 27, 1907.

50. FAM to Stanley Richardson, October 18, 1906, Correspondence Richardson Family 1906–07, II C 10, A500-190.

51. FAM to George Marston, November 22, 1907, Correspondence 1907 November, I A 22, A500-190.

Chapter Sixteen: Much Sweetness of Character

1. *RDP*, February 7, 1908.

2. FAM to S. C. Evans, January 27, 1908, Correspondence January–March 1908, I A 24, A500-190. The Socialist was Nelson O. Nelson, an activist promoting the consumer cooperative movement and a garden-cities exponent. Kim McQuaid, "The Businessman as Social Innovator," *The American Journal of Economics and Sociology*, 34: 4 (October 1975), 411–422.

3. *RDP*, February 1, 6, 7, 8, 25; March 1, 1908. The city took over a chamber labor exchange, enrolled over three hundred unemployed, and succeeded in finding work for many. The Women's Christian Temperance Union, that steady watcher of public behavior, thought all these efforts touched only part of the unemployment before the office closed in late March.

4. FAM to Edwin S. Williams, December 10, 1907; FAM to A. W. Hodgdon, December 24, 1907, Correspondence 1907 December, I A 23, A500-190.

5. *RDP*, April 7, 24, 1908.

6. *RDP*, April 17, 24–30, 1908.

7. Charles F. Lummis, "Getting Together," in *Out West*, January–June 1908, 28. Lummis materials are at the Braun Research Library, Autry National Center, Los Angeles.

8. *RDP*, January 7, 16, 1908.

9. Letters between FAM and F. C. O'Kelly, March 16 through March 19, 1908, Correspondence January–March, I

A 24, A500-190; Tom Sitton, *John Randolph Haynes: California Progressive* (Palo Alto, California: Stanford University Press, 1992), 13, 14.

10. Not even a hint of the nature of Isabella's illness emerged in the public or private record, not surprising at a time when modesty veiled much to assure personal privacy—something even more elusive for so public a person as the Mistress of the Inn.

11. FAM to J. H. Reed, July 1, 1908, I A 28, A500-190; Rose Hardenberg to Allis Miller, no date, Condolences 1908, II C 18, A500-190.

12. FAM to AHM (telegram), July 21, 1908, Condolences July 21–22, 1908, II C 13, A500-190.

13. *RDP*, July 21, 22, 25, 1908.

14. Certification of Vital Record, Registered Number 2321, Isabelle Demarest Miller, July 21, 1908, Registrar/Recorder/County Clerk, County of Los Angeles (California).

15. *RDP,* July 26, 1908; Condolences July 21–22 1908, II C 13, A500-190; FAM to Charles Hardy, July 25, 1908, Correspondence 1908 July–September, I A 28, A500-190.

16. Condolences, July, August, September, dated and undated 1908, II C 13–18, A500-190.

17. *Los Angeles Times*, July 21, 1908.

18. Memorial Book, II D 13, A500-190.

19. *The Fra*, 1: 6 (September 1908), 85–86.

20. W. A. Purrington to FAM, July 22, 1908, Condolences 1908, II C 13, A500-190.

21. Tracy Drake to FAM, November 17, 1908, Condolences 1908, II C 17, A500-190.

22. Gale, *Miller*, 66.

23. Memorial Book, II D 13, A500-190; Albert Shaw to FAM, October 17, 1908, Condolences 1908, II C 17, A500-190.

24. *RE*, July 26, 1908.

25. "MNC" to Allis Miller, July 27, 1908, Condolences 1908, II C 12, A500-190.

26. Charles M. Loring to FAM, no date (1908), Condolences 1908, II C 12, A500-190.

27. Chas. Ohlmeyer to Ed E. Miller, July 24, 1908; E. Newman to FAM, July 26, 1908, Condolences 1908, II C 12, A500-190. Emphasis in the originals.

28. Gale, *Miller*, 116. The sentence in the original manuscript, page 99, ran, "This violent personality, which of course sometimes kindled enmities, was the vesture and spirit of the 'natural leader.'" See also pages 134, 167, 168, 99, 100. Gale wrote with the family looking over her shoulder.

29. Sarah Seger to Allis Miller, no date, Condolences 1908, II C 18, A500-190. Internal evidence places this undated letter after May 30, 1909, Memorial Day, ten months after Isabella's demise.

30. Gale, *Miller*, 63.

31. Emma Newman to Allis Miller, July 26, 1908, Condolences 1908, II C 15, A500-190.

32. David Starr Jordan to FAM, February 14, 1905, Correspondence David Starr Jordan 1905–1931, I E 21, A500-190; David Starr Jordan, *Days of a Man* (New York: World Book, 1922), 1: 301, 302. I have difficulty in putting a date on the depression. Miller spent six weeks in Tahoe, in Yosemite, and visiting in San Francisco and Santa Barbara following Isabella's death. His travels would have allowed visits to Jordan in Palo Alto during that time. He visited San Francisco briefly again in September. The fall and winter months in Riverside were busy, with Miller juggling personal and civic projects, anything but an unmotivated schedule.

33. Allis Miller to Marion Clark, no date, Jane Cullen Clark Collection, MIFMA. Most of the letters consulted in this collection were undated. Internal evidence places this letter following Isabella's death in July 1908 while Marion Clark was Miller's secretary and before Marion Clark's departure for Pomona College in August 1909.

34. Miscellaneous Poems, etc., Manuscripts, II A 17, A500-190. The poem, in Burrough's handwriting, is signed and dated March 10, 1909, although originally written much earlier.

35. Bond visited on May 10 and August 25; the verses appeared in *RDP*, September 18, 1909.

36. FAM to Charles M. Loring, September 21, 1908, Correspondence Charles M. Loring 1907–1908, I C 16, A500-190.

37. Harry Candler in *Los Angeles Times*, June 30, 1935.

38. Pliny Evans to FAM, October 3, 1908; FAM to Pliny Evans, October 4, 1908; FAM to R. H. Ingram, October 12, 1908, Correspondence October–December 1907–1909, I A 29, A500-190; *RE*, October 29, 1908; *Los Angeles Times*, June 16, 1908; *RDP*, February 17, 1909. The *Los Angeles Times* notes a bid from P. T. Evans, Miller's antagonist in the earlier conflict.

39. *RDP*, January 16, 1909; Jeffrey Brown, "Statewide Transportation Planning in California," Institute of Transportation Studies, University of California Los Angeles, 2000, ii; California Statutes, 1909, 383. There was abundant reason for Miller's concern. As early as 1894, Governor H. H. Markham had written about corruption in "Good Roads Movement in California," *Good Roads Magazine*, 5: 13–16, (January–June) 1894.

40. *RDP*, February 17, 1909.

41. *RE*, April 6, 1909, reprinting from the *Los Angeles Times*, April 3, 1909; *RDP*, December 21, 1910.

42. Michael McGerr, *A Fierce Discontent: The Rise and Fall of the Progressive Movement in America* (New York: Oxford, 2003).

43. *RDP*, May 21, October 4, 1910.

44. McGerr, "The Shield of Segregation," *A Fierce Discontent*. Miller's ethnic views are now too often set inappropriately in twenty-first-century concepts and language.

45. Notes, 22, 29, MIFMA.

46. *Los Angeles Times*, quoted in *RDP*, April 25, 1910.

47. See *RDP*, January 5, 11, 1911, for a typical report on the arrival of winter guests.

48. Jacob Riis to FAM, August 7, 1908, Condolences on Isabella (Mrs. F.), Miller's Death August 1908, II C 6, A500-190.

49. Walter Raymond to FAM, December 3, 1908; FAM to Walter Raymond, December 4, 1908; Allis Miller to Walter

Raymond, December 22, 1908, Correspondence, I A 29, A500-190.

50. *RDP*, December 22, 26, 1908.

Chapter Seventeen: Propinquity Does It

1. *RDP*, January 2, June 2, 1909.
2. *RDP*, May 12, 1909.
3. *RPE*, June 27, 1951; January 2, 1909. DeWitt Vermilye Hutchings, File Box 276, pages 26–50, Alumni Undergraduate File, Alumni Office, Princeton University. Hutchings first arrived in Riverside from Colorado Springs. His family, reputed to be among the descendants of the Old Dutch of New York and New Jersey, had sent him to the select Lawrenceville School then to Princeton, where he graduated in 1901. Going from there, he taught school for a year and attended theological seminary in New Jersey and at the Union Theological Seminary in Manhattan. Next, he spent a year at Balliol College in Oxford, England. For two years prior to coming to the West, he had tried his hand in insurance and bond sales in New York, then vaguely reported turning to "ranching in the West," but where and for how long, he gave no details.
4. Gale, *Miller*, 84.
5. *RDP*, September 13, 1909; *Los Angeles Times*, September 14, 1909. The *Los Angeles Times* picked up the story from the local papers, indicative of Miller's prominence and Allis's popularity.
6. Wenzel, *Anecdotes*, 193, 221.
7. Wenzel, *Anecdotes*, 193, 221.
8. The souvenir, measuring four and three-eighths by two and one-half inches, is filed in Ribbons, 1895–1909, 2 C 5, A500-190.
9. Wenzel, *Anecdotes on Mount Rubidoux and Frank A. Miller, Her Promoter* (Riverside, California: published by the author, 2010). Chapter 9 provides a reliable chronology and copious illustrations.

10. Mary Riis to Alice Richardson, February 20, 1915, I A 3, A500-190. This appraisal comes much later and from Riis's wife.

11. Hall, *Doors*, 1: 56–58; *RE*, March 31, April 1, 1909.

12. *RDP*, April 7, 1909; DeWitt Hutchings to John Reinhart, March 26, 1927, Easter Sunrise Service 1927, VI 14, A500-190.

13. Freeman, "A Pilgrimage," FB 75, F 2000 .56 .1, MIFMA.

14. Charles Francis Saunders, *Finding the Worthwhile in California* (New York: McBride, 1937), 47. First published in 1916.

15. Notes, 19–21, MIFMA.

16. Notes, 22, MIFMA.

17. *RDP*, June 9, 1909; FAM to Alexis Bjornsen, September 4, 1904, Letter Book 4, I H 4, A500-190; FAM to Gustav Stickley, October 29, 1904, Letter Book 4, I H 4, A500-190.

18. *RDP*, June 9, 1909; *RDP*, June 6, 9, August 14, 1909. As nearly as can be determined, Miller and Benton visited Pala Asistencia, San Luis Rey, Carmel, San Gabriel, San Juan Capistrano, and the distant San Miguel Mission.

19. W. A. Purrington to FAM, August 6, 1909, Series I Subseries A, Folders 1–5, Letter Books, LHRC, RPL.

20. *RDP*, June 27, 1909.

21. Marion Clark to FAM, June 1, 1910, JCRC. Marion Clark reminded Miller of their declaration a year later while they were separated, she in New Jersey and he in Riverside. The date is taken from the postmark on the envelope and is, at best, probable. See Note 25, following.

22. FAM to Marion Clark, October 24, November 17, 1910, JCRC.

23. FAM to Marion Clark, December 22, 1908.

24. Flyleaf inscription, *The Mission Inn*, F2000 1884 86.7.25, Found Box 121, MIFMA.

25. Allis Miller to Marion Clark, no date, JCRC.

26. Untitled biography manuscript, 32, 34, Cullen Collection JCCC 86.8.22, MIFMA.

27. FAM to Emma B. Messer, November 19, 1910, JCRC.

28. *RDP*, September 21, 1909. Marion, at twenty-six a little older than most entering Pomona students, enrolled as a degree-bound student for English, biology, vocal music, and the required physical education. She entered well qualified by Riverside High School graduation that included above average performance in English, history, mathematics, and Latin. Pomona College was near home and popular among her fellow graduating high-school students; certainly Miller's involvement with the college since its beginning and his friendship with Rev. E. F. Goff, corporate secretary there, would influence her choice.

29. Marion Clark to FAM, November 29, 1909; FAM to Marion Clark, October 28, 1910; FAM to Marion Clark, October 18, 1909, JCRC.

30. FAM to Emma B. Messer, November 19, 1910, JCRC.

31. *RDP*, September 12, 1910; Hesperides, "Dwight School for Girls," *A Handbook of American Private Schools, 1916* (Boston: Porter Sergeant, 1916), 177. The Dwight School, established in 1859, offered college-preparatory and finishing-school programs to fifty residential and a hundred day students. The school catalog spoke of a happy, homelike life where women could cultivate self-respect and self-control with only the most necessary restrictions. The surroundings offered every incentive to outdoor sports and pleasures.

32. Papa to Miss Marion Clark (telegram), September 18, 1910, JCRC.

33. FAM to Marion Clark, October 19, 1910, JCRC.

34. Jane Adams to Marion Clark, November 15, 1910, JCRC; Jacob Riis to FAM, December 21, 1909, JCRC; Emma Newman to FAM, November 1909, JCRC. JCRC letters contain references to Marion Clark's enjoyment of such recreations in Riverside, Pomona, and Englewood.

35. Ben C. Truman to FAM (telegram), November 4, 1908, Correspondence 1908 October–December 1908, I A 29, A500-190. Planning began in 1908, two years before the visit. The telegram confirming the visit offered "Congratulations. Have a big chair and presidential suite ready for him." Miller

complied: a large chair (still in the hotel lobby a hundred years later) and a large bed, if later reminiscences are to be relied on, awaited the large president. *RDP*, October 2, 1909; Ray George, "Atmosphere Surrounded by Service," in *National Hotel Review* (December 24, 1927), 24; "Order of Precedence," Correspondence 1909–1913, I A 30, A500-190.

36. Klotz, *Mission Inn*, 23–26; *RDP*, October 12, 13, 1909.

37. FAM to Bishop Thomas Conaty, July 26, 1909, Letter 1995, Archival Center, Archdiocese of Los Angeles.

38. *RDP*, November 5, 18, 1909.

39. *RDP*, December 1, 1910; *Los Angeles Times*, February 28, 1911.

40. Frank V. Pollock to FAM, May 3, 1906, Correspondence 1906 May, 1 A 10, A500-190.

41. For descriptions of the Music Room, see Gale, *Miller*, 56–60; Francis Borton, *Handbook of the Mission Inn*, 19–21, and the companion *Bells and Crosses of the Mission Inn*. Copies are available at MIFMA and RMM.

42. The superb triptych was the work of Harry E. Goodhue (1873–1918).

43. Gale, *Miller*, 58, 59.

44. Hubbard, "The Mission Inn—An Ad," *The Fra*, December 1909; A. B. Benton responded, rejecting similar comments in his essay "The Architecture of the Mission Inn," giving fully half of the essay to the Cloister Wing and its relation to the Franciscan missions. Mission Inn Brochures (Large), Hotel Memorabilia, 3 E 7, A500-190.

45. *RDP*, June 18, 1910; Arthur D. Nichols, "A Mission Ballad." The author, Arthur D. Nichols, a writer of published verse, lived at sometime in Riverside. The nearby presence of a praise-laden piece in the newspaper does nothing to dilute the bitter inferences of the verse, and the verse does much to confirm the presence of Miller's antagonists. The only other scornful verses I found in the newspapers had to do with the county supervisors' corruption in building the courthouse.

46. Gale, *Miller*, 60.

47. *RDP*, August 14, 1909.

48. Brown and Boyd, *History*, 2: 671.

49. *RDP*, December 5, 7, 1910.

50. Miller and Marion had planned but not announced their wedding for June 1911. Her father's rapidly failing health caused them to choose a December date, considerate of his wishes.

51. Jean Rumsey Williams to MCM, August 18, 1949, JRCC.

52. *RME*, December 9, 1910; *Los Angeles Times*, December 9, 1910.

Chapter Eighteen: Big, Jovial, and Genial

1. Rose Hardenberg to FAM, no date, JCRC; FAM to Rose Hardenberg, December 2, 1910, JCRC. For other expressions of confidence, see FAM to MC, October 24, November 17, December 2, 1910, JCRC.

2. Gale, *Miller*, 117.

3. Gale, *Miller*, 117; JCCC, 86.8.22: 35–36; MIFMA.

4. *RDP*, May 22, 1967.

5. FAM to Mrs. Emma B. Messer, November 7, 1909, JCRC.

6. JCCC, 86.8.22; MIFMA, 33, 36–37. The manuscript is of uncertain authorship. Internal evidence suggests its existence during Miller's lifetime, late 1932. Family correspondence reports its existence and a reluctance to publish it. Surviving family letter books, correspondence, and memoirs contain little indeed. There must have been verbal congratulations, however obligatory—many of the season's guests were regulars, well known to Miller, but the absence of cards of greeting, the sentiments of well-wishers, or even incidental comment in letters about other interests is now surprising, if it was, indeed, that way in the first months of 1911. Even decades later, two local searchers expressed surprise at the skimpy sheaf of clippings in the family collections, unaware, perhaps, that except at the time of her death, Isabella also received rare public notice. Beth Teters, *RDP*, June 1956; George Ringwald, *RPE*, May 22, 1967.

7. *RDP*, December 27, 1910.

8. *RDP*, January 4, 5, 8, February 4, 1911.

9. A surprising void now exists where we would expect the family records to contain comments and cards of greeting, even incidental mention in letters from friends and the regularly returning guests. Marion may have collected them separately as she did with other items still preserved.

10. Kate Overton to FAM, November 7, 1910; Rose Hardenberg to FAM, no date, 1909, JCRC.

11. FAM to Rose Hardenberg, December 2, 1910, JCRC.

12. JCCC, 86.8.22: 37, 34, MIFMA; Notes, 13, 19, 26, MIFMA.

13. *RDP*, January 13, 1911.

14. *RDP*, February 14, 1911.

15. David Starr Jordan, *The Human Harvest* (London: Alston Rivers, 1907). Annual reports of the Mohonk Conference began in 1894. Whitney summarizes the American Peace Society. For the spectrum of interests illuminating peace movements, see John Whiteclay Chambers (ed.), *The Eagle and the Dove: The American Peace Movement and United States Foreign Policy 1900–1922* (New York: Garland, 1976) and Charles Chatfield (ed.), *Peace Movements in America* (New York: Schocken, 1973). Jordan, in *Days of a Man*, gives personal glimpses of his own peace advocacy, likely shared with Miller.

16. Notes, 27, MIFMA.

17. *RDP*, February 21, 25, 27, 28, 1911; *Los Angeles Times*, February 28, 29, 1911.

18. *RDP*, March 3, 1911.

19. Michael McGern, *A Fierce Discontent* (New York: Oxford, 2003). Part 2, Progressive Battles, presents the main lines of Progressive reforms in the national context.

20. Gale, *Miller*, 124.

21. *RDP*, March 27, 1911, quoting an unnamed Los Angeles wire source.

22. Francis A. Groff, "Friendliness that Dwells in an Inn," *Los Angeles Times Magazine*, August 1914.

23. Notes, 19, MIFMA.

24. Franklin Hinchborn, *The Story of the Session of the California Legislature, 1911* (San Francisco: James H. Barry,

1911). Chapter 20 and page 246ff describe the legislative history in scrupulous detail. California's constitution assured an eight-hour workday in public employment, but women in private employment worked ten to twelve hours, even six days a week, and with lower wages. In 1911 about 60 percent of trades employing men had eight-hour days, Los Angeles lagging behind San Francisco. See Lucille Eaves, *A History of California Labor Legislation* (Berkeley: University of California, 1910), 225. Advocacy of shorter workdays in trades and crafts had sounded for many years, and concessions had been gained.

25. *RDP*, March 27, 1911.

26. *RDP*, June 5, 1911; Cal. 1912, Ex. parte Miller, 162, 124: 427; L.R.A. 1915F, 829, 35 S.Ct.342.

27. Gale, *Miller*, 124.

28. JCCC, 86.8.22, 34, MIFMA.

29. *RDP*, June 1, 1911.

30. *RDP*, July 10, 24, 1911.

31. FAM to MC, December 2, 1910, JCRC. See also October 19, November 22, 1910, JCRC.

32. Notes, 12, MIFMA.

33. JCCC 86.8.22 MIFMA, 42. Some decorative iron still in the Spanish Wing and the Rotunda Internacional is believed to be from Spain.

34. *Los Angeles Times*, November 23, 1911; *RDP*, November 22, 1911.

35. JCCC 86.8.22: 44, MIFMA. Gale, his biographer, saw these facets of raw personality, artfully concealing them in her text. For examples see, Gale, *Miller*, 50, 54, 88, 99, 100, 116, 126, 134.

36. Patterson, 187, 219, 317, 321. For Crewdson's role in Riverside business, see Joan H. Hall, *Pursuing Eden* (Riverside, California: Highgrove, 2010).

37. JCCC, 86.8.22: 44–49, MIFMA. The date of this encounter is uncertain. I place it here toward the end of Miller's trip, because the inconclusive arrangements left to Crewdson and the US consul might have been clarified after Miller left England.

38. DeWitt Hutchings (ed.), *Bells and Crosses of the Mission Inn* (Riverside, California: Mission Inn, no date), Bell Number 54. The bell still attracts attention at the Mission Inn.

39. *RDP*, November 22, 1911.

40. These fragments of Miller's dream appeared also in Manhattan's Madison Square Garden (1890), on San Francisco's Ferry Building (1892), and later, in Chicago's Wrigley Building (1920); Wrigley Building, Chicago (1920).

41. The curator, Francis Borton, is the likely author. The booklets included several editions of *Bells and Crosses of the Mission Inn* and *Handbook of the Mission Inn*. After Borton's retirement in 1928, DeWitt Hutchings became editor of all subsequent editions.

42. Marie Walsh, *The Mission Bells of California* (San Francisco: Harr Wagner, 1934), 309–311.

43. In 1911 the novel appeared in serial in the *Riverside Daily Press* and in *Sunset* and later in hard cover.

44. Edmund Mitchell, *The Call of the Bells* (New York: Menzies, 1916), 412.

Chapter Nineteen: A Play, a Hotel, and a Gallery

1. *RDP*, March 25, 31, 1909; June 13, 1910; *San Francisco Dramatic Review*, 22: 10 (April 30, 1910).

2. *RDP*, March 25, 31, 1909.

3. John Steven McGroarty (1862–1944) was an employee of the *Los Angeles Times* for forty years, prolific in boosting California and facile in adjective-laden prose. Kevin Starr, *Inventing the Dream: California Through the Progressive Era* (New York: Oxford, 1985), 186–188, sets the mission play in the wider context of the mission myth of California and gives costs and income for the play's twelve-year run. William Deverell, *Whitewashed Adobe* (Los Angeles: University of California, 2004) gives a chapter to the play. See also Frandlin Walker, *Literary History of Southern California* (Berkeley: University of California, 1950), 242–245; FAM to John Steven McGroarty, June 7, 1909, Mission Play Archive, MIFMA.

4. By the contract, McGroarty would receive 15 percent of the gross receipts for each performance; Miller and his heirs would own the script. This attention to detail in the contract reflected Miller's earlier Loring Opera House management years.

5. *RDP*, June 13, 28, 1910; *San Francisco Dramatic Review* 22: 10 (April 30, 1910).

6. FAM to Bishop Thomas Conaty, February 6, 1912, Letter 2761, Archival Center Archdiocese of Los Angeles; Gale, *Miller*, 144; Patterson, *Colony*, 249. Patterson is not as convinced as Gale that the play was written at the inn.

7. Starr, *Dream*, 87–89; FAM to JCMcG, August 10, 1910; *Los Angeles Examiner*, August 10, 1910.

8. Gale, *Miller*, 145.

9. FAM to Frederick Heath, May 31, 1918.

10. Gale, *Miller*, 55, 94.

11. FAM to Secretary of the Interior, December 10, 1910, Yosemite December, I C 28, A500-190.

12. Archival collections are noticeably thin for 1912.

13. *Los Angeles Times*, October 22, 1912.

14. W. H. Childs to FAM, October 17, 23, 1912.

15. Secretary of the Interior to FAM, November 5, 1912, Yosemite November 1912, I C 28, A500-190.

16. Department of the Interior to FAM, December 30, 1912, 180 Frank A. Miller Addendum, Old Central Files, Yosemite National Park Archives. The Miller file on these topics comprises fifty-five documents.

17. George Zentmeyer, *The Lighted Cross*. Miller knew Myron Hunt well from Hunt's visit in 1905 and from working with him as Hunt successfully competed with Arthur Benton in designing the new Congregational Church on Seventh Street, completed in 1912.

18. H. W. Child to FAM, March 15, 1913, Yosemite March 1913, I C 30, A500-190.

19. Charles M. Loring to FAM, July 12, 1913, Yosemite January 1913, 1 C 29, A500-190. Myron Hunt's detailed

descriptions went also to the Department of the Interior. Archival folder, I C 29, A500-190.

20. *RDP*, February 15, 1913.

21. FAM to George Lamar, February 26, 1913, Yosemite 1913, I C 30, A500-190. Miller had already benefited from Lamar's effective intervention in the legislative process.

22. H. W. Childs to FAM, October 23, 1912, Yosemite October 1912, I C 29, A500-190. The Yosemite file in A500-190 fills thirty-six folders. FAM to F. K. Short, December 30, 1912, Yosemite 1912, 1 C 28, A500-190.

23. FAM to H. W. Child, March 30, 1914, Yosemite March 1914, I C 36, A500-190.

24. George H. Lamar to FAM, January 21, 1914, Yosemite 1914, I C 36, A500-190.

25. FAM to George H. Lamar, January 29, 1914, Yosemite 1914, I C 36, A500-190.

26. *RDP*, June 8, 1914.

27. FAM to E. O. McCormick, January 29, 1913, Yosemite January 1913, I C 29, A500-190.

28. Archer Huntington was Henry E. Huntington's stepbrother.

29. Notes, 11, 12.

30. JCCC 86.8.22, 37, MIFMA; Gale, *Miller*, 116, 117.

31. *RDP*, May 16, 1913.

32. *Architect and Engineer*, May 8, 1913. Benton "had withdrawn from further connection with Mr. Miller's architectural projects in Riverside and elsewhere." Miller, however, wanted him as a consulting architect. *Building Review*, clipping, undated, in: Mission Inn Articles and Clippings, Hunt and Chambers, 1913–1919, University of California Santa Barbara.

33. *RDP*, November 4, 1913.

34. Gale, *Miller*, 61.

35. *RE*, June 3, 1916.

36. *RDP*, January 2, 1914. Popular journals and magazines almost always mention the dining facilities but usually offer adjectives rather than factual details. Somewhat better is

Henrietta Mellar Mullan, "Glimpses into Los Angeles Hotels," *Midwest Hotel Reporter* 21: 47 (April 6 1928), 3-5, and 21: 48 (May 5, 1928), 3, 4. Charles W. Goddard, "The Spirit of True Hospitality," *Hotel Management*, III: 2 (February, 1923), 91–96. *RDP*, April 28, 1914. The paintings exhibited early included William Wendt (1865–1946), the dean of California *plein air* painters; Gardner Symonds (1862–1930); A. C. Tanner; and Conway Griffith (1863–1924)—thirty-four canvases in all from respected landscape and architectural artists. Tanner, at the time, lived in the Carmel Tower of the inn, gave a series of art lectures, prepared architectural plans for several local homes, and painted California's history in large murals in the new kitchen. *RDP*, January 14, 1914; Klotz, *Mission Inn*, 37, 38. Even as the Spanish Art Gallery moved toward completion, distinguished visitors coming to the hotel included author and Princeton professor Henry Van Dyke, artist Ernest A. Peixotto, novelist Gertrude Atherton, and Owen Wister, author of *The Virginian*, the cowboy story that launched westerns as a literary genre. All stayed as guests, and almost all performed in one way or another for other guests—a reading, a lecture, a short performance—as happened at selective resort hotels. *RDP*, March 24, September 27, October 5, 30, 1912; March 25, 1913. For FAM's interest in William Keith's paintings, see FAM to Brother Cornelius, April 12, 1935, Correspondence 1935, I B 23, A500-190.

    37. *RDP*, September 17, 21, 1914.

    38. FAM to Bishop Thomas Conaty, April 22, 1914, Letter 2996, Archival Center, Archdiocese of Los Angeles.

    39. *RDP*, September 7, 21, 1914.

    40. *RDP*, August 1, 4, 1914. See editorials in *RDP* and *RE* following August 1, 1914.

    41. *RDP*, September 1, November 14, 1914; Hall, *Doors*, 1: 18–20.

    42. *RDP*, September 14, 1914.

    43. *RDP*, March 14, 1913; W. R. Hearst to FAM, September 19, 1914, Correspondence 1914–1917, I A 31, A500-190.

44. *RDP*, May 1913.
45. *RDP*, November 10, 1917.
46. Hall, *Doors*, 1: 105–108.
47. *RDP*, August 1, 1914.
48. *RDP*, November 23, 1914.
49. *RDP*, December 26, 1914.
50. *RDP*, December 26, 1914.

Chapter Twenty: Peace, Race, and Ceremony
1. *RDP*, January 15, 1915.
2. *RDP*, January 14, 23, 25, February 17, 20, 1915.
3. *RDP*, June 28, 1915.
4. *RDP*, April 14, 1915. A five-day package tour including rail fares cost about forty dollars. In the general local enthusiasm for attendance at the exposition, the fortieth anniversary of the local navel orange, the basis of local prosperity, passed by noticed but uncelebrated. But for many a surge in unemployment prevented such pleasures. Miller called a Southern California conference on resident and transient unemployment, attracting representatives from all the larger cities. The paper reported "hopes for a plan," but nothing regional emerged. *RDP*, September 24, 1915. Memorandum (typescript) "Riverside California September 23, 1915," Concerning Problems of Unemployment 1915, I C 39, A500-190.
5. *RDP*, April 27, 29, May 4, 1915.
6. *RDP*, July 2, 1915.
7. President, Panama-Pacific Exposition to FAM, September 9, 1915; G. W. Goethals to FAM, September 16, 1915, Correspondence 1914–1917, I A 31, A500-190; *RDP*, September 17, 1915.
8. Tarbell's first visit to Riverside was in February 1911 at the Peace Conference.
9. R. V. S. Berry, *The Dream City: The Art, Story and Symbolism* (San Francisco: Brunt, 1915); *RDP*, December 29, 1915.
10. *RDP*, May 27, 1916; *RE*, June 10, July 3, 5, 1916.
11. *RDP*, December 31, 1915.

12. FAM to Brother Cornelius, April 12, 1935, Correspondence 1935, I B 23, A500-190.

13. The city hall would eventually be built on that site in 1924.

14. *RDP*, July 13, 21, 27, August 10, September 7, 1915. The "one man" was not identified. Perhaps the target was C. S. Evans, realtor, twice mayor of Riverside, and Water Company executive.

15. FAM to John A. Allen, July 8, 1926, Correspondence 1926 July–September, I B 6, A500-190. A few years later Miller alluded to the arrival of the war and his loss of control of the council. He may have been thinking of this troubled time when several of his proposals to the council had a rocky reception, but there's no evidence of control in these years. Indeed, the feisty council would be difficult to control.

16. *RDP*, February 4, 1922; *RE*, February 4, 1922.

17. If we calculate banquet attendance based on Riverside's 2011 population, there would be about 7,500 guests. The comparison is a fiction, of course; so many other aspects have changed.

18. *RDP*, November 8, 1915; *RE*, November 9, 1915. The *Press* thought the Millers knew about the event beforehand; the *Enterprise* thought they didn't.

19. *RE*, November 9, 1915. James Mills to Marion Clark Miller, February 12, 1938, Zona Gale Collection, 90.16.64.1, 2, 3, MIFMA. James Boyd, who in his own grief had been welcomed at the inn to revive his "sad and lonely heart," confirmed Miller's quiet, brotherly kindnesses extended to many others, "given not ostentatiously for 'his right hand knoweth not what his left hand doeth.'" Brown and Boyd, *History*, 2: 674.

20. James Mills to Marion Clark Miller, February 12, 1938, 90.16.64.1, 2, 3, Zona Gale Collection, MIFMA; *RE*, November 9, 1915.

21. *RE*, July 11, 1916.

22. *RDP*, August 8, 1916; *Los Angeles Times*, September 10, 1916; reprinted in *RDP*, September 11, 1916.

23. *RDP*, March 3, 14, 1917. Loose Sheet Summary of Plans, L.H. Mission Inn Documents, Correspondence I, MIFMA; *RDP*, December 21, 1916; January 2, 1917; Louise George (ed.) *The Californian* 13: 7 (January 6, 1916) Tournament Number Odds and Ends, I B 30, A500-190.

24. *RDP*, March 6, 1918; FAM to Frank Vegely, Orange County Assessor, June 19, 1903, Letter Book 2, I H 2, A500-190; Clippings in Laguna Beach Public Library Local History files; www.tfaoi.com/newsm1/n1m664.htm, Accessed March 27, 2007.

25. FAM to James T. Phelan, November 1917, Phelan James T. Papers 1857–1941, CB 800 BANC-MSS Phelan, Bancroft Library. The *Charge Up San Juan Hill* hangs prominently in "Duane's," the prestigious Mission Inn restaurant.

26. *RDP*, February 25, 1915; Wenzel, *Anecdotes*, 68.

27. Typescript, E. E. Goff Scrapbook, 223, Series III H, A500-190.

28. Wenzel, *Anecdotes*, 197, n.32.

29. *RDP*, February 2, 25, March 23, 24, 31, April 3, 4, 1915. Wenzel, *Anecdotes*, gives the programs in impressive detail.

30. *RDP*, April 8, 1915; Wenzel, *Anecdotes*, 68, 69.

31. *RDP*, March 18, 1919; *RE*, March 19, 1919.

32. *RDP*, April 19, 25, June 17, 18, 26, 1917.

33. *RDP*, October 15, 18, 20, 25, 1917.

34. *RDP*, November 1, 1917. As a member of the Food Conservation Committee, Miller would keep involved and informed.

35. *RDP*, November 1, 6, 1917; *RE*, November 1, 1917. The agreement temporarily put an end to United States and Japanese tensions over China. Miller regarded the agreement as a triumph of peace through negotiation and as supporting his sentiments toward Japan, two causes for rejoicing.

36. *RDP*, November 17, 1916. Two Japanese-speaking American women in Riverside visited in the Japanese community to welcome newcomers, meeting the often reticent Asian women and encouraging neighborly feeling and awareness

with the two Japanese congregations, one Methodist, one Congregational.

37. *RDP*, January 6, 29, 1916; Mark Rawitsch, *The House on Lemon Street* (Denver, Colorado: University Press of Colorado, 2012); *RE*, June 22, 23, 1915; *RDP*, April 8, 1916; Morrison Gideon Wong, "The Japanese in Riverside, 1890–1945: A Special Case in Race Relations," (PhD diss., University of California Riverside, 1977), 144–146.

38. Gale, "Beauty Pays," *The American Magazine*, April 1918, 85: 52 MIFMA.

39. Hall, *Doors*, 1: 108; *RDP*, November 17, 1915.

40. *RDP*, January 8, 1916.

41. P. David Sentance, *Cricket in America*, Jefferson, North Carolina: McFarland, 2006, 187, uses this idea from Leo Kuper's *Race, Class and Power in Plural Societies* (1963). See also chapter 6, "The Shield of Segregation," McGerr, *Fierce Discontent*. The Progressive impulse favored a strategy of segregation as the better way to bring about the uplifting and educational changes sought. Records suggest that Riverside's nonwhite population had doubled since 1890 to 11.21 percent in 1910. For most, the melting-pot idiom calmed fears and projected a vaguely harmonious future; others saw a more contentious vision as different ethnic groups vied for social position and hegemony within the power structure.

42. R. Bruce Hawley, "Beginnings of March Field," in *Southern California Quarterly* 53: 2 (March 1971), 147–158; *RDP*, January 16, 18, February 7, 28, March 12, 23, 1918; Patterson, *Colony*, 355; San Bernardino County Recorder, Maps, Book 11, 10, Map Number 1, November 3, 1890; County of Riverside, Robert A. Fitch Archives, Deeds Book 527, 308; Book 528, 298–299, 300–301. I am indebted to Jim Hofer, Riverside, California, county archives manager, for guidance through these labyrinths.

43. Gale, *Miller*, 106–108; John H. Holmes, "Gentle Frontier Host," in *Books*, 31 (July 31, 1938), 7; Charles A. Goddard, "The Spirit of True Hospitality," in *Hotel Management*, III: 2 (February 1923), 95.

44. Gale, *Miller*, 106, 107.
45. FAM to Frederick Heath, May 31, 1918, A500-190.
46. Armistice Day 1919–1920, VI A 1, A500-190; Glenn Wenzel, *Anecdotes*. Wenzel's *Anecdotes* provides a careful chronology of Armistice events.
47. Armistice Day, 1919–1920, V A 1; Armistice Day 1921, VI A 2, A500-190; *RDP*, November 12, 1921.
48. *RDP*, October 29, 1919; *RE*, October 29, November 12, 1919; November 11, 12, 1921; Wenzel, *Anecdotes*, 165.

Chapter Twenty-One: A Gorgeous Creation
1. Zona Gale, *Tomah Journal*, June 20, 27, 1919.
2. *RE*, June 13, August 19, 20, 1919.
3. JCCC, 86.8.22, 35, 36, MIFMA.
4. Brown and Boyd, *History*, 2: 637.
5. Marion Clark Miller Archives, Found Box 106, F2000.1869, MIFMA. In addition to the property at Arch Beach, Marion had been deeded a house on Fourth Street, in Riverside, by Mrs. W. A. Purrington, widow of Miller's attorney. The deed was dated May 2, 1918.
6. John R. Gabbert, Miller's newspaper-publishing friend, wrote in 1922 that Miller "had a vision of the possibility of creating a great building which would preserve in solid masonry all the outstanding architectural features of the missions of the padres." No doubt that opinion reflected what Miller shared with Gabbert at that time. But in the building Miller revealed a penchant for variety even more than any vision of the starkly functional Franciscan missions or the assembly of an eighteenth-century California architectural encyclopedia. Brown and Boyd, *History*, II: 669ff. See also Roy George, "Atmosphere Surrounded by Service," *National Hotel Review*, II: 6 (December 24, 1927), 62, 68.
7. *RE*, November 29, 1919. Oral history: Ernest Wilson & Mabyl Bareham, June 10, 1992, 14, MIFMA.
8. Eloise Roorbach, "Romance and History," *Touchstone* 8 (October 1920), 13–18.

9. *RE*, November 9, 1915.

10. JCCC 86.8.22, 37, MIFMA.

11. *RDP*, March 23, 1920; FAM to William Irving, December 29, 1903; Patterson, *Colony*, 112, 217; FAM to Edward E. Miller, August 31, 1904; *RDP*, February 16, 1906. At nineteen and for five years, he drove the stagecoach between Riverside and Colton. Among his later ventures, he invested in livery stables, riding stables, and a horse-trading business. He also played side drum in the Riverside Cornet Band, worked as tree planter for the city, and managed the Loring Opera House for two years to public praise.

12. See Letter Book 6, I H 6, Number 218, 257; Correspondence 1907, May–October, I A 19; Correspondence June–September, I A 20, A500-190; *RDP*, January 9, 1917.

13. FAM to Sarah Seger, April 18, 1906; FAM to Rose Hardenberg, April 22, 1906; Correspondence April 1906, I A 9, A500-190; Gabbert, *History*, 374; Brown and Boyd, *History*, 2: 817; FAM to Sarah Seger, April 22, 1906, Correspondence 1906, I A 9, A500-190; FAM to C. L. Pardee, May 4, June 2, 1906, Correspondence 1906, I A 11, A500-190; FAM to George Pearson, July 10, 1906, Correspondence 1906, I A 12, A500-190; FAM to Josephine Seger, January 3, 1907, Miller Family Correspondence 1907–1908, II C 11, A500-190. Miller set up the interest-free Hardenberg Loan Fund. He built a home for Marion's mother and cared for various of members of his in-law's family and mental-health needs.

14. Notes, 6, 7, 13, 25, MIFMA.

15. Gale, *Miller*, 84.

16. FAM to Alice Richardson, May 4 1907, Correspondence Richardson Family 1906–07, II C 10, A500-190.

17. "Dear Father" letter, April 8, 1924, Correspondence Concerning Murillo and Other Art Works 1924, III F 12, A500-190.

18. *The Bells and Crosses of the Mission Inn* (Riverside, California: Mission Inn, 1912); *Handbook of the Mission Inn* (Riverside, California: Mission Inn, 1947). These were Mission

Inn publications, and after Borton's retirement, DeWitt Hutchings took over as editor, his name appearing in the 1947 edition. DeWitt Hutchings, *The Story of Mt. Rubidoux. Riverside, California* (Riverside, California: Mission Inn, 1926).

19. DH to FAM, April 8, 1924, Correspondence 1920–1927, III F 12, A500-190.

20. *Helena (Montana) Daily Independent* (hereafter *HDI*), January 2, 1920. The Riverside papers made no mention of DeWitt's summer activities in Helena, Montana.

21. *HDI*, April 3, 20, 1920.

22. *HDI*, April 3, 15, 1920.

23. *HDI*, April 18, 20, 22, 23, 1920.

24. *HDI*, April 29, May 15, 16, 24, 29, June 14, 1920.

25. *HDI*, October 28, 1920.

26. *RDP*, December 20, 1920; Elmer R. Murphy, "Mexico," *Rhode's Colossus*, January 1921, 1–8. Miller and Hutchings stayed fifteen days in Mexico, returning on December 10, 1920.

27. *RDP*, December 8, 10, 11, 1920.

28. For the correspondence, see Concerning the Rayas Reredos 1920–21, III F 6, A500-190.

29. *RE*, August 21, 1921; *RDP*, August 29, 1921.

30. Arturo Parra Moreno, "La Capilla Domestica del Marques de Rayas: Estudio de su Iconologia" (master's thesis, School of Architecture, University of Guanajuato, Mexico, 1984). MIFMA has a 2010 translation of this document.

31. *RDP*, May 3, 12, 13, August 8, 21, 1921; Concerning the Rayas Reredos 1920–1921, III F 6, A500-190.

32. FAM to M. Crane, August 27, 1921, Concerning Rayas Reredos 1920–1921, III F 6, A500-190.

33. Mary Crane to FAM, August, 27, 1921; FAM to Mary Crane, August 27, 1921, Concerning the Rayas Reredos 1920–1921, III F 6, A500-190.

Chapter Twenty-Two: Hospitals and Egotism

1. *RE*, April 25, 1922. Bank clearings for the first quarter increased 17 percent over 1921.

2. *RDP*, August 15, 1922.

3. *RDP*, March 31, 1921. The occupancy rate for the first three months that year hovered between 50 and 70 percent, not counting visitors coming for meals only. Well into the twenties, the inn attracted almost as many as could be cared for. In the holiday season and on Easter week, all rooms were filled, with uncared-for guests being sent to other hotels.

4. *RDP*, April 11, June 6, December 14, 1921. A large contingent of Eastern hoteliers, the regional Civil War veterans of the Grand Army of the Republic, the Women's Relief Corps, and a Japanese delegation en route to Washington, DC, made an informal visit. He mended local fences, entertaining the Riverside Municipal Band and nearly a hundred of their supporters in honor of performances on Armistice Day, Easter, and Christmas, not events organized by Miller.

5. *RDP*, February 14, 1921.

6. *RDP*, October 10, 1922.

7. Even before visiting Mexico with DeWitt Hutchings in 1920, Miller had been offered a painting, *The Assumption of the Virgin*, by Bartolome Esteban Murillo (1618–1682). He declined, offering a catalog of banal reasons while confessing elsewhere that he was out of his financial depth and that he did not know a good picture when he saw one. Hutchings became interested in the painting, thereby starting himself on a tortuous involvement in buying it, exhibiting it in the East and West, trying in vain to sell it, and, finally, against his preferences, hanging it at the Mission Inn, where he thought it superior to all other paintings. See Correspondence Murillo, III F 10-12, 1920–1927, A500-190; Correspondence, I B 1, 1920–1921, A500-190; Correspondence, III F 11, A500-190. Hutchings developed other interests, none enduring. His management involvement lay more than a decade ahead.

8. *RE*, April 14, 1922.

9. *RDP*, November 14, 22, 1922; December 1, 1925.

10. *RDP*, November 25, 1919; November 1, 1921. Home building for the newcomers and thrifty residents increased in pace to the point of one new home completed every day for several months in 1928. Tract building was not part of the picture yet.

11. *RDP*, January 6, February 5, 1919.

12. *RDP*, May 20, 21, 22, 1920; *RDP*, November 15, 1921.

13. D. H. Meyer, *The Instructed Conscience: Shaping the American National Ethic* (Philadelphia: University of Pennsylvania, 1972).

14. US Congress, Senate, Special Committee to Investigate the Munitions Industry, Seventy-Third, Seventy-Fourth Cong. Pursuant to S. Res. 206, 1930 (Washington, DC: US Government, 1937). The committee began reporting in 1930. See also H. E. Englebrecht, *Merchants of Death* (New York: Dodd Meade and Company, 1934).

15. *Los Angeles Times*, April 20, 1923. Local physicians favored a community hospital where they could send and attend their patients. Community leaders and businessmen favored a hospital governed by a lay executive board responsive to a lay board of trustees rather than a proprietary doctors' hospital owned and managed by doctors. Further, a community hospital could train nurses economically, provide continuous nursing services, and eliminate the cost to patients of special nurses, well trained, perhaps, but expensive for hospital or home care.

16. *Los Angeles Times*, April 20, 1923.

17. Gale, *Miller*, 94.

18. FAM to Msg. McCarthy, April 6, 1923, Community Hospital 1923, 1 D 8, A500-190. Miller was naïve if he expected the Catholic congregations to rally. They had their own commitments to Catholic hospitals. The two tiny Seventh-day Adventist congregations in Riverside already had administrative links to supporting Loma Linda Sanitarium and their newly established Southern California Academy in La Sierra, which would grow to become La Sierra College, later La Sierra University.

19. FAM to Mrs. C. Loring, April 19, 1923, Correspondence 1923, 1 B 2, A500-190.

20. *RDP*, February 25, 1921.

21. *RDP*, February 27, March 1, 1921.

22. The Carnegie Foundation and the Rockefeller Foundation both had enormous effect in speeding up much-needed change in medical education, especially with the publication of Abraham Flexner, *Medical Education in the U.S. and Canada* (New York: Carnegie Foundation, 1910). Nursing education also became professional in these years, itself exerting profound changes in hospitals and colleges and on physicians.

23. *RDP*, February 21, 22, 23, 25, 1921.

24. *RDP*, May 21, 1923.

25. *RDP*, January 10, 1922. Though not reported at the time, many saw Miller's influence at work in securing the attractive property from within the family.

26. Memorandum for the Family, Community Hospital 1923, I D 8, A500-190, 4, 7, 8, 12–13, 30.

27. Memorandum for the Family, op. cit., 7, 8, 15.

28. Memorandum for the Family, op. cit., 18.

29. FAM to T. C. Peck, August 3, 1923, Correspondence T. C. Peck 1906–1907, I E 23, A500-190; Notes, 12, 13, MIFMA; Hall, *Doors*, 2: 110; FAM to HEH, May 19, 1925, Correspondence HEH 1912–1924, I E 19, A500-190.

30. Hall, *Doors*, 2: 115.

31. JCCC 86.8.22, 65–66; MIFMA. DeWitt Hutchings to Maurice Lavanoux, editor of *Stained Glass*, February 6, 1933, tells the story of the acquisition, attributing the sale to the committee of the Madison Square Presbyterian Church on advice from Louis Tiffany and either Santa Barbara resident Lockwood De Forest, a former Tiffany partner, or his brother Robert De Forest, president of the Metropolitan Museum of New York.

32. D. W. Pontius to FAM, December 19, 1923, Correspondence 1923, II C 1, A500-190. The writer did not specify

the Mayos, but his use of the capital letter and his knowledge of Miller's visit makes the reference highly likely.

33. *RDP*, December 8, 1922.

34. Correspondence, Philanthropy 1923–1925, 1 D 24, A500-190. I have chosen these three years as typical. The list included the American Child Health Association, the Salvation Army, Japanese Relief, American Education in the Levant, Piney Woods Life School, the Mission Restoration Fund, and the Churches of Christ.

35. FAM to Horace Porter, February 3, 1926, Correspondence Concerning Philanthropy 1926–1927, I D 25, A500-190.

36. The *Press* in 1918 described "the industrial center" of Riverside as "well developed and extensive," implying adequacy to local needs. The buildings were strung along the railroad tracks for a mile, from First Street to Fourteenth—eleven citrus-packing houses, two iron foundries, four bulk-storage warehouses, six lumberyards, three railroad warehouses, and processing plants for meat, fruit, ice, flour, and dairy products, as well as gas and electric plants. *RDP*, January 4, 1918. Miller's antagonism to expanding the industrial base was well enough known in the family to become part of the oral history given by Davis Newman, G. O. Newman's grandson, in his oral history: Davis Newman interview by Thomas Patterson, June 1, 1978, Tom Patterson File, RMM.

37. FAM to Alfred M. Lewis, October 2, 1923, Correspondence 1923, II 1 B 3, A500-190.

38. *RDP*, November 2, 1923.

39. FAM to Ross Hammond, October 2, 1923; FAM to Ray Lyman Wilbur, October 13, 1923; FAM to A. H. Halstead, October 13, 1923; FAM to Frank Wiggins, November 28, 1923, Correspondence 1923, II 1 B 3, A500-190.

40. *RDP*, May 26, 1921; *A Story of the Inn; Riverside, California* (Riverside, California: The Mission Inn, c.1919), 8.

41. Joe Skidmore to FAM, February 8, 1923, Correspondence 1923, 1 B 2, A500-190.

42. *RDP*, August 23, 1923.

43. *Hotel Management*, III: 2 (February 1923), 91; see also *RDP*, February 24, 1923, and *RE*, February 25, 1923.

44. *RE*, February 25, 1922.

45. *Los Angeles Times*, December 26, 1922.

46. *RDP*, February 4, 1922; *RE*, February 4, 1922.

47. *RDP*, September 17, 1921.

48. *RE*, December 5, 1921.

49. *RE*, January 6, 1922.

50. *Los Angeles Times*, March 13, 1922; *RDP*, March 12, 1922.

51. FAM to Clarence Barton, May 3, 1924, Correspondence Politics 1922–1924, I D 26, A500-190.

52. *RDP*, August 23, September 22, 26, 1924; FAM to Paul Shoup (telegram), October 8, 1924, Correspondence Politics 1922–1924, I D 26, A500-190.

Chapter Twenty-Three: Go on a Long Sea Voyage

1. M. H. Sherman to FAM, February 6, 1925, General M. H. Sherman 1924–1931, 1 E 25, A500-190; *RDP*, August 22, 24, 26, 1924.

2. FAM to J. S. McGroarty, May 13, 1925, Correspondence and Materials, Mission Play 1917ff, I D 2, A500-190.

3. *RDP*, December 4, 1925; January 28, 1925.

4. *RDP*, January 10, 27, 1925.

5. Notes, 18, MIFMA.

6. Vincent Moses, "Machines in the Garden," in Esther Klotz (ed.), *History of Citrus in the Riverside Area* (Riverside, California: Museum Press, 1982), 61.

7. Notes, 19, JCCC, 86.9.22, MIFMA.

8. Ralph Cram, *Walled Towns* (Boston: Marshall Jones, 1919), 19.

9. *RDP*, October 16, 1930.

10. FAM to J. T. Van Rensselaer, May 18, 1922, Correspondence 1921–1922, 1 B 2, A500-190.

11. *RDP*, May 12, 1923.

12. Patterson, *Colony*, 284; *RDP*, January 3, 8, April 3, December 12, 1924.

Chapter Notes

13. Harry Chandler to M. H. Sherman in Sherman to FAM, February 6, 1925, General M. H. Sherman 1924–1931, 1 E 25, A500-190; FAM to HEH, May 19, 1925, Correspondence HEH 1917–1927, 1 E 19, A500-190.
14. *RDP*, May 15, 1925.
15. Gale, *Miller*, 102.
16. Legal Agreement May 21, 1925, Correspondence Municipal Auditorium 1925–1932, I D 22, A500-190; *RDP*, May 23, 1925.
17. FAM to M. H. Sherman, November 30, 1925, General M. H. Sherman 1924–1931, I E 25, A500-190.
18. Legal Agreement, May 21, 1925; Conference Report, May 22, 1925, Correspondence Municipal Auditorium 1925–1932, 1 D 22, A500-190. The group met at the inn, used the hotel's notepaper, and later provided Miller a copy of their resolutions "for your records." *RDP*, May 23, 26, 1925.
19. FAM to Y. Sakine, August 7, 1925, Japanese Correspondence up to 1925, I F 8, A500-190.
20. Wu Tai Tsang to FAM, September 15, 1925; FAM to Tai Tsang (no date); Quan Quong to FAM, October 12, November 5, December 4, 1925, Correspondence 1924–1925, I B 4, A500-190. See Miller's later involvement with Quon's artist son, Kwan Kim-Gaul, in Correspondence Concerning Portrait Painter Quon Kim Gaul 1928–1934, 1 E 22, A500-190.
21. FAM to James Shaw, April 27, 1925, Correspondence Mission Play 1917, 1 D 21, A500-190; FAM to A. M. Lewis, May 18, 1925, Correspondence 1924–1925, 1 B 4, A500-190; FAM to Edward E. Ayer, May 19, 1925, Correspondence Edward E. Ayer 1916–1927, 1 E 5, A500-190; FAM to HEH, May 19, 1925, Correspondence HEH 1917–1924, 1 E 19, 1 E 5, A500-190; FAM to W. K. Ettner, May 23, 1925, Correspondence Concerning Politics 1925, I D 27, A500-190.
22. M. H. Sherman to Alice Richardson, June 12, 1925, Letter 157, Sherman Collection April 29, 1925–March 21, 1926, Sherman Library and Garden, Corona del Mar, California.
23. *RDP*, June, July, August 3, 1925.

24. *RDP*, August 14, 1925.
25. *RDP*, June 25, 1925.
26. *RDP*, November 18, 1925.
27. *RDP*, June 27, 1925.
28. *RDP*, October 22, 1934.
29. *The Japan Advertiser* (Japan), July 3, 1925. Japanese Correspondence up to 1925, I F 8, A500-190.
30. *The Japan Times and Mail* (Tokyo, Japan), July 8, 1925, Japanese Correspondence up to 1925, I F 8, A500-190.
31. Alice Richardson commented to the *Press* reporter that she had been in Japan three years earlier. See *RDP* September 19, 1925. I found no confirmation of the visit in the available records. She had visited Hawaii previously.
32. *Shanghai Times* (Shanghai, China), October 2, 1925.
33. FAM to M. H. Sherman, November 30, 1925, General M. H. Sherman, 1924–1931, I E 25, A500-190.
34. M. H. Sherman to FAM, November 30, 1925, General M. H. Sherman 1924–1931, 1 E 25, A500-190.
35. Names vary in local publications. I have chosen to use the name printed in the dedicatory program. See Wenzel, *Anecdotes*, 111, 112, and chapter 5.

Chapter Twenty-Four: The Things We Believe In
1. *RDP*, December 14, 1925; Wenzel, *Anecdotes*, 106–112, 279–280.
2. FAM to E. E. Ayer, December 15, 1925, Correspondence Edward E. Ayer, 1916–1927, I E 5, A500-190; *RDP*, December 14, 1925.
3. FAM to M. H. Sherman, December 18, 24, 1925; January 13, 1926, General Sherman 1924–1931, 1 E 25, A500-190.
4. *RDP*, December 14, 1925,
5. FAM to K. Uyeda, August 16, 1926; FAM to Henry Yamaguchi, August 18, 1926, Japanese Correspondence 1926, 1 F 9, A500-190; *RDP*, August 6, 1926.
6. JCCC, 86.8.22, 52, 53, MIFMA.
7. See Peace Movement Correspondence, I F 5, A500-190.

Chapter Notes

8. Wilson Crewdson, *Japan Our Ally* (London: MacMillan, 1915).

9. See, for example, "Responsibility of the Motion Picture Industry in International Relations," in the proceedings of the Institute of International Relations, December 1927.

10. FAM to Cecil B. De Mille, February 2, 1926; De Mille to FAM, February 6, 1926, Correspondence 1926 January–March, 1 B 5, A500-190.

11. FAM to John D. Rockefeller Jr., July 6, 1926, Japanese Correspondence 1926, 1 F 9; Correspondence 1926 July–September, 1 B 17, A500-190; Notes, 28, MIFMA. The opinion was widely shared. See Jon Thares Davidann, "Colossal Illusion: U.S.-Japanese Relations in the Institute of Pacific Relations, 1919–1938," *Journal of World History*, 12: 1 (2001), 155–182; Jon Thares Davidann, *A World in Crisis: The American YMCA in Japan* (Cranbury, New Jersey: Associated Universities Press, 1998).

12. *RDP*, May 15, 1926; FAM to Ross Hammond, April 20, 1926, Peace Monument and Tower 1925–1926, 1 F 2, A500-190.

13. *Tidings* (Los Angeles Diocese), June 25, 1926.

14. Laura L. Klure and Ron Gallup, "The Educator and the Hotel Man" (unpublished manuscript; author's draft, 2007).

15. John E. Harley, *International Understanding Agencies* (Palo Alto: Stanford University, 1931). In the twenties many institutes, summer sessions, vacation schools, academic programs, and international organizations had organized. One author published over 250 pages of program descriptions, Riverside's among them.

16. *RDP*, November 27, 1925.

17. *RDP*, November 27, 1925.

18. FAM to A. G. Wells, November 27, 1925, Correspondence 1924–1925, 1 B 4, A500-190.

19. FAM to W. K. Etter, November 27, 1925, Correspondence Municipal Auditorium 1925–1928, 1 D 22, A500-190.

20. FAM to Riverside Board of Education, July 6, 1926, Correspondence 1926 July–September, 1 B 7, A500-190.

21. FAM to E. E. Ayer, May 19, 1925, Correspondence Edward E. Ayer 1919–1927, I E 5, A500-190.

22. "Riverside's Great Cement Plant," in *As You Find It*, I: 4 (October 12, 1907), 8–23, LHRC, RPL.

23. W. I. Hollingsworth to FAM, May 24, 1926; FAM to W. I. Hollingsworth, June 27, July 3, 1926, Correspondence Mission Play 1917f, 1 D 21, A500-190; *Los Angeles Times*, March 5, 1927. Some memberships that Miller shed were of long standing, though honored in name more than in attendance. The mere diversity of them was indicative of how he was regarded in the community and his own need to be in and be seen in many interests. His *firstness* did not evaporate with maturity. He withdrew from the Auto Club of Southern California Advisory Board, the Catholic Welfare Board, the California Junior Republic Advisory Board in Chino, and even the local Chamber of Commerce, though he saw to it that DeWitt Hutchings's appointment to the chamber gave him a listening post. When offered a vice-presidency in the regional League of Nations, he declined on the very valid bases of not knowing the work and his illness. He had resigned from the Mission Play board earlier; he ended even his association with the play itself when the secretary solicited his presence to plan for land purchase. He declined; "not well enough," he said. Then, with a flourish, he cleared his subscription obligations by canceling the debt the play owed him and reminded the secretary, in listed detail, of all his donations of cash and kind that had, in his view, kept the play afloat. His eagerness to see the new $650,000 Mission Play Theater, however, carried him and many glittering notables to the gala reopening of the play in 1927.

24. FAM to Willis Baum, July 1, 1926, Correspondence Politics 1926–1927, 1 D 28, A500-190; FAM to Flora M. Hastings, July 6, 1926; FAM to P. D. Swing, July 6, 1926, Correspondence 1926–1927, I D 28, A500-190; *RDP*, September 19, 1926.

25. RDP, December 8, 1922; FAM to Alex Fleisher, March 18, 1926; P. Boquet to E. D. Rourke, March 18, 1926; Ray [Newman?] to Uncle Ross [Hammond?], March 16, 1926;

Riverside Community Hospital 1926, I D 10, A500-190; Ronald L. Numbers, *Almost Persuaded: American Physicians and Compulsory Health Insurance* (Philadelphia: Johns Hopkins University, 1978), chapter 7. Miller put his best efforts into assuring financial health for the school and the hospital, particularly to safeguard patient access to the improved care—a benefit offered to middle-class patients. The wealthy had options in Riverside and elsewhere. He knew that annual gifts to the hospital would not continue at the level of the first enthusiasm. Another source might be endowment income generated from investments, paying about a 5 percent return, usual at the time. Insurance plans with prepaid contributions to the hospital were another source. Miller looked toward insurance plans for triple benefit—for himself as an employer, for his employees as patients, and as predictable income to the hospital. He talked to his insurance acquaintances—he himself had been in the business of writing policies for several major companies—but found no help. His own private proposal, based on wide consultation, suggested $1,200 annually to hospital income from the inn, funded at one dollar monthly for each of the one hundred employees, intended to assure their free treatment. No community-wide or other comprehensive-insurance provisions developed, all incentives in California having disappeared following the defeat, largely from physicians' influence, of a compulsory insurance referendum vote in 1918.

26. Carolyn E. Gray to FAM, July 26, 1926, Riverside Community Hospital 1926, I D 10, A500-190; Prospectus, *Riverside School of Nursing* (Riverside, California: Riverside Junior College, 1925), Community Hospital 1926, I D 10, A500-190. The proposed affiliation impressed Gray, more so, no doubt, because of the "rule or ruin" belligerence of the MDs, something well aired in Riverside and within her awareness of medical affairs, even at the national level. Here, indeed, the new departed from what physicians had been used to. Carolyn E. Gray to FAM, July 26, 1926; August 11, 1926, 1 D 10, A500-190. The nursing program succeeded in its training intentions, even though the lines of administration and

finance fluctuated in the settling-in stages. In 1927 the school transferred fully to the junior college while sustaining a close relation to the community hospital. Gilbert Jimenez and Thomas M. Johnson, *Riverside City College, 1916–1981, A 65-Year History* (Riverside, California: Board of Trustees Riverside City College, 1981), 59, 60, 102.

27. *Long Beach (California) Press*, May 12, 1926.

28. FAM to John D. Rockefeller, July 8, 1926, Japanese Correspondence, I F 9, A500-190; Correspondence 1926, July–September I B 17, A500-190.

29. *Tidings* (Los Angles Diocese), June 25, 1926.

30. Found Box 135, F 2000 1898, 1999.56.1, MIFMA; Mary W. Tileston, *Daily Strength for Daily Needs* (London: E. M. Dent, 1904). This annually published personal devotional book is still in publication. Only the 1904 volume is documented in use, but incidental comments in other documents suggest a lifetime habit. FAM to Olive Newman, December 8, 1904, Letter Book 4, I H 4, A500-190.

31. "Plan for Securing Permanent Peace Among the Nations," (undated typescript), Peace Movement Correspondence, I F 5, A500-190. His proposal was first aired in the Committee of Fifty. Their endorsement, and the local newspaper's, encouraged him to present it at the 1927 meeting of the Institute for Pacific Relations in Hawaii. Miller could appreciate this timely public approval, having been publicly criticized by "militarists and some alleged 100-per-centers" for his advocacy of world peace. The proposal urged appointment of national ministers for peace, counterparts to the customary ministers of war. He suggested their appointment by nonpolitical organizations, recommending the Association for International Understanding, a neutral selector already widely accepted among civic and religious organizations. Miller's notions stirred interest as one of many proposals aimed at turning aside growing militarism and continued as a subject of correspondence three months later. Devotees of *realpolitik*, however, all too often the majority, gave such ideas short shrift.

32. *RDP*, January 1, 1926; http://www.papalencyclicals.net/Pius11/P11ARCAN.HTM.

33. Charles M. Sheldon, *In His Steps: What Would Jesus Do?* (Chicago: Advance, 1897); Walter Russell Bowie, *The Inescapable Christ* (New York: Scribner's, 1925).

34. FAM to Walter Russell Bowie, August 6, 1927, Community Hospital 1927, I D 12, A500-190.

35. David Starr Jordan, *The Religion of a Sensible American* (Boston: American Universalist Society, 1909), 23, 78.

36. FAM to C. C. Johns, January 27, 1934, Japanese Correspondence 1934–1926, I F 13, A500-190.

37. FAM to John D. Rockefeller, July 8, 1926, Japanese Correspondence I F 9; Correspondence 1926 July–September, I B 17, A500-190.

38. Elsie Carlson to Marion Clark Miller, July 23, 1937, Zona Gale Collection, 90.16.68, MIFMA.

Chapter Twenty-Five: Peace Plans and Straws in the Wind

1. Wenzel, *Anecdotes*, 174.

2. DH to Harry Robertson, November 6, 1926, Armistice Day 1924–1926, VI A 5, A500-190.

3. FAM to Harry Chandler, October 19, 1926, Correspondence to Harry Chandler *L A Times* 1906–1929, I E 6, A500-190.

4. DH to K. E. Schwinn, November 6, 13, 1926, Armistice Day 1924–1926, VI A 5, A500-190.

5. This member of the German Club was, in fact, a credited diplomatic representative but refused to appear as such with a mere professor.

6. *Los Angeles Times*, November 12, 1926.

7. *Los Angeles Times*, November 1, 1925; November 12, 1926; *RDP*, November 12, 1925; November 12, 1926.

8. Wenzel, *Anecdotes*, 174–182.

9. Wenzel, *Anecdotes*, 177.

10. The annual conferences survive in Riverside in the World Affairs Council of Inland California, sponsored still by the Historic Mission Inn. The eight annual public lectures on

current world issues, delivered by nationally regarded experts, are an intellectual and cultural legacy from Miller's long devotion to international peace and his encircling hospitality.

11. University of Southern California, *Proceedings of the Institute of International Relations* (Los Angeles: University of Southern California, 1926), v. 1–15. KleinSmid published the proceedings for the next fifteen years. Miller's own gatherings about the Institute of International Relations are collected now in Scrapbook 1926, 1 F 4, A500-190. James Rockwell Hunt, "The Twelve Apostles of California," *History Society of Southern California Quarterly* 38: 1 (March, 1956), 65. Miller's chief claim to inclusion as an apostle, in Hunt's opinion, was his zeal for international peace.

12. Arthur Turner, April 23, 2003, personal communication with the author. See also histories of the University of Southern California.

13. Conflated from photographs in Charlotte Ann DuBois, "Tribute to Riverside," *The United States Publisher*, October 1926, reprinted from *RDP*, October 1920; FAM to L. J. Defani, May 26, 1926, Correspondence 1926 April–June, I B 6, A500-190; Gale, *Miller*, 114, 134.

14. "Frank A. Miller to his Successor," II C 23, A500-190. The presumption is that Miller wrote this undated and unaddressed memorandum in March or April 1935 for his daughter, Allis, who would become chairman of the hotel board appointed by his will.

15. FAM to M. H. Sherman, December 7, 1926, General M. H. Sherman 1924–1931, I E 25, A500-190.

16. Notes, 3, MIFMA.

17. *New York Times*, January 2, 1927.

18. *New York Times*, January 2, 1927; *RE*, January 7, 1927; *RDP*, January 11, 1927.

19. FAM to T. J. Sheehy, April 1, 1927, Correspondence 1927 April–June Frank A. Miller, I B 11, A500-190.

20. *RDP*, January 1, March 1, 1927; FAM to E. E. Ayers, April 17, 1927, Correspondence Edward E. Ayer 1916–1927, I E 5,

Chapter Notes

A500-190; S. C. Evans to FAM, September 30, 1927, Correspondence Municipal Auditorium 1925–1928, 1932, I D 22, A500-190; FAM to S. C. Evans, November 25, 1927, Correspondence Municipal Auditorium 1925–1928, 1932, I D 22, A500-190.

21. L. C. Waldman to ABB, March 24, 1927; L. C. Waldman to FAM, August 13, 1927, Correspondence Municipal Auditorium 1925–1928, 1932, I D 22, A500-190.

22. FAM to Harry Chandler, December 17, 1927, Correspondence Municipal Auditorium 1925–1928, 1932, I D 22, A500-190.

23. *RDP*, March 7, 15, 1929.

24. FAM to Edward Filene, November 24, 1928, Correspondence 1928, I B 13, A500-190.

25. *Los Angeles Times*, November 18, 1928.

26. *RDP*, August 7, 1916.

27. *RDP*, August 20, 21, 22, 23, 1912; *RDP*, December 11, 1924, January 27, 1925. Long-term residents could remember the public outcry of 1912 when, close to the Grant School, flyblown manure, pit toilets, and trash piles jolted the city into action for its slum-living underclass and the disgrace of low school services and abnormally high infant-death rates in Casa Blanca.

28. Miller reached beyond the Mile Square to the community hospital, the park in Arlington, and the much-praised Magnolia Avenue leading to it.

29. Notes, 18, 19, MIFMA.

30. Notes, 3, 5, MIFMA.

31. Alice Richardson to Zona Gale, January 8, 1938, 90.16.81, MIFMA. Miller himself later listed Albert S. White, Charles Loring, David Starr Jordan, and Wilson Crewdson as significant friendships, all of whom were deceased by 1927. Notes, 4, MIFMA.

32. FAM to HEH, April 17, 1906; HEH to FAM, April 19, 1906, Correspondence HEH 1899–1907, I E 15, A500-190.

33. FAM to HEH, December 22, 1926; HEH to FAM, December 30, 1926, Correspondence Henry E. Huntington 1917–1927, I E 19, A500-190.

34. *Los Angeles Times*, September 19, 21, 1927.

35. Arthur B. Benton, *The Mission Inn* (Los Angeles: Segnogram Publishing, 1908). Benton's literary gifts found beguiling expression also in a hymn for the Easter service and a booklet publication, *The Mission Inn*, a fanciful and inspirational myth of California missions and the inn. He hand inscribed the narrative's troubled iambic couplets on pages bordered by William Alexander Sharp's pen illustrations and printed on suitably antique-looking parchment paper.

36. *RDP*, September 19, 1927.

37. *RDP*, February 5, 6, October 28, 1926.

38. Memorandum, "Dear Father," September 19, 1927, 2 pages, L.H. Mission Inn Documents, Correspondence I, MIFMA; FAM to A. E. Hubbard, February 26, 1927, Correspondence 1927 January–March FAM, I B 10, A5400-190. My sample of daily room counts for 1927 through 1932, on the same dates each year, is very small but justifies a conclusion that in every instance of comparable dates the guest count declined steadily, even steeply, from 1928 through 1933. My data came from the backs of daily room-count record forms used for carbon copies of correspondence, suggesting Depression-era frugality.

39. "Dear Father," April 8, 1924, Correspondence Concerning Murrillo and Other Art Works 1924, III F 12, A500-190.

40. FAM to David Hardenberg, January 20, 1928, Correspondence 1928, I B 13, A500-190. A local observer, Thomas Patterson, thought the inn never did recover its halcyon days. Patterson, *Colony*, 422.

41. Some of Miller's competition in the twenties and thirties came from a scattering of cheaper spas set up around thermal pools in Riverside County and the growing lure of Palm Springs: "When it comes to a winter resort the desert has put a crimp in us that is going to last," he said about 1934 after citing a 60 percent decline in Mission Inn business over the previous eight years. Financial records for the inn are fragmentary, but Miller's continued building appears to have

involved heavy borrowing. See: Speech Notes, Correspondence Civic Center 1928–1936, I D 17, A500-190. For an illustrated survey of Riverside County spas and resorts in the period, see Steve Lech, *Resorts of Riverside County* (San Francisco: Arcadia, 2005).

42. Gale, *Miller*, 84, and chapter 6, "Devoir to Riverside."

Chapter Twenty-Six: Medals, Minarets, and Flying Buttresses

1. Robert Freestone (ed.), *Urban Planning in a Changing World* (New York: Routledge, 2000); *RDP*, May 3, 1915; Charles H. Cheney and Elvon Musick, "Architectural Control of Private Property," papers presented at the National Conference of City Planning, 1927 (Boston: City Planning, 1927). A comprehensive review of city-planning writing appears as chapter 1 in Freestone's *Urban Planning in a Changing World*.

2. SB 585 (McKinley 1927), Chapter 874, Statutes of 1927; SB 614 (McKinley 1929), Chapter 837, Statutes of 1929; SB 615 (McKinley 1929), Chapter 838, Statutes of 1929; Charles H. Cheney to FAM, May 29, 1927; FAM to Governor C. C. Young, May 27, 1927, Correspondence 1927 April–June, Frank Miller, I B 11, A500-190.

3. Richard Fitzgerald, "Land Use Planning in Southern California: The Matter of Sears, Roebuck and Co. and The City of Riverside," *Southern California Quarterly* 52: 4 (December 1970), 382–405.

4. FAM to H. E. Chambers, January 28, 1930, Correspondence Civic Center 1928–1936, I D 7, A500-190.

5. *RDP*, February 4, 1930.

6. FAM to C. E. Bobert, February 24, 1930; FAM to Ford Howell, February 24, 1930, Correspondence 1930, I B 15, A500-190; *RDP*, November 8, 1930.

7. Zona Gale quoting FAM, 90.16.55.4, Zona Gale Collection, MIFMA.

8. Notes, 28, MIFMA.

9. Smith, *Must We Have War?*, 317.

10. The local *Daily Press* found extensive reporting and editorial comment necessary to spell out to its readers just what this significant international recognition meant. See: *RDP*, December 22, 1928; March 7, 18, 22, May 4, 1929. Other Americans, including David Starr Jordan of Stanford University, had been honored previously. Newspaper clipping, *Pan-Pacific Progress*, January 29, 1928, Japanese Correspondence 1927–1932, I F 10, A500-190; *RDP*, March 19, 1929. The *Los Angeles Times*, March 23, 1929, also described the day's events and the investiture, quoting parts of several speeches.

11. *RDP*, December 22, 1928; March 6, 7, 18, 21, 22, 1929; Joan H. Hall, "Rising Sun in Riverside," *Riverside Museum Associates Report*, February 1989, RMM.

12. *RDP*, March 22, 1929.

13. *RDP*, May 4, 6, 1929.

14. *RDP*, August 28, 1930; Klotz, *Mission Inn*, 83. Henry De Varigny, "The Institute in France," *Nature* 1350: 52 (September 12, 1895), 460. Authorization had come to the consul general from the French Department of Public Instruction in Paris, the award itself made selectively overseas, though widely given in France to teachers and scholars of distinction.

15. Diploma, MA (honorary), June 7, 1930, Correspondence 1930, I B 15, A500-190; Zona Gale Collection 90.16.87, MIFMA; *Los Angeles Times*, June 8, 1930. No record of the citation survived. The program of the day and the newspapers merely listed names.

16. *RDP*, January 1, 1930.

17. *RDP*, May 19, 1926; *RDP*, March 21, 31, 1927.

18. Harry Chandler to FAM, August 6, 1929, Correspondence Harry Chandler 1906–1929, I E 6, A500-190.

19. FAM to W. M. Garland, March 7, 9, 1927; FAM to Harry Chandler, February 26, 1927, Correspondence Standard Finance Corporation 1927, I D 33, A500-190.

20. *RDP*, January 1, 1930. See also *Los Angeles Times*, January 8, 1930; Klotz, *Mission Inn*, 79. Construction continued piecemeal, with seven building permits and probably as many loans.

21. FAM to Stephen T. Mather, January 23, 1929, Bancroft C-B 535, Box 2, Mather, Stephen Tyng, Letters to Mather G-M, Bancroft Library.

22. FAM to ZG, January 20, 1930, Correspondence Zona Gale 1917–1929, I E 10, A500-190. M. H. Sherman to FAM, January 7, 21, 29, February 8, 1926, Range April 29, 1925–March 21, 1930, Number 759, 790, 811, 858; Sherman to FAM, June 7, 1927, Range April 1, 1927–December 23, 1929, Number 235. Miller's letters to and from General M. H. Sherman contain specific comments about his and Miller's bladder troubles, daily irrigations, and Sherman's refusal to undergo surgery.

23. L. H. Mission Inn Documents, Correspondence I, May 1, 1933, to November 30, 1935, MIFMA.

24. FAM to Carl A. Gray, June 20, 1933; FAM to James B. Duffy, July 8, 1933, Correspondence 1933, I B 19, A500-190.

25. *RDP*, November 11, 1930; May 31, 1932.

26. *RDP*, January 16, 1933.

27. *RDP*, April 22, 1933.

28. Elsie [Younggren] Carlstrom to Mrs. Hutchings, August 27, 1933; Mrs. DeWitt V. Hutchings to Mrs. C. E. Carlstrom, August 29, 1933; FAM to Elsie [Younggren] Carlstrom, September 4, 1933, Correspondence 1933, I B 18, A500-190.

29. *RDP*, January 1, May 27, 1930.

30. The painting cannot be identified with certainty. An appraisal, "General Appraisement [sic] of the Mission Inn Riverside California," by the General Appraisals Co. of Los Angeles, October 5, 1938, lists "Near the Wall of the Monastery," Number 22, by K. Vroblevski, 307. Clarkson Dye's "Church Interior in Durango," Catalog Number 618 was listed in an inventory of objects for sale from the inn in 1957: *Catalog: Valuable Paintings...Property of the Mission Inn Riverside California*. Part I, Roy J. Goldberg Galleries 9244 Wiltshire Blvd., Beverley Hills, CA, 1957. These two paintings are attractive candidates only by reason of their titles; I've seen neither.

31. *RE*, January 1, 1932.

32. Cottrell's biographical essay (see note 50), written about the time the Rotunda was under consideration, says, "In 1930 he prepared to spend a million dollars or more in the building of the Rotunda International: a lasting monument to the dream of peace." JCCC, 86.8.22, 60. The exact cost has escaped record and recall.

33. The author was probably Ida Dorothy Ottley Cottrell (1902–1957); see folder "G. O. Newman" in the Tom Patterson Collection, RMM. The manuscript, donated to the Mission Inn Foundation Museum Archives by Mrs. Edward M. Cullen, Marion Clark Miller's niece, comprises all of JCCC 86.8.22, MIFMA. It bears an ascription, "possibly Dorothy Cottrell," based on comparable passages in the manuscript and a booklet by Cottrell, *Little Chapel of Memory* (no place, no publisher, no date), which has the date 1932 written on a flyleaf. The handwritten initials on each page of the manuscript most resemble a conjoined *d* and *c*. Another contender as author is Mary Hester McCoy, a Los Angeles author writing identical prose, though much less of it, in *RDP*, April 9, 1931, under the headline, "Local Sidelights, from Louis Rubidoux to Frank A. Miller" in a section called "Ascent of Mt. Rubidoux." Was there borrowing, sharing, or plagiarism? On Cottrell, see *Australian Dictionary of Biography–Online Edition*, http://adbonline.anu.edu.au/blogs/A080134b.htm.

34. Davis Newman interview by Thomas Patterson, June 1, 1978, Thomas Patterson File, RMM.

35. FAM to ZG, February 17, 1934, Correspondence Zona Gale 1930s, I E 11, A500-190.

36. The manuscript is, at best, a winsome essay, generally chronological, episodic, and sympathetic to its subject, and it is only one among many impressionistic pieces written about the Master and his inn, though longer than others. It differed also in occasional novelistic detail, its sharp focus on the Master of the Inn, and the absence of the usual catalog of places, decorations, and architecture that impressed so many writers and visitors. Whatever the other reasons, this tribute failed the test of

biography as the recreation of a life, an exploration of personality and motivations, and mention of Miller's major interests and material achievements, and their inclusion is probably what Miller had in view. His comment about lack of support for the biography is in FAM to ZG, February 17, 1934, Correspondence Zona Gale, 1930s, I E 11, A500-190.

37. MCM to ZG, August 7, 1935; L. H. Biography Miller Marion, C I, MIFMA.

38. Sears, "California's Mission Inn," *California Arts and Architecture*, 40 (September 1931), 16–21; *RDP*, January 1, 1931; Gale, *Miller*, 75–76, 148–154.

Chapter Twenty-Seven: Advancing Years

1. Jason Root to FAM, February 15, 1927; FAM to Jason B. Root, February 18, 1932, Correspondence 1927 January–March, Frank A. Miller, I B 10, A500-190; *Ontario (California) Daily Report*, February 24, 1932.

2. Handwritten notation in a partial transcription of FAM's March 1873 diary entry mentioning Mattie Weed, prepared in connection with the Zona Gale biography. Found Box 77, 1990.16.75 MIFMA.

3. *RDP*, May 23, 1932; *RE*, May 23, 1932.

4. *RE*, May 23, 1932; *RDP*, May 23, 1932; *Roseville (California) Evening Recorder*, February 20, 21, 1933.

5. FAM to Harry Carr, August 27, 1932, Humane Society Tablet, 1932–34, I F 12, A500-190.

6. *RDP*, August 20, 31, September 15, 1934; *Los Angeles Times*, September 14, 1934.

7. *RDP*, December 14, 1925.

8. *RDP*, July 18, 1928; February 8, 1930; January 16, May 6, 1935.

9. *RDP*, June 30, 1931.

10. *RDP*, February 20, 1932.

11. *RDP*, January 31, February 8, June 26, 1933.

12. Fred B. Smith, *Must We Have War?* (New York: Harpers, 1927), 316–317.

13. *RDP*, June 1, 1932.

14. Gale, *Miller*, 127.

15. FAM to Lee Shippey, February 7, 1935, Correspondence 1935, I B 23, A500-190.

16. *RDP*, April 20, 21, 1933.

17. Japanese Exhibition Association to FAM, August 15, 1933, Japanese Correspondence 1927–1933, I F 11, A500-190; *Los Angeles Times*, August 18, 1933. The two battledores had been prominent in the Japanese exhibit at the Chicago Century of Progress International Exhibition in 1933.

18. Brown and Boyd, *History*, 1: 305.

19. FAM to ZG, May 29, 1933, Correspondence Zona Gale 1930s, I E 11, A500-190.

20. *Los Angeles Times*, June 12, 1929.

21. *RDP*, April 28, 1930.

22. M. H. Sherman to Marion Clark Miller, December 25, 1928, Number 692, Sherman/Miller Correspondence, Range 12/27/27–9/21/29, Sherman Library and Garden, Corona del Mar, California.

23. FAM acquaintances dying in 1932 included E. P. Clarke, C. S. Evans, Pliny T. Evans, and Agnes Overton in Riverside, Henry Van Dyke in Princeton, New Jersey, and Louis Comfort Tiffany in New York.

24. The poem, abbreviated here, is by Eunice Tietjens (1884–1944), published first in 1920 and included in *Leaves in Windy Weather* (New York: Knopf, 1929). Undated tear sheet marked "from Rose, Christmas 1934," Correspondence 1934 October–December, I B 22, A500-190.

25. Notes, 13, 19, MIFMA; JCCC, 86.8.22, 34, 35, MIFMA.

26. FAM to Eugene Clark, February 24, 1934, Correspondence 1934 January–March, I B 19, A500-190. See also L.H. Mission Inn Documents, Correspondence I, between May 1931 and November 30, 1935, MIFMA.

27. Memo, FAM to Alice Richardson, Albert Miller, M. Saint Clair, A. Hutchings, June 30, 1932, Correspondence 1932, I B 17, A500-190.

Chapter Notes

28. *RDP*, October 30, 1933; Davis Newman Oral History, 7, A500-190.

29. FAM to All Heads of Departments, February 28, 1934, Correspondence 1934 January–March, I B 19, A500-190.

30. FAM to G. Gottlob, April 23, 1934, Correspondence 1934 April–June, I B 20, A500-190; *RDP*, April 1, June 4, 1935. The year 1935 brought swelling groups of tourists and added conventions to the inn; the optimism of the previous year seemed to be rewarded. Lower rates helped: $3.50 for a single with bath, $5.00 for a double. These were the rates of the early twenties. California *plein air* painter and Miller's Laguna neighbor William Alexander Griffith exhibited in the adobe; nationally known artist Martin Borgord followed in February with what was to be his last exhibition. Then, in succession, Frederick Johnson, James Redmond, and sculptor Peter David Edstrom exhibited. In March nearly a thousand young men of the De Molay Society met in Riverside and the inn. Notables allowed a newspaper headline of "Famous People at a Famed Hostelry," and July reservations exceeded a thousand from the tour agencies and railroads, a brisk upturn from previous years.

31. FAM to Henry Schwanecke, October 1, 1934, Correspondence 1934 October–December, I D 22, A500-190.

32. See, for example, FAM to Henry M. Robinson, March 16, 1935, Correspondence 1935, I B 23, A500-190.

33. FAM to C. C. Chapman, July 10, 1932, Correspondence Politics 1932, I D 29, A500-190.

34. FAM to Marshal Hale, May 5, 1932, Correspondence Politics 1932, I D 29, A500-190.

35. *RDP*, August 13, 1932.

36. *RDP*, October 13, 1934.

37. FAM to ZG, May 29, 1933, Correspondence Zona Gale 1930s, I E 11, A500-190; FAM to Aurelia Reinhardt, April 17, 1934, Correspondence 1934 April–June, I B 20, A500-190.

38. *RDP*, October 3, 1932. The name International Institute of World Affairs replaced Institute of International Relations.

39. Martin Keating to FAM, October 19, 1933, Correspondence 1933, I B 18, A500-190; Aurelia Henry Reinhardt to FAM, October 3, 1934, Correspondence 1934 June–December, I B 20, A500-190; *RDP*, November 16, December 9, 1934.

40. *RDP*, March 12, 1928.

41. FAM to Chamber of Commerce Mattoon Illinois, June 16, 1933; FAM to Phil Stanton, October 4, 1933; FAM to Harry Chandler, October 5, 1933; Mike Westerfield to W. A. Sullivan (telegram), October 6, 1933; FAM to Harry Chandler, October 7, 1933, Correspondence Highway 60 1933, I D 18, A500-190; *RDP*, October 30, 1934; *Los Angeles Times*, November 26, 1933.

42. FAM to Phil A. Stanton, October 7, 1933, Correspondence Highway 60 1933, I D 18, A500-190.

43. M. J. Westerfield to W. A. Sullivan, October 14, 1933; W. A. Sullivan to M. J. Westerfield, November 3, 1933, Correspondence Highway 60 1933, I D 18, A500-190.

44. Robert Ashworth to FAM, January 3, 1935, Correspondence 1935, I B 23, A500-190.

45. Blaisdell Papers M. Miscellaneous 1935, Drawer 12: 42, Pomona College Archives.

46. *RDP*, March 26, 1935.

47. FAM to ZG, May 29, 1933, Correspondence Zona Gale 1930s, I E 11, A500-190.

48. *RDP*, March 10, 1934.

49. See Walter P. Parks, *The Famous Fliers Wall of the Mission Inn* (Riverside, California: Harwarden, 1986).

50. Marion Dixon to FAM, January 3, 1935, Correspondence 1935, I B 23, A500-190.

51. DH to Marion Dixon, January 5, 1935, Correspondence 1935, I B 23, A500-190.

52. DH to Marion Dixon, January 5, 1935, Correspondence 1935, I B 23, A500-190. There are two separate letters to Dixon on this date.

53. Will of Frank A. Miller (hereafter Will of Frank Miller), Dated January 25, 1934, Probate No. 6900, Office of the County Clerk, Riverside, California.

Chapter Twenty-Eight: Master No More
1. *RDP*, March 6, 8, 1935.
2. Notes, 23, MIFMA.
3. FAM to ZG, February 17, 1934, Correspondence Zona Gale 1930s, I E 11, A500-190. There are several letters; the one cited runs to four pages, single spaced.
4. Marco R. Newmark, "Early California Resorts," in *Historical Society of California Quarterly* 35: 2 (June 1953), 140–141.
5. The available transcript at MIFMA comprises twenty-nine pages with the handwritten title "Notes for an autobiography, dictated at Laguna Beach, March 1935, by Frank Miller." Internal evidence adds dictation dates of April 6 on page ten, April 17 on page eighteen, and April 27 on page twenty. Also included are letters dated April 24 and April 28, 1935, and referred to in the text. Gale, *Miller*.
6. Notes, 1, MIFMA.
7. Notes, 2, MIFMA.
8. Notes, 6, 13, 16, MIFMA.
9. *Diaries*, July 15, 1877.
10. FAM to Frank Miller Hutchings, June 25, 1933, Correspondence 1933, I B 18, A500-190; FAM to Rose Hardenberg, December 2, 1910, JCRC.
11. Notes, 13, 15, MIFMA.
12. Miller had as lucid an exposition of these views as could be found in an autographed gift copy of David Starr Jordan, *Religion of a Sensible American* (Boston: American Unitarian Society, 1909), 13–17.
13. Notes, 3, MIFMA.
14. Notes, 20, MIFMA.
15. Notes, 25, MIFMA.
16. Henry van Dyke, "God of the Open Air," line 31.
17. FAM to C. H. Emmons, February 20, 1935, Correspondence Civic Center 1928–36, I D 7, A500-190; T. J. Jackson Lears, *No Place of Grace* (Chicago: University of Chicago, 1983).

18. MCM to K. Igarashi, April 9, 1935, Japanese Correspondence 1934–1935, I F 13, A500-190. Which hospital he patronized is not known, whether the community hospital he had done so much to establish or the Loma Linda Sanitarium that he admired greatly, as demonstrated, for example, in a letter from FAM to Harry Chandler, July 15, 1933, Correspondence Harry Chandler 1930–1938 I E 7, A500-190.

19. Fully reported in *RDP*, April 27, 1935; Wenzel, *Anecdotes*, 217.

20. JCCC, 86.8.22 MIFMA, 67, 68. Notes, 20, makes clear that Miller remained at the hotel during the 1935 Mount Rubidoux Easter service, later visited there by Harry Chandler, who had been on the mountain, his first visit to the service. See Harry Chandler to FAM, April 24, 1935, inserted in Notes between pages twenty-two and twenty-three.

21. Notes, 20, MIFMA.

22. FAM to ZG, February 17, 1934, Correspondence Zona Gale 1934, I E 11, A500-190.

23. Notes, 29, MIFMA.

24. "Frank A. Miller to his Successor," typescript, II C 23, A500-190. The presumption is that Miller wrote this undated, unaddressed memorandum in March or April 1935 for Allis Hutchings, who would become board chairman on his death.

25. Few details of Miller's last two months of life appear in available records.

26. Zona Gale, "Master of the Inn," in *Christian Century*, June 1935, 1347; L.H. Biography: Miller, Marion C. I, MIFMA.

27. Marco Newmark, "Early California Resorts," *Historical Society of Southern California Quarterly*, 35: 2 (June 1935) 140–141.

28. *Los Angeles Times*, June 16, 1935.

29. FAM to ZG, November 17, 1934, Correspondence Zona Gale 1930s, I E 11, A500-190.

30. JCCC 86.8.22, 8, MIFMA.

31. Zona Gale comment, L.H. Biography: Miller Marion C. I, MIFMA; *Time*, May 13, 1935.

32. *RDP*, June 6, 12, 1935; Zona Gale, "Makers of the Inn," *Christian Century*, 1374; L.H. Biography: Frank A. Miller II, MIFMA.

33. *RDP*, June 15, 1935. Almost the only records of Miller's death, funeral, and burial come from newspapers—*Los Angeles Times*, *RDP*, and *RE*. The June 15, 1935, *San Francisco Chronicle* carried a half-dozen-line obituary that named his pioneer origins, peace advocacy, the Institute of World Affairs, work for United States–Japan relations, and his decoration with the Order of the Rising Sun.

34. *RDP*, June 17, 1935.

35. *RDP*, June 17, 1935.

Epilogue

1. *Los Angeles Times*, June 21, 1935.

2. *RDP*, September 21, 23, 1935.

3. *RDP*, September 3, 1935.

4. *Los Angeles Times*, June 30, 1936. Intentional or not, the title indicated indirectly that talk of a statue of any kind had gone nowhere.

5. *RPE*, August 1, October 12, 1936.

6. Documents about Gale's Miller Biography, I E 12, A500-190.

7. DH to Harry Chandler, March 26, 1938; Harry Chandler to DH, April 1, 1938, Correspondence Harry Chandler, 1930–1938, I E 7, A500-190.

8. Chapters 8 through 13 of Esther Klotz's *The Mission Inn: Its History and Artifacts* offer largely chronology; see also chapter 23, "Hard Times at the Mission Inn," in Patterson's *A Colony for California*.

9. *RPE*, May 22, 1967.

10. *Los Angeles Times*, July 17, 1972; *RP*, May 22, 1967; *RPE*, July 15, 1972.

11. Marion Clark Miller's collection passed to family members and subsequently to the Mission Inn Foundation Museum, becoming the Jane Cullen Clark Collection.

12. *RDP*, October 8, 1952; *RE*, October 8, 1952. The articles are in Subseries II B, Allis Miller Hutchings, II B 2, Scrap Book: AMH Publications, A500-190.

13. DH to E. B. Criddle, September 25, 1936, Subseries VI, Easter Armistice VI 20, A500-190. *RDP*, March 5, 1943. Hutchings seems to have rejoined the planning committee by 1943.

14. *RDP*, February 16, 1953; *RE*, February 16, 1953; *Los Angeles Times*, February 17, 1953; *RPE*, October 8, 1952; *RPE*, February 16, 1953. Allis Miller Hutchings died October 8, 1952, and DeWitt died February 16, 1953.

15. These now comprise the Frank Miller Hutchings Collection, A500-190 at the Riverside Metropolitan Museum; Patterson, *Colony*, 397.

16. Alice Richardson to Mary Shepherd, October 21, 1936, Thomas Patterson File, John W. North, RMM.

17. Klotz, *Mission Inn*, 98; *RDP*, August 22, 1938.

18. *RPE*, October 23, 1952.

19. *RDP*, January 20, 1925.

20. *RPE*, June 24, 25, 26, 27, 1956.

21. Notes, 1, MIFM.

22. *RDP*, July 3, 1956; Klotz, *Mission Inn*, 128–129.

Bibliography

Some of the books included here are not quoted but were directly helpful to the narrative.

Abbot, Willis J. "Chicago Newspapers and their Makers." *Review of Reviews* 11: 6 (June 1895).
"A Pictorial Digest of California's Best Architecture." *Architectural Digest* 6: 2 (Spring 1926): 11–25.
A Story of the Inn, Riverside California. Riverside, California: Mission Inn, 1919.
Adams, John Anthony. *Rialto*. San Francisco: Arcadia, 2004.
Aldrich, Mark. "Train Wrecks to Typhoid Fever: The Development of Railroad Medical Organizations." *Bulletin of the History of Medicine* 2001 75: 254–289.
Apps, Jerry. *One Room Country Schools: History and Recollections from Wisconsin*. Amherst, Wisconsin: Amherst Press, 1996.
Baker, LaFayette C. *History of the Secret Service*. Philadelphia: Baker, 1867.
Baker, Ronald J. *Serving Through Partnership*. Riverside, California: Riverside City and County Public Library, 1988.
Bailey, J. M. *Life in Danbury*. Boston: Shephard and Hill, 1873.
Barsness, Richard W. "Iron Horses and an Inner Harbor at San Pedro Bay, 1867–1890." *Pacific Historical Review* 34: 3 (August 1965): 299.

Battles, Mrs. F. Daniel (compiler). *Diary of Two Decades*. Riverside, California: the compiler, 1967.

Bauer, John. "The Health Seekers and Early Southern California Agriculture." *Pacific Historical Review* 20: 4 (November 1951): 347.

Beck, Warren A. and Ynez D. Haase. *Historical Atlas of the West*. Norman, Oklahoma: University of Oklahoma, 1992.

Benton, Arthur B. "Architecture for the Southwest." *Land of Sunshine* 4: 3 (February 1896): 37.

Benton, Arthur B. "The California Mission and its Influence on Pacific Coast Architecture." *The Architect and Engineer of California* 24: 1 (February 1911): 35–75.

Benton, Arthur B. *The Mission Inn*. Los Angeles: Senogram, 1908.

Berlin, Edward A. *Ragtime: A Musical and Cultural History*. Berkeley, California: University of California Press, 1980.

Berry, R. V. S. *The Dream City: The Art, Story and Symbolism*. San Francisco: Brunt, 1915.

Borton, Francis. *Bells and Crosses of the Mission Inn*. Riverside, California: Mission Inn, 1916.

Botolin, Norman and Christine Laing. *World's Columbia Exposition*. Champaign Illinois: University of Illinois, 2002.

Bowie, Walter Russell. *The Inescapable Christ*. New York: Scribner's, 1925.

Brackett, F. P. *History of Pomona Valley California*. Los Angeles: Historic Record, 1920.

Brinkerhoff, Roelf C. *Supplement to the Family of Joris Dicksen Brinkerhoff, 1628*. Riverside, California: the author, 1902.

Brown, James and James Boyd. *History of San Bernardino and Riverside Counties*. Chicago: Western Historical Association, 1922. 3 volumes.

Burgess, Lawrence. *The Smileys*. Redlands, California: Moore Historical, 1991.

Case, Walter. *History of Long Beach*. Chicago: S. J. Clarke, 1927. 2 volumes.

Cataldo, Joseph. *San Bernardino*. San Francisco: Arcadia, 2002.

Cheney, Charles H. and Elvon Musick. "Architectural Control of Private Property." *National Conference on City Planning.* Boston: City Planning, 1927.
Choules, J. O. *Young Americans Abroad or Vacations in Europe.* Boston: Gould and Lincoln, 1852.
Clinchy, Everett R. *All in the Name of God.* New York: John Day, 1934.
Clover, S. T. *Constructive Californians.* Los Angeles: Saturday Night Publishing, 1926.
Club Women of California, Official Directory and Register 1906–07. San Francisco: C. C. Hoag, 1907.
Coleman, Satis Narrona. *Bells, Their History, Legends, Making and Uses.* New York: Greenwood, 1971.
Cook, Increase. *The American Orator.* Boston: The Intelligencer, 1828.
Cottrell, Dorothy Ottley. *Little Chapel of Memory.* Riverside, California: Mission Inn, n.d.
Cram, Ralph. *Walled Towns.* Boston: Marshall Jones, 1919.
Crewdson, Wilson. *Japan Our Ally.* London: MacMillan, 1915.
Cross, Ira B. *A History of the Labor Movement in California.* Berkeley, California: University of California Press, 1935.
Current, Richard N. *History of Wisconsin, the Civil War Era, 1848–1873.* Madison, Wisconsin: Wisconsin State Historical Society, 1976.
De Meglio, John E. *Vaudeville U.S.A.* Bowling Green, Ohio: Ohio State University Popular Press, 1973.
Department of Indian Affairs. *61st Annual Report, Commission on Indian Affairs.* Washington, DC: US Government, 1892.
———. *Report of the Superintendent of Indian Schools, 1903.* Washington, DC: US Government, 1903.
Derleth, August. *Still Small Voice.* New York: Appleton-Century, 1938.
Deverell, William. *Railway Crossing: California and the Railroad, 1850–1910.* Berkeley, California: University of California Press, 1994.

Deverell, William. *Whitewashed Adobe*. Los Angeles: University of California Press, 2004.

Dickens, Charles. *Bleak House*. New York: Penguin Signature Classics, 1964.

Dodge, Grenville. *How We Built the Union Pacific*. Council Bluffs, Iowa: Monarch, 1910.

Duell, Marshall. "Frank Miller and the International Expositions." Master's thesis, University of California Riverside, 1987.

Dumke, Glenn. *The Boom of the Eighties in Southern California*. San Marino, California: Huntington, 1944.

Eaves, Lucille. *A History of California Labor Legislation*. Berkeley: University of California, 1910.

Elliott, Wallace. *History of San Bernardino and San Diego Counties*. Riverside, California: Riverside Museum Press, 1965. (A reissue of an 1883 publication.)

Eggleston, Edward. *The End of the World*. New York: Judd, 1872.

———. *The Mystery of Metropolisville*. New York: Judd, 1873.

Fahey, David M. *Temperance and Racism: John Bull, Johnny Reb and the Good Templars*. Lexington, Kentucky: University of Kentucky, 1996.

Fallows, Alice K. *Everybody's Bishop*. New York: Seares, 1927.

First Congregational Church of Riverside, California. "Historic Meeting Documents, 1871–1922." Riverside, California: First Congregational Church of Riverside, California Archives, n.d.

Fletcher, Robert Samuel. *A History of Oberlin College From Its Founding Through the Civil War*. New York: Arno, 1971. 2 volumes.

Flexner, Abraham. *Medical Education in the U.S. and Canada*. New York: The Carnegie Foundation, 1910.

Freud, Ralph. "Frank Miller: Theater Manager." *Southern California Quarterly* 41: 1 (February 1988): 43–46.

Gabbert, J. R. *History of Riverside City and County*. Phoenix, Arizona: Record, 1935.

―――. "Tribute to a Visionary." *Arizona Highways* (November 1936): 27–32.
Gale, Zona. *Frank Miller of Mission Inn.* New York: Appleton-Century, 1938.
―――. "Master of the Mission Inn." *Christian Century* 52: 43 (June 1935): 27–34.
Garfield, Ellery Irving. *Knights Templar Tactics and Drill.* Detroit, Michigan: E. B. Smith, 1871.
Garland, Hamlin. "Up the Coulee." *Main Traveled Roads.* New York: New American Library, 1962.
Gibson, Campbell J. and Emily Lennon. *Historical Census Populations of Counties, Towns and Cities of California, 1850–1990.* Washington, DC: US Bureau of the Census, 1999.
Gleye, Paul. *The Architecture of Los Angeles.* Los Angeles: The Los Angeles Conservancy, 1981.
Gliman, Charlotte Perkins. *The Living of Charlotte Perkins Gilman.* New York: Appleton-Century, 1935.
Gonzales, Nathan. "Riverside, Tourism and the Indian: Frank A. Miller and the Creation of Sherman Institute." *Southern California Quarterly* 84: 3/4 (November 2003): 193–222.
Greene, Sarah Pratt McLean. *Winslow Plain.* New York: Harper and Brothers, 1902.
Haas, Lisbeth. *Conquest and Historical Identities in California, 1796–1936.* Berkeley: University of California Press, 1995.
Haglund, Roy L. *One Hundred Years of Masonry, 1879–1979.* Riverside, California: Evergreen Lodge, 1979.
Hall, Joan Herrick. *Pursuing Eden.* Riverside, California: Highgrove Press, 2010.
―――. *Through the Doors of the Mission Inn.* Riverside, California: Highgrove Press, volume 1 (1996), volume 2. (2000).
Hall, Kelly Patricia and Steven Ruggles. *Restless in the Midst of Their Prosperity: New Evidence on Internal Migration of Americans, 1860–2000.* Minneapolis, Minnesota: University

of Minnesota Department of History and Minnesota Population Center, 2004.

Harley, John E. *International Understanding Agencies*. Palo Alto, California: Stanford University Press, 1931.

Harley, R. Bruce. "The Beginnings of March Field." *Southern California Quarterly* 53: 2 (March 1971): 147–158.

Hayward, Alice McCaul. *The Story of Tomah*. Tomah, Wisconsin: Journal Printing, 1955.

Headley, J. T. *The Great Rebellion: A History of the Civil War in the United States*. Hartford, Connecticut: American, 1866. 2 vols.

Hesperides. *A Handbook of American Private Schools, 1916*. Boston: Porter E. Sergeant, 1916.

Hill, Thomas E. *Hill's Manual of Social and Business Forms: A Guide to Correct Writing*. Chicago: Moses Warren, 1875.

Hinchborn, Franklin. *The Story of the California Legislative Session, 1911*. San Francisco: James H. Barry, 1911.

Hinckley, Edith Parker. *On the Banks of the Zanja*. Claremont, California: Saunders, 1951.

Hodgen, Maurice. *The Organ at the Mission Inn*. Riverside, California: Friends of the Mission Inn, 2003.

———. "The Romance of the Rain Cross." *Journal of the Riverside Historical Society* 9 (February 2005): 12–35.

Holmes, Elmer W. *History of Riverside County with Biographical Sketches*. Los Angeles: Historic Record, 1912.

Holmes, J. Lewis. *Riverside Directory 1889*. Riverside, California: Daily Press, 1889.

Holtz, Maude. "Cleveland University." Master's essay, Case Western Reserve University, 1930.

Honnold-Mudd Library, Special Collections. *Claremont Inn Register 1910*. Claremont, California: Claremont Inn, 1910.

Hubbard, Elbert. *Selected Writings of Elbert Hubbard: On My Way*. New York: Wise, 1922.

Hutchings, DeWitt. *The Bells and Crosses of the Mission Inn*. Riverside, California: Mission Inn, 1952.

———. *The Story of Mt. Rubidoux, Riverside, California.* Riverside, California: Mission Inn, 1926.

Ingersoll, Luther A. *Ingersoll's Century History: Santa Monica Bay Cities.* Los Angeles: the author, 1908.

International Railway and Steam Navigation Guide. Montreal, Quebec, Canada: n. p., 1880.

James, George Wharton. *The 1910 Trip of the H.M.M.B.A. to California and the Pacific Coast.* San Francisco: Bolte and Braden, 1911.

Jensen, Joan M. *Calling This Place Home: Women on the Wisconsin Frontier 1850-1925.* Saint Paul, Minnesota: Minnesota Historical Society Press, 2006.

Jiminez, Gilbert and Thomas M. Johnson. *Riverside City College, 1916-1981: A 65 Year History.* Riverside, California: Board of Trustees of Riverside City College, 1981.

Jones, Roger. *The History of Villa Rockledge, a National Treasure in Laguna.* Laguna, California: American National Research Institute, 1991.

Jordan, David Starr. *Days of a Man, Being the Memories of a Naturalist, Teacher and Minor Prophet of Democracy.* New York: World Book, 1922. 2 volumes.

———. *The Human Harvest.* London: Alston Rivers, 1907.

———. *The Religion of a Sensible American.* Boston: American Unitarian Society, 1909.

Keller, Jean. *Empty Beds.* Ann Arbor, Michigan: University of Michigan, 2002.

Kemble, John Haskell. *The Panama Route, 1848-1869.* Berkeley: University of California, 1943.

Klotz, Esther (ed.). *A History of Citrus in the Riverside Area.* Riverside, California: Riverside Museum Press, 1969.

———. *The Mission Inn: Its History and Artifacts.* Corona, California: UBS Printing, 1981.

———. *Riverside and the Day the Bank Broke.* Riverside, California: Rubidoux Press, 1972.

Laing, Christine. *World's Columbia Exhibition.* Champaign, Illinois: University of Illinois, 2002.

Lawton, Harry Wilson. "History of Real Estate in Riverside." Typescript. Riverside Metropolitan Museum, Riverside, California. n.d.

Leavitt, James McD. *The American Cardinal*. New York: Dodd Mead, 1871.

Lech, Steve. *Along the Old Roads: A History of the Portion of Southern California that Became Riverside County, 1772-1893*. Riverside, California: the author, 2004.

———. *Resorts of Riverside County*. San Francisco: Arcadia, 2008.

———. and Kim Jarrell Johnson. *Riverside's Mission Inn*. San Francisco: Arcadia, 2008.

Leonard, Delavan. *The Story of Oberlin College*. Boston: Pilgrim, 1898.

Le Roy, Bruce (ed.). *H. M. Chittenden: A Western Epic*. Tacoma, Washington: Washington State Historical Society, 1961.

Lewis, Richard and Vincent Moses. *The Riverside Fire Department Presents a Century of Services*. Riverside, California: Riverside Fireman's Benefit Association, 1983.

Liebert, Marie. *Observations*. Arlington, California: Teresa Gordon, 1982.

Limerick, Jeffrey. *America's Grand Resort Hotels*. New York: Pantheon, 1979.

Love, William DeLoss. *Wisconsin in the War of the Rebellion*. Chicago: Church and Goodman, 1866.

Lummis, Charles F. "Getting Together." *Out West* 28: 1 (January-June 1908): 2.

Matthews, William. *Getting on in the World*. Chicago: Griggs, 1874.

May, George W. *Charles E. Duryea: Automaker*. Chillicothe, Illinois: River Beach Publishing, 1996.

McArthur, Benjamin. *Actors and American Culture, 1880-1920*. Philadelphia: Temple University, 1984.

McDougal, Dennis. *Privileged Son: Otis Chandler*. Cambridge Massachusetts: Perseus, 2001.

McGerr, Michael. *A Fierce Discontent: The Rise and Fall of the Progressive Movement in America.* New York: Oxford, 2003.

McKenny, Charles E. *Educational History of Wisconsin.* Chicago: Delmont, 1912.

McKenny, L. M. *McKenny's Pacific Coast Directory 1880–1881.* San Francisco: L. M. McKenny, 1881.

McQuaid, Kim. "The Businessman as a Social Innovator." *The American Journal of Economics and Sociology* 34: 4 (October 1975): 411–422.

Matthews, William. *Getting on in the World or Hints on Success in Life.* Chicago: S. C. Griggs, 1874.

Metcalf, Richard. *Letter and Spirit.* Boston: American Unitarian Society, 1870.

Meyer, D. H. *The Instructed Conscience: Shaping the American National Ethic.* Philadelphia: University of Pennsylvania, 1972.

Miller, Frank A. "Plan for Securing Permanent Peace Among Nations," Peace Movement Correspondence, 1 F 5, A500-190, RMM.

———. Diary, 1871–1884. Mission Inn Foundation Museum Archives. Mission Inn, Riverside, California.

Miller, Judy. *Claremont: A Pictorial History.* Claremont, California: Historical Resource Center, 1980.

Mitchell, Edmund. *The Call of the Bells.* New York: Menzies, 1915.

Monroe County, Wisconsin Bicentennial Committee. *Monroe County Wisconsin Pictorial History, 1976.* Tomah, Wisconsin: Journal Publishing, 1976.

Monroe County, Wisconsin, Local History and Research Room. "1860 Monroe County (Wisconsin) Census—Tomah Village." "1870 State Census Transcription." Sparta, Wisconsin: Monroe County Local History and Research Room, n.d. Typescripts.

———. Real Property Records. Monroe County, Wisconsin, County Records Office, Sparta, Wisconsin.

Morris, Edmund. *Colonel Roosevelt*. New York: Random House, 2011.

Murphy, Elmer R. "Mexico." *Rhode's Colossus* (January 1921): 1–8.

Newmark, Marco N. "Early California Resorts." *Southern California Quarterly* 35: 2 (June 1953): 140–141.

Nordoff, Charles. *California: A Book for Travelers and Settlers*. New York: Harper and Brothers, 1873.

Norris, Frank. *The Octopus*. New York: New American Library, 1964.

Noyes, A. D. *Forty Years of American Finance*. New York: Putnam's, 1898, 1909.

Numbers, Ronald. *Almost Persuaded: American Physicians and Compulsory Health Insurance 1912–1920*. Philadelphia: Johns Hopkins, 1978.

Nunis, Doyce B. *Women in the Life of Southern California*. Los Angeles: Historical Society of Southern California, 1966.

Oberlin College Catalog. Oberlin, Ohio: the College. 1836, 1847–48, 1848–49, 1850–51, 1851–52.

Official Army Register of the Volunteer Force of the United States Army for the Years 1861–1865, Part VII, Washington, DC: Government Printing, 1867.

Orsi, Richard. *Sunset Limited*. Berkeley: University of California, 2005.

Parks, Walter P. *The Famous Fliers Wall of the Mission Inn*. Riverside, California: Harwarden, 1986.

Patterson, Thomas W. *A Colony for California*. Riverside, California: Press Enterprise, 1971.

Perkins, J. R. *Trails, Rails and War*. Indianapolis: Bobs Merrill, 1929.

"Picturesque Riverside." An undated presentation portfolio at the Braun Research Library, Southwest Museum, Los Angeles, California.

Poling-Kempes, Leslie. *The Harvey Girls*. New York: Paragon House, 1994.

Pomona College, Admissions Office. *Pomona College Student Register, 1909–1910.* Claremont, California: Pomona College Admissions Office.

Powell, Alexander. *By Camel and Car to the Peacock Throne.* New York: Century, 1923.

Press Reference Library. *Notables of the West.* New York: International News Service, 1915.

Proceedings of the Institute of International Relations. Los Angeles, California: University of Southern California, 1926. 15 volumes.

Rawitsch, Mark Howland. *No Other Place: Japanese American Pioneers in a Southern California Neighborhood.* Riverside, California: Department of History, University of California Riverside, 1983.

Richards, Randolph A. *History of Monroe County, Wisconsin.* Chicago: Cooper, 1912.

Rider, Fremont (ed.). *Rider's California: A Guidebook for Travelers.* New York: MacMillan, 1925.

Riverside County Directory 1901. Riverside, California: Weed and Payne, 1901.

Riverside, California Public School Records. Series V: Public School Registers. Local History Resource Center, Riverside, California Public Library.

"Diary of Two Decades." Compiled by Mrs. F. Daniels Battles. Riverside, California: the compiler, c.1967. Typescript.

Leech, Charles. Diary. Cage 7:2:2, Eastman Papers [RPL-35].

Riverside School of Nursing. Riverside, California: Riverside Junior College, 1925.

San Bernardino, California County Archives, San Bernardino California Deed Book 21. San Bernardino California County Records.

Sandoval-Strausz, A. K. *Hotel: An American History.* New Haven, Connecticut: Yale, 2007.

Saunders, Charles Francis. *Finding the Worthwhile in California.* New York: McBride, 1916.

Saxton Alexander. *The Rise and Fall of the White Republic: Class Politics and Mass Culture in 19th Century America*. London: Verso, 1990.

Schlereth, Thomas J. *Victorian America: Transformations in Everyday Life, 1876–1915*. New York: Harper, 1991.

Schulz, Peter and Sherri M. Gust. "Faunal Remains and Social Status in 19th Century Sacramento." *Historical Archaeology* 17: 1.

Scott, Paula. *Santa Monica: A History on the Edge*. San Francisco: Arcadia, 2004.

Scott, Walter. *The Lady of the Lake*. Boston: Little Brown, 1853.

Seward, William H. *Travels Around the World*. New York: Appleton, 1873.

Sheldon, Charles M. *In His Steps: What Would Jesus Do?* Chicago: Advance, 1897.

Simondson, Harold. *Zona Gale*. New York: Twayne, 1962.

Sitton, Tom. *John Randolph Haynes: California Progressive*. Palo Alto, California: Stanford University, 1992.

Skinner, Otis. *Footlights and Spotlights*. New York: Blue Ribbon, 1924.

Smith, Fred B. *Must We Have War?* New York: Harper and Brothers, 1929.

Snelling, W. J. *West of the Mississippi*. Boston: Gray and Brown, 1830.

State of California. Statutes of California, 20th (1873–1874) Session. S.B. 405, Chapter 516. Sacramento, California: Gov't Printer, 1874.

Starr, Kevin. *Inventing the Dream: California Through the Progressive Era*. New York: Oxford, 1985.

Stearnes, J. W. *The Columbian History of Education: Wisconsin*. Milwaukee, Wisconsin: State Educational Exhibit for Wisconsin, 1893.

Stiles, T. J. *The First Tycoon: the Epic Life of Cornelius Vanderbilt*. New York: Vintage, 2010.

Stonehouse, Merlin. *John Wesley North and the Reform Frontier*. Minneapolis, Minnesota: University of Minnesota, 1965.

Sumner, Charles B. *The Story of Pomona College.* Boston: Pilgrim Press, 1914.

Tewkesbury, Donald. *Founding of American Colleges and Universities Before the Civil War.* New York: Anchor, 1965.

Tracy, Sarah W. *Alcoholism in America.* Philadelphia: Johns Hopkins University, 2005.

Turner, James. *A History of Roller Skating.* Lincoln, Nebraska: Roller Skating Rink Operator's Association of America, 1975.

US Census, 1850. Russia, Lorraine. Ohio. Roll M432, Page 275, Image 33.

Vail, Mary C. *Both Sides Told: of Southern California As It Is.* Pasadena, California: Star Job Printing, 1888.

Walker, Frandlin. *A Literary History of Southern California.* Berkeley, California: University of California Press, 1950.

Ward, Earl C. *A Godly Heritage.* Riverside, California: First Church of Christ Scientist, 1973.

Weitz, Karen. "Arthur B. Benton" in *Toward a Simpler Way of Life*, Robert Winter (ed.), Berkeley: University of California Press, 1997.

Wenzel, Glenn. *Anecdotes on Mount Rubidoux and Frank A. Miller, Her Promoter.* Riverside, California: the author, 2010.

Winter, Robert (ed.). *Toward a Simpler Way of Life: The Arts and Crafts Architects of California.* Berkeley: University of California, 1997.

Wong, Morrison Gideon. "The Japanese in Riverside, 1890–1945: A Special Case in Race Relations." PhD dissertation. University of California, Riverside, 1977.

Wright, Harold Bell. *God and the Grocery Man.* New York: Appleton, 1927.

———. *The Re-Creation of Brian Kent.* New York: Book Supply Company, 1919.

Wyss, Johann David. *Swiss Family Robinson.* London: Nelson, 1871.

Zentmeyer, George A. *The Lighted Cross: The First Hundred Years of Riverside's First Church, 1872–1972*. Riverside, California: First Congregational Church, 1972.

Newspapers and Periodicals

Two papers served Riverside, California, for most of Miller's life, the *Daily Press* (with some changes of name) and the later-arriving *Enterprise*. Whatever their differences in politics or otherwise, they drew directly on the Miller family and the Master of the Inn and the front desk in their reporting. I have made extensive critical use of these newspapers and a variety of others:

Arlington (California) Times
Boston Sunday Journal
Citrograph (Redlands, California)
Helena (Montana) Daily Independent
Hemet (California) News
Long Beach (California) Press
(Los Angeles) Daily Hotel Gazette
Los Angeles Daily Herald
Los Angeles Examiner
Los Angeles Times
Milwaukee (Wisconsin) Journal
Milwaukee (Wisconsin) Sentinal
Milwaukee (Wisconsin) Sentinel
New York Times
Porterville (California) Evening Record
Riverside (California) Daily Press
Riverside (California) Enterprise
Riverside (California) News
Riverside (California) Press Enterprise
Riverside (California) Press and Horticulturalist
Riverside (California) Reflex
Riverside (California) Weekly Press

Riverside (California) Weekly News
Roseville (California) Evening Recorder
San Bernardino (California) Times Index
(San Bernardino, California) Weekly Times Index
Sparta (Wisconsin) Herald
Tokyo (Japan) Advertiser
(Tokyo, Japan) Times and Mail
Tomah (Wisconsin) Journal
Tomah (Wisconsin) Weekly Journal
Truckee (California) Republican
Victorville (California) Record

Index

Note:
F.M. stands for Frank Augustus Miller
Italics indicate photos
"n" indicates an endnote.
Square brackets indicate endnote references.

A
Abbott, Lyman, 220
Arcadia Hotel, 97–99, [99n7], 356–357n7
Arlington Hotel, 69
Association for International Understanding, [271n31], 412n31
Atherton, Issac W. & Adelia S., 24, 30
automobiles, 91, 143, 243–244

B
Barton, Clarence (C. W.), 145
Benton, Arthur B.
  character, 279–280
  collaboration with F. M., 120–121, 133–134, [217n32], 279–280, 393n32
  The Mission Inn, 416n35
  mission style architecture, 113, 279–280, 365n10

Berry, Rose V. S., 223
Bjornsen, Alexis, 148, 169
Blue Front Store, 49–51, 58–59, 61
Bond, Carrie Jacobs, 181
Borton, Francis, 236–237
Bowie, Walter Russell, 271
Boyd, James, [10n10], 24, [36n13], 331n10, 336n13
Broadwater Hotel, 237–238
Brown, Mayor L. V. W., 252
Burroughs, John, 181

C

California Electric Company of San Francisco, 102
Casa Palma Hotel, 114
Chandler, Harry, [100n13], 301, [309n20], 357–358n13, 426n20
Cheney, Charles H., 285
Chittenden, Captain Hiram, 143, 165–166
Commercial Travelers Association, [130n7], 367n7
Conaty, Bishop Thomas, 167, 177
Congregational Church, 31, *160*, [215n17], 392n17
Conkling, Mr. & Mrs., 8
Cram, Ralph, 255
Crane, Margaret, 239–241
Cross, Rev. & Mrs. W. H., 31

D

De Mille, Cecil B., 266
Depression of 1929, 290–291
Duryea, Frank, 91

E

Eastman, Annie, 36, 41
Evans, Pliny, [145n35], 374n35
Evans Jr., Mayor Samuel Carey, 84, [145n35], 256–257, 257–258, 374n35

F

Fairbanks, Charles W., 204
First Americans. *see* Native Americans
Fisher, Secretary Walter L., 213–214
Fort Chittenden, 166
Frank Miller of Mission Inn, 306, 315–316
Froleman, Gustav, 211

G

Gabbert, John R., [234n6], 399n6
Gale, Zona, 11, 131, 305–306, 315–316
Garland, Hamlin, 304
Glenwood Cottage/Tavern. *see also* Mission Inn (formerly the New Glenwood Hotel)
  advertising, 58
  construction, 35–36, 336n11, 336n13
  entertainment, [63n38], 65, 344n38
  Glenwood Investment Company, 110
  guests, 57–58, [63n38], 65–66, 344n38
  ownership, 53, 65–66, 69
  renovations, 45–46, 49, 60, 61, [63n38], 344n38
  staff, 90
Glenwood Garage, 143
Goethals, G. W., 223
Goff, Reverend E. F., 167, 193–194
Good Templars Lodge, 16
Gray, Carolyn E., 269, 411–412n26
Greves, James P., 26

H

Hague Peace Conference, 173
Harada family, 227
Hardenberg, Isabella. *see* Miller (née Hardenberg), Isabella (wife)
Hardenberg Loan Fund, [236n13], 400n13
Harriman, Edward H., 144

Hearst, William Randolph, 220
Highway 60, 244, 301
Hollister, Mamie Runkle, 295
Holmes, Elmer, 89
honors
   French, 289, 418n14
   Japanese, *156*, 264, 286–289, 296, 298, 315
   Master of Arts, *156*, 289
   Riverside, California, 224, 262–264, 272, 297, 319
Hubbard, Elbert, 179, 220
Hunt, Myron, [214n17], 217, 234–235, 392n17
Hunt, Reverend T. C., 134–135
Huntington, Archer, 217
Huntington, Collis P., 44–45, 57–58, 108–109
Huntington, Henry E.
   friendship with F.M., 278–279
   Mission Inn (and New Glenwood), 115–116, 119–120, 130, 364n3
   Mount Rubidoux, 144–145, 167, 374, 374n35
   Riverside, California county separation, 81–82
   Riverside, California trolleys, 105–106
Huntington Park Association, 144–145, 165, 374n35
Hutchings (née Miller), Allis (daughter)
   aviation, 303
   birth (1882), 61
   business advice from F. M., 310
   death (1952), 317
   education, 140
   family vacation, 143
   Isabelle Miller's death, 178–181
   Mission Inn (and New Glenwood) management, 281–282, 317
   photo, *155*
   Scandinavian trip, 171–173, 379n41
   wedding, 190–191
   World's Columbia Exposition (1893), 86

Hutchings, DeWitt Vermilye
  Armistice observance, 273–274
  The Assumption of the Virgin, [243n7], 402n7
  aviation, 303
  Broadwater Hotel management, 237–238
  death (1953), 317
  education, [189n3], 384n3
  Mexico trip, 238–239
  Mission Inn management, 236–237, 281–282, 317
  Mission Inn publications, 235–236, 400–401n18
  Tahoe Tavern management, 189
  wedding, 190–191
Hutchings, Frank Miller (grandson), *155*, 318
Hutchings, Helen (granddaughter), 318
Hutchings, Isabella (granddaughter), *155*, 318

I
Indian school (Sherman Institute), 99–100, 107–110, *159*, 357–358n13, 362n12
Institute for Pacific Relations, [271n31], 412n31
Institute of International Relations, 267, 270, 275, 413–414n10

J
James, Louis S., 131
Japan relationship
  economic partnership, 286–287
  Harada family, 227
  Japan trip, *156*, 257, 260–261
  honors, *156*, 264, 286–289, 296, 298, 301, 315
  Order of the Rising Sun, *156*, 287–288
  peace advocacy, 264–266, 270, 286–287
  royal visit, 296
Johnson, Hiram, 183
Jordan, David Starr
  death, 299
  friendship with F.M., 181

Indian conference, 176–177
peace advocacy, 204, 263–264, 271–272

K
Keeley Institute, 87
King, George H., 295
KleinSmid, Rufus von, 267, 270, 275, 289

L
Landmarks Club, 173, 177
Langtry, Lilly, 72
League of Nations, 273
Long Beach Hotel, 62
Loring, Charles M., 73–74, 146–148, 176, 214–215
Loring Building and Opera House, 73–74, 76–77, 146–148, *159*, [235n11], 400n11
Lummis, Charles, 173, 176–177

M
March Air Field, 229–230
Mariona, 233–234, 280, 317
Markham, Governor Henry Harrison (H. H.), 82, 83
Mayo, Charles, 248
McClellan, John Jasper, 203
McDonald, James A., 204
McGroarty, John Steven, 211–212, 263–264, 391n3, 392n4
McKinley, President William, 57, 88
Miller, Alice (sister). *see* Richardson (née Miller), Alice (sister)
Miller, Allis (daughter). *see* Hutchings (née Miller), Allis (daughter)
Miller, Christopher Columbus (father)
    California bound, 19
    death (1890), 77
    Glenwood Cottage, 35–36, 53
    Mason, 12, 28, 77
    photo, *150*

return from war, 11
   Riverside tin mine, 9, 23
   schooling Frank, 14
   social position, 12
   surveying, 12, 16, 28, 59, 150
   unplanned disguise, 59–60
Miller, Edward (brother)
   death (1922), 252
   Loring Building and Opera House, [235n11], 400n11
   Mission Inn (New Glenwood Hotel) management, 171–172, 235–236
   odd jobs, 111, 400n11
   photo, *151*
   surveyor, 67
   wife & children, 318
Miller, Emma (sister). *see* Newman (née Miller), Emma (sister)
Miller, Frank Augustus: character & characteristics
   abstinence, 16–17, 40
   appearance in 1920s, 275–276
   appearance in 1930s, 298
   baseball, 39–40, 337–338n28
   civic righteousness, 19, 40
   competitiveness, 15
   culture, 122
   diaries, 32, 48, 340n25, 340n26
   frugality, 35
   illnesses--bladder problems, 419n22
   illnesses--cancer, 310–311
   illnesses--death, 312
   illnesses--diagnostic work, 308
   illnesses--fatigue, 259
   illnesses--hemorrhoid surgery, 70
   illnesses--Mayo Clinic, 248
   illnesses--migraines, 6, 19, 264, 330n4
   illnesses--multiple complaints, 34, 136–137
   illnesses--unidentified, 290

imagination, 212-213
letter writing, 7, 31-32, 33
moralizing, 40, 112, 169
philanthropy, 87, 250, 405n34
photo, *149, 151, 154, 155, 156, 163*
playacting, *155*, 212
politicking, 141-142, 300-301
puberty, 17-18
reading selections, 8, 14-15, 204, 270, 271, 332-333n7
recognition need, 166, 276, 297-298, 307, 375n3
religiousness--Christ philosophy, 270-272, 307
religiousness--Church of Christ, Scientist, 93
religiousness--moral resolve, 39
religiousness--Quakerism, 75
religiousness--Sabbath observance, 37
social status, 56
time management, 39-40
Miller, Frank Augustus: events 1857-1880
  birth (1857), 11
  father's homecoming, 11
  boyhood chores, 12-13, 332n2
  early education, 14-15
  Lyceum debating, 15
  Shakespeare encounter, 15-16
  Good Templars Lodge, 16
  surveying with father (1872), 16
  puberty, 17-18
  education (1872-73), 19-20
  Riverside move (1874), 4-10, 24
  boards with Athertons, 30
  surveying, 28
  Cross campaign, 31
  surveying (1874), 34
  land purchase (1875), 34-35, 38
  Hills Manual of Social and Business Forms, 35
  Glenwood labors, 35-36, 336n13

mule driver (1875), 36–37
odd jobs, 38
dating, 41–42
Lyceum debating, 42
Hardenberg friendship (1876), 43–44
Hardenberg trip to Tustin(1877), 45
land deed possession (1877), 46
survey crew supervisor, 47, 339n17
Blue Front Store purchase (1879), 49–51
Glenwood ownership (1880), 53
Miller, Frank Augustus: events 1880-1902
wedding (1880), 54–55
wedding trip (1881), 56–57
Blue Front Store sale, 61
birth of Allis Miller (1882), 61
Republican convention delegate (1884), 62
Glenwood for sale (1885), 65–66
Miller & White real estate & insurance office (1876), 67
Palomares Hotel preparations, 68
San Diego trip (1888), 70
Church of Christ, Scientist eviction, 71
Loring Building and Opera House (1890), 73–74
death of Christopher Miller (1890), 77
Riverside county lobbying (1891-93), 78–82
county offices proposal, 84
World's Columbia Exposition (1893), 86
Republican convention (1896), 88
Glenwood waitress strike, 90
death of Mary Ann Miller (1895), 92–93
Arcadia Hotel management (1897), 97–99
Riverside county courthouse/hotel proposal (1897), 93–95
Indian school petition, 99–100
Riverside and Arlington Railroad (R&A) (1886), 101–106, 107, 358–359n17, 359n20
Indian school lobbying, 107–109, 362n12
Glenwood Investment Company incorporation (1898), 110

Miller, Frank Augustus: events 1902-1908
  Mission Inn shopping trip (1902), 122
  Mission Inn opening (1903), 129–130
  women's college proposal (1901), 140–141
  state convention (1904), 141
  state citrus experiment station, 142
  family vacation (1905), 143
  President Roosevelt meeting (1905), 146
  Loring Building and Opera House sale (1906), 146–148
  death of Alexis Bjornsen (1906), 169
  death of Frank Richardson (1906), 169
  Mount Rubidoux cross (1907), 166–167
  Scandinavian trip (1907), 171–173, 379n41
  Hague Peace Conference, 173
  Native American conference (1908), 176–177
  death of Isabelle Miller (1908), 178–181, 382n32
  Christmas at Raymond Hotel (1908), 184

Miller, Frank Augustus: events 1909-1935
  Mission Inn renovations, 192–193, 203
  courting Marion Clark (1909), 193–195
  wedding of Allis Miller (1909), 190–191
  Pres. Taft's visit (1909), 195, 386–387n35
  mission play commission (1909), 211–212, 392n4
  marries Marion Clark (1910), 198–199, 201–203, 388n6, 388n50
  Peace Conference (1911), 196
  labor law court case (1911), 205–206
  European trip (1911), 206–208
  Washington D. C. trip (1912), 217
  Spanish Art Gallery opening (1914), 218
  World War I, 219
  Yosemite Hotel abandoned (1914), 216
  Pan-Pacific Expo trip (1915), 222–223
  March Air Field, 229–230
  Mariona opens (1920), 233–234
  Mexico trip, 238–239

hospital support trip & Mayo Clinic stay (1920), 247–249
Hawaii trip, 253
city hall proposal (1923), 256
Hawaii/Japan trip (1925), *156*, 258–259, 260–261
Mission Inn (formerly the New Glenwood Hotel) 20th anniversary party (1926), 251–252
Peace Tower and Bridge dedication (1926), 262–264
Riverside Peace Committee of Fifty, 266
Republican County Central Committee, 269
Armistice observance (1926), 273–274
World War I memorial auditorium (1929), 277
Order of the Rising Sun conferred (1929), *156*, 286–288
Master of Arts conferred (1930), 289
Officier d'Academie conferred, 289, 418n14
California Standard Finance Corporation board, 290
Tomafornian reunion (1932), 295–296
Japanese royal visit (1934), 296
Highway 60 lobbying, 301
Union Pacific streamliner train ride (1934), 302–303
Gale visit (1935), 305–308, 309
death (15 June 1935), 312
funeral, 311, 312–313, 427n33
Miller, Frank Augustus: views
 alcohol, 40, 71–72, 112
 architecture, 268, 292
 Christ philosophy, 270–272, 307
 Church of Christ, Scientist, 71, 93
 civic righteousness, 19, 40, 268, 270–271
 common citizen, 309
 diaries, 11
 games, 7
 imagination, 234, 399n6
 inclusiveness, 228
 labor laws, 205–206
 love, 306–307
 marriage, 112

Native Americans, 108
newspapers, 112–113
Progressive movement, 182–183
railroad support, 20
Republican Party, 343n33
unemployment relief, 89–90
U.S.--Japan relations, 257, 264–266, 286–289
vision for Riverside, 254–255
war vs. peace, 173, 204, 221–222
women's suffrage, 75, 205

Miller (née Hardenberg), Isabella (wife)
death (1908), 178–181, 382n32
family vacation, 143
F.M. friendship, 41–42, 43–44
F.M. trip to Tustin, 45
Hardenberg Loan Fund, [236n13], 400n13
illnesses, 70, 169, 177–178
Mission Inn shopping trip, 122
photo, *152, 153, 154, 155*
Pomona move, 68
Pres. Roosevelt meeting, 146
Republican convention (1896), 88
Riverside departure, 47–48, 339–340n21
Saint Cecilia chapel, 184, 192–193, 196, 220
Scandinavian trip, 171–173, 379n41
sisters, 55, 112, 202–203, 299
social status, 56
teacher, 55
wedding, 54–55
wedding trip, 56–57
World's Columbia Exposition trip (1893), 86

Miller (née Clark), Marion Louise (wife)
death (1972), 317
education, 174, 194, 386n28, 386n31
European trip, 206–208
F. M. courting, 193–195

Index

   hospital research & Mayo Clinic trip, 247–249
   illnesses, 301
   Mariona, 233–234, 280, 317
   memorabilia collection (later Jane Cullen Clark Collection), 317, 427n11
   Mission Inn (formerly the New Glenwood Hotel) board, 317
   mother, [236n13], 400n13
   photo, *152, 153, 154, 155*
   retirement, 317
   Washington D. C. trip, 217
   wedding, 198–199, 201–203, 388n6, 388n50
Miller (née Clark), Mary Ann (mother)
   advocating abstinence, 16–17
   birth (1882), [92n43], 356n43
   children's schooling, 29
   death (1895), [71n26], 92, 348n26
   education, 12
   illnesses, 6–7, 12
   photo, *150*
   Redlands visit, 29
   religion, 71, 92, 348n27
   Riverside move, 4–10
Mission Inn (formerly the New Glenwood Hotel). *see also* Glenwood Cottage/Tavern
   20th anniversary party, 250–252
   architect. *see* Benton, Arthur B.
   artist exhibitions, [300n30], 423n30
   The Assumption of the Virgin, [243n7], 402n7
   bell collection, 172–173, 196, 207–208, 209–210, 248–249
   Benton, Arthur B. *see* Benton, Arthur B.
   Bjornsen, Alexis, 148, 169
   Cloister Wing, *157*, 195–198
   construction, 122, 124, 136
   Court of the Orient, 293, 310
   Depression of 1929, 299–300, 423n30
   design, 120–121, 125–128, [135n40], 365n10, 369–370n40

entertainment, 131, 196, 204–205, 212, 220
Frank Miller of Mission Inn, 306, 315–316
funeral of F. M., 312–313
funeral of Isabelle Miller, 178
furnishings, general, 122–123
Giralda Tower, 310
guests--distinguished, 130–134, 219–220, 296, 302
guests--tourists, 222, 243–244, 367n7, 402n3, 402n4
Ho O Kan, 293
Huntington, Henry E., 115–116, 119–120, 130, 364n3
Hutchings, DeWitt Vermilye, 235–236, 236–237, [243n7], 281–282, 317, 400–401n18, 402n7
Institute of International Relations (later World Affairs Council of Inland California), 267, 270, 275, 413–414n10
ironwork, 207, 390n33
Japanese royal visit, 296
Japanese tea garden, 265
logo, 137
macaws, *163*, 319–320
Mexican invasion article, 215–216
Miller, Edward (brother), 171–172, 235–236
Miller (née Hardenberg), Isabella (wife). *see* Miller (née Hardenberg), Isabella (wife)
Miller (née Clark), Marion Louise (wife). *see* Miller (née Clark), Marion Louise (wife)
The Mission Inn, [280n35], 416n35
Mission Play, 211–212, [269n23], 391n3, 392n4, 410n23
Mission Wing, *157*
Music Room--Institute of International Relations, 275
Music Room--interior design, 195–198, 203, 206
Music Room--nativity production, 212
Music Room--Saint Cecilia chapel, 184, 220, 260
naming of, 137
occupancy shrinkage, 281–282, 416n38, 416n41
opening events, 129–130

paintings, 218, [218n36], 223–224, 226, [243n7], 394n36, 402n7
parking lot debate, 224
Peace Conference, 196, 204–205
Pres. Roosevelt's visit, 132–134
Pres. Taft's visit, 195, 386–387n35
proposals & financing, 114–116, 119–120, 364n1, 364n3
publications, 236–237, [280n35], 400–401n18, 416n35
renovations (1905 start), 142–143
renovations (1909 start), 192–193, 196–198, 203, 385n18, 387n42, 387n45
renovations (1913 start), 217–219
renovations (1930 start), 290–293
reredos/altarpiece, 239–241
Richardson (née Miller), Alice (sister), 58, 111, 235, 318
roof tiles, 223
Rotunda Internacional, 291–292, 292–293
Saint Cecilia chapel, 184, 195–198, 220, 260
Saint Francis Chapel, 292
Saint Francis chapel, *158*
Saint Francis of Assisi, 137–138
Spanish Art Gallery, *158*, 217–218, 223, 239–241, 393–394n36
staff, 124–125, 205, 228, 299–300, 389–390n24
Tiffany windows, *158*, 248–249, 404n31
Weber, Peter, 291
Wilson, G. Stanley, 291
Mission Play (Oberammergau of America), 211–212, [269n23], 391n3, 392n4, 410n23
Mitchell, Edmund, 210
Modjeska, Madame, 147
Mohonk Mountain House, 122, 176
Morgan, Mrs. J. Pierpont, 132
Mount Rubidoux
   Armistice observance, 230–231, 273–274
   Easter sunrise service, 191–192, 226–227, 309

F. M.'s mystical change, 371n3
Huntington Park Association, 144–145, 165, 374n35
Japanese royal visit, 296
memorial service for F. M., 315
Mount Rubidoux Hotel, 69, 70, 348n24
park proposal, 144–145, 374n35
Peace Tower and Bridge, 262–264, 272
photo, *162*
plans for, 139–140
Pres. Taft's visit, 195
surveying, 143, 165
Mount Rubidoux Hotel, 69, 70, 348n24

N
Native Americans, 99–100, 107–110, 176–177, 211–212. see *also* Indian school (later The Sherman Institute)
Needham, Congressman James C., 108–109
Nelson, Nelson O., 175, 380n2
New Glenwood Hotel. see Mission Inn (formerly the New Glenwood Hotel)
Newman (née Miller), Emma (sister), [12n2], 30, *151*, 252, 318, 331–332n2
Newman, Gustavus Olivio
  death, 252
  employment, 53, 342n2
  Glenwood Cottage, 35–36
  Los Angeles, California, 318
  marriage, 30
Nichols, Arthur D., [197n45], 387n45
North, John W., 24, 25–27

O
Oberammergau of America (Mission Play), 211–212, [269n23], 391n3, 392n4, 410n23
Oceanside Hotel, 99
Otis, Harrison Gray, 109

P
Pabst, Mr. and Mrs. Fred, 132
Pacific Electric Railway Company, 106, 107
Pacific Improvement Company, 97–98
paintings, 218, [218n36], 223–224, 226, [243n7], 394n36, 402n7
Palomares Hotel, 68
Panama-California Exposition 1915-1917, 222
Panama-Pacific International Exposition 1915, 222–223
Park Hotel, 62, 67
Peace Tower and Bridge, 262–264, 272
Pomona College, 68
Pullman, Mrs. George, 132

R
railroads
   emigrant car accommodations, [5n3], 330n3
   entertainment, 7
   fares, 5
   Huntington, Collis P., 44–45
   Huntington, Henry E., 81–82
   Riverside and Arlington Railroad Company, 101
   Santa Fe Railroad, 216
   Southern Pacific Railroad, 79, 81–82, 83, 216
   Spadra, California terminus, 9–10
   tourism, 101
   Union Pacific Railroad, 302–303
   Worthington, B. A., 83
Raymond, Walter, 65, 91
Raymond and Whitcomb Tour Company, 65
Raymond Hotel, 184
religion
   Catholic, 27, 266, 271
   Church of Christ, Scientist, 71, 93, 220
   Congregational Church, 31, *160*, [215n17], 392n17
   Mount Rubidoux. *see* Mount Rubidoux

Protestant, 27, 28, 71, 75
Riverside hospital support, 246
Seventh-Day Adventist, [246n18], 403n18
Republican Party
  background, 343n33
  county delegate, 62
  influence, 141–142, 300
  Progressive Republicanism, 182–184
  Republican County Central Committee, 269
  Republican National Convention, 88
Reynolds, George, 113–115, 364n33
Richardson, Frank, 68, 97–99, 168–169
Richardson (née Miller), Alice (sister)
  death (1938), 318
  death of Frank Richardson, 169
  girlhood chores, [12n2], 331–332n2
  Good Templars Lodge, 16
  Lyceum debating, 15, 42
  marriage, 68
  Mission Inn (New Glenwood Hotel) management, 58, 111, 235, 318
  moves to Pomona, 68
  photo, *151*
  politicking, 142
  religion, 92–93, 169
  Tahoe Tavern management, 168–169, 171–172, 189
Riis, Jacob, 166, 205
Ripley, E. P., 132
Riverside, California
  advertising by F. M., 88–89
  agriculture, 27
  American Peace Society, 221
  Armistice observance, 230–231, 273–274
  automobiles, 143
  Blues team (baseball), 39, 337–338n28
  businesses, 40, 50, [250n36], 405n36

citrus business decline, 316
city beautification, 267, 278, 415n27
city hall, *161*, 256–257
city management, [68n17], 347n17
city planning, 285–286
city services, 257–258, 260
Congregational Church, 31, *160*, [215n17], 392n17
county courthouse/hotel proposal (1897), 93–95
county separation, [68n17], 78–82, 347n17
Depression of 1929, 290–291
early settlement, 24, 25, 26–27
economic decline, 316
electrification, 101, 106, 107
entertainment, 73–74
ethnic divide, 104, 227–228, 397–398n36, 398n41
ethnic mix, 27
F. M. honors, 297
Fort Chittenden, 166
foundation of, 25–27
Glenwood Cottage/Tavern. *see* Glenwood Cottage/Tavern
Glenwood Garage, 143
Greves, James P., 26
growth (1880s), 51–52, [65n1], 345n1
growth (1920s), 243–244, 403n10
Harada family, 227
Highway 60, 244, 301
hospital, community--nurse training program, 249–250, 269, 411–412n26
hospital, community--photo, *161*
hospital, community--planning for, 245–248, 403n15, 410–411n25
Institute of International Relations, 267, 270, 275, 413–414n10
Keeley Institute, 87
land sale of 1887, [67n12], 346–347n12
Lawrence Pavilion (formerly Riverside Opera House), 72

library, 73
Loring Building and Opera House, 73-74, 76-77, 146-148, *159*, [235n11], 400n11
March Air Field, 229-230
Mile Square, 26
Mission Inn. *see* Mission Inn (formerly the New Glenwood Hotel)
Mount Rubidoux. *see* Mount Rubidoux
Municipal/Memorial Auditorium, *162*, 255-258, 260, 267-268, 277, 280
North, John W., 25-27
Peace Tower and Bridge, 262-264, 272
prohibition (1888), 71-72, 349n30
Raymond and Whitcomb Tour Company, 65
Red Cross Society, 227
religion, 26, 71, 246, [246n18], 271, 403n18
Riverside and Arlington Railroad (R&A), 66, 101-106, 107, 358-359n17, 359n20
Riverside Banking Company, 85
Riverside Land and Water Company, 28, [145n35], 374n35
Riverside Peace Committee of Fifty, 266, [271n31], 412n31
road improvements, 166-167, 301
  Roberts, Florence, 132
  Rockefeller, John D., 266
  Rockefeller, Mrs. John D., 132
  roller-skating, [65n3], 345-346n3
  Roosevelt, President Theodore, 132-134, 146
  Root, E. M., 8
  Rose Parade, Pasadena, 225-226
  Rubio, President Ortiz, 301
  Rumsey, C. E., 176
trolleys, 101-106, 107, 109-110, 124, 358-359n17, 359n20
U. S. Post Office, *160*, 182
unemployment, 89, 175-176, 354-355n29, 380n3
Women's Christian Temperance Union, [72n30], [176n3], 349n30, 380n3

women's college, 140–141
World War I memorial auditorium, 244–245, 255–256, 257–258, 260, 277
YMCA, 70–71

S
San Bernardino, California, 9, [65n1], [68n17], 78–82, 345n1, 347n17
Santa Fe Railroad, 216
Schley, Admiral Winfield Scott, 132
Sheldon, Charles M., 271
Sherman, General M. H., 299
The Sherman Institute. *see* Indian school (later The Sherman Institute)
Smiley, Albert K. and Alfred H., 122–123, 139, 176
Smiley Heights, 139
Southern California Hospital for the Insane and Inebriates (later Patton State Hospital), [83n38], 352n38
Southern Pacific Railroad, 79, 81–82, 83, 216
Spadra, California, 9–10
Spanish Art Society, 225–226
stage, 8
state citrus experiment station, 142
Stewart, General Thomas J., 132
Stubbs, J. C., 132

T
Taft, President William Howard, 195, 386–387n35
Tahoe Tavern, 168–169, 189
Tarbell, Ida, 223
theater. *see* Loring Building and Opera House
Tiffany Louis Comfort, 248–249, 404n31
Tomah, Wisconsin
  birth of F. M., 11
  education system, [41n25], 338n35
  entertainment, 15

Millers move from, 4–10
  Red Front Store, [50n38], 341n38
  Tomafornian reunion, 295–296
  Tomah Institute, 14
  wedding trip of F. M.'s, 56–57
  Weed, Mattie. *see* Weed, Mattie
transportation. *see* automobiles; railroads; stage; trolleys
trolleys, 101–106, 107, 109–110, 124, 358–359n17, 359n20

V
Vincent, George Edgar, 248

W
Warde, Frederick, 132
Washington, Booker T., 220
Weber, Peter, 291
Weed, Mattie
   courtship with F. M., 7, 18, 33, 335n22
   marriage, 31, 41
   reunion with F. M., 57, 295–296
Westerfield, Michael, 300
White, Albert S., 67, 73–74
Wilson, G. Stanley, 217–218, 265, 277, 291
Wooster, Anna, 41
World War I
   Armistice observance, 230–231, 273–274
   Harada family, 227
   Lansing-Ishii Agreement, 227, 397n35
   memorial, 244–245, 255–256, 257–258, 277
   public reaction, 219, 221, 229–231
Worthington, B. A., 83

Y
YMCA, 70–71
Yosemite National Park, 145–146, 170–171, 213–215, 216, 392n17

www.ingramcontent.com/pod-product-compliance
Lightning Source LLC
Chambersburg PA
CBHW050059170426
43198CB00014B/2390